The Dinosaur Films
of Ray Harryhausen

The Dinosaur Films of Ray Harryhausen

Features, Early 16mm Experiments and Unrealized Projects

ROY P. WEBBER

with forewords by
Jim Aupperle *and* Bill Maylone

McFarland & Company, Inc., Publishers
Jefferson, North Carolina, and London

The present work is a reprint of the illustrated case bound edition of The Dinosaur Films of Ray Harryhausen: Features, Early 16mm Experiments and Unrealized Projects, *first published in 2004 by McFarland.*

LIBRARY OF CONGRESS CATALOGUING-IN-PUBLICATION DATA

Webber, Roy P., 1961–
The dinosaur films of Ray Harryhausen : features, early 16mm experiments and unrealized projects / Roy P. Webber ; with forewords by Jim Aupperle and Bill Maylone.
p.   cm.
Includes bibliographical references and index.

ISBN 978-0-7864-6936-9
softcover : acid free paper ∞

1. Harryhausen, Ray — Criticism and interpretation.
2. Dinosaurs in motion pictures.
I. Title.

PN1998.3.H369W43   2012   778.5'345'092 — dc22   2003027764

BRITISH LIBRARY CATALOGUING DATA ARE AVAILABLE

© 2004 Roy P. Webber. All rights reserved

No part of this book may be reproduced or transmitted in any form or by any means, electronic or mechanical, including photocopying or recording, or by any information storage and retrieval system, without permission in writing from the publisher.

On the cover: Harryhausen with a dinosaur puppet from the 1956 *Animal World*; large dinosaur image © 2012 Digital Vision

Manufactured in the United States of America

McFarland & Company, Inc., Publishers
Box 611, Jefferson, North Carolina 28640
www.mcfarlandpub.com

To Mom,
who instilled her love of
knowledge and learning

Acknowledgments

I would like to thank the following for providing a tremendous amount of support to this book project:

- Jim Aupperle
- John M. Ballentine
- Mark F. Berry
- Ted A. Bohus
- Ronald V. Borst
- Tim S. Cole
- Chris Endicott
- Donna Franklin
- Rolf Giesen
- Simon Greetham
- Ray Harryhausen
- Wayne Kinsey
- Douglas Klotz
- Gregory Kulon
- David M. Massaro
- Bill Maylone
- Richard Mirissis
- Susanna Moross Tarjan
- Loren Portillo
- Charles H. Schneer
- Donald K. Strole, Jr.
- John V. Ulakovic
- Marian C. Webber
- S.S. Wilson

Contents

Acknowledgments vii
Foreword by Jim Aupperle xi
Foreword by Bill Maylone xiii
Preface 1

1. Early Experiences, Experiments and *Evolution* 5
2. The Beast from 20,000 Fathoms 45
3. The Animal World 87
4. One Million Years B.C. 111
5. The Valley of Gwangi 152
6. The 1970s and Beyond 192

Ray Harryhausen Dinosaur Filmography 209
Casts and Credits 211
Bibliography 215
Index 219

Foreword
by Jim Aupperle

Like many youngsters I developed a fascination with dinosaurs at an early age. I saw their skeletons displayed at the L.A. County Museum and their likenesses, as captured by paleo artist Charles Knight, reproduced in books from our local library. When *The Beast from 20,000 Fathoms* ran on television in the early 1960s, my fascination turned to wonder at seeing this living prehistoric creature that by all accounts should not exist. My parents explained that these things were done with trick photography, but beyond that, information at the time was sketchy, to say the least.

On the lookout for anything that might explain further how these marvels were accomplished I chanced upon a copy of Forry Ackerman's *Famous Monsters of Filmland* on a drugstore's magazine rack. In those pages I learned that the "trick photography" my parents had alluded to was actually a process of animating models and puppets called stop motion and that the master of that art was a man by the name of Ray Harryhausen. From that point, my fascination evolved into an obsession and by high school I was experimenting with making my own dinosaurs and animating them on a borrowed 16mm Bolex.

Around 1970 I was most fortunate to be invited, along with a gathering of other fans, to meet Ray Harryhausen one glorious afternoon at the original Ackermansion in Los Angeles. It was there that I first met fellow Harryhausen fan Stephen Czerkas, who remains one of my closest friends to this day. Stephen and I collaborated on numerous animated tests and eventually we both became involved in creating the effects for a low-budget feature titled *Planet of Dinosaurs*. Acknowledging the immense debt of inspiration received from Ray Harryhausen, we included a cameo appearance of a dinosaur that was modeled after his own *Beast from 20,000 Fathoms* in a battle with the Tyrannosaur villain of our little epic.

I consider myself very fortunate indeed that I've followed a career that was planted by a dream and that dream in turn resulted from the creations and inspiration of Ray Harryhausen. Thanks, Ray!

Foreword
by Bill Maylone

Back in 1956, sandwiched between television commercials for Wheaties and Ramblers, Ray Harryhausen's dinosaurs walked, leaped, stampeded and fought their way into my young life. Televised previews for *The Animal World* featured the most realistic dinosaurs I could imagine, and as usual, my parents indulged my happy obsession with prehistoric animals and took me to see the film. I was impressed with how the creatures looked, moved and interacted, but I also suspected that unseen hands had somehow crafted the dinosaurs and given them the convincing appearance of life. Realizing this, I began to dream about making my own film about dinosaurs.

As my drawings and clay sculptures of dinosaurs evolved into rough 8mm stop-motion experiments, articles in fan magazines revealed it was Ray Harryhausen who not only brought the dinosaurs of *The Animal World* to life but had also created the strange and captivating monsters of *7th Voyage of Sinbad*. The designs of his creatures, the way they moved and how he blocked the action inspired many of my early animated experiments.

Those were the days before home video and digital distribution. Once a Harryhausen picture completed its opening run in the theaters, the chance to see it again was a rare treat. I scanned the TV movie listings and Saturday matinee schedules to not miss a showing of *Beast from 20,000 Fathoms*, *One Million Years B.C.*, or *Valley of Gwangi*. I couldn't get enough of his animated creatures. They sparkled with predatory alertness and possessed a stylistic economy of motion, startlingly original design and subtle quirks of behavior that stamped each character with a distinct and memorable personality. Every shot contained a lesson for an emerging animator.

In 1975, with my desk already bulging with rejection letters from museums, oil companies and film production companies, I walked into the National Film Board of Canada with a storyboard under my arm and a stop-motion dinosaur in a brown paper bag. The NFB embraced the idea and agreed to eventually fund my eleven-and-a-half minute animated dinosaur project. Released in 1981, it entered classrooms with the title, *64,000,000 Years Ago*, and I'm gratified it remains popular to this day.

When *64,000,000 Years Ago* came out, the approach to the subject—a day in the life of a community of dinosaurs—was novel, but the dinosaurs themselves were inspired by and dedicated to the work of the master.

Since then, I've been fortunate to work on many animated dinosaur projects. These include a feature (*Simon les Nuages*, aka *Simon and the Dream Hunters*), a *Nova* episode, various short educational spots for television, sequences for museum and planetarium shows and a public service announcement featuring a dinosaur made of rusted automobiles. In these, as well as in my non-prehistoric animation projects, I'm keenly aware of the source of my inspiration and of how much of my approach to the art of stop-motion was learned from watching Ray Harryhausen's amazing dinosaurs.

Preface

Dinosaur. When I hear this word, my mind becomes filled with images of a variety of large and grotesquely-shaped reptiles, dwelling in steamy jungles of a volcanic world before the beginning of recorded time. The term itself is derived from the combination of two Greek words and means (literally) "terrible lizard"—indeed these giants from eons past were usually equipped with teeth, claws and other such fearsome weaponry, and more than likely bore a temperament to match. They existed during three geological periods that together constitute the Mesozoic Era (the Triassic, Jurassic and Cretaceous), flourishing from about 225 million years ago until their final extinction around 64 million years ago. Collectively, dinosaurs were Earth's most successful group of land vertebrates, dominating the prehistoric landscape so thoroughly while they reigned that mammals, which come into being nearly as long ago, never evolved to be larger than a house cat. While "dinosaur" to some people is synonymous with the outdated or that which is doomed to failure, most people think in terms of the actual monstrosities that walked on either two legs or four legs.

All true dinosaurs were land animals, and those reptiles that had wings (pterosaurs) or that had flippered feet and paddled with in the ocean weren't saurians, though together with pterosaurs and crocodilians these dinosaurs composed the archosaurs, or "ruling reptiles." Taxonomically they are arranged in orders, made up of many families that are in turn composed of an even greater number of genera. The "names" of most familiar dinosaurs like tyrannosaurus, stegosaurus, brontosaurus (now apatosaurus) and triceratops each represents a genus, which contains a group of closely related species. An example of a specific epithet (the Latinized lower-case noun or adjective that follows a capitalized genus name in binomial nomenclature) is the "rex" of Tyrannosaurus rex, indicating a particular species within that genus. This is logical for purposes of identification, since it would be like someone having to know the house number (species) on a certain street (genus) to be able to find the sought-after address. It should be noted that the word "variety" is used throughout this book in the context of distinguishing groups of animals; technically the term is synonymous with "subspecies" in the biological sense, but here it is applied as a more general definition.

Since no human has ever seen a living dinosaur, they have become natural subjects of curiosity. Artists were the first to reconstruct dinosaurs in drawings and paintings, and several of these illustrators, including Charles R. Knight, were renowned for their depictions of these long-extinct creatures. When the moving image developed into a celluloid art form in the early part of the twentieth century, it didn't take long for them to be resurrected in this new flickering medium; one of the earliest examples is the British silent short *Prehistoric Peeps* (1905), which has been followed by hundreds of other shorts, documentaries and feature-length films featuring authentic or somewhat fanciful monsters from antiquity.

Like the old cliché "There's more than one way to skin a cat," moviemakers have discovered numerous methods of putting saurians on the screen, with results of widely varying quality. Owing to budget restriction and/or the inadequacy of the then-current technology, two techniques in older dinosaur features in which the effect calls too much attention to itself were the use of mechanical props and men in rubber suits. Most of the time these "dinosaurs" really don't look good and, even when I think their looks are acceptable, the movements seem so awkward and restricted that any semblance of realism is instantly destroyed (modern animatronics have make this a non-issue in recent pictures). Another way in which saurians were brought to life on the silver screen was by using photographically enlarged lizards and other reptiles as stand-ins. It is usually more effective than mechanics or costumes, since these four-legged thespians do crawl around under their own power, but even dressed up with horns and fins they still come across to me being too recognizable as living organisms. Probably the very best of these is *One Million B.C.* (1940), with dinosaurian imposters looking so convincing that it has become a classic and has served as the source of stock footage which ended up within a number of low-budget dinosaur flicks. Yet another means of creating filmic prehistoric beasts was cartoon animation. Still in use today, it dates back all the way back to *Gertie the Dinosaur* in 1914. The Disney opus *Fantasia* (1940), with its beautiful "Rite of Spring" segment featuring dinosaurs, represents a high point in cel animation artistry.

Traditionally the most convincing way of realizing saurians, in my and most other folks' opinion, was via stop-motion animation. Sometimes referred to as dimensional animation, this method differs from cartoons in that a 3-D model or puppet is moved into progressive positions instead of a series of flat drawings. The term itself is an oxymoron, since "stop" and "motion" certainly are completely opposite concepts though they belong together here since the results are actually a paradox of sorts; the "movement" seen is actually the stationary positions that are photographed between incremental adjustments made to the model, projected at so many frames per second to generate a moving image. Closely related to "Claymation" effects, stop-motion animation generally employs figures immutable in exterior features that can only change poses and not form. Usually composed of foam latex rubber, these puppets (which is functionally a more descriptive word than "models," though it may connote to some more doll-like appearances rather than miniaturized replicas) are constructed around an armature consisting of machined ball-joints or wire, or sometimes a combination of the two to allow for naturalistic hinging or swiveling motions. Tie-downs, which are keys that are twisted into slots in the bottom of armature feet and then screwed down from the underside of the floor it is being staged upon, serve to support heavier models and help facilitate the walking cycles of bipedal characters like tyrannosaurs.

Because the stop-motion process is highly derivative of time-lapse photography (that is, what is seen in the resulting footage took place in a period of time much greater than perceived), control measures must be in place to insure quality results. Any non-linearities in the staging of such frame-by-frame manipulation, like shifts in lighting intensity or minute disturbances to a miniature set, will be greatly exacerbated by the compression of real time through its screening. There are several other fundamental shortcomings with the stop-motion protocol, which count among them the lack of a "blur" which would naturally be seen during rapid movements, and the inability of miniature puppets to convey the extraneous ripples and undulations of large animals. However, despite its obvious limitations, this technique definitely produced the best results in dinosaur films up until the computer age.

Even in the wake of the dazzling computer-generated saurians of *Jurassic Park* (1993) and *Walking with Dinosaurs* (1999), stop-motion prehistoric beasts still have great appeal to the public even if they no longer represent "cutting-edge" prestidigitation. There are some who feel that these animation effects have been totally upstaged by the perfection of digital dinosaurs, but in my thinking they are missing the aesthetical virtues inherent in this methodology. I believe a good analogy to explain this is how a painting of a landscape can convey an artistic sentiment in a fashion that a photograph cannot. Much like a painter's canvas, dimensional animation allows the person in charge of production to set down a personal vision and make it however faithful to realism he desires. Since animation never appears 100 percent authentic, viewers are therefore seeing something that is interpretive to at least some degree, and therefore will elicit a reaction based on taste and personal preference.

Although many animators have achieved dinosaurs one frame at a time, two names stand above the rest in this category. One of them is Willis O'Brien, considered by many as the father of the traditional type of animation which utilizes these flexible figures that are built around a jointed armature. O'Brien was one of the first to have done this moving and photographing of puppets, making such early shorts as *Dinosaur and the Missing Link* (1915), *R.F.D. 10,000 B.C.* (1917), *Prehistoric Poultry* (1917) and *The Ghost of Slumber Mountain* (1919). His later feature films include *The Lost World* (1925) and *King Kong* (1933), both teeming with Mesozoic reptiles which are impressive to this day.

The other name, the man considered O'Brien's successor in the field and the subject of this book, is Ray Harryhausen. Harryhausen has animated many saurians in a number of early experimental films, an uncompleted project that was envisioned to have been much longer than these called *Evolution*, and several full-length motion pictures: *The Beast from 20,000 Fathoms* (1953), *The Animal World* (1955), *One Million Years B.C.* (1966) and *The Valley of Gwangi* (1969). His life was forever changed after seeing *King Kong* in his youth, putting him on a career path in the special effects field that owed to his affinity for these terrestrial titans of yore.

As this book's title indicates, its purpose is to discuss Harryhausen's lifelong involvement with the dinosaur in film, from fledgling efforts all the way to the (at the time) state-of-the-art prehistoric beasts. Reading from front to back will take the reader through his projects, spanning quite a few decades, in a fairly chronological order. However, the scope here isn't simply limited to what Harryhausen has actually accomplished in a dinosaur film. Productions that never got past the preliminary preproduction phases are discussed, along with his ideas for films which might have consisted of but a single conceptual drawing. Ray's four dinosaurian movies are extensively discussed from all aspects of the staging of their stop-motion content of course, but many additional facets of the overall production are covered in significant depth also. Besides the movies with bona fide saurians present, others which bear some relationship to either them or any antediluvian life form, such as those observed in titles like *20 Million Miles to Earth* (1957), *Mysterious Island* (1961) and *Sinbad and the Eye of the Tiger* (1977), are valid subjects as well.

Additionally, there is an earnest attempt on my part to chronicle Harryhausen's formative years and development as an animator, from the late 1930s into the early 1940s, with more substantial coverage than this exuberant period usually receives in print. Besides the content and making of these early films, people and events that proved inspirational to this highly motivated young man are also duly noted. Since this is after all, a book about dinosaurs, the paleontological accuracy of his dinosaurs from a modern perspective and also how they fared at the time are given treatment. Perhaps most importantly, a portrait of the man himself will emerge throughout these pages that should give some insights to his deep-rooted affection for prehistoric animals.

In the process of writing this book, I consulted a number of previously published works on Harryhausen and incorporated all the pertinent information from these within, but a certain amount of knowledge included here is also of an exclusive nature. A great attempt has been made to get the facts right, in spite of discovering that some small details are contradicted between two or more credible sources. Even though at times I point out specific bits of data that are incorrect in preceding publications, the aim of this is not to denigrate their authors but instead simply set it right "for the record." While several individuals have proven to be of incalculable benefit to this project, I want to especially commend Dr. Rolf Giesen. He has provided a wealth of esoteric data for this work, including measurements for a great preponderance of Ray's models, and continually demonstrated to me such unconditional support and patience that it deserves my deepest appreciation.

What you see here in print represents more than two years' worth of incessant research, but the experience has been very rewarding on a personal level and I now reflect upon this endeavor as being a labor of love. It is therefore my hope that *The Dinosaur Films of Ray Harryhausen* will be looked upon as a comprehensive and compelling book about this patriarchal cinemagician by his legions of fans and, really, *anyone* who is awed by these marvelous monsters of long ago.

—Roy P. Webber
March 2004

1. Early Experiences, Experiments and *Evolution*

Raymond Frederick Harryhausen was born in Los Angeles, California on June 29, 1920, to Fred and Martha Harryhausen, the only child of these American natives of German ancestry. Father Fred was a machinist by trade and supported the family through his skilled labor, allowing for an adequate if not affluent lifestyle. Regardless of income, the parents brought up their son in a loving and nurturing environment, often taking him on weekend trips to places that he enjoyed frequenting. From a very tender age, Ray was fascinated by prehistoric life and loved to visit museums and sites where these long-extinct creatures could be seen.

One such location was Hancock Park, home of the world-famous Rancho La Brea Tar Pits. This attraction, presently in downtown Los Angeles along Wilshire Boulevard, began forming 40,000 years ago when petroleum seeped up to ground level; over many thousands of years this gradual process resulted in the creation of cone-shaped asphalt deposits. During warmer months, the substance would soften up enough to become very sticky, and when covered by leaves, dust and water nearly invisible to the native fauna. When an animal unwittingly walked onto this pool, it would become hopelessly mired in the viscous material. Predators and scavengers were lured to this hapless creature caught in the tar pit, and more often than not they became victims themselves. Other carnivorous animals might be attracted to the scene and wind up being stuck there as well. Since there are many more fossil remains of this type than herbivores (even though meat-eating types are found in nature as only a small percentage of an ecosystem's total make-up), this is an example of a "predator trap." The La Brea Tar Pits have yielded life forms from the late Pleistocene epoch of around 20,000 years ago, which include ancient mammalian varieties such as the saber-tooth tiger, dire wolf, mammoth, giant ground sloth and camel.

Another place where the youth liked to visit, even more than the Tar Pits, was the Los Angeles County Museum of Natural History. This facility housed displays of extinct beasts coming not only from La Brea but also bona fide Mesozoic reptiles; Ray admits that he "haunted" the galleries of the museum when he was young. When Martha Harryhausen bought her son a book illustrated with Charles R. Knight dinosaur paintings, it put a "face" on the fossilized poses he viewed on exhibit. Knight, born in 1874, was for decades the foremost artist of prehistoric reconstructions, bringing back to life scores of saurian genera through his vivid renderings. Although modern paleontology has deemed that many of the depictions are inaccurate, his imagination and expressions are still appreciated by dinosaur fans today. He provided the best blueprints available for early filmmakers (including Harryhausen himself), which were conspicuously present in *The Beast from 20,000 Fathoms* (released in 1953, the year Knight passed away). Ray talked to Knight on the phone once but never met him in person. He noted the importance of this man while talking on the Criterion *Jason and the Argonauts* laserdisc audio commentary, saying, "I got my influence of dinosaurs, of course, by reading books and seeing Charles Knight's wonderful paintings that he made for the American Museum of Natural History."

In addition to museums, the young boy was enthralled with the moving image of the cinema. Harryhausen has indicated that there was a room in the basement of the Los Angeles County Museum dedicated to displays having to do with film processes, including the traveling matte; this no doubt helped enlighten him and give him an appreciation of motion pictures. Back in the 1920s, Ray saw plenty of silent pictures which are still well-known today, among them *Metropolis* (1927) and at least one version of *The Golem*. Probably the one best remembered by him is the original version of *The Lost World* (1925). Adapted from the 1912 Sir Arthur Conan Doyle novel, this First National film starred Bessie Love, Lewis Stone, Wallace Beery, Lloyd Hughes and Arthur Hoyt.

The Lost World takes place in a contemporary setting, beginning in England inside the office of the metropolitan publication *London Record-Journal*. The editor is requesting legal advice: He wants to know if Prof. Challenger (Beery) can sue them for expressing doubts regarding his tale of living dinosaurs. He also notes that Challenger attacked three reporters who were trying to interview him. Looking to be given a dangerous assignment, Edward Malone (Hughes) literally falls through the editor's door and is handed the task of reporting on Challenger's lecture at the Zoological Hall even though reporters are barred. At the Hall, Malone meets Sir John Roxton (Stone), a renowned hunter and explorer, and goes in on his pass. Prof. Challenger is informed that his colleagues cannot support his claims since he lacks proof but is afforded an opportunity to clear his name. Standing before the assembly and continually heckled by students, the professor says he cannot defend his account of existing prehistoric monsters but invites anybody present brave enough for a return trip to the South American region where these beasts were found. Accepting his challenge are Prof. Summerlee (Hoyt), Roxton and Malone. But Malone lets slip he works for the *Record-Journal*, sending Challenger after him in a rage. Since this abruptly ends the meeting, the volatile professor returns to his Kensington residence.

Malone follows him home and sneaks in through a window, eager to be included in any expedition. Seething at the intrusion, Challenger lunges at the newspaperman and both end up rolling out the front door. Making peace and going back inside, they are soon met by Roxton. Challenger shows Malone the diary of Maple White, a fellow scientist who went on the expedition to the remote part of the Amazon basin with him but was unfortunately left behind. Paula White (Love), Maple's trained assistant and daughter, who was with him on the journey, enters the room. She recounts how she was stricken with jungle fever in camp while her father climbed the plateau with the dinosaurs; when the bearers saw them they fled, marooning him there and carrying her

1. Early Experiences, Experiments and Evolution 7

back to the coast. Malone sees illustrations of the plateau and two Mesozoic reptiles in the notebook. Malone announces that the newspaper will finance a rescue party, whether or not any saurians can be found in the area. Won over by this business proposal, Challenger shakes Malone's hand.

In the Amazon, the explorers see all kinds of indigenous wildlife, including a dangling snake that frightens Jocko the monkey. Making camp at the base of the great plateau for the night,

Several dinosaurs, including a stegosaurus and a brachiosaurus, flee from volcanic fury in *The Lost World*. The tabletop set seen here is extremely large. Photograph courtesy of Greg Kulon.

they nearly get crushed by a boulder dropped down the sheer side of the tableland and watch a pteranodon eating its meal. In the morning, they climb a stand-alone pinnacle next to the main plateau (the plateau itself is too steep to directly ascend, so this neighboring formation must be scaled). In order to reach the plateau, they fell a tree across the chasm (as Maple White had done) and cross over to the prehistoric realm. But just after they all get across (except Jocko), a foraging brontosaurus sends the log bridge crashing down the cliff, trapping Challenger, Roxton, Summerlee, Paula and Malone there. While they settle down for the evening, an allosaurus kills a duck-billed dinosaur but loses the carcass when it tumbles into a quagmire, and then gets stabbed by a horn during an unsuccessful attack upon a mother and baby triceratops. The two-legged monster then bursts through dense foliage and enters the encampment. Repelled by several bullets and a hurled torch, it retreats back through the trees. As the allosaur fights yet another horned saurian, an ape-man, who has been watching the explorers' every move (and pushed the large rock off the cliff earlier), is perched in a tree right above them. Wounded by a gunshot to the arm, this missing link leaps into the brush. Meanwhile, the allosaurus is killed by its ceratopsian adversary, which is then defeated by a larger Tyrannosaurus rex that also snags a pteranodon gliding past it.

Jocko the monkey has returned to the camp at the plateau base, where two assistants have been waiting behind. The ape-man treats his injured arm at a pool of water.

The next day, Challenger devises a catapult from a couple of supple tree trunks, and Roxton goes exploring inside of a cave. Roxton finds some human skeletal remains and a pocket watch bearing the monogram "M.W." and a picture of Paula. He also discovers a cave opening right upon the precipice of the tableland and sees the two helpers down below, firing his revolver to signal them. Spotting Roxton, they yell up to him that they are making a rope ladder out of the hammocks and will work all night to finish it, with Jocko being the means of getting it up to them. In another part of the cave, Malone and Paula are discussing their future together; their affection for each other has been growing steadily ever since they met. He asserts that his engagement back home is now null and void as far as he is concerned, and kisses the pretty woman. Roxton approaches and is informed by Malone that they will get married soon, since Prof. Summerlee was once a minister, and congratulates the couple though a look of disappointment shows on his face; it is clear that his interest in her is more than just platonic. After Malone walks off, Roxton produces the pocket watch and gives it to her. Realizing that her father is dead, Paula starts to sob.

Both professors are trailing a brontosaurus, grazing while it walks along. An allosaurus suddenly approaches and confronts the giant herbivore. A brief struggle ensues, ending when the brontosaur steps backward and falls off the edge of the plateau into a pool of water; it survives the plunge but is mired in thick mud. Roxton and Paula wait for the others to return to the cave, noting the nearby volcanic mountain-top venting furiously. Soon, a full-blown eruption sends forth rivers of molten lava. Many dinosaurs stampede through the jungle in a panic to escape the searing heat and burning vegetation. Malone frantically races through the inferno to find the professors, who are just as busy running around to avoid being killed. The next day, the sun rises on a great number of saurians concentrated in a small area of the plateau, with a pack of allosaurs sharing a meal.

Challenger, Summerlee and Malone head to the opening looking directly down the steep side of the tableland. There Paula, with Roxton, coaxes Jocko to bring a line attached to the rope ladder up. They all climb down from the plateau, Malone descending last. The ape-man appears and begins violently yanking on the ladder, making him swing wildly. But his antagonist is shot dead by Roxton, allowing the newspaperman to finish his descent and rejoin the others. Just as they are starting to set out, they come across the fallen brontosaur (still stuck in the muck) and a major from the Brazilian Geodetic Survey. The major, who arrived there after observing a cloud of smoke above the plateau, promises help to get the dinosaur floated out on a raft.

Much later, back in London, Challenger is again appearing before a Zoological Hall audience when Malone phones him with the news that the brontosaurus has escaped; as the cage was swung out from the chartered ship the cables broke, smashing it in the fall and setting the creature loose in the streets of the city. Challenger announces this startling turn of events to the audience at the Hall; they react angrily at the presumed hoax and shake fists as Challenger hastily leaves to retrieve his specimen. Outside the building, terror-stricken masses try to run from the oncoming sauropod. Swatting people with a flick of its tail and demolishing a number of London structures, the brontosaur lumbers out onto the famous Tower Bridge. Challenger, Summerlee, Roxton, Malone and Paula arrive just as the dinosaur crashes through the middle of the bridge's roadway and drops into the Thames below. As a dejected Roxton looks on, the young lovers ride away in an automobile. With his prehistoric exhibit proceeding to swim downriver and heading towards its home, Challenger slumps down on an embankment in a posture of utter defeat.

This version of the 1925 film is the most familiar to fans, at just over an hour. It was restored and tinted in alternating hues for a 1991 Lumivision laserdisc release by the George Eastman House in association with Disney archivist Scott MacQueen, an improvement upon the very grainy B&W edition. It still represented an abridged edition. On its original theatrical release, *The Lost World* was a total of 9,209 feet of 35mm film, running somewhere near a time of 104 minutes (indicating a projection speed nearly that of sound movies, about 23 frames per second (FPS).

However, all known subsequent prints are much shorter. As explained in supplemental notes found in the Lumivision incarnation of *Lost World*, it was cut in 1930 prior to its non-theatrical distribution to schools and churches. "With few exceptions, Kodascope prints were shortened to five theatrical reels in length, running just under an hour," the liner notes reveal. "A 35mm lavender positive printed from the camera negative would be edited to 5 reels. From this, a 35mm nitrate dupe negative was made for reduction printing 16mm safety film release prints." Since the domestic negative is missing or decomposed, the Kodascope became the archetypal version more or less by default. While this surviving portion is actually well-edited (though rather tightly in places), the storyline is condensed and suffers in that certain characters and situations are now left hanging. Even worse was the excision of some stop-motion effects, probably considered too "gory" for the intended school and church group audiences.

But recent developments have changed the picture quite literally. In the early 1990s, a Czechoslovakian print came to light in the early 1990s which was over 8,000 feet long, and about 12 minutes of animation outtakes were also discovered in a New York film archive. Using the Czech version, several tinted Kodascopes and material from other sources, David Shepard put together a new 93–minute "restored" *Lost World* for DVD release in 2001, with the outtakes included as an added bonus. Unfortunately, this new edition isn't perfect, as an A-B comparison with the Lumivision DVD reveals a number of brief clips missing here and there (especially of the brontosaurus in London). Still, the extra footage makes this endeavor a must-have version for fans. Until a complete print or negative of *Lost World* is located, it will remain a "lost" film, since there is no way to determine with 100 percent certainty the exact order of every cut based on what is now known. An interesting point about this picture is that the animation appears to have been photographed for a projection speed of 16 FPS, with the live-action sequences recorded at a speed close to 20 FPS.

Harryhausen remembers seeing *Lost World* during its theatrical run, carrying away a memory of the brontosaur on a rampage through London. In a letter reprinted on the Lumivision *Lost World*, Ray wrote, "Looking back still further in time, I remember vividly the first time I saw *The Lost World* in 1925 at the tender age of five. The great brontosaurus wallowing pathetically in the mud lake at the bottom of the cliff was an image that kept re-appearing in my mind's eye to this very day." This classic of the silent era was produced by Earl Hudson and directed by Harry O. Hoyt. Arthur Edeson, who worked on Douglas Fairbanks films including *The Thief of Baghdad* (1924), was cinematographer and Marion Fairfax wrote the screenplay, which is relatively faithful to the Doyle novel.

Of course, what stands out about *The Lost World* is the special effects content, featuring stop-motion dinosaurs moving around in convincing miniature tabletop sets. Most of the animation was done on four foot by six foot miniatures, with the eruption and stampede being done on a very large 75-foot by 150-foot set. The man primarily responsible for these effects (assisted only in animating the stampede sequence), who would later have a profound influence on the life of young Harryhausen, was Willis H. O'Brien. Born in 1886 in Oakland, California, O'Brien (called "Obie" by his friends) worked in a variety of jobs and had quite a varied résumé: He had briefly been a cowboy, trapper, newspaper cartoonist, boxer and stonecutter, among other occupations. Then one afternoon when he was in his late twenties, while tinkering with clay figures of boxers and repositioning them in differing poses, the idea of dimensional animation came to him. After constructing clay dinosaur and caveman models, and having a newsreel cameraman photograph these figures in progressive poses within a miniature setting, a new art form was born.

Eventually 80 seconds of animation effects was realized, and Obie felt that his invention could be turned into a marketable endeavor. So he approached filmmaker and entrepreneur Herman Wobber, who was impressed enough by O'Brien's results to give him $5,000 to remake his short subject. Accepting the money and laboring for two months, these efforts yielded what is known today as *The Dinosaur and the Missing Link* (1915). Even though this production is extremely crude by modern animation standards, it was a big improvement upon his previous footage owing to puppets built out of rubber and animated on sturdier sets. O'Brien was soon employed by the Edison Studios, where he made a number of shorts under the Conquest Pictures banner, among them *Morpheus Mike* (1917), *Prehistoric Poultry* (1917) and *R.F.D. 10,000 B.C.* (1917). Obie then joined forces with Major Herbert M. Dawley, who paid the effects man $3,000 to make a film with saurians. The result was his most ambitious feature to date, *The Ghost of Slumber Mountain* (1919). This work, unlike the earlier Edison shorts, is a combination of stop-motion and live-action elements, with O'Brien making his only acting appearance as "Mad Dick," the ghost of a deceased hermit. *Slumber Mountain* was initially about 45 minutes long, but Dawley had cut it down to only a fraction of that length for its release; what remains of the film features a number of prehistoric animals, including a brontosaurus, diatryma, a pair of triceratops and an allosaurus. Unfortunately, this experience turned out to be quite bitter for Obie: Dawley not only refused to give any credit for his visual contribution, he also claimed to have "invented" the animation process and later took out patents to that effect. Luckily for O'Brien, soon after ending his relationship with Dawley, he met Watterson R. Rothacker. A Chicago businessman and promoter, Rothacker was impressed by Obie's work and had followed his career ever since his Conquest Pictures shorts. They made several "novelty films" together before starting to develop *The Lost World* during the early 1920s (apparently it was brought to Rothacker by O'Brien). But several lawsuits were initiated at this time against those trying to make this movie, including one by Major Dawley seeking $100,000 from Rothacker for using "his" stop-motion techniques. This was squelched by proof consisting of the early films and signed affidavits stating who really devised stop-motion photography.

Two other personalities were very important in the making of *The Lost World*. Marcel Delgado, a young Mexican-born artist Obie met in an evening art class, was talked into leaving his grocery clerk job and joining the production. His contribution was in modelmaking, constructing the 50 dinosaur puppets used for animation through a "build-up" procedure he developed himself. It gave these figures realistic musculature and skin texture, making them more than satisfactory for their roles. Ralph Hammeras was an independent effects man who eventually teamed up with First National, not only for the security of working for a large film company but also the opportunity to collaborate with O'Brien. Hammeras' great development was the glass shot, a simple yet very effective method to extend or enhance scenery for a movie. Lined up with a set that needs modification from the camera's perspective, it provides a tremendous budgetary savings to the filmmaker since no physical objects need be built if seen only from a distance. Many wonderful vistas seen in the feature only existed as paintings on glass. Carefully executed, they can appear extremely convincing in a two-dimensional image.

Even if *The Lost World* was a memorable experience for a little boy like Harryhausen, it didn't provoke any substantial change in him. Harryhausen would, for several more years, be pretty much a "normal" child with typical interests. Young Harryhausen showed artistic talent from an early age, initially working with pencils and ink before discovering a different medium with which to express himself. On the Criterion *Jason* laserdisc, Ray relates a significant event which took place while he was a student:

> I think in my early days at school, in grammar school, I remember our teacher gave us a mission of making the Missions of California in three dimensions. And that was one of the projects I think I did, about four or five in clay, of the various Missions along the coast of California. And that really, when I look back, stimulated me into having more of an interest in dimensional objects rather than flat drawings. So that was largely responsible, I think, for my interest in sculpture.

Harryhausen would apply this experience to make dioramas of prehistoric creatures, shaping his monsters out of clay and giving them teeth made from toothpicks.

During the 1920s, several expeditions into the Gobi Desert led by Roy Chapman Andrews of the American Museum of Natural History (a swashbuckling personality who possibly was an indirect inspiration for Indiana Jones) made some extremely interesting paleontological finds; in addition to locating some fossilized bones there, they discovered a number of well-preserved saurian eggs, the first ones ever found. Reports of this exotic travel and bone-digging excited and fascinated Harryhausen, who dreamed of doing pretty much the same thing himself. But throughout the 1920s and into the early 1930s, Ray lived a normal childhood, full of imagination for things he loved but doing nothing especially out of the ordinary. However, during the middle of 1933 a pivotal event took place that forever changed the outlook Ray Harryhausen would have on life.

It started out, innocently enough, with his aunt taking care of an elderly lady. Her patient was the mother of Sid Grauman, owner of the ornate and world-famous Grauman's (now known as Mann's) Chinese Theatre in Hollywood. Sid gave his mother's nurse three tickets to a matinee at his movie house, so she took both Martha and Ray along to the show. The movie was *King Kong*, which the boy knew from newspaper ads had something to do with a gorilla. Upon their arrival, he saw a wonderful display in the forecourt: an enormous, moving bust of the giant ape (the same prop used for live-action close-ups when Kong chews on hapless human beings). It was surrounded by tropical plants; several pink flamingos strolled about this jungle setting. Once inside, young Ray observed publicity photos of the film and a live prologue with native dancers performing a stage show. In *Cinefantastique* Volume 11 Number 4 (1981), he describes how this warm-up excited him: "It somehow appealed to my Gothic or Germanic background" (26). Now that the pageantry had raised his level of enthusiasm, Harryhausen was perfectly conditioned when the feature began flickering on the theater screen.

King Kong is an RKO (Radio-Keith-Orpheum) production which stars Fay Wray, Robert Armstrong, Bruce Cabot and Frank Reicher, produced by Merian C. Cooper and directed by Ernest B. Schoedsack. It begins in New York Harbor, where the tramp steamer *Venture* is docked. Aboard the ship, Capt. Englehorn (Reicher) talks to filmmaker Carl Denham (Armstrong) about plans for shoving off first thing in the morning. Englehorn is worried that some explosive gas bombs brought aboard may prompt the insurance companies to investigate, and Denham wants to arrive at his faraway destination before the monsoon season begins so he can shoot his new picture.

Just then, a theatrical agent (Sam Hardy) shows up, escorted by First Mate Jack Driscoll (Cabot). The agent tells Denham he cannot send a girl to him for his movie, since Denham refuses to reveal what the assignment will involve or how long it will last. Both the captain and first mate admit that even *they* aren't exactly certain where this voyage will take them. Protesting that the public demands a pretty female in films, Denham heads into the city to find his gal.

Getting out of a cab near a women's mission, Denham is unimpressed by the rough and haggard examples of femininity waiting in line. But then he finds a beautiful lass (Wray) accosted by a shopkeeper who thinks she is attempting to steal an apple from him. Saving her by giving the belligerent owner a dollar, he is immediately taken by her beauty and brings her to a cafe for a cup of coffee. Learning that her name is Ann Darrow and that she has some acting experience, he introduces himself and asks her to star in his next picture.

As the *Venture* leaves port the next morning, Driscoll is clearly uneasy about Ann's presence on the vessel. Before long, however, he starts to fall in love with her. Denham tells Ann to get ready for an on-deck camera test and she leaves to put on a costume.

On the bridge, Denham tells the captain to head southwest from their

A distinctive-looking prehistoric mammal with two horns on its snout, the arsinoitherium was to have appeared in the unrealized O'Brien project *Creation*. It was going to chase sailors out onto a log bridge, a scenario recycled into *King Kong*.

present location west of Sumatra. When Englehorn protests that there is nothing but ocean for thousands of miles, Denham produces a hand-drawn map of an uncharted island. He obtained it two years earlier in Singapore from the skipper of a Norwegian bark, who created it from information provided by a dying native blown out to sea in a canoe. Only accessible through an opening in a reef, the landmass is sheer cliffs hundreds of feet high on all sides except for a small peninsula where the islanders live. This area is separated from the rest of the island by a great wall, which they keep in repair to protect themselves from something on the other side. With the curiosity of the two men piqued, Denham notes that on this island there is a legendary entity called "Kong" which *he* believes is a living creature rather than myth. Denham has come halfway around the world to photograph this colossal being, neither man nor beast, and has brought the gas bombs along just in case his subject is camera-shy.

A short while later, Ann comes out on deck in her "beauty and the beast" costume and positions herself for Denham to shoot some camera tests. After telling her to look up at something towering and terrible, something she is unable to turn away from, he instructs the starlet to cover her eyes and scream, which she does quite convincingly. Driscoll observes this and becomes very concerned; what exactly does the filmmaker expect that she will witness on the exotic shoot?

The ship is soon surrounded by a thick mist as it draws near the uncharted island. While a crew man takes soundings to make sure they don't run aground, Englehorn notes that they were indeed very close to the island when the fog settled around them. Ann asks Denham how they will know, by observation, if the land they sight is what they are looking for; he replies that there is a mountain there shaped like a skull, hence the name "Skull Mountain." Even though they can't see a thing, a sound is heard carrying across the water: drums beating out a tempo. When the enveloping shroud clears, the enormous skull-shaped outcropping and barrier wall are plainly visible, identifying the island as their destination. Englehorn hears drums again but doesn't see a living soul on the low-lying peninsula.

Going ashore with his camera equipment and a handful of men, Denham, Englehorn, Driscoll and Ann, head for the native village and marvel at the impressive wall. Hearing noises up ahead, they cautiously encroach until they see a ritual is in progress, with the tribesmen attired in gaudy makeup and furry robes dancing around with ape-like gestures. A native girl covered with flowers is obviously soon to be sacrificed to whatever they are worshipping. Seeing this spectacle from behind some bushes, Denham gets excited and sets up his camera out in the open to begin filming. He is quickly spotted by the fierce-looking tribal chieftain, who shouts to alert his subjects of the intruder's presence.

After everyone from the *Venture* steps out into plain view, Englehorn, who knows some native dialects, attempts to communicate with their leader. He learns that the girl with the floral decoration is to be the bride of Kong. The witch doctor then runs over to the chieftain, obviously quite upset, saying that the intruders have ruined the ceremony by witnessing it. Denham calls out their word for friend, "bala," to help ease the situation but this doesn't work. Englehorn now translates the chieftain's offer to trade six of his females for the blonde "golden woman," intended as a gift to Kong. After refusing the offer, Englehorn senses they are now in great peril and instructs everybody to leave before the natives think of cutting them off from the beach. Offering to come back tomorrow, they all walk away very uneasily, constantly looking over their shoulders.

That night, back on the ship, with the pounding of native drums heard carrying over from the island, Ann is out on deck when Driscoll comes over and chats with her. He admits that he is very worried about her well-being, and also that he has fallen in love with her. He is called up to the bridge just as they begin to kiss and embrace, leaving her swooning in the darkness. But while she is distracted by these passionate feelings, several tribesmen in outrigger canoes paddle up to the tramp steamer and noiselessly abduct Ann. However, she pulls a bracelet off an abductor's wrist so evidence of what has happened remains on deck. Driscoll looks around for his sweetheart but can't find her on deck or in her cabin. The Chinese cook discovers the bracelet and excitedly shouts "All hands on deck!" After a quick search by the crew, they realize that Ann has been taken by the villagers and hurriedly grab guns and gas bombs for a rescue mission.

Right in front of the great wall, the islanders are dancing more festively than before, jumping around and waving torches in their revelry. With the "golden woman" securely in their clutches, they slide the huge bolt that seals the colossal double doors in the middle of the wall. After this portal has been swung open, she is led to an altar on the other side and tied to posts. The native retreats back through the doorway. The doors are then quickly closed, the bolt slid back in place and the natives climb to the top of the wall to get a view of their staked-out sacrificial victim. Flanked by his jubilant tribesmen, the chieftain stands directly above the gateway next to a large gong. Shouting a ritualistic invocation ("Rama Kong") he waves his staff and the gong is struck. It isn't long before roars are heard coming from the foliage. A moment later, a gigantic ape pushes several trees away to get to his offering. Ann sees Kong's leering expression and is terrified out of her wits, screaming convulsively as he plucks her from the altar. Growling at the natives arrayed above him on the wall, King Kong leaves with the woman clutched in his paw.

By this time, the men from the *Venture* have come ashore and race through the village. Driscoll catches a glimpse of Kong through an opening at the bottom of one of the doors, and winces at the sight of the monstrous gorilla heading back into the jungle.

The rescue party quickly opens the passage leading to the interior of the island. Driscoll and Denham take a number of men and go through the doors, with Englehorn waiting behind with the rest of the crew men to protect the entrance. Trailing the simian in the darkness, the rescuers are able to follow him by finding broken branches and sizable tracks. Just after dawn breaks, the pursuers spot a stegosaurus across a clearing in the distance. As they try to lay low, the plated dinosaur ambles out of view, then re-emerges closer to their position. It notices them and charges with a roar, but is stopped with a volley of bullets and a gas bomb. Firing again at the fallen stegosaur brings the beast back on its feet, but it collapses a moment later and is kept down with a round shot into its eye. Denham, Driscoll and the others file past the supine stegosaurus and are awestruck by the prehistoric monster. Its spiked tail flickers in a post-mortem reflex.

Moving on, they hear and follow the grunts of Kong to the edge of a great swamp; through the fog they can perceive him splashing through it just ahead of them. After building a raft, the group poles over to where they heard the towering ape making his

1. Early Experiences, Experiments and Evolution   15

way. Meanwhile, a brontosaurus is cruising towards their log raft, surfacing periodically like a submarine. This long-necked dinosaur appears suddenly like a sea serpent in the gloom next to the men, who react by shooting at the monster. It quickly dives back below the surface. The brontosaurus then comes up directly underneath the craft, capsizing it and spilling all the men into the water. It seizes several men in its jaws before they can swim to shore. Running for their lives through a marsh, the survivors flee before the gigantic sauropod that has followed them onto land. Denham, Driscoll and most of the others outdistance the lumbering dinosaur, but one sailor lags behind. As the brontosaurus closes in on him, the man desperately climbs a dead tree to escape his pursuer but the attempt fails; the brontosaur plucks the screaming crew man out of the tree and shakes him like a rag doll.

The survivors of the rafting adventure race through the jungle as Kong crosses a mossy log bridge over a crevasse with Ann still clenched in his paw. Setting her in the fork of a tall tree trunk, the gorilla goes back and menaces the men on the log bridge. Denham is hung up on a branch on the far side, and Driscoll shimmies down a vine into a recess in the rocks just below the charging simian. The rest of the men are caught on the middle of the log. Roaring ferociously at the crew men, Kong picks up one end of the log and twists it back and forth until all fall to their deaths in the crevasse. Kong finally drops the entire log down the ravine with a mighty crash.

Driscoll witnesses all this in horror from his perch right below the towering gorilla. Now Kong leans over the edge and tries to grab him. With his knife, Driscoll stabs the gigantic groping fingertips. He also cuts loose a creeper that a sizable lizard was using to crawl up towards him.

While this is taking place, Ann sees a tyrannosaurus from her treetop perspective and screams loudly, drawing the ape away from her trapped boyfriend. Kong arrives to face this menace and a very spectacular and acrobatic fight breaks out, with both combatants being tossed around by one another. During the battle, the dead tree holding Ann is toppled and she is pinned under its weight. Defeating the tyrannosaur by pulling its jaws far enough apart to break bones, a victorious Kong pounds his chest and retrieves the blonde from under the fallen tree.

Denham sees Dris-

The tyrannosaurus model from *King Kong* and styracosaurus figure from *The Son of Kong* posed on a table. The former was originally built for *Creation*; the latter was to have been in *Kong* but was cut before the film's release. Photograph courtesy of Greg Kulon.

coll climb out of the crevasse and shouts to him. The first mate says he'll follow after Kong to figure out a way of saving Ann, and instructs Denham to return to the native village. Hearing the grunts of the tremendous ape, he heads in that direction and notices the tyrannosaurus carcass, with blood still oozing from its mouth.

Denham returns to the great wall and fills in Englehorn. Denham wants to take some more gas bombs and cross the crevasse in the morning, saying they will definitely stop King Kong. Asked if there has been any trouble with the islanders, Englehorn says they fled to their huts like "scared rabbits" after a couple of rounds were fired over their heads.

Driscoll has followed Kong along a river to Skull Mountain. Inside a great cavern with rising mist and a pool in the middle, Kong sets Ann down in a small recess in the rocks for safe keeping but she gets attacked a moment later — a plesiosaurus has emerged from the water and slithered over to her. Kong grabs the serpent-like monster but it quickly wraps itself around his throat and nearly strangles the mighty gorilla with constricting coils. Kong manages to pull the plesiosaur off and then bashes its head on the rocks by swinging it around by the tail. With this menace disposed of, Kong picks up Ann and leaves the grotto.

Stepping out onto a ledge with a panoramic view of the island and ocean, Kong looks out over his domain, roars defiantly and then begins to playfully peel away some of his blonde captive's outer garments. Driscoll accidentally dislodges a boulder inside the cavern, and Kong investigates the source of the crashing noise. Ann is now attacked by a swooping pteranodon and nearly carried away but Kong nabs the flapping reptile and quickly dispatches it. While the colossal simian is distracted, Ann and Driscoll begin climbing down a vine dangling from the ledge. Kong tosses the lifeless pteranodon over the side, then spots them fleeing down the creeper and starts reeling the pair back in. Ann and Driscoll let go of the vine and plunge into the river beneath. Kong sets out in pursuit of the tiny object of his affection.

When Ann and Driscoll arrive back at the native village, Englehorn begins preparing to head back to the ship, when Denham protests; the intrepid filmmaker says they came there for a moving picture and the gorilla is worth more than all the movies in the world. Denham implies that Ann can be used as bait to lure Kong to where he might be caught; Driscoll flushes with anger at the suggestion. Just then, a man on the wall cries out that Kong is coming towards them, spurring them to quickly close the door and secure the entrance with the massive timber. Banging the gong brings the natives running with the male villagers racing over to help hold the giant door shut. But despite their combined efforts, Kong splits the wooden bolt and the doors swing open. Everybody runs for his life as Kong enters the village and goes on a rampage. Some of the islanders are crushed by tossed debris or underneath his gigantic hairy feet, while others grabbed by the gorilla are gnawed between his tusk-like teeth. Denham hurls a gas bomb at Kong which swiftly renders him unconscious. Denham now calls for chains and material to build a raft for Kong, promising to share the wealth with all of the crew men.

Later, in New York, the "Eighth Wonder of the World" is about to go on display in a large theater; the patrons waiting in line and taking their seats have been kept in the dark about the nature of the attraction. Off stage, Denham, Driscoll and Ann formally dressed for the premiere showing of their monstrous captive, are meeting with the press; Denham suggests they emphasize the "beauty and the beast" aspect of the amazing story. The moviemaker now walks out on stage in front of the curtain before the packed house and begins to tell the story of their voyage as the curtain rises, revealing the titanic gorilla chained to a crossbar on a steel girder platform. After calming down the theatergoers (frightened by the sight of Kong), Denham introduces Driscoll and Ann to the audience, announcing that the couple will soon be wed. Denham next invites a number of photographers to take the first photos of Kong and his captors. They start snapping flashbulb pictures, agitating the giant ape. The gorilla begins violently wrenching against his restraints, since he thinks the flashes are an attack on Ann. Denham tells the photographers to stop but they continue until Kong breaks his bonds and leaps off the metal platform.

As the theater attendees fall over themselves escaping, Kong chases Ann and Driscoll. Bursting out the side of the building, the monstrous simian grabs a man, chews on him and then tosses his body aside. Hearing a lady scream up above, he now starts to climb a hotel exterior.

When the ape peers in the window of a sleeping woman, he mistakes her for Ann, reaches in and snatches her from bed; dangling her in his paw many stories above the street, Kong realizes his error and lets the woman drop to her death. The gorilla continues his ascent with

In remarkably good shape for its age, the *Kong* stegosaurus in a fairly recent photograph taken at the home of Forrest J Ackerman. Photograph courtesy of Loren Portillo.

The armature from one of the Kong models. Note that two of the digits are missing from its left hand. Photograph by the author.

masses of humanity gathered beneath him and comes across the room to which Driscoll and Ann have retreated. Kong shoves his furry paw in through a side window. Driscoll is knocked down, and Ann is grabbed and lifted out through the window.

Escaping with Ann, Kong comes across a trestle as an elevated train rolls past; he pummels a section of track with his fists as another train races towards the wrecked rails. Seeing both the damaged trestle and stupendous ape up ahead, the operator tries to brake but cannot stop in time. One of the cars crashes into the gaping hole next to Kong, who proceeds to pull it down to the street and pounds on it as passengers scream in terror. The ape now begins climbing a building next to the scene of the derailment.

At a police station, Denham and Driscoll listen to a radio news bulletin announcing that Kong is climbing the Empire State Building. Driscoll suggests that airplanes can possibly pick Kong off without harming Ann. Four World War I–vintage biplanes soon take off from a nearby airfield.

Kong is nearing the top of New York's tallest building as the squadron closes in. Preparing for their attack, he puts Ann down as the biplanes circle overhead. One by one, they shoot at him in strafing runs. Some of the aircraft fly dangerously close to the gorilla; one plane comes too close and is snagged by Kong, who sends the craft crashing to the street below. But after a number of fly-bys, Kong has blood on his chest and is clearly in pain. Sensing that death is near, he picks up Ann one last time, then sets her down as his energy is waning. Another burst of gunfire finishes off Kong, who plunges over 100 stories. As Driscoll comforts Ann, a crowd gathers around the broken carcass of Kong. When a policeman says that Kong was done in by the airplanes, Denham muses that it was actually beauty who killed this legendary beast.

King Kong was not only a successful motion picture financially (saving RKO from bankruptcy during the depths of the Depression) but is universally considered one of the best ever made. Its basic storyline has been repeated in many subsequent offerings, but none come close to matching its atmospheric build-up and powerful visual effects. The idea for the movie was dreamed up by producer Merian C. Cooper, who along with director Ernest B. Schoedsack made several documentary-type adventure films during the 1920s, which include *Grass* (1925), *Chang* (1927) and *The Four Feathers* (1929). Cooper wanted to make a picture dealing with gorillas, an interest that developed as a result of his involvement with *Four Feathers*. Elements from these were incorporated into their latest production, which was originally going to showcase a battle between a real gorilla and a Komodo dragon. However, the studio heads were not interested in the expense of going to both Africa and then the island of Komodo for the animals and locations required. Fortunately, Cooper saw footage from a shelved O'Brien project, *Creation* (1931), about dinosaurs inside a dormant South American volcano that are discovered by a group of people swept there aboard a submarine. The premise of *Creation* really didn't appeal to Cooper, but the technology impressed him.

The existing animation, of a baby triceratops wandering around and eventually being shot by a man (who then gets chased by its angry mother) shows a great artistic improvement upon *The Lost World*. Obie pitched to Cooper the idea of using stop-motion effects for the gorilla project.

Most of the technical staff from *Creation* were retained for this new production, including talented artists such as Byron Crabbe, Marcel Delgado and Mario Larrinaga. Some of the already constructed miniatures also ended up in *Kong*. Several of these prehistoric creatures, like the triceratops models and an arsinoitherium, never made it into the finished film, but the tyrannosaurus that fights Kong did. All the puppets built by Delgado for *Creation* and *Kong* show an immense leap in quality over those he made just a few years earlier, both in design and exterior detailing. Two 18"-tall figures of the titular ape and several new dinosaurs were constructed. A few of these still exist, either badly deteriorated or (like one of the gorilla puppets) only an armature.

Harryhausen, in a letter to the author, admits, "The 1933 *King Kong* has some very bad jerks in the animation if you run it over and over and only look for the faults. ... But it did not matter to the average public as the dynamic over all entertainment value of the film made one forget these details."

Kong was quickly followed by a sequel that was released before the end of 1933, *The Son of Kong*. Starring Robert Armstrong, Helen Mack and Frank Reicher, it is about a return trip to the uncharted island, where a much smaller and highly anthropomorphic giant ape is discovered—the offspring of Kong. *Son of Kong*'s animated monsters include a styracosaurus (which was cut from the original *Kong* shortly before its release), cave bear, dragon-like saurian and sea serpent. The movie ends with the utter destruction of the island and the friendly simian's death, but most of the picture is of a highly farcical nature completely unlike the preceding feature. Ray doesn't particularly care for this offering, stating in the 4th edition of his *Film Fantasy Scrapbook*, "Although certain sequences had some merit, the picture as a whole was a great disappointment for the many fans of the mighty *King Kong*. To me, the white 'baby' gorilla seemed completely out of character, from his very appearance to the many cartoon-like gestures he exhibited throughout the story."(6)

But back at Grauman's Chinese that summer day in 1933, a boy just shy of his teens was totally absorbed by the spectacle flickering before his eyes and ringing in his ears. Young Harryhausen went in to see *King Kong* a normal child but emerged a changed person, deeply affected by the experience. He was impressed by the gargantuan simian as well as the dinosaurs, particularly the stegosaurus and tyrannosaurus. The movie filled his impressionable mind with sights and sounds that made their indelible mark on his receptive psyche; on countless occasions Ray has quipped that he "hasn't been the same since" viewing *Kong*. Of course, many people have been steered toward celebrated careers by either a single event or a series of events. Many struggling entertainers had lucky breaks or were simply in the right place at the right time. But they were already following a career with a talent created by a natural inclination or developed through the influence of others like parents. Harryhausen's vocational calling was indisputably the result of a tumultuous experience that afternoon in mid–1933, putting him on a path to an occupation that he positively wouldn't have pursued otherwise.

Ray returned to see *King Kong* over and over again during its original theatrical run. He was haunted by the feature, but didn't understand what techniques were used in order to achieve the effects (he knew it wasn't a man inside of a gorilla suit). Fueled by a passion to understand what he had seen, the curious fan began putting together pieces of information about this movie's special effects. This couldn't have been an easy undertaking, since in the 1930s precious little was written about the nuts and bolts of special effects wizardry. Ray noted in *Collectable Toys & Values* #16 (1993), "Then there was a big article in *Look* magazine about Kong. It was a two-page spread with details and various other things" (17).

Besides finding published information on the movie, young Harryhausen happened to hunt up some who were involved in its making. Even though they served in minor functions and therefore didn't have extensive knowledge on the stop-motion process, they did give Ray an idea of how intricate and time-consuming it is. In *Wonder* #5 (1991), he divulged, "My dad had

Two prehistoric models crafted by a young Ray Harryhausen on display at Forrest Ackerman's home, a papier-mâché brontosaurus and an arsinoitherium sculpture. Photograph by the author.

worked at RKO just briefly as a machinist and he met one of the men that had worked on it. So he got some inside dope. That was my first initiation to stop-motion photography" (29). This gleaning of little scraps of wisdom progressed at an imperceptible pace and it took several years for him to accrue enough data to even think of trying anything on his own. One thing he managed to do soon after this stimulating occurrence was build a fairly sizeable sauropod figure. It is described in *Cinefantastique* Volume 31 Number 1 / 2 (1999) by writer Dan Feilberger as "a four-

One of the earliest bits of animation Harryhausen ever did with his cave bear puppet. Ray and his dog Kong are visible below the tree in the lower part of the frame image, inserted via a static matte. Photograph courtesy of David M. Massaro.

foot long paper-mache Brontosaurus, made in the early 1930's, shortly after first seeing *King Kong*" (36). But after this period of discovery had run its course, Ray, now a gangly teenager, was poised to attempt some model animation of his own.

Ray's first animation film was made some time during the early part of 1938 when he was 17 years old. Most fans know that the first creature he animated frame-by-frame was a cave bear that he constructed himself. The budding effects man appropriated from a closet a fur coat which his mother didn't wear anymore (contrary to several magazine articles, he maintains that he had permission to use it as the bear's hairy exterior). Built over a wooden armature like many of Willis O'Brien's earliest puppets, the cave bear was obviously crude compared to subsequent stop-motion figures he made but on its own level was quite decent. To record this first attempt, friend Jack Roberts' 16mm Victor camera served his purposes. Ray recalls in *From the Land Beyond Beyond* (1977), "At the time, I didn't have a place to do these experiments. I had no lights, so I built the sets outside in the sunlight, and then borrowed a 16-mm camera from a friend of mine. He kindly came over and we shot a number of scenes. We weren't sure whether we'd get one frame or not: you'd touch your finger on the camera and maybe two or three frames would go by. But when we got the film back a few days later, the excitement of actually seeing this bear move was quite satisfying, which encouraged me to do more. Of course, the one thing I'd forgotten was the fact that shooting outside, taking several hours, the sun would move. So you'd see all the shadows changing. But still, that didn't dissuade me" (54).

Even though the result was quite jerky, it still demonstrates a skill and panache which would grow steadily over the years. This first film featured a stop-motion

Figure A

Figure B

Figure C

How a static matte is made. Figure A: Frame image of animated figure is photographed or rephotographed with matte (unexposed black area) in place. Figure B: Live-action lower section is then exposed into the previously unexposed section, with the animated figure now concealed by a matte. Figure C: The finished composite, with the dotted line indicating the boundary between the previously separate film elements. Illustrations by Douglas Klotz and used by permission of S.S. Wilson.

human scaled to the size of the cave bear, chased by this prehistoric ursine. Later tests with the bear included Harryhausen himself. Moving inside the family garage for a more controlled environment, he and his pet German shepherd Kong appear in the frames of these experiments (along with the miniature) through a technique known as static matte. A device used since the very earliest days of filmmaking, static matte is a means of combining two separately recorded objects in a composite image. It is done by photographing something but leaving a portion of the frame unexposed (matted), then exposing a different image onto this blank section on another pass through the camera, with the previously filmed part covered to prevent any double exposure. So now Ray and his dog could be "attacked" by the ferocious cave bear by simply being in the frame along with it. The bear, who swipes a paw at Harryhausen and his dog, then ambles back to its cave, is well-matched with these real-life opponents. (A variation of this procedure, one which involves rear-projection, would years later become the crux of his combining animation with live-action elements.)

Of course, his rapture with *King Kong* made doing dimensional animation a dream come true, but these tests could have easily been abandoned for other interests or remained only a hobby. Harryhausen, a teenager about to graduate from Manual Arts high school at this point in time, enjoyed these experiments yet felt some trepidation about them; the field of stop-motion was very limited, and he feared that trying to make a profession out of it might become an exercise in futility.

While still in high school, just after beginning to work on his animation films, he was fortunate to meet Willis O'Brien. It was indeed an influential event for the young fan of the effects man behind *The Lost World* and *King Kong*. Ray remembers this while talking on the Criterion *Jason and the Argonauts* laserdisc audio commentary:

> I first met Willis O'Brien I think when I was first in high school, long before I worked with George Pal. I was sitting in the study room, I remember this vividly in high school, and I saw a girl in the distance with a book she was reading, and it had big illustrations of *King Kong*. And of course I almost went out of my mind, and I went over and introduced myself and she showed me that it was a script from *King Kong*. And of course I almost went bananas and I thumbed through it, and she said that her father had worked for Willis O'Brien at RKO, and she said "Why don't you call him up if you're that interested in it? He works at MGM." So I did that, I went home and the next day I called

A static model of a stegosaurus rendered by a youthful Harryhausen decades ago, along with a triceratops cast from *One Million Years B.C.* Photograph by the author.

him at MGM, and he was in the process of making a film called *War Eagles*. And I told him of my intense interest and I said I made several dinosaurs, and he kindly offered to have me come over and see all his preparation for *War Eagles*. And I'll never forget that day. So I piled a lot of my dinosaurs in a suitcase and went over to visit him at MGM.

When I walked into his office, I was overwhelmed: There was about 200 gorgeous drawings of the whole process of *War Eagles*, the whole pattern of the story. Big oil paintings of War Eagles standing on the spikes of the Statue of Liberty's helmet, and I often wondered what happened to all those paintings, because an enormous amount of preparation was put into that. He had a staff of about three or four artists who were doing nothing but creating images for the story that was being developed at the time. It never left my mind. But Willis O'Brien was very courteous, and he encouraged me and gave me bits of advice. He looked at my stegosaurus and he said "He's got legs like a sausage," and he says "You ought to study anatomy." And that was a great piece of advice because I did go to art school and studied anatomy, and tried to develop legs that didn't look like sausages.

The stegosaurus model, one of his earliest figures, was also equipped with a wooden armature like the cave bear. This model that had been criticized by O'Brien had earned Ray an award from the Los Angeles Museum of Art when it was entered in a young artist's competition.

War Eagles never made it past the preproduction stages though models had been constructed and some animation tests made. Basically, *War Eagles* was about a Viking society that still existed in the contemporary Arctic. An American history professor and pilot on an expedition crash in their realm and find that the climate is remarkably temperate. The Vikings, living in a village on a plateau high up on a mountainside, haven't been touched by any outside influences for a number of centuries. The professor and pilot befriend the Norse chieftain and learn that these people get around using enormous white snow eagles, 12–15 feet tall, as their primary mode of transportation. Ridden with saddles like horses, they have to be tamed in the manner of a bronco. To obtain food, the Vikings occasionally fly to a fertile valley inhabited by a number of dinosaurs, so extreme caution is taken during these operations. With the pilot accompanying them there, the group encounters a brontosaurus and then is attacked by a pack of vicious allosaurs that kills many men and some of the tethered birds. The rest of the group are saved through a pitched attack on the savage saurians. Eventually, after repairing the radio and learning that the United States is about to encounter hostilities from an aggressive Teutonic nation, the Vikings rally behind the two Americans. Winging their way to New York City with the pair, they defeat the enemy's aircraft in a spectacular battle over this major metropolis.

The real-life advent of warfare in 1939 immediately rendered the theme of *War Eagles* passé and thus contributed to its abandonment. It was another disappointment in the career of O'Brien.

Urged by Obie to study anatomy, Harryhausen enrolled in Los Angeles City College (LACC), near Hollywood, in 1939 and took courses in art, anatomy and drama — courses which would give his models more character and improve his filmmaking abilities. His art classes included drawing, sculpture and ceramics, providing valuable training. Some examples of his youthful sculpting work still exist, among them a small stegosaurus and a beautifully designed arsinoitherium built over a wire form. (Photos of both are included in a section on Harryhausen props and models on the Criterion *Jason* laserdisc.)

It was Harryhausen's drama class that proved the greatest challenge, since it demanded that he put himself in touch with deep feelings and express them. This proved very difficult for the introverted student. Instructor Charlotte Knight worked with her pupil to help him bring forth animalistic emotions such as fear, rage, bewilderment and hunger, as opposed to more human expressions, which she found rather puzzling. But the young man soon grew close to his teacher, confiding dreams to the older woman. Ms. Knight, an actress, director and playwright, would be of invaluable help to Harryhausen; not only did her dramatic lessons find their way into his puppets' superlative characterization, she also assisted him years later with the scripted narration on several of his Fairy Tales and on the screenplay for *20 Million Miles to Earth*.

Harryhausen also attended night classes at USC. He recalls in *Land Beyond Beyond*, "They had just started their series of film courses: editing, art direction and photography. I studied with Lou Physioc, who was one of the photographers in Hollywood who was teaching a cinematography course at night. All phases of trick photography, from matte shots to double exposure were discussed at length. I didn't quite know what I was going to do with all of this information, but I knew I was immensely interested in it" (55).

Besides furthering his education to improve his artistry and technical abilities, other developments helped to insure that his stop-motion efforts would rise in caliber. One very important refinement was switching from wooden to metallic armatures. Models constructed on a jointed wooden skeleton weren't very durable, but those of steel could stand up to significantly more manipulation. In his *Film Fantasy Scrapbook*, Ray states, "The Agathaumas and Triceratops were my first fully jointed metal 'skeletal build-up' rubber figures. The exterior flexible material was carefully shaped over the steel armatures, which had been padded with cotton and rubber muscles" (13). A ceratopsian dinosaur loosely resembling a cross between a styracosaurus and centrosaurus, the agathaumas was a genus based on dubious fossil evidence and thus never existed. However, it played a prominent role in the 1925 *Lost World* and a part in young Harryhausen's experiments, owing to a wonderfully detailed Charles Knight painting.

Ray's prehistoric menagerie grew steadily in number and also included a mammoth, brontosaurus, allosaurus, pteranodon, eryops and dimetrodon. Fred Harryhausen machined the armatures for these puppets and would continue to do so for his son until his passing many years later (at the time of *Jason and the Argonauts*). Even with the involvement of his father, Ray would sometimes have to be resourceful when it came to the composition of his puppets. A case in point is the utilization of bendable stems from lamps to serve as the malleable armature neck and tail for one of his earliest brontosaurus models. Another fortunate occurrence for the animator: getting his own facility. Recalling this in *Land Beyond Beyond*, he says, "My dad and I built a studio in the back of our garage. It was a big one in which I could leave things set up without having to take it all down when the cars were run into the garage at night. So that new studio really helped and encouraged me. My parents, God bless 'em, were always very interested in what I was doing" (55). This building, which he refers to as his "hobby house," is still in existence and is somewhat larger than a two-car garage. It permitted Ray not only to create his motion pictures in an uninterrupted environment but also allowed space for him to fabricate his miniature models and sets, which he previously did in an area on the back porch.

Ray's mother and father were an incalculable benefit to his embryonic career but others, met through his affinity for *King Kong* and prehistoric beasts, would be highly influential as well. Through Willis O'Brien, Harryhausen was introduced to the work of an illustrator whose visual influence was strongly felt in *Kong*. That person was Gustave Doré, a nineteenth century French engraver. Doré is famous for illustrating literary classics such as *Dante's Inferno* (1861), *Don Quixote* (1863), *Paradise Lost* (1866) and *The Bible* (1866). His singular style, which is characterized by striking vistas and intricate landscapes, made him France's foremost illustrator by the 1860s. Many early movies owe their visual design to Doré, and then in the 1930s some of *Kong*'s most memorable images. The log bridge (from *Atala* 1863) and the spectacular view from the Skull Mountain cliff (*Paradise Lost*), were taken directly from Doré book renderings. Ray has openly embraced the artist as a mentor in the way he does Obie, even adopting Doré's unique approach when creating beautifully detailed preproduction art. He has often referred to the Frenchman as "the original motion picture art director" for his predominance of numerous productions' visual designs, and marveled at the extraordinary output (into the many thousands) of illustrations in a fairly brief lifetime. Doré only lived to the age of 51.

Other indispensable influences were young men close to his age, who became friends and remained so over the decades. While *King Kong* was still showing around 1937, Harryhausen went to see it at a "flea pit" theater in the Los Angeles suburb of Hawthorne. Seeing some 11 × 14 stills of the film on display he remembered from Grauman's Chinese caused him to inquire about possibly borrowing them for making copies. The theater manager pointed Ray to the owner of the stills, a collector named Forrest ("Forry") J Ackerman, now known to legions of science-fiction fans as the editor of *Famous Monsters of Filmland* magazine; Ackerman loaned the stills to the teenager. Through Forry, Ray found a group of young people with similar interests who met weekly in the Little Brown Room of Clifton's Cafeteria. This was the Los Angeles Science Fiction Society, which included among its members Robert Heinlein and another great future author, Ray Bradbury. At the time, Bradbury was a

Forrest J Ackerman, Ray Bradbury and Ray Harryhausen appearing together at a convention. They have been friends for quite a number of years. Photograph courtesy of Greg Kulon.

struggling writer who kept getting rejections from magazines but was published in the club's mimeographed *Imagination*, for which Harryhausen did a couple of "ghoul" cover illustrations.

The two Rays forged an alliance through their common love of dinosaurs, talking on the subject for hours. He reminisces about these days on the Criterion *Jason* laserdisc audio commentary: "Ray lived in one section of town and I lived quite a distance away, so we used to do a lot of our conversations by telephone. Fortunately, in those days the telephone prices per minute was not very strong and we talked for hours about our thoughts and our dreams. He wanted to be one of the world's greatest writers, and I wanted to follow in the footsteps of Willis O'Brien and make the definitive dinosaur picture. So all our dreams were aired over the telephone a great deal. That was our bond between us, our interest in dinosaurs, prehistoric animals, strange qualities of 'Never-Never Land' creatures. When I look back, it was one of the best parts of my life, I suppose." He also discusses this in VISFX (June, 1998), saying here, "He had a great yen for dinosaurs. When he saw my dinosaurs we became buddies. We used to talk on the phone for hours. You could talk for half an hour for five cents. He lived in Venice; I lived in the Baldwin Hills" (21). Bradbury went over to visit his friend's home, seeing the studio and all the fantastic creatures.

Ackerman, Bradbury and Harryhausen all remain friends to the present day, representing a very important trio in the science fiction and fantasy genre. In addition to being introduced to influential folks via *Kong*, Ray continued to demonstrate his rapture for the movie. In *Wonder* #5, he remembers, "Another wonderful Sunday excursion back then was to go down to Culver City and see the old *Kong* wall in the backlot of the studio. It stood there for a long time and you could look at it—the door and the gong and everything" (30). The barrier wall was torched for the Atlanta fire scenes in *Gone with the Wind* (1939).

In *Land Beyond Beyond*, Ray says, "I had this strange notion—and, as I look back, maybe it was somewhat distorted—but that I was wasting time if I weren't doing something constructive every minute. And when I didn't find too many people who felt like this, I began to think I was a little abnormal. But every waking hour I felt that I should be doing *something*, either studying or experimenting. I suppose that that was part of my driving force. But to apply this drive, a small area was set aside on our back porch for my workshop, and I would work until two o'clock in the morning on various projects. It would take weeks to make a prehistoric animal and then you'd have to tear it down if it didn't look right. At times it was discouraging. There seemed to be so many dead ends and little, if any, helpful information to be found in print. But once you passed that discouraging aspect, you were ready to reach your goal. And a lot of people get discouraged during that period; for some reason, I just didn't. I can't put my finger on just *why*—but I felt compulsion, I suppose, to keep making these things" (55). His success, even with the support of family and friends, mainly came from his very powerful enthusiasm and determination to do stop-motion effects.

Much already has been written here of the circumstances leading up to Ray's amateur dinosaur films, but exactly what did he do while he was making them? During the late 1930s and early '40s period, Harryhausen was in his "hobby house" studio equipped with lights, sets and camera. Over the metallic chassis he built up his models, devising a method of sculpting the foam rubber directly on these frames without any molds.

Working in the manner of O'Brien, he placed his puppets in tabletop miniature settings dressed to look like long-past geological periods. Trees and plants were made from cut tin and other metals for sturdiness, with shaped plaster of Paris (covered with rocks and sand) serving as the dinosaurian terrain. Painted canvas to the rear were backgrounds; strategically placed glass paintings gave these antediluvian landscapes a sense of depth and a feeling of lushness. Small birds, made from cut tin, would often fly past on horizontally stretched piano wires; though the supports are certainly visible, they are not obtrusive. He also used wires to suspend his figures in mid-air if they leapt or otherwise were off the ground. Besides placing his dinosaurs in miniature trappings, Ray would sometimes use static mattes to combine them with filmed live-action elements. The projection speed of his animation experiments was 16 FPS, which was comparable of that of *The Lost World*. Obviously, this projection rate demanded broader movements than those typical in his feature-length productions and thereby insured that the results would be less smooth by comparison.

Along with his physical filmmaking techniques, Harryhausen used his artistic abilities to sketch concepts for future projects. Some examples of discarded projects include *David and Goliath*, a retelling of the famous Biblical story; as seen in his *Film Fantasy Scrapbook*, the rendering for this unrealized short subject is extremely well-drawn and shows a definite Doré influence. Another unmade film was *Lemuria*, which was about a faroff "lost continent" landmass. In one detailed drawing, a brontosaurus attacks an ancient city. Apparently *Lemuria* never went beyond this single sketch, though Ray's fascination with "Lemuria" and other fabled regions were prominently included in *Golden Voyage of Sinbad* and *Sinbad and the Eye of the Tiger*.

Another project which never came to pass dealt with a "creature from Jupiter." Harryhausen worked on this in 1939, drawing a conceptual sketch of the monster approaching a landed spacecraft and building a miniature set and a model of the Jupiterian. The creature appears several times in his experimental footage, so at least Ray got some use out of this remarkably well-constructed and quite sizable (nearly two feet tall when fully upright) puppet. A bipedal organism sporting a total of six limbs, the Jupiterian possesses an unmistakably dinosaurian head, webbing stretched between four arms (ending in digits resembling pincers) and a tail like that of a carnosaur. Equipped with canine-like fangs, the monster's cranium bears a striking similarity to the rhedosaurus in *The Beast from 20,000 Fathoms*. In *Cinefantastique* Volume 11 Number 4, writer Ted Newsom notes that it "shows the influence of his membership in the Los Angeles Science Fiction Society" (29). Although this is true, what is far more important about the Jupiter creature is what it represents with respect to Ray's subsequent productions: Not only is it his initial stab at creating an animal of pure fantasy, it is also a prototype for many of his later animated characters. One could loosely describe this alien as a "reptilian humanoid," a term that can applied to a number of other composite creatures like the Elementals, Ymir, Harpies, Homunculus and Kraken (which also bears four arms). From these early days, Harryhausen had seemingly invented his archetypal monstrosity and reused portions of it within a number of models across his entire professional career.

As mentioned previously, all of Ray's earliest experimental footage was animated at a projection rate of 16 FPS. Collectively, these extant tests are in the possession of David Massaro, a longtime friend and collector living in Cleveland, Ohio. Massaro acquired this material from its creator a number of years ago and later wrote an article describing the clips in FXRH #4 (1974), entitled "I Was a Teenage Harryhausen." Here he discusses the brief vignettes comprising this 16mm work, which he has shown at science fiction conventions on several occasions, and includes many still frames as illustrations. The film of this footage is obviously a hodgepodge of brief stop-motion bursts, nearly four and a half minutes in length, quite enthralling even though it is rather crude and amateurish when compared to his subsequent output. Massaro observes that this was all done with a camera lacking a proper single-frame capacity for doing stop-motion; he writes, "Mr. Harryhausen is somewhat diffident over his earliest work as he could not regulate the exact number of film frames that might be exposed for each bit of action. He could only press the button and hope for the best — sometimes getting, upon exposure, one, two, or three frames of the model, depending upon the speed of his reflexes."(46)

Despite the lack of polish, one can see a spark of creativity and unbridled enthusiasm in the way these puppets are made to do things, sometimes with seeming spontaneity. It begins with a shot of the triceratops model that instantly becomes the agathaumas while ambling along, followed by a close-up of the triceratops' head grazing on vegetation that suddenly changes into a tiny human figure. After this the Jupiterian steps into the frame, with the next shot displaying the puppet's expressively sneering mouth and twitching eyebrow. Spinning around, it grabs a spaceship out of mid-air in one cut and bites down upon the rocket in the following cut. (These three shots of the creature from Jupiter appear in the 1991 Midwich Entertainment video *Aliens, Dragons, Monsters & Me*).

Following this is a battle between a brontosaurus and an allosaurus, with the sauropod being vanquished by the meat-eater, who then tears off and devours huge chunks from its quarry. A sharp eye can see the crouching teen animator (or perhaps one of his friends) in the lower left portion of the frame image, an area included through the use of static matte. The allosaur is next seen in a forest clearing, walking with a bounce in its stride, scratching the side of its head like the tyrannosaurus did in *King Kong* and later Ray's Gwangi figure. It ges-

The head of the agathaumas in one of the early tests. This dinosaur, like the one in *The Lost World*, was designed from the beautiful painting of it made by Charles R. Knight. Photograph courtesy of David M. Massaro.

tures as if issuing a roar before moving off. Then with its jaws it seizes a tiny human frantically trying to escape; in the following shot, the allosaur violently shakes him from side to side, then briefly clutches him vertically in a clawed hand before biting and swallowing him headfirst. He slides through its tilted mouth and down the gullet. This extended shot ends with the dinosaur moving its huge head around slightly as if showing morbid satisfaction over consuming the squirming morsel (this is also seen in *Monsters & Me*). Here is an early sequence which shows a delightfully macabre scenario, displaying a sense of black humor that would well up now and then in his feature film effects.

Next is a cut of the triceratops plodding along through miniature undergrowth, with a quick cut of its large horned cranium. Following is a lengthy shot of the cave bear attacking Harryhausen and his pet dog Kong. The bear emerges from an opening in a large rock formation and moves towards the young man and his pet, rearing up and pushing large sticks and stones aside along the way. Reaching a large tree immediately above him, the ursine swipes a paw at the youth through a crotch in the trunk but can't quite get at its intended target. Moving around to one side of the tree while Kong runs to and fro, the bear tries clawing Ray again and fails, then sullenly walks back towards the lair, shaking itself off seemingly in disgust. The top half or more of the frame image (where the animation stage had been) turns black before the shot concludes, leaving only the live-action lower section in which Ray and his dog are located. This part was obviously filmed along a rural stretch of road past a curve, with Ray getting his four-legged companion to move about to match the action he was going to animate later on. From the camera's perspective, the static matte composite image is seen from an extreme distance and therefore it is difficult to clearly perceive everything going on, but the results are nevertheless still interesting. This vignette is also included in *Monsters & Me*, labeled "one of many early Cave Bear experiments"; apparently the footage on the Massaro reel is all that remains of these numerous stop-motion tests.

Next are several shots of the agathaumas trudging through foliage in front of a painted backdrop; a slate identifies it as a "monoclonius." There is also a cut of its head and a close-up showing the mouth alone. After this, a pteranodon rigged by wires to fly flutters down and is then attacked and killed by the brontosaurus. Immediately afterwards, next to an enormous boulder, is the allosaur, who moves off. Then the brontosaur steps out from behind this rock and moves its neck around while a small bird flies past in the background. Then there are a couple of shots of the crested pteranodon flapping down and grabbing a small human puppet, with the second shot much closer as seen from the camera's vantage point. This specific event is quite intriguing, for it is reworked in both *One Million Years B.C.* and *Valley of Gwangi* as key stop-motion sequences.

Following this is another cut of the flying reptile swooping down toward a tiny person. Before he is grabbed, the Jupiterian rushes out and seizes both the pteranodon and the man. After gnawing on the crested flier and letting it drop to the ground, the creature from Jupiter passes the luckless fellow between its pincer hands and mouth, chewing mercilessly on his body. Next is a tighter shot of the alien holding both of them captive, with the pteranodon on its left side and human to the right. After this, the brontosaurus and wooden armature stegosaurus tramp past each other. Just when the plated dinosaur walks out of view, the creature from Jupiter rushes out at the brontosaur, then acrobatically leaps on its back. Lashing out savagely at the sauropod, the monster from another planet defeats its adversary, flipping it over like a turtle.

Animating at 16 FPS tends to make movements jerkier than at a faster projection speed. This, along with Harryhausen's lack of experience, certainly insured that these tests wouldn't be particularly polished. But there are a couple of other anomalies that can be observed within these clips. At times the lighting flickers a bit as a shot progresses; this is particularly noticeable when the agathaumas strolls over his tabletop stage in several consecutive shots. Since these were experiments, Ray possibly could have moved his lights around, as opposed to voltage fluctuations causing the detectable shifts. Several cuts, including the pteranodon being grabbed by the brontosaurus, and the allosaurus and brontosaur by the massive rock, are partially or completely washed out over half or more of the frame image. Ray blames the "cheesy [film developing] lab," but the raw stock used may not have been of the highest quality to begin with.

In spite of all their minor imperfections, the stop-motion tests were a worthwhile venture for young Harryhausen, and also proved to be an excellent demo reel. In attendance at a recent Massaro presentation, he commented that it has been so long he doesn't remember doing a number of these scenes. During an interview in *Monsters & Me*, Darlyne O'Brien, the widow of Willis O'Brien, stated that she remembered seeing some:

> Obie told him to bring his work and come up to our house sometime soon, which he did and brought his mother and dad and his portable screen, and ran a bit of the film and brought his little dinosaur with him. And he was real young and sparkly-eyed, and a nice boy. I just patted him on the back and praised him, and after they left Obie looked at me sort of strangely and he said "You realize you're encouraging my competition, don't you?"

But an even more practical audience for this work than his mentor, at least in the short term, was George Pal. He is widely known as a major force in the fantasy film genre, having produced such effects-laden pictures as *The War of the Worlds* (1953), *The Time Machine* (1960) and *7 Faces of Dr. Lao* (1964). Born in Hungary in 1908, Pal was a European filmmaker who lived in Berlin, Paris and Holland before permanently moving to the United States in 1939 in the face of Nazi expansion. Arriving in California in 1940, he went to work for Paramount making a series of one-reel films called "Puppetoons," which he had created at his "Dollywood" studio in Eindhoven, Holland.

A combination of the words "puppet" and "cartoon," Puppetoons aren't two-dimensional cartoons but rather three-dimensional animated shorts. Unlike conventional stop-motion that involves a single model which can be repositioned into an infinite number of poses, the technique instead involves a great number of wooden figures of a given character, each one in a slightly different progressive position. Known as "replacement animation," this method guarantees flawless results if the figures are placed on the set one by one and photographed in the proper order, but requires a substitution for even the tiniest movement. Some motions are cyclic (like walking) and can be repeated over and over with only a handful of puppets, but normally thousands of these carved individual representations are required for the gyrations in a single Puppetoon. Because so many figures are necessary for achieving animation this way, their design is required to be both stylized and simplistic. Hearing that Pal was bringing his Puppetoons to America, Harryhausen decided to apply for his first professional job. Pal saw these early experiments and dinosaur models and hired the home-grown animator for his Puppetoon series. Ray's compensation started at $16 per week, which wasn't a bad wage in those times, but his salary rose over time when Pal got to know him better and noticed his talent.

Some of the Puppetoons he labored on included several in the "Jim Dandy" and "Jasper" series. The latter features a little African-American boy in a manner that many would consider to be stereotypical and racist, and indeed he is somewhat represented as a clichéd "darkie" by his mischievous antics. However, the character is never mawkish or ridiculous though definitely possessing the "expected" behavioral traits of a Negro youth. Harryhausen found the overall Puppetoon experience positive and rewarding, learning more about filmmaking and production as well as making friends with artist Wah Chang (who would later work on the effects in several of Pal's features). However, he found the assembly-line production of these shorts to be quite unsatisfying from an aesthetic point of view; since every single nuance was immutably etched across the entire wooden progression of figures, it was impossible for him to add even the slightest bit of spontaneity to the animation. Another thing that must have been at least a little unsettling for Ray was seeing O'Brien work there during the early 1940s. His stint at the Pal studio was brief, lasting only a few weeks while he was between other jobs. Harryhausen remembers though that Obie was in good humor and found it wonderful to animate alongside him, even if the senior animator was unhappy about having to take this assignment.

Ray stayed on the Puppetoons for about two and a half years. He was forced to drop out of classes at LACC because he now had a day job, but he continued going to night classes at USC to further his education in cinematography. The young man was now quite busy with his employment, which sometimes demanded he work until midnight or later to get a scene finished. He also tried to do some stop-motion projects in his meager spare time.

Harryhausen's earliest tests lasted into 1940, but in that year he started a new undertaking that demonstrated a remarkable improvement in his animation. Much of this noticeable rise in quality resulted from his purchase of a new 16mm camera, a Kodak Cine II that was equipped with the crucial single-frame mechanism for making these stop-motion films.

This feature-length motion picture, titled *Evolution of the World* (now known only as *Evolution*), was envisioned to run 60–90 minutes and be released to schools as a documentary. The subject, obviously, was the origins of life on the planet. Jeff Rovin notes in *Land Beyond Beyond*, "Making a rough outline of the film, Ray had intended to tell the entire story of life on earth, from the birth of the stars through the coming of Homo sapiens" (56). Ray started off with his favorite section of the production, as one would expect him to do, scenes depicting the era of the dinosaurs. Another thing that helped make the *Evolution* animation look smoother was increasing from only 16 FPS to the standard projection speed of 24 FPS. It was necessary to do this for the addition of a possible soundtrack, but it also forced him to retool his manipulation for smaller incremental moves due to the faster projection rate. Another change was the use of color film. If the earliest tests were an embryonic phase of his stop-motion accomplishments, then *Evolution* was clearly stepping up to the next level through a number of technical enhancements to attain superior results.

A sequence from *Evolution* shows the travels of a brontosaurus along a shoreline (A), framed in a misty glade (B), then surprised and stalked by an allosaurus (C–E). Shot in color and at 24 FPS, it shows a level of refinement not seen in the previous experimental films.

Included in the *Harryhausen Chronicles* DVD as a bonus feature, the unedited *Evolution* footage runs exactly four minutes in length (there is an edited version here as well). The series of clips begins with a brontosaurus crawling out of a large body of water onto shore. This was actually a nearby lake filmed and matted into the image, with the wading dinosaur even kicking up some superimposed spray where it meets the water; the shot was seen previously in black-and-white in *Monsters & Me*, flopped in reverse with respect to what is seen here. Next there is a very quick cut of the brontosaurus strolling through a jungle, which is followed by the sauropod as it makes its way along an embankment above the shoreline. Again, the lapping ripples below the brontosaur are genuine and look convincing alongside the miniature set. The sauropod, very alert and responsive, looks around with some rapid swinging of its serpentine neck. It flicks its tail back and forth across the ground, and a small stone is sent tumbling down to the water's edge in an effective

1. Early Experiences, Experiments and Evolution   33

Dynamic struggle between a triceratops and tyrannosaurus in *Evolution*. Lots of movement plus low camera angles makes this a very exciting episode in the never-completed project.

incidental action. Another touch which infuses character in the gigantic reptile is its looking at the pool's surface, appearing to recognize the reflection. Two small piano wire birds fly through, one just before the saurian walks up the bank over the shore and the other passing right in front of its body. Even at a quick glance, it is clear that this model isn't the one used in his earliest experiments but rather a new and improved brontosaurus, with a body proportioned closer to the accepted reconstructions of this dinosaurian genus at that time.

The brontosaur is seen at a distance in a forest glade, framed by some hanging vegetation as it ambles with a forward thrusting of the neck. A couple of more birds wing through the air as the sauropod stops and glances over its shoulder before finally shuffling off out of view. In this shot, Ray employed a glass painting for the foreground foliage in this shot to foster a feeling of great depth perception here. In *Cinefantastique* Volume 11 Number 4, Ted Newsom states that here "Harryhausen shows his debt to Gustave Doré and *King Kong*" (29). There is no doubt that by the time Ray was toiling on *Evolution* he was well aware of Doré; the background painting where the brontosaur wades ashore include shafts of sunlight beaming through gaps in the clouds, a trademark of the French artist.

After this, the sauropod is in the far side of a clearing nibbling on plants growing on the ground as still more birds can be seen flitting past. It looks cautiously around, then begins to rear up on hind legs to forage high in a tree. Just then, an allosaur suddenly lands on its feet across from the startled brontosaurus, immediately in front of the camera in the foreground.

The unexpected arrival of this predatory saurian is an effective visual (it was seen practically in silhouette when first encroaching upon the peaceful herbivore). The allosaurus viciously snaps and swishes its tail very rapidly to signal an aggressive temperament. Ray obviously thought enough of this wire-rigged insertion to reuse it in *Animal World* years later (a ceratosaurus jumps into a shot to challenge another of its kind). Next is a cut of the allosaur stalking its gigantic prey, moving with a noticeable bounce. A small, intriguing detail: This dinosaur was modeled with four fingers, one of which is situated where it would serve like an opposable thumb for grasping. Again, the posture demonstrates that it has a ferocious disposition and is preparing for an attack. The sauropod nervously bellows with a lowered neck and slides away sideways while keeping watch on its enemy. Harryhausen conveys a sense of anxiety very well in the sauropod's retreat, which is a credit to him since it could have been done only through broad movements and "body language"–type expressions in such a reptilian creature. Much of this footage is featured in *Monsters & Me*.

After this are several shots of a battle that is raging between a triceratops and a tyrannosaurus. The very first thing glimpsed is quite dynamic in terms of staging: The allosaur is literally riding on the ceratopsian's back, biting on its horns and frill all the while. Blood can be seen staining the triceratops' upper body as it stumbles beneath the antagonist's weight. Since the camera is moved incrementally as these dinosaur figures travel across the tabletop (to keep them centered in the frame image), this is what is known as a tracking shot. Finally the horned quadruped tilts its back, launching the tyrannosaur off. Flailing in a prone position for a few seconds, the carnosaur then gets on its feet. Ray used a wire to facilitate the puppet's picking itself up; a sharp eye can detect it for a few frames (the wires supporting the triceratops can also be seen at times). The two dinosaurs lunge at each other in the remaining cuts of this sequence, with neither one really gaining an advantage. The two-legged saurian is clearly quicker and more agile, at times even leaping in to confront its opponent. This segment ends with the tyrannosaurus clamping onto the long brow horns of the triceratops, which struggles to get free.

Harryhausen made this encounter extremely captivating with very good camerawork; besides the tracking shot, the fight is observed at floor level of the miniature stage to place the audience right beside the combatants. Adding to the intimate feel of these proceedings is an abundance of tropical flora that the monsters weave in and around during their confrontation. The stop-motion figures serve quite well here. Though it possibly could have been touched up slightly, the triceratops looks like the same one constructed in 1939 that makes some brief appearances in the experimental films.

However, the three-fingered tyrannosaur is recognizable as a unique incarnation of the cretaceous predator, different from the allosaurs in the early tests or that which is hunting the brontosaurus. It is both gracile and lithe, and in motion is a fleet-footed and nimble animal. Covering much of its body are many fine, pebbly protuberances, with the neck and head distinguished by a pattern of furrows arranged to form a lattice-like skin texture. Overall, it comes across as a highly efficient killer. The tyrannosaur often twitches an eyebrow and curls the upper lip to give a menacing leer, a facial sophistication achieved by wires below the epidermis that allows it to convey several different emotions. This was also included in the head of his creature from Jupiter, as noted earlier, to give it a measure of personality along with those traits incorporated in the composite physiognomy. Like the alien, this tyrannosaurus has become a quintessential Harryhausen design that originated in this formative animation period and would resurface later in his feature film work. He has a vastly similar allosaur terrorize the Shell camp in *One Million Years B.C.*, unmistakably owing its countenance to this puppet circa 1940. Many fans consider the small allosaurus in *One Million* the very best of his dinosaurs, whose completely monstrous characterization is greatly abetted by its singularly sinister guise.

Following the triceratops and tyrannosaurus tussle, there is another altercation, this time between the ubiquitous Jupiterian and a woolly mammoth. This cut is a static matte composite, with the right and lower section of the frame image an actual steep, rocky hillside, and the left and upper fraction a miniature set. During this scrap, the alien pushes the prehistoric elephant over on its side and then climbs onto the massive flank; however, the shaggy pachyderm is almost immediately able to pick itself back up, knocking the creature off. The pachyderm then nervously and rapidly backs away to the left then disappears from the frame, and its grotesque adversary exits the scene to the right. Witnessing all this, hunkering on the slope, is a school friend of the animator serving here as an actor.

Suddenly the Jupiterian pops back into view and eyes the tiny human on the hillside, growling and lashing out its numerous arms at him in a threatening manner, then turning and bolting off in the direction of the mammoth. Besides the wonderfully expressive face, this monster shows superb characterization just before chasing after the fleeing mammal; its arms hang loose at its sides as one pair of pincers click together, as if indicating there is a thought process going on. The woolly mammoth is actually the oldest model in Ray's possession and was employed in only a few tests.

Right after is a another cut which includes the young actor-friend, now facing the fierce-looking tyrannosaur. As the saurian savagely snaps at him, the youth slides down the side of a rock face to escape but is seized in its powerful jaws and swallowed whole. Although at first blush it sounds like Ray repeated a vignette from the preceding black-and-white sessions, this shot is achieved in a totally different fashion and therefore simply isn't a rehash. Harryhausen used rear-projection behind the tyrannosaurus puppet (a fern-like small-scale shrub was also placed in the foreground with this model); the background plate a static matte composite of live-action and miniature elements. For the actual consumption, he substituted a tiny human figure after his friend slips from sight at the bottom of the frame image, which wouldn't fool anyone but is a nice effect nevertheless. Shown in a medium shot, the tyrannosaur is a delightfully sinister entity, befitted with a maniacal "grimace" as a permanent and characteristic facial expression. It even scratches the side of its face after eating its victim, once again paying tribute to *King Kong* in showing a measure of smug satisfaction. The graininess of the rear screen image exposes an inherent problem when rephotographing this projection along with the model: The background element tends to be much less sharp than the stop-motion puppet. It is strange that this and the previous shot appear in the *Evolution* raw footage, since they are undeniably not "documentary" by any stretch of the imagination. Most likely what is observed on the *Harryhausen Chronicles* DVD represents a compilation of not only bona fide animation for this project but also extraneous experiments undertaken at the time as well. This is borne out by the fact that these clips are not included in the "edited" version of *Evolution* which is included here.

Next seen is a cut which would be legitimate for an educational film, the seminal tyrannosaur standing over and tearing a chunk of flesh from a duck-billed dinosaur. In a slightly gruesome touch, the prey isn't dead yet since it moves the head and mouth slightly while being ripped apart by the razor-like teeth. Chewing with a grinding motion, the tyrannosaur opens its jaws to take a bite, then suddenly stops and looks straight towards the camera, with eyes glowing. It growls at the lens and resumes eating the hadrosaur as the cut fades to black. Concluding the raw footage on the *Chronicles* DVD is a shot of a lemur or primitive monkey scratching its side and sitting on a tree limb, and two shots of a Neanderthal man holding a club posed in front of rear-projected backgrounds; one of these is a spectacular waterfall, and the other is rapids of a fast-moving river. Walking with an appropriately shuffling gait, the thick-bodied caveman strolls upon a miniature foreground (which is clearly delineated while he is in front of the waterfall after the projector is turned off, lasting about a second or so).

Evolution is a significant improvement over Ray's earlier output. Of course, going from B&W to color photography gives an added ambience to these cuts, and going from 16 FPS to the standard 24 FPS projection speed allows for smoother movements as well. Since a single second of animation now required more and smaller progressive movements of his dinosaur figures to accomplish the same action, it would have demanded a greater degree of patience on Ray's part. He was also made painfully aware that one should keep his emotions under control. In *Cinefantastique* Volume 11 Number 4, Ted Newsom writes, "Harryhausen was so 'unflappable' because he'd learned a valuable lesson while making *Evolution*. While setting up a glass painting for a shot of his brontosaurus model in a misty glade, he became frustrated at something and threw a hammer to the floor of his garage workshop. The hammer bounced up and smashed the glass painting on which he had labored for so long. Harryhausen called the incident his 'lesson in patience,' and vowed never again to let his work's petty annoyances get the better of him" (30).

The young animator's achievements here also demonstrate that more pre-planning and preparation went into this work than the previous stop-motion efforts. There is a definite succession when watching the cuts of the brontosaurus coming ashore and traveling across the prehistoric landscape. What is on the *Chronicles* DVD is supposedly all there is, but Massaro has one shot that is not part of the raw footage, a brief encounter between the Jupiterian and agathaumas. Also, the lead-in to the sauropod strolling along the embankment is slightly longer here, with one more bird seen flying across. In the *Scrapbook* are two sketches credited to *Evolution*, one of a carnosaur (looking most like the early experiments allosaur) and the other a triceratops defending itself against two smaller predators (one of them is impaled on a brow horn).

Ray spent around a year on this project when time permitted, until the release of the Disney feature *Fantasia* (1940). A wonderful blending of cel animation and classical music, *Fantasia* consists of a number of such synergistic segments. One of the episodes, set to "The Rite of Spring" by Igor Stravinsky, canvasses exactly what Harryhausen was attempting: the evolution of life on Earth to the extinction of dinosaurs. Disney had beat him to the punch, and Ray realized that the atmospheric splendor of these antediluvian visions couldn't be surpassed, so *Evolution* was abandoned. Most likely this occurred in early 1941, since *Fantasia* came out at the end of 1940 and wasn't screened in Los Angeles until the following year. In hindsight, Ray feels that although the scope of *Evolution* was realistically beyond the possibility of completion, this experience was indispensable for "raising the bar" of his creative powers; in trying to overachieve, he improved his animation abilities in the process.

Around the time of the dissolution of *Evolution*, young Harryhausen received his first recognition in a nationally published magazine. A three-page article in the April 1941 issue of *Popular Mechanics*, titled "Cashing in on a Fantasy," features Ray at work in his garage studio. Overall, the piece is excellent in describing what the animator does before and during the making of a stop-motion subject, going from its preproduction planning to building jointed models and miniatures sets, and finally the frame-by-frame shooting of the puppets. A number of photographs show several of his dinosaurs, the creature from Jupiter and the woolly mammoth. The article says of the latter, "Shaggy mammoths are covered with goat's wool, their tusks being carved from wood and painted to resemble ivory" (126A). Another interesting point is that the article states, "Beginning with inexpensive photographic equipment plus an ability to draw and sculpture, this man worked for eight years to perfect his technique" (568), which undoubtedly refers all the way back to the original viewing of *King Kong* in 1933. Even more intriguing here is the limited discussion of how he puts sponge (foam) rubber over an armature; all it says is that "the method is Harryhausen's secret" (126A). At face value this statement may not seem like much, but presently it shows the beginning of his now-famous (some might say infamous) penchant for secrecy regarding his methods.

Ray continued with the Puppetoons for about another year. During this time, he kept in touch with O'Brien and visited the elder special effects creator at work on a new project called *Gwangi*, which never went beyond the early preproduction phases by the time it collapsed in 1942; Ray saw some of the conceptual art and was very impressed by what was proposed for the aborted production (this is discussed in more detail in the *Valley of Gwangi* section). His stint with the Puppetoons ended suddenly in 1942; America entered World War II following the sneak attack on Pearl Harbor, and Harryhausen was drafted by the U.S. Army. Realizing that they made films for training purposes, he decided to put his talents to use while in the service, ending up in the Signal Corps under Frank Capra. In Capra's unit, he did bits of stop-motion for the *Why We Fight* series; he had made a short animated subject called *How to Bridge a Gorge* that impressed Capra and his assistants. The young inductee also served as an assistant cameraman and sculpted several figures of the "Private Snafu" character, his work appearing on the cover of *Yank* magazine. Another wartime project achieved during his spare time was *Guadalcanal*, highlighting the events taking place during this famous battle and demonstrating the potential of dimensional animation.

Harryhausen was mustered out of the Army in 1945, and from New York traveled to Cuba and the Yucatan Peninsula before returning to California. Pal offered him a position on the Puppetoons but Ray declined, wanting to do something on his own. While in the Army he had come across outdated Kodachrome film that the Navy threw away, taking and storing the film for safekeeping until deciding what to do with it. Soon he settled upon creating Fairy Tales, which resulted in *Mother Goose Stories* (1946), the first in his wonderful series of animated shorts. Little Miss Muffet, Old Mother

Hubbard, the Queen of Hearts and Humpty Dumpty, appear in these shorts with Mother Goose, who is seen at the beginnings and ends. Harryhausen considers them his "teething rings" for story and character development. He adopted a replacement animation method for changing the heads of his figures to allow them to change facial expressions over eight frames, by dissolving from one to the other rapidly.

Meanwhile, Willis O'Brien was engaged to

Ray with one of the main Joe Young figures. He has confessed to being particularly fond of the model, which he feels best exemplifies "the very essence of gorillahood."

make another gorilla picture with Merian C. Cooper. Tentatively called *Mr. Joseph Young of Africa*, it was to be somewhat of a recapitulation of *King Kong*, though with a lighter tone. Cooper reassembled many of the principals responsible for making *Kong*, including Ernest Schoedsack, Ruth Rose and Obie. The senior animator figured he would need assistance with the actual stop-motion because of the technical difficulties that this production would entail, so he thought of young Harryhausen. Ray showed his mentor some of his *Evolution* footage and the recently made *Mother Goose Stories*, and was hired as a result.

Released as *Mighty Joe Young* by RKO, the movie has a gorilla only about ten feet tall instead of a monstrously huge individual à la *Kong*. *Mighty Joe Young* was produced by Cooper and John Ford (executive producer) through Argosy Pictures, a partnership formed by these two men. Ford is famous for having directed and produced numerous Westerns starring John Wayne, including *Stagecoach* (1939), *Fort Apache* (1948) and *The Man Who Shot Liberty Valance* (1962). Schoedsack was director and wife Ruth Rose wrote the screenplay, as they both did some 15 years earlier on the original giant ape feature. Terry Moore, Ben Johnson and Robert Armstrong star in *Mighty Joe Young*, an agreeable fantasy that has become a Thanksgiving holiday tradition on TV over the years.

The story begins in Africa, where little Jill Young sees two native porters passing by her house carrying a basket slung beneath a pole. She gets excited after peering inside the basket and anxiously wants to buy its contents, gathering several objects (including her father's shiny flashlight) to exchange. After offering all these items, Jill gets what she desires, a baby gorilla that is quickly taken inside as her father arrives home. He finds the tiny ape hidden in bed and, in a firm and fatherly way, tells his little girl she can't keep him. But he relents, since she is later seen playing "Beautiful Dreamer" on a piano-shaped music box to her hairy pet (she has christened him Joe), lulling him to sleep. The father feels bad for his girl, since her mother as passed away and she has no playmates.

Twelve years later, in New York, promoter Max O'Hara (Armstrong) is planning a trip to Africa in conjunction with a new nightclub he is opening in Los Angeles. He hires cowboy Gregg (Johnson), who arrived at his office looking for a job, taking him along to the Dark Continent. In Africa, O'Hara is writing some highly exaggerated accounts of the expedition (a number of lions have been captured for the nightclub). Suddenly they hear a distinctive roar and see a very large gorilla approaching the camp. The men chase after the ape and attempt to rope him, but he proves too powerful for their lassos. O'Hara is grabbed by the now enraged animal but his owner arrives in time to save him; this is Jill Young (Moore), now grown up and in charge of a quite enormous Joe. She angrily chastises Gregg, who had been ready to shoot her beloved pet, about the way they treated Joe and the fact that they are trespassing on her land. Soon O'Hara and Gregg arrive at her house and discover that Joe is all the family she has, since both parents are now deceased. O'Hara is intrigued by the mighty yet loyal gorilla and pleads Jill to come with Joe to Hollywood, even though the sight of the huge ape outside her fence terrifies him.

Jill agrees, and they end up at O'Hara's club The Golden Safari. Decorated in a jungle motif, the lounge features a treetop orchestra, lions in a glass-enclosed area behind the bar and performing "natives." The patrons are buzzing about who "Mr. Joseph Young," the starring attraction, is. Soon O'Hara introduces Jill to the audience; as she performs "Beautiful Dreamer" on a piano, both piano and player seem to float in the air until the gigantic simian Joe is illuminated, holding her and piano above his head while standing on a turntable. Other acts follow, including a "tug-of-war" between Joe and a number of strong men, wrestlers and boxing champion Primo Carnera.

The weeks pass, and Joe becomes very depressed and listless since he is locked in a cage when not performing. Jill threatens to take her gorilla back to Africa due to his condition, but the fast-talking O'Hara convinces her to stay longer. Now in the seventeenth week, Jill and Joe play an organ grinder and monkey in a skit while large "coins" are tossed by the audience members at the pair. Three drunks behave rudely toward everyone they meet; one of them throws a bottle at Joe, which angers the colossal ape. Taking liquor with them, the trio sneak down to his cell and inebriate the gorilla with their booze. When one of the men burns Joe's paw with a lighter, all the pent-up rage boils over in an instant. Breaking out from behind bars, Joe goes on a rampage and destroys the nightclub, swinging from one end of the lounge to the other in the manner of Tarzan. All the lions get out after the thick glass is broken by hurled debris, with several pouncing on the rampaging ape (he manages to toss them off). Joe also literally brings down the house by toppling some of the interior props and supports.

A judge decrees that the gorilla is to be destroyed. However, before the police can carry out this order, O'Hara helps Jill and Gregg (who are now very fond of each other) escape with their buddy. Loading Joe in the back of a moving van, they manage to elude the authorities and drive into the countryside. Stopping at a burning orphanage, Joe helps save several small children from certain death and is injured by the collapsing structure. Spared from the firing squad by his heroism, the enormous gorilla returns to Africa with Jill and Gregg. Back at his office in New York, O'Hara receives a reel of film from their home in Africa in which all appear happy as they wave "goodbye" to the camera.

It is safe to say that it was a dream come true for Harryhausen to be working on a picture with O'Brien which bore great similarity to *King Kong*. During pre-production, Ray assisted his mentor by doing relatively menial tasks (mounting sketches, sharpening pencils and cutting mattes). But in late 1947, the apprentice animator was finally able to start doing the frame-by-frame effects for the film, starting with a scene of a forlorn Joe in its holding cell. He ended up doing about 85 percent of the stop-motion chores himself, with most of the remaining work done by Pete Peterson. A grip who was trained by O'Brien to help speed up the production of the movie's stop-motion footage, Peterson most notably did the scenes of Joe in the back of a stolen truck and the "Beautiful Dreamer" debut at the Golden Safari. Requiring dozens of tests to properly match the live-action and stop-motion elements, it proved to be the most difficult scene of all. Although Obie did very little himself, he animated the scenes of miniature horses and riders passing in front of Joe during the roping sequence, some of Joe's nightclub rampage and other portions.

There were six main animation figures of Joe Young. Four were about 15 inches tall, one was ten inches and the other four inches. All their armatures were very intricate, consisting of around 150 moving parts, 60 of them in the hands and fingers alone. Wires gave movement to the eyelids and eyebrows, and an allen screw under the chin incrementally controlled the opening and closing of the ape's mouth. An upper-body-only model of Joe, about the height of the four larger ones, was fabricated and mounted on a board that could be swiveled. These, along with the small-scale horses, riders, lions and people, were built-up by Marcel Delgado, the extraordinary talent who rendered many for *The Lost World* and *King Kong*. The design of Joe Young was based upon an actual gorilla named Gargantua, a famed circus attraction of the era. Since each puppet was individually modeled, there is some variation in physiognomy between them. Ray had a favorite model (seen outside the fence in Africa frightening O'Hara and in the Golden Safari holding cell). In his *Scrapbook* he notes this preference: "It was the only figure I really felt at home with and which I could successfully manipulate into the

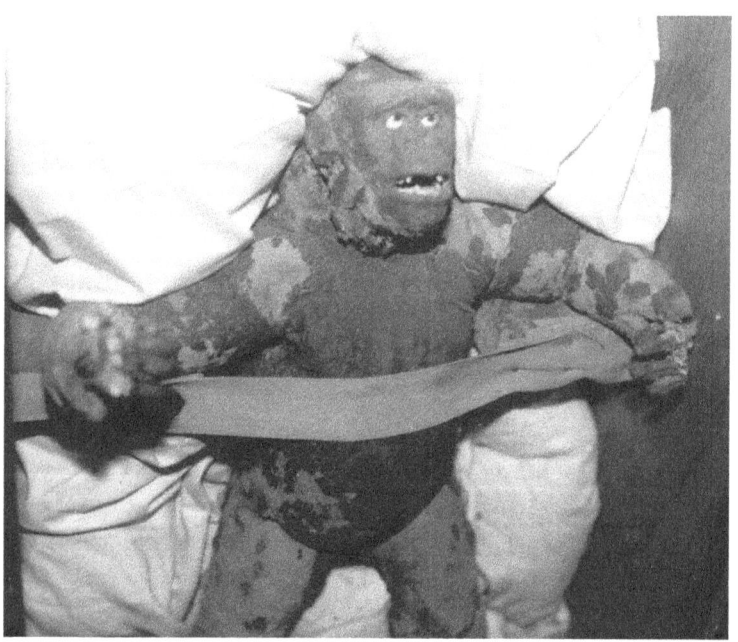

One of the Joe Young figures, as seen on display at the MOMI in London. This model was used for the orphanage fire sequence. Photograph by the author.

many complicated poses I visualized in my mind. It is really quite fascinating how one can become attached to a mass of metal and rubber. It may be that it was all in my own mind but there was something about this one model that seemed to reflect the very essence of gorillahood" (7–8). Ray even had a name for this particular figure; he called it "Jennifer" after Jennifer Jones, who appeared in the 1946 movie *Duel in the Sun*.

A noticeable improvement with Joe is that his fur doesn't "ripple" as Kong's rabbit pelt exterior does throughout the 1933 feature; this was achieved by taxidermist George Lofgren (who would later assist Harryhausen on some of his 1950s productions) through a process of taking unborn calf hide and "rubberizing" the hair (an ingenious technique of replacing the skin with rubber) to make it resilient when handled. A number of tabletop sets were employed for *Mighty Joe Young*; they were situated between large 8 × 10 foot glass paintings to give a multi-layered look to these shots. A number of studio artists, including Jack Shaw, Fitch Fulton and Lou Litchenfield, provided a number of matte paintings. Miniature rear-projection was used very frequently in *Mighty Joe Young*, notably to place a live lion in a cage next to the simian when it is seen for the first time. Front-projection and opticals were also called upon to realize various shots in the picture.

Mighty Joe Young allowed Harryhausen to create many marvelous characterizations for the central figure. Of course, a fairly anthropomorphic creature like an ape allows for infinitely more possibilities for instilling personality traits and behaviors than does a dinosaur. But Harryhausen also wanted to distinguish this gorilla from *King Kong*; instead of having Joe pound his chest like Kong, he devised an equally expressive gesture when the ape strikes the ground with a fist. One such defining episode shows the huge simian being given bottles of liquor in his holding cell. Harryhausen says in the *Scrapbook*, "I was really anxious to get to the 'drunk' sequence. Three men in the story try to get Joe intoxicated with whiskey. This offered some wonderful possibilities for interesting patterns of movement" (10). The animation of Joe was previously rendered and then full-scale rear-projected behind the actors during this episode. During one cut of the gorilla in its cell, there are even shadows of the drunks falling through the bars and moving slightly on the wall as an effective detail within this set-up. However, some other scenes were far more mundane and required great patience on Ray's part. The first ones he did for the feature, with the ape being put back into his cage, demanded movements so incrementally small that it took three days to realize 15 seconds worth of stop-motion. Most shots showing the more comical side of the gorilla were created by Peterson (Joe spitting from the back of the truck and strumming his fingers on his knees while sitting there). Ray objects to *Mighty Joe Young*'s lighter tone in comparison to *King Kong* where he adds, "I personally felt it was the 'tongue-in-cheek' approach that destroyed the full box-office potential" (11). He has also said that this picture, due to its comical elements, is more like a sequel to *The Son of Kong* rather than the original opus.

There were a number of concepts proposed for *Mighty Joe Young* that never materialized on the screen. They include a tug-of-war with an elephant instead of a row of strong men and Jill as a "jungle girl"-type who was raised by apes. In *The Men Who Made the Monsters* (1996), Paul M. Jensen relates that "O'Brien 'wanted to have another ferocious gorilla escape from its attendants in the cellar (of the nightclub) and come

Harryhausen's conceptual drawings for the unrealized feature *Valley of the Mist* show the unequivocal influence of Gustave Doré in their style. Photographs courtesy of Rolf Giesen.

up on stage where Jill Young is performing. Her screams were to have reached Joe, who was then to have broken out of his cage and engaged in a destructive battle with the other gorilla.' Cooper overruled O'Brien on this point, and rightly so, for this action — like many aspects of O'Brien's unproduced plots — lacks originality: It is too much like Kong's theater scene, whereas Cooper's version omits the visual redundancy of a second gorilla, lets Joe's drunken stagger add to his personality, and ultimately arouses more sympathy for the animal" (88). Jensen continues, "For the film's climax, according to Harryhausen, O'Brien argued to have Joe and a second gorilla 'let loose in San Francisco on top of a cable car, beating the heck out of one another as the cable car broke loose going down the hill!' Cooper also rejected this visually striking but farfetched idea and replaced it with the more emotionally involving orphanage sequence, even though it meant that the film lacked an all-out fight between giant creatures, something which O'Brien clearly desired" (88–89). Additionally, the author of this book has observed several of Obie's extremely esoteric concepts from *Mighty Joe Young*, which were in the possession of one of his relatives who was in attendance at a convention. These include the simian standing inside an open arena next to a wall below adoring spectators who are throwing flowers as a pack of leopard-like cats stealthily approach, and a man getting tossed high in the air by Joe and landing in a gigantic glass aquarium.

But what remains in the final version are several dynamic vignettes which include the roping sequence, stage acts in the Golden Safari, the inebriated rampage and the spectacular orphanage fire (featuring a very impressive miniature building about the height of a man, filmed at high speed as it was destroyed by both real and superimposed flames). This film has a connection to O'Brien's *Gwangi*, lifting the attempted lassoing on horseback of the starring ape and the battle with lions from the aborted 1941–42 production. For all its highly impressive visuals (and perhaps a belated recognition of *King Kong* as well), Willis O'Brien was honored with an Oscar for best special effects of 1949. Even though it was a great personal triumph for the film's technical creator, it also represented the last "grandiose" stop-motion production; studio padding of expenses and overhead drove *Mighty Joe Young* to a bottom line cost of around $2.5 million, making subsequent filmmakers wary of the procedure. Ray himself saw the waste and excessive crews (dictated by the studio system) that Obie needed to craft his animation imagery, and decided that in order to survive in the business, many of these aesthetics would unfortunately have to be dispensed with.

Not long after the release of *Mighty Joe Young*, O'Brien set about making another motion picture. This was based upon a story idea co-written some years earlier with his wife Darlyne, *Emilio and Guloso*. Emilio is a 12-year-old boy who has a pet bull named Guloso that is sold by his father to a dealer of animals for the ring. This upsets the lad. Extracting a promise to swap Guloso for money and a fabled giant reptile living in the region, Emilio sets out with some local Indians and captures this creature. But it escapes while being hauled back to town (where the bullring is situated) and makes its way into the arena through the bullpens, killing several animals there. Emilio manages to free Guloso, who is able to kill the monster but is severely wounded and dies in the boy's arms. Later, the title was changed to *El Toro Estrella* (The Star Bull) as the concept developed into a prehistoric epic with dinosaurs à la *The Lost World* set in a Mexican jungle. The latter treatment calls for more expansive stop-motion and features a misty valley located beyond the mountains that is populated with some flying reptiles, two allosaurs which fight to the death and a triceratops. An allosaurus is captured and brought back to town, where it escapes and kills a couple of bulls in the arena before facing Star. A spectacular match carries out of the arena and into the streets, and ultimately the bovine prevails. Both Emilio and his bull head for home after the victory.

Obie spent about six months working on conceptual illustrations for the outline (which was bound together with a cowhide cover, like he did previously for *Gwangi*), and Jesse Lasky, Sr. become very interested in this proposed film. Lasky, who was one of the founders of Paramount Pictures and its first vice-president, arranged to have this production (now named *The Valley of the Mist*) shifted to that studio. The screenplay was written by Jesse Lasky, Jr. (a draft, if not the final one, calls this feature *Valley of the Mists* and is dated December 22, 1949), with Richard Landau credited as an "additional scriptwriter," and brother William Lasky to be the associate producer. However, Lasky, Sr., couldn't get financing for the project after about a year of trying and so it collapsed in 1950, with the rights reverting back to O'Brien.

Ray was tapped to serve in the same capacity as he did on *Mighty Joe Young*, as assistant and chief animator. He also rendered several beautiful conceptual drawings for *Valley of the Mist* (which have been available from Dark Horse Comics as high-quality, signed prints), their style again showing the heavy Gustave Doré influence. Something that is very curious about the unmade story is that a highly derivative film, *The Brave One* (1956), was released only a few years later after Obie sold the rights to it to the Nassour brothers. *The Brave One* received an Oscar for Best Original Story, but the award went unclaimed for many years because the writer was apparently blacklisted. Even though the storyline is very similar to *Emilio and Guloso*, this is probably a case of parallel constitution, since the *Brave One* pressbook cites an actual bullring occurrence in 1936; *Emilio* was worked up by Mr. and Mrs. O'Brien in 1944.

In the *Starlog* publication *Dinosaur*, Paul Mandell states that there was another potential saurian movie in the works at the time;

> In 1950, Harryhausen and O'Brien were hankering to get their mitts on a dinosaur movie, and two massive projects were in development. O'Brien would

storyboard and design the shots; Harryhausen would do the bulk of the animation. The first was *The Great Adventure*, based on a story written in 1949 by Ruth Rose (of *Kong* and *Joe Young* fame). The script by Cyril Hume told of a bring-'em-back-alive showman whose ship and crew are marooned on an island inhabited by prehistoric monsters. The project hit a brick wall when *Joe Young* failed to recoup its production costs and producer Merian Cooper decided to devote his energies to the Cinerama process, of which he was a prime bankroller [66].

None of these ever got off the ground and Ray returned to his garage studio to make more of his Fairy Tale films. But only a couple of years would pass before he would come into his own by doing the animation effects solo for a dinosaur picture. Overcoming low-budget constraints and developing a new photographing means of combining man and monster, Harryhausen admirably achieved the central character for the 1953 release *The Beast from 20,000 Fathoms*.

2. The Beast from 20,000 Fathoms

In 1952, producers Hal Chester and Jack Dietz set about to make a monster movie in the wake of several successful science fiction flicks of the early 1950s. Their idea was to have a frozen-solid creature reawakened by an atomic blast and eventually ending up terrorizing New York City. In association with Eugene Lourié, a highly respected production designer who had agreed to direct the fledgling project, they decided upon stop-motion as the means of achieving their creature. Even though *Mighty Joe Young* had earned the animation process an undeserved reputation as overly costly, at least two films with these dimensional effects were made shortly after *Mighty Joe Young*: *The Great Rupert* (1950) and *Lost Continent* (1951).

Perhaps with one or both in mind, they set about looking for an animator for the developing production. They considered O'Brien but he was passed over in favor of his young apprentice mainly for budgetary reasons. In *Cinefantastique* Volume 11 Number 4 (1981), Lourié remembers that Chester said, "I've heard of this animator who worked with Willis O'Brien, and we can get him cheap!" (34). Unlike Obie, who sat back and waited for the phone to ring, Ray Harryhausen was more proactive. Dietz went over to his house and watched his *Evolution* footage and then invited young Harryhausen over to his office to discuss making their upcoming monster movie. Reading a script, the animator was intrigued by the premise and stated that he felt he could handle the stop-motion for this project. Ray had never before been solely in charge of a motion picture's special effects, but his experiences up to this point had certainly made him capable of handling such an undertaking.

After serving on *Mighty Joe Young*, he had been primarily involved in making more of his Fairy Tale short subjects; he invested the money he earned on the giant ape film in improved miniature sets and better staging. This period saw three more of these wonderful puppet animation features come into being: *Little Red Riding Hood* (1949), *Hansel and Gretel* (1950) and *The Story of Rapunzel* (1951). Even though they were all made back at the "hobby house" studio built next to the garage and had been entirely a family affair, they demonstrate a remarkable complexity on their own level and benefit from the addition of a narrative voice-over.

Hired to provide *Beast*'s effects, Ray worked on script revisions with Fred Freiberger and Lou Morheim (writers for TV's *Star Trek* and *The Outer Limits*, respectively), who included story elements suggested by him, and began sketching out the effects sequences.

The story begins somewhere above the Arctic Circle, at a secret U.S. base; a military research project with the code name "Operation Experiment" is in progress for the testing of an atomic weapon. A plane takes off and heads to a rendezvous point 200 miles away from there; 58 minutes later it arrives at this location, now only about a minute before the detonation. This place is a forward observation post equipped with radar and a number of personnel; among the men are scientist Tom Nesbitt (Paul Hubschmid) and Col. Jack Evans (Kenneth Tobey), who are outside and observe the aircraft as it passes by. Many others are also stationed outdoors with various kinds of recording instruments. The nuclear device explodes in a blinding flash of light and releases a mushroom cloud of searing vapor. Tons of ice and snow instantly melt, causing avalanches.

After the effects of the blast have subsided, Nesbitt and fellow scientist George Ritchie (Ross Elliott) measure the effects close to ground zero. After they inspect Post 16, they decide to split up to obtain the data from Posts 17 and 18. Walking across the frozen terrain as a blizzard is approaching, Ritchie hears a growl and sees something moving in the distance; he calls out to Nesbitt but gets no reply. He then climbs a sloping slab of ice just above a small chasm, and when he reaches the top a shadow suddenly and completely engulfs him. Turning around to look, he sees a monstrous reptile only a short distance away. Frightened out of his wits, he screams and falls backward into the opening.

Nesbitt returns to Post 16 and sees no sign of his companion but soon hears a gunshot ring out. Following the sound, he finds Ritchie at the bottom of the crevasse and descends to help. His friend has an injured leg and cannot climb out, so Nesbitt promises to go and bring others back to assist in his rescue. But just as the scientist pulls himself back up onto the flat slab of ice, the gigantic Beast appears once again, now along the edge of an icy cliff looming above this locale. As it shuffles along the precipice, the creature's immense weight causes the cliff's edge to collapse into the chasm. Ritchie is crushed and Nesbitt barely survives.

Brought back to the outpost building on a stretcher, the delirious scientist mumbles, "The monster! ... The monster!" He is flown to New York City and Hartley Hospital, where Dr. Ingersoll (King Donovan) tries to convince him that his "monster sighting" was in fact a hallucination. Nesbitt counters that Ritchie was alive when discovered and that *he* shared the same "hallucination." Col. Evans enters the room to visit the recuperating physicist, who is happy to see his associate; however, he is disappointed when the colonel informs him that he didn't report the animal to the authorities in Washington. Ingersoll tells his psychiatric patient that the growl he heard was the wind and nothing more, but this statement does little to convince Nesbitt that the event was imaginary.

Meanwhile, the fishing ketch *Fortune* is cruising the dark waters off the Atlantic seaboard. In the blackness outside the port window, pilot Jacob Bowman (Jack Pennick) sees something rising out of the ocean and releases the steering wheel; the giant reptile looms up and smashes into the vessel, submerging it in a matter of moments. Back in New York, the recovering Nesbitt is reading the newspaper and sees an item regarding this tragedy. He is startled to read that Bowman, the lone survivor, thought that a sea serpent attacked his boat. Though the nurse quips the item belongs exactly where he found it, on the comics page, the scientist seeks out Thurgood Elson (Cecil Kellaway), a paleontologist at the local university. Elson is very skeptical about the possibility this "Beast" is a frozen creature that survived from the Mesozoic Era, but his assistant Lee Hunter (Paula Raymond) is more receptive to the idea, noting that mastodons have been so preserved from the Ice Age. A week later, back at the hospital, Nesbitt and his physician hear a radio news report from Marquette, Canada, about a second "sea serpent" attack upon a boat. This bulletin makes the scientist crack a sarcastic grin.

Now back to work at the Atomic Energy Commission, Nesbitt has a visitor, Lee Hunter. Invited to her apartment to look at dinosaur sketches, he discovers a dead (or not so dead) ringer for his sighting. Deciding to phone captain Georges LeMay regarding the second attack, Nesbitt finds that the French-speaking seafarer refuses to discuss the matter. The operator explains he has been ridiculed for claiming to have seen a sea serpent.

Taking a flight north of the border, Nesbitt arrives in the seaport of Marquette but

Poster from *The Beast from 20,000 Fathoms* (Warner Bros., 1953).

just misses the captain, who has decided to travel far into Canada's uninhabited interior. Deciding to go 100 miles down to St. Pierre to talk to the mate from the first maritime incident, Nesbitt looks up the injured Bowman in a hospital ward. When a sister asks the pilot if he would speak to a visitor, he becomes paranoid that this is another who only wants to make fun of him, but the scientist puts his fears to rest. Telling Bowman that he too has seen the monster, Nesbitt convinces the mate to accompany him back to New York where there are scientists who will listen and believe.

Waiting for the pair to arrive at the university, Elson muses to Lee that he is excited about taking his first holiday in 30 years. Soon Nesbitt and Bowman arrive. Lee has the helmsman look through a stack of prehistoric animal renderings which includes the sketch identified by Nesbitt, and he quickly comes up with the same artistic concept. Elson indicates that this Mesozoic animal is a rhedosaurus, a variety extinct for 100 million years; the only known fossil remains were found in a drag of the Hudson Submarine Canyons off New York. No longer a skeptic, Elson phones Col. Evans and says he is persuaded there is something to these "sea serpent" reports and is willing to stake his reputation on it.

That night, in a lighthouse situated off the coast of Maine, two men stationed there wile away the long hours. In the darkness, the gigantic Beast emerges out of the sea and rears up at the revolving beacon. Seeing the Beast through the window, the men try to escape down the spiral staircase but the monster topples the tower, crushing the pair under tons of stone and mortar.

Col. Evans stops by the office of Capt. Phil Jackson (Donald Woods) and asks his old friend to check on a suspected prehistoric creature plying the North Atlantic; the captain is incredulous but agrees to the request. Nesbitt takes Lee to a ballet performance, but the date is interrupted when an usher hands him a note, and they immediately depart. The couple meets Dr. Elson, Col. Evans and Capt. Jackson in the latter's office. By now, the destruction of the lighthouse has been reported as well as that of some isolated buildings wrecked along the Massachusetts shore; a farmer has also been found, crushed to death. As the paleontologist listens with keen interest, he realizes there is a chronology to these disasters; walking over to a large wall chart, he theorizes that the rhedosaurus is following the route of the Arctic Current — and predicts that the Mesozoic reptile is heading towards the Hudson Canyons. Evans suggests mining the submerged canyons to kill the creature while Elson recommends instead that it should be captured for scientific purposes. Since it needs to be observed before a method of capture can be formulated, Elson requests a diving bell to go down into these deep recesses.

Soon a ship is anchored off New York with the bathysphere sitting on deck. As he is being sealed into the bell, Elson is clearly excited about the prospect of seeing a living dinosaur, but both Nesbitt and Lee worry for his safety. The diving bell is swung off the deck and lowered into the depths. Going almost to the very bottom of the abyss, the paleontologist and a crew member watch a fight between an octopus and a shark. The battle is suddenly interrupted by the rhedosaurus, who swims over and swallows both of the sea creatures in one gulp. While Elson begins to pass along a physiological description of the Beast, the monster begins to advance on the bell. Nesbitt and Lee react with shock when the communication is cut off in mid-sentence. Later back at the university, Lee gathers Elson's personal effects together and tearfully recalls to Nesbitt some of Elson's slightly eccentric, endearing mannerisms.

Longshoremen are moving cargo on a lower Manhattan pier when the Beast's gigantic head emerges from the water right in front of them. The Beast climbs onto the dock as workers flee for their lives. As it moves inland, a wave of people running up the street create a scene of mass hysteria. Traffic heading in the direction of the throng comes to a halt and the occupants abandon their vehicles. A cop empties his revolver into the dinosaur. Only annoyed by the bullets, the Beast plucks the screaming policeman up into the air and swallows him whole. Destroying cars along the way, the Beast is met by a squad of policemen on a narrow street. They shoot at the thrashing monster, but it escapes the barrage by crashing through a building, crushing a number of people on the opposite side with falling rubble. Soon newspaper headlines scream Monster Death Toll Mounts!, stating just below that there are 180 known dead and 1500 injured.

That night, the monster is found lurking in a cordoned-off part of the city. Shooting a large caliber bullet between the eyes does little damage; Lee believes it has a skull some eight inches thick. Evans says it would take a three-inch shell to penetrate the thick cranium. Moving forward, the Beast faces a garrison of troops behind high-voltage wires and stacked bags of sand. Lunging forward at the soldiers, the snout of the invader touches the energized lines and makes them spark furiously. The colonel orders the bazooka squad to fire. Nesbitt advises the gunners to aim at the neck when the creature raises its head; they hit this tender flesh with a missile, eliciting a cry of pain from the prehistoric reptile. Wheeling in circles while illuminated in the arcing electric light, it suddenly vanishes as these flashes subside.

The rhedosaurus on the prowl in lower Manhattan in *The Beast from 20,000 Fathoms.*

With a smoky haze still hanging in the air, the troops begin a foot search down the empty street. They discover large drops of Beast blood on the asphalt. Evans cautions his men via walkie-talkie that it is twice as dangerous now because of the injury. Soon the soldiers begin dropping like flies from a mysterious affliction. The animal is the carrier of a virulent germ, and exposure to its blood can be fatal. A doctor (Michael Fox), advises that it not be shelled, as this action could spread the blood throughout the entire metropolitan area. Nesbitt rejects the idea of incinerating it with flame throwers, saying the smoke would carry the blood particles far and wide. Just then, word of a sighting comes in: The Beast has reappeared at Manhattan Beach and is heading towards Coney Island. Hearing this, Nesbitt suggests they kill the Beast with a radioactive isotope; shot into the animal, this would destroy all the diseased tissue and reduce the creature.

Nesbitt, Lee and Evans head over to the amusement park, meeting up with a large military contingent. They see the rhedosaurus in the middle of the roller coaster, tearing out sizeable chunks of its superstructure. The radioactive material arrives in a large shielded cart. Nesbitt is introduced to Cpl. Stone (Lee Van Cleef), a sharpshooter who assures the scientist he can use the grenade rifle necessary to deliver the isotope; Nesbitt tells him to make sure he hits his target, since there isn't any more of the radioactive material available.

Walking towards the roller coaster with the cart in tow, Stone tells Nesbitt that he cannot hit the monster through the framework of the roller coaster. To get a clear shot, Nesbitt and Stone (now clad in protective clothing) ride the roller coaster to the summit. The scientist places the isotope in the barrel of the rifle and motions for the marksman to shoot at the neck. When the creature raises its head, the oozing throat wound is exposed and quickly hit by the nuclear projectile. Convulsing and roaring in pain, the rhedosaurus strikes the wooden structure and shakes the cars so they roll off the hill. The freewheeling vehicles soon crash to the ground, starting a fire that rapidly spreads and surrounds the Beast. Nesbitt and Stone climb down the side to safety and rejoin Evans and Hunter. The Beast destroys a section of the burning structure and escapes from this ring of fire, but dies almost immediately outside the holocaust. New York is saved from the reawakened prehistoric menace.

Designed to be more like a monster than any actual type of dinosaur, the rhedosaurus is a fictitious variety configured to look both unique and ferocious. Instead of being based upon a recognizable saurian body type, Harryhausen patterned his monster as a kind of composite animal; in *Cinefantastique* Volume 11 Number 4 (1981), Ray notes in the career article by Ted Newsom, "We felt that a real dinosaur would have been too small for our purposes, so I made it a combination of several" (35). In *The House That Hammer Built* #15 (2001), he describes his creation: "It was a combination of things. I didn't want a brontosaurus, because it would make the thing look too much like *The Lost World*, and I didn't want an Allosaurus, so I combined the features of the two and used my imagination" (357). His description of the Beast is slightly different in *The Prehistoric Times* #18 (1996); there he indicates that it "had the head of a Tyrannosaurus and the body of an iguana more or less" (7). This melding of reptilian characteristics was in fact nothing new for the animator, as the creature from Jupiter seen in his late 1930s experiments was also a blending of body parts to concoct something completely fantastic. Indeed, this extraterrestrial's head and that of the rhedosaurus bear a striking similarity. It originally was conceived as a sort of giant octopus, but its look was essentially Ray's own conception; according to Paul Mandell in the *Starlog* publication *Dinosaur* (1993), "For the look of his beast, Harryhausen eschewed traditional dinosaurs and the concept sketches that had been drawn by Lourié" (67) to come up with something unique.

The animator wanted a more esoteric design since his prehistoric Beast would be much larger than any known extinct genera. The weight of this massive creature is inferred very early in the picture; after it passes before a radar antenna after being liberated from the ancient field of ice, an operator observes that the blip "silhouetted like 500 tons at least." Its length (around 200 feet from nose to the tip of the tail) makes the rhedosaur much longer than even the largest variety of sauropod known to paleontology. Overall, the quadruped is really a sort of modified crocodilian, possessing the torso and limbs which are very identifiable in this order of reptiles. Though the hind legs have a sprawling stance, the clawed front legs are longer and hold the chest higher off the ground, a semi-upright position that crocodiles can in fact carry themselves around in. Another attribute in common is the flattened end of the tail, which would serve it very well swimming under the water's surface all the way from the Arctic to New York. The rhedosaurus normally goes about on four feet, but it has the ability to rear up on its back legs owing to the strength of its dragging posterior. In addition, the skin pattern of the model's underbelly came from a real alligator hide that was cast and applied to its lower body section.

But overall, the fabrication of the monster's physiognomy makes it appear remarkably similar to the tuatara (Sphenodon punctatus). The only surviving member of an order (Rhynchocephalia) of reptiles which predates the dinosaurs, the tuatara is now only found on small islands off the New Zealand mainland. Grouped by its having a "beak-head," a tuatara can live up to 100 years and survive in a nearly freezing climate. So this unintentional likeness in the rhedosaur's general morphology to this "living fossil" seems to vindicate the unorthodox configuration and role in being the last of its ilk. An additional item which further augments the personality of this titular monster are its vocalizations; for the most part, it issues a throaty cat-like growl but when in distress or pain roars with a sound like a braying horse. (This unique sound can also be heard during the first few minutes of 1983's *Romancing the Stone*.)

Measuring about 30 inches from its snout to the end of the tail, the rhedosaurus model served very well as the film's title character. Ray constructed this figure himself, starting with ball-joints and pieces of cannibalized armatures machined by his father Fred (with a custom-built metallic cranium for this figure). The elder Harryhausen had long made these articulated internals for his animator son, beginning in the late 1930s and continuing all the way up until the time of his passing (the early 1960s). In the time-honored fashion of Marcel Delgado, the master craftsman who made the puppets for *The Lost World* and *King Kong*, Ray built-up his rhedosaurus model. This procedure, which can vary somewhat depending on the materials used and the type of animated figure being made, is detailed in S.S. Wilson's authoritative work *Puppets & People* (1980). Basically, after the armature has been tinkered into its final assembly, the interior cavity space is padded with cotton or cut foam rubber to provide the "bulk" of the character's body; the exterior (usually textured latex for dinosaur skin) is then applied. As mentioned before, an alligator hide was cast and applied in segments to the rhedosaur's belly section. Even though this crafting was his own effort, the stop-motion animator did receive a bit of help in its making. In the June 1998 issue of VISFX, Harryhausen says, "I got an alligator skin from a taxidermist and then made a textured skin and transferred it into rubber. I did all of it myself" (22). A scaly epidermal pattern covers the rest of the monster, and a row of glued-on dorsal plates running from its head down to the tail tip further dresses up the puppet. It took him several weeks to complete the rhedosaurus model.

The design reflected the intent of both satisfying the needs of the script and not making it recognizable as a known prehistoric type. However, there are those who objected to this conversion into a creature of fantasy. In his engrossing book *The Stop-Motion Filmography: A Critical Guide to 297 Features Using Puppet Animation* (1999), Neil Pettigrew opines, "Harryhausen claims that a fictitious creature was invented because real dinosaurs were too small. Somehow this doesn't ring true; an animation puppet can be made to look any size an animator chooses to make it. Is the real reason that he didn't feel confident enough in his animation to have a swift-moving biped as the star? Or is it because a biped would look unnatural walking around on the bottom of the sea? Whatever the reason, he chose a slow-moving quadruped with the vicious head of a carnivore" (62). The rhedosaurus puppet is no longer in existence, having been cannibalized for other stop-motion figures. Ray recalls that these ball-joints went into a "dinosaur" or something of the kind. Many fans believe that the dragon of *7th Voyage of Sinbad* represents a direct substitution of the rhedosaur's metallic chassis for this newer reptilian. In *Colossa* Vol. 1 #2 (1995), Mike Hankin writes in a condensed *7th Voyage* chapter from his impending tome *Ray Harryhausen: Master of the Majicks*, "The modelling of the dragon is wonderful. Built over the armature of the Rhedosaurus from *The Beast from 20,000 Fathoms*, it naturally has the wide lizard-like gait of the earlier beast, but there the resemblance ends." Indeed, there is a strong similarity between the abdominal areas of these two animals, but the dragon (at 40" in length) was probably scaled a bit larger

All that remains of the Beast is its armature head, as seen on display in Bottrop-Kirchhellen, Germany. Most likely, parts were cannibalized for the dragon in *7th Voyage of Sinbad* and perhaps other figures. Photograph courtesy of Greg Kulon.

than his rhedosaur so this wouldn't have been possible. But there is the distinct probability that some pieces from his titular saurian did end up in the fire-breathing reptile of *7th Voyage*. Hankin indicates that the prehistoric Beast was equipped with an air bladder to simulate breathing, though he says that it was "rarely noticed in the earlier film"; it is indeed virtually imperceptible if in fact present within the model.

During the portion of *Beast* set in the Arctic, the rhedosaurus is only included in three shots. Ritchie's first sighting of the creature is really nothing more than a glimpse; the lower body of its body travels behind a couple of blocks of ice to obscure the view. In *The Stop-Motion Filmography*, Pettigrew writes, "The blocks look like miniatures, or perhaps just cut-outs, placed in front of the puppet" (63). These definitely were not part of the live-action plate from behind the tramping monster and probably had been created by splitting the screen and using a different image in the foreground; the "ice-blocks" are most likely from a projected icy cliff shaped by the matted-out areas. Soon afterward, the rhedosaurus is sighted again by Ritchie. Even though it has started to snow, the dinosaur is much more discernible behind the startled scientist. Both the blowing snow and upper body of this man are superimposed over the background animation footage. (Since he is much better lighted at the bottom of the frame image than the rest of this scene, it belies the fact he really doesn't "belong" in the composite.)

Shortly after Nesbitt finds his injured comrade, the Beast makes its final appearance on the frozen terrain. The rhedosaur is spotted by the physicist on the edge of a precipice straight above their position. When the monster begins to stroll away, the motion dislodges loose ice and snow beneath the rim to fall right on top of the men, killing Ritchie and nearly killing his would-be rescuer. While on the cliff, seen from a low angle shot, the Beast was placed into the scene by static matte rear-projection composites; as it walks off, a keen eye can detect that the matte line, following the top of the icy ledge, suddenly disappears as the model moves out of the frame image.

The other interesting thing about this cut is its pedigree; it was stock footage from a movie that is one of Harryhausen's personal favorites, the 1935 version of *She*. Starring Helen Gahagan, Randolph Scott and Helen Mack, it is about a lost civilization in the Arctic region that is ruled by the immortal "She" (Queen Hash-A-Mo-Tep of Kor). Scott, a descendant and the reincarnation of her 500-year-old love, journeys to this legendary realm, where she mistakes him for his forebear. Ray first saw this picture in his youth during its initial release and was affected enough to later pay homage in two of his color films, *First Men in the Moon* and *Sinbad and the Eye of the Tiger*. But he is probably just as proud to have been able to incorporate this piece of film in *Beast*. Besides the cut of the icy precipice, the following shot of the tumbling frozen chunks was lifted from *She* as well.

Later in the movie, the rhedosaurus emerges from the ocean and attacks a fishing ketch. The encounter begins with a close-up of the monster in front of the boat's pilot house. In his *Stop-Motion Filmography*, Neil Pettigrew states, "Two cuts are silhouettes of the beast's head and neck rising up in front of a static photo of the ship" (63). This isn't correct, since the background image does change during these shots. It then rears up about halfway out of the sea and bites out a mouthful of the wooden structure while trying to push the vessel under the surface. Although a fairly brief episode, the surprise attack by the dinosaur is quite well done. Harryhausen's animation of the rhedosaurus pouncing on the capsized ketch is convincingly smooth, with the bobbing miniature boat popping back up after each shove below the waves in an especially effective manner. Even the lighting on the Beast, as if by bright moonlight, perfectly matches that on the ocean in these static matte rear-projection composites. But one element of the final image is somewhat less impressive: At the point where the ship and monster meet the water (where the matte line occurs), the spray from waves breaking along a shoreline is superimposed in a less than realistic fashion. Since there is no corresponding splashing or rippling in the projected background, it only makes the mist look artificial. To place this over the stop-motion animation, it was double-printed over the appropriate area by Harryhausen himself through the use of a process screen. (The mist probably would have been shot separately and situated within a black background.)

Besides the articulated puppet filmed in stop-motion, another means was used to portray the rhedosaurus during this incident. Seen through a water-drenched window of the boat, the creature's head here was actually a hand puppet photographed through a distortion glass to achieve this bleary view. The hand prop was about seven inches long and twice the size of the main model's head, and functioned quite well as a stand-in to save time and money.

Following another hiatus, the rhedosaur crawls up out of the sea at night and attacks a lighthouse off the coast of Maine. Although it is somewhat understated in its presentation, the incident still rates as one of the most memorable of Harryhausen's career. Seen virtually in silhouette, the whole episode is really quite haunting and impressive. When coming up onto the small island, the shadowy creature is seen in long shot within a wonderfully dark panorama with waves crashing all around the isolated signal; nearly all of the offensive taking place is shown in several long shots, ending with the Beast roaring in another extreme shot. Some highlights here include the Beast rearing up to its maximum height and peering in the window (which is the final appearance of the nicely detailed hand puppet), then grasping and shoving the tower until it crumbles and falls to the rocks below. To depict the lighthouse during this encounter, a convincing scaled-down model made of plaster brick served to perfection, with its revolving light truly the icing on the cake. Rotated by steady animation, the shining beacon provides sharp contrast to these otherwise dimly lit scenes until knocked out by the dinosaur's assault.

To facilitate the falling pieces of plaster in a stop-motion manner, they were rigged on wires and lowered to the animation stage frame by frame. Of course, this method of making buildings and like structures collapse will look unrealistic to some extent, since there would always be some degree of blurring when filming a real one toppling over. Ray animated the destruction of many edifices in *Earth vs. the Flying Saucers* but admits that this method was used because high-speed photography simply wasn't affordable; this certainly would be the case here as well. But such a barely detectable flaw does little to harm the overall impact of the stunning sequence; though it doesn't really advance the story at all, the vignette is unforgettable for both its dramatic staging and actually being the cornerstone of *Beast*'s development into a full-length feature.

The Beast's next sighting is a short while later, in the Hudson Submarine Canyons off New York City. There are a few cuts of Elson's diving bell descending; These exterior shots were all done in miniature; Paul Mandell (*Cinemagic* #36, 1987) writes, "The moody shot of the bathysphere descent was stop-framed on a wire in front of a painted backing, and a ripple glass made 'dry for wet' seem real" (60). If so, the animation here is so slick it doesn't even look like stop-action photography. A similar sequence can be observed in *The Black Scorpion* (1957), where a basket is lowered by crane into the inky depths of an enormous underground cavern. This animation is also very good but not flawless enough to disguise that fact. Behind the diving bell, the stalagmite-like spires thrusting from the ocean floor give a labyrinthine appearance to this known haunt of the prehistoric survivor.

In the midst of the battle between the octopus and shark, the rhedosaur is observed swimming with a paddling action towards the combatants; a slight rippling effect can be seen over this cut, giving an underwater feel to it as well. It is obvious these scuffling marine animals were simply fighting inside of an aquarium (the glass is extremely easy to spot in a couple of shots of the cephalopod alone; this was possibly culled from different stock footage than the altercation itself). This lessens the impact of the vignette since it obviously had been staged. Soon, both contestants are scooped up in the monster's maw, looking extremely large through the use of miniature rear-projection. While this cut is adequate, the reversing of the rear screen film in order to keep the sea creatures in position to be so snatched forewarns the audience that something is just about to happen. Right afterwards there is a long shot of the Beast lurking in the submarine canyons and then one of the Beast below the suspended diving bell, which gives an idea of its immensity even though only the uppermost parts of the body can be seen.

Concluding the disastrous deep-sea encounter are two cuts showing the gaping reptile making towards the bathysphere, clearly to seize this object in its jaws. These shots use lighting to effectively convey how much danger Prof. Elson is in, in spite of his composure in describing the rhedosaurus; the searchlight of the bell first brightly illuminates the encroaching creature's mouth, then it goes dark from being too close to be hit by the shining beam. Along with the ever-growing size of the head as it approaches, this animation works quite cleverly in suggesting the paleontologist's fate without having visualized any physical attack on the bathysphere.

The miniature lighthouse model in *The Beast from 20,000 Fathoms* that was attacked by the rhedosaur in the gloom of night off the coast of Maine, as seen at Forrest J Ackerman's home many years ago. Its spiral staircase can be seen above the beacon, and a cast of the Ymir and *One Million Years B.C.* triceratops flank this signal. Photograph courtesy of Ronald V. Borst / Hollywood Movie Posters.

Just a minute or two passes in the movie before the rhedosaurus is on the offensive again, popping up next to a lower Manhattan dock. Coming into view with a startling suddenness, its fearsome head weaves behind the pier in these static matte rear-projection composites as if being moved about by the water's buoyancy. Further refining the aquatic feel is the glistening flesh on its head, made to look wet by the application of glycerin.*

Climbing onto a miniature set of the dock, the monster is now seen from a greater distance in a medium shot. Here it lifts its front foot up in a state of alertness, then

---

*A colorless, viscous liquid (a byproduct of the soapmaking process), it can simulate moisture when applied to a model's latex surface. Since this substance is hygroscopic (absorbs water vapor from the air), it helps prevent rapid drying and thus makes it suitable for animation purposes.

scurries after the longshoremen fleeing the scene, crushing a boxcar underfoot in the process.

Passing by a bridge in a couple of brief cuts, the rhedosaur is then seen stepping out into the middle of a wide street. Again, it picks up a forefoot to indicate attentiveness towards all the bustling activity in these unfamiliar surroundings. It is interesting to see the traffic and even a few pedestrians in the background plate moving nonchalantly, not knowing of course that they would be placed next to a dinosaur. Next, it strolls down the middle of a street in several medium shots; these are convincing because the Beast's head and neck move in and out of shadows as if cast by the towering high-rises lining the thoroughfare. These particular cuts were dolly shots that were very well executed. The Beast soon faces the lone policeman firing his handgun. Recoiling from the sting of his bullets, it plucks this hapless lawman off the pavement kicking and screaming. To create this visual, the actor was hoisted up from the street in a physical effect; the live-action film was later miniature projected behind the model's snout to make it look extremely massive. Another medium shot of the dinosaur's head and neck follows, with the policeman's legs (now a tiny prop) protruding from the side of its jaws. While a horrified lady watches, he is swallowed with a single gulp. This scene has become famous for being the most gruesome in the movie, a delightfully macabre incident to invoke some response from the viewer.

While the Beast is still prowling down the same avenue, another memorable bit takes place: The creature smashes an automobile under one of its front legs. Although it doesn't sound extraordinary by any means, Harryhausen manages to make this minor occurrence very interesting by the way in which it plays out. Mandell writes in *Cinemagic* #36, "a car made of sheet lead crunched under the monster's foot" (60). To concoct this superb visual, the model car and also the lower section of the frame image (which includes the sidewalk and roadway below the model) were in miniature as well. The Beast casts a distinct shadow here, making this more believable. After crushing the car, the Beast paws the wreckage like it is curious as to what had given out underfoot, then continues over the crumpled automobile. Where its dragging tail hangs down far enough below the hips, the underside catches and pulls the twisted hunk of metal along down the street. Miniature rear-projection was used again to make the prehistoric monster look very large.

The rhedosaurus is then seen entering an intersection among abandoned cars and panicked citizens, thrusting its head out from behind the corner building. Achieved through the use of static matte rear-projection composites, it is seen in the next several cuts sticking out even further into the open. Neil Pettigrew (*Stop-Motion Filmography*) makes note of a curious thing in the first cut here: "Several extras run past in the foreground and their heads clearly pass in front of the monster's legs. This, of course, is impossible to do with a conventional static matte set-up, so Harryhausen must have placed a sheet of glass in front of the puppet and painted each of the heads on it frame by frame as they move across the image" (65). This would of course be a possibility, but since the heads don't seem to change very much if at all, a more likely explanation is that Ray either concealed their noggins in each frame to put them below the split and exposed over the model, or by enlarged photo cutouts; either way could put the heads over the rhedosaur. Pettigrew also points out, "In the background, it also looks as though he has animated (very crudely) a puppet or a cut-out trying to get out of one of the cars; only registered by us subliminally, this effect is over in a fraction of a second" (65). Because this is indeed very crude, perhaps it is only an artifact created by somebody crossing a matte line. In the following shots, the rhedosaur plucks a miniature car and shakes it with a lateral head movement, then drops the crunched prop with a roar. This animation is intercut with live-action of a man (not looking terribly frightened) sitting behind the wheel, and a derelict passenger vehicle dropped from a height to smash on the pavement; the editing together of shots for this occurrence is passable if not completely satisfying.

The Beast is next seen in a long shot from down an avenue as frightened people scurry away towards the camera, followed by another medium shot. The rhedosaurus is then seen in a sequence of very stunning cuts within a miniature set representing a city block. In the first shot, it struts head-on at the camera in a distracted manner, sideswiping and knocking over a lamp post along the way. There are a number of toy vehicles by the Beast's feet; at least two trucks and a "woodie" station wagon, the latter making a cameo appearance in *Earth Vs. the Flying Saucers* a few years later, can be spotted on the street. In the next pair of shots of this miniature replica, the giant creature stops when it sees the policemen arrayed in front of it, then rears backwards as it feels the sting of their shotgun blasts. The monster spins around and flicks its tail at the tiny tormentors, who are still rapidly firing volleys; this cut is interesting, since the depth-of-focus gives a slight blur to the swishing posterior that seems so extremely close it might actually brush against the lens. After being hit by a number of rounds, it escapes by crashing through a building in the concluding shots of the encounter, standing up on its hind legs and pressing hard into the outer wall.

To achieve these impressive visuals, the miniature structure (looking quite realistic as well as detailed, with a credible-looking fire escape running down its side) was pre-cut for the purpose of being damaged by the reptile's retreat. Like the lighthouse earlier in the film, all the animated pieces that fall from the small-scale building were attached to wires and incrementally lowered to the stage. When it comes out the other side of the edifice, this stop-motion footage is intercut with a small group of live-action men being crushed under a collapsing brick wall; though it doesn't perfectly match the stop-motion of the rhedosaur punching through the opposite side, the overall result is still very good. These last two shots of the Beast exiting the ruined structure, with superimposed dust further enhancing the sense of realism, are rendered quite expertly by Harryhausen. (The only quibble here would be that some of the falling debris definitely has a "jigsaw puzzle" look about it.) The entire episode with the policemen and the building is entertaining and demonstrates the strength and ability of the prehistoric animal.

The Beast continues down an avenue in still another medium cut of the head and neck, moving into an especially dark shadow. Now within the heart of the financial district, it appears within a canyon-like street in a pair of long shots, first roaring towards the tops of the towering edifices and then continuing on its way. These shots are followed by another of the rhedosaurus coming down the same path, only seen from a low-angle inside a subway entrance. A composite shot done with full-scale rear-projection, it shows a number of people trying to race down the enclosed staircase in front of the rapidly approaching monster. When it seems to have enveloped this entryway with a looming silhouette, a wooden post breaks through a side of the partition right above them in a well-staged maneuver. Although the similarity is quite superficial, it does look something like the rampaging King Kong in the native village seeming to step over the camera's position. This cut not only concludes the first segment of its on-screen Manhattan invasion, but is also the final time the prehistoric Beast is seen in daylight.

Spotted by the lead characters from a rooftop, the Beast now lurks in a desolate street as seen from a high angle. Again, the rhedosaurus model is situated in a miniature set furnished with buildings that are quite realistic (the "woodie" can be spotted again next to its front foot). There are several shots of the Beast in this man-made ravine, moving slightly back and forth; an animated searchlight can be noticed working its way slowly across the massive body of the dinosaurian intruder. An effective bit is the reaction to the shell aimed between the monster's eyes, causing it to draw back in pain upon impact. It next approaches troops positioned behind an electrified barricade. During this episode, there are a number of cuts showing the creature behind sandbags and high-voltage wires, ranging from long shots all the way to extreme close-ups. The first one is a full-scale rear-projection of footage created by Harryhausen using miniature projection to make his dinosaur look gigantic as it strolls towards the barrier. After this, it is shown in long shot through static matte rear-projection composites; the sandbags and poles immediately before the rhedosaurus are tiny props upon the animation stage (the row of sandbags closest to the soldiers is real). Followed by a quick medium cut of the Beast behind this miniature barricade, the vignette finishes with several more full-scale rear-projection shots done with a dramatic flair like before. Ray excelled in rendering the Beast's gyrations, implying a sense of confusion along with pain it is experiencing as a result of being both electrocuted and blasted by a bazooka. Some other touches which help make these images quite effective are a bright light (representing the radiant electrical arcs) on the puppet and the exploding shell double-printed over the agitated dinosaur. A sharp eye can notice that a stop-motion clip of it circling around behind the barricade is immediately repeated, but this reuse is neither obvious nor obtrusive.

The rhedosaurus is next seen, in a couple of long shots, in the midst of the Coney Island roller coaster. These are static matte rear-projection composites, with a small-scale roller coaster section matted into the live-action film of the amusement park. It is then seen in a pair of medium cuts within the lattice-work of this elevated amusement, tearing pieces of the timbers out in mighty bites. Since it is seen here entirely within a miniature set, there were no mattes needed. While both these shots are good, there is a slight jerkiness to the rhedosaur's head as it swings about and the lighting upon the puppet fluctuates a bit (perhaps due to the voltage supplying the lights). Right afterward there is another long shot of the monster moving in a circle, taking another huge mouthful of the roller coaster and then tossing the timbers off to the side. Its sliding tail and falling debris, seen behind the girder-like structure, proves the ride miniature extends at least to the middle of the frame image. Following this is a medium shot from the perspective of Prof. Nesbitt and Cpl. Stone, again with the model situated within a small-scale section of the ride. This is another excellent piece of animation work from Ray, very busy even if quite short: The Beast's head rises just above the roller coaster, then the camera pans down as the Beast blinks an eye and turns a little, as if observing them, while a bright searchlight slides over it. There is one more medium cut of the Beast ripping out a chuck of the coaster, different from the other two in that here this bite is taken from the rear with its back turned.

Having taken up a position on top of the high roller coaster hill, Nesbitt and Stone are seen in long shot as the dinosaur rears up almost vertically. Pettigrew points out in *Stop-Motion Filmography*, "One half of this matte shot jiggles for a second because of a slip in the registration" (66). It exposes the fact that a miniature and full-scale set were combined here. Next is a close-up moving from the monster's cranium down to its neck, showing the bleeding throat wound created by the bazooka shell; the oozing liquid is again glycerin, which also simulated liquor dribbled down the chin of the inebriated Mighty Joe Young. When the radioactive isotope is fired into its neck, the Beast convulses in extreme agony and careens into the side of the wooden risers, causing huge vibrations to emanate throughout the serpentine structure. These actions are first viewed in long shot, then in several non-matte medium cuts. The shock ripples reach the cars parked on the hill, knocking loose the two men's means of transport when they roll down the tracks unattended. Racing over hills in several live-action shots, the empty cars are seen as a smaller prop where they reach a gap in the tracks and fall. Stop-motion is employed for the miniature cars striking the ground (probably the same ones as seen immediately before), igniting barrels of a flammable substance.

Trapped within the rapidly spreading inferno, the anguished rhedosaur contorts in a series of well-conceived medium shots. To stage these spectacular images, a miniature precut roller coaster about eight feet high and coated with flammable rubber cement was ignited and pulled apart by thin wires to match the Beast's thrashing around; this film was rear-projected behind the model as an effective backdrop. A noticeable flicker illuminates its skin, seeming like the glow produced by the leaping flames. It is more pronounced in *Earth Vs. the Flying Saucers* a few years later as a saucer hovers above a raging forest fire. Of course, there really wasn't anything ignited in front of the puppet during animation; the fire on the foreground prop roller coaster section was printed to make it look ablaze.

One very impressive visual shows the boxed-in dinosaur spinning around and then bashing a pile of burning timbers with a swish of its tail, causing an explosion of flame and sparks; this was achieved by photographing a bonfire at night and double-printing the conflagration over the animation footage. S.S. Wilson writes about this in *Puppets & People*:

> The rhedosaurus is wounded and trapped in the mazelike structure of a burning roller coaster. As it thrashes about, its tail collides with a pile of burning wood in the foreground, blasting the pile into the air with a shower of sparks. The pile was placed in the foreground through double exposure, and since it was filmed originally as a separate element, it could be full-scale wood and fire (miniature fire almost never looks convincing), thrown into the air by some appropriate means. With its action timed to the movement of the rhedosaurus's tail, the full-scale fire greatly enhances the illusion of the beast's size (114).

Harryhausen did this himself through an in-camera technique utilizing rear-projection, as opposed to using an optical printer to superimpose the conflagration. The optical printer, which has been around for decades and is a very versatile tool to achieve a myriad of special effects, is a camera-like apparatus whose purpose is to create a new composite image printed onto raw stock from separate film elements (though digital compositing has replaced this device in most current releases).

Pettigrew points out a slight flaw within a shot late in the sequence just before the rhedosaurus escapes from the wall of fire: "Keen-eyed viewers will notice that the puppet's head briefly passes behind the woodwork and disappears, although it should still be visible through the scaffolding" (67). It is obvious from the manner in which the creature butts the structure that Harryhausen was very aware that the matte line would chop off whatever part of his figure extended beyond it. Although it is significant enough to note, the glitch is very minor and lasts not much over a second or so in length. Outside of the collapsing amusement park ride, the Beast feebly walks around in circles in an open area and then drops to the ground. With a final burst of ebbing strength, it rears up on hind legs and makes an agonized roar before succumbing to the lethal dose of radioactive isotope. While this searing finale is certainly one of the most memorable episodes in the entire feature, it serves to complement but not overwhelm the other vignettes which include this central character. Ray's handling of the dimensional animation effects makes the rhedosaurus as well-rounded as can be expected here. Its demise is met with both a sense of relief and regret from being developed into an thoroughly ferocious yet relatively expressive antagonist.

While there is no doubt that the Beast is supposed to be a dinosaur, its physiognomy incorporates traits which unequivocally don't belong to this order of reptiles. One non-dinosaurian attribute that is quite apparent is the rhedosaurus is its sprawling stance; no known saurian variety walked around with its legs protruding from the torso at right angles. Much of this is a function of size; a gigantic animal needs to have its vertical, pillar-like limbs in order to support its weight and move about. It was proved in the early part of the twentieth century that sauropodal dinosaurs, such as the brontosaurus, must have had an elephantine posture, since otherwise its ribs would have extended lower than the feet (thus requiring a rut in the ground for its abdomen). During the early 1950s, some of the four-legged dinosaurs (like ceratopsians) were often reconstructed with their front limbs in a sprawling attitude. However, the rhedosaur's hind legs sprawl more than its forelimbs, making it the opposite of these illustrated Mesozoic reptiles. Another detail comprising the rhedosaurus which dinosaurs didn't actually possess is canine teeth. Usually referred to as "fangs," this type of dentition originated in a prehistoric group of "mammal-like reptiles" which were unrelated to the dinosaur. Known collectively as pelycosaurs, these creatures flourished during the Permian period, about 245–285 million years ago, and were early synapsids. The most famous pelycosaur was dimetrodon, a tetrapod with a pronounced "sail" sitting upon its back. Therefore, due to its sprawling stance and dental configuration, the rhedosaurus seems more classifiable as one of these instead of a saurian.

Another non-dinosaurian anomaly worthy of note manifests itself only once in the movie, when the Beast flicks out a forked tongue in a snake-like manner while strolling down the New York street just before it encounters the lone policeman. This was also considered 40 years later as a characteristic of the ferocious velociraptors in *Jurassic Park* (1993) but was dropped when it was decided that the trait would be paleontolgically inaccurate for this particular type of prehistoric creature.

Dr. Elson unequivocally identifies the underwater monster as a dinosaurian genus and even gives a scientific description; he tells Lee, "It's a paleolithic survival ... exactly as we pictured it. Except that the dorsal is singular, not bilateral. And the clavicle suspension appears to be ... cantilevric! But the most astonishing thing about it is that—" He is never heard from again. Of course, while his statements are colorful though ultimately meaningless, they can be loosely translated as "there is only one row of plates running down its back instead of two" and "the structure supported from the collarbone seems to be attached at only one end." This last observation is rather vague, but because he stated earlier that he could only see the creature's leg and shoulder, it probably has to do with the clavicle's connection to the shoulder.

It is interesting to see the numerous dinosaur artistic concepts and fossil mount photos strewn around Lee's apartment. Most of the artwork are reproductions of famous Charles R. Knight paintings but there are also some rough sketches torn out of an artist's spiral-bound pad. There is one other reconstruction here, an original concept of the rhedosaur rendered specifically for the feature. From the manner it is edited twice into the film and shown only close up, it is apparent that the portrait was created some time after principal photography was completed (a sharp eye can see that this wasn't the illustration handed to Nesbitt before being flashed on the screen). Perhaps the most interesting idiosyncrasy within *Beast*, in light of the monster's pedigree, is the fact that "dinosaur" is never uttered by any character. Perhaps it was scripted this way to make the reptilian invader appear much less familiar. This peculiarity is also detectable in *The Valley of Gwangi*, probably to make that movie's allosaurus come across less ordinary as well.

All in all, *Beast* is a success on the stop-motion level not only because of the rhedosaur's singular design but just as much for its wonderful characterization. This was fairly easy to do in *Mighty Joe Young* with an anthropomorphic gorilla, but here he had the much more difficult task of pulling it off with a quadrupedal reptilian. Characterization should be a paramount concern for any animator, since such a puppet in a dramatic presentation must connect sympathetically to the audience or will prove useless in its leading part. Harryhausen seems to have done this through subliminally imbuing his prehistoric creature with familiar animal mannerisms. Throughout its on-screen appearances, there are numerous instances where Ray's nemesis expresses certain traits which most pet owners would recognize; he clearly based much of its behavior upon that seen in a dog. Examples of these common gestures include the lifting of a front limb to indicate alertness, and its rearing up at times to stand on two legs. Looking even closer at the animation, other perhaps less apparent canine-like expressions can be detected in this marauding reptile. One such instance is the attack on the fishing ketch at night; pouncing on the hull of the capsized boat, its frenzied moves actually remind one of a puppy playfully jumping on a ball. Also, after the rhedosaurus escapes from the roller coaster inferno, its circular movement recalls that often seen just before a dog lies down on a rug. These small refinements to the character of the rhedosaur make it more identifiable, even though it remains wholly monstrous, thus helping to foster empathy for this basically ferocious life-form.

Another factor which also contributes to the Beast becoming a sort of tragic figure is the understanding that it is a "stranger in a strange land." Like Ray's later Ymir and Gwangi characters, the rhedosaurus is a creature that arrives in an environment that is completely alien and entirely hostile to its fundamental nature. While this may not completely excuse its aggressive antics, it does explain why the dinosaur reacts rather

This is a static matte rear-projection composite set-up. A dinosaur puppet, center, is on a stand in front of a translucent screen upon which a rear projector, right, is shining a frame of film from the opposite side. Between the animation camera, left, and the model is a sheet of glass with a matte (black area) mounted on it. Illustration by Douglas Klotz and used by permission of S.S. Wilson.

violently towards a number of man-made objects. Of course, the Beast travels to New York City of its own accord, but this migration to the largest U.S. city is implicitly an innate behavioral pattern. It also isn't any fault of the prehistoric reptile that it happens to carry a Mesozoic microbe that, although seeming to have no ill effects on its host, is deadly to humans. However, the fact remains that the rhedosaur's resurrection was spawned by atomic testing, so Man must therefore bear the consequences of his experimentation. Owing to the excellent characterization Harryhausen infused in his model and a comprehension of the circumstances that lead up to its reawakening in a modern world, the intruding saurian's killing brings with it a touch of pathos. Obviously this conclusion is decreed by the film's storyline, but even with an acceptance of the monster's inevitable death there is still a measure of remorse in its passing. Lacking this, it would make the killing of the film's dinosaur simply an extermination and thus lacking a sense of duplicity stemming from its being thrust into these unaccustomed surroundings.

In order to achieve the picture's special effects content, it fell upon young Ray Harryhausen to invent a method of combining stop-motion animation with live action footage to satisfy the very low budget. He knew how Willis O'Brien put together live elements with animation from serving in the role of 1st assistant on *Mighty Joe Young*; these techniques included glass paintings and miniature rear-projection. Although there isn't any doubt that these visuals are aesthetically quite pleasing, unfortunately they are very labor-intensive and demand a retinue of artists and craftsmen to paint and construct sets. This contributed to *Mighty Joe Young's* bottom line reaching more than $2 million (along with the padding of studio overhead and expenses on this production to yield an inflated figure), causing these particular technical processes to be considered exorbitant to achieve. To insure that he would work professionally in his chosen vocation, Ray created a proprietary means of placing animated figures within real photographic settings. These are called static matte rear-projection composites, a fundamentally simple and low-cost yet effective means of immersing a model within a piece of separately shot live-action film.

After shooting the appropriate footage on location, this film is then projected on a translucent screen from the side away from the camera a single frame at a time (flopped left to right so it will be reversed on the camera side). In front of the still frame shining through this projector screen, the animation model stands on a support floor in the desired position. Between the model and animation camera is a sheet of glass, with the area just below the puppet's feet (from the camera's perspective) covered in opaque black to create a matte. By masking out the foreground area of the frame image, this rear-projection plate is "split" into two components: the background component with the model along with everything "behind" it, and the foreground component that is unexposed behind a matte (photographing black will

How a static matte rear-projection composite is made. (*Top*): The first pass through the camera conceals everything below the model's feet (support floor) and the bottom of the background plate. (*Middle*): In the second pass, a countermatte allows the lower background plate section to be exposed in the camera and protects the upper area previously photographed. (*Bottom*): Completed static matte rear-projection composite, with the matte line shown by the dotted line. Illustrations by Douglas Klotz and used by permission of S.S. Wilson.

not expose film). After the given sequence is animated in this set-up, the film in the animation camera and the rear screen projector are both backwound to their starting points, and the model and support are removed from the area in front of the camera. The original matte is replaced by a counter-matte before the camera lens, which is exactly the opposite of and perfectly complimentary to the matte. So now the situation is reversed: the fraction of the rear screen image which the puppet was photographed against is now concealed from the camera's perspective, and the lower foreground portion (which was also obscured by the floor support) can be exposed. A second pass is made to complete the animation frame, with the foreground projection image now filling in the remainder of the camera's unexposed emulsion.

This is a very elementary description of a static matte rear-projection composite; these can also be achieved with more sophistication. For instance, the matte doesn't have to travel across the bottom of the composite image in a straight line but rather can be contoured to match the landscape in the rear screen projection. Any object, like a building or boulder, can be masked out to become foreground elements the model seems to pass behind instead of before. Also, a floor inlay can be inserted on the animation stage directly beneath the puppet and set within the live action terrain of the composite; this miniature floor allows the figure to cast shadows and to seemingly make solid contact with the ground. But there are other considerations which demand the animator's attention when executing these particular images. Certain problems may arise, such as decreasing definition and both increasing contrast and grain, from the necessary duplicate printing of film demanded in this procedure. Another difficulty can be frame-to-frame fluctuations in the film's position behind the camera lens or being projected on a screen; these minute variations can cause a pronounced jiggle in footage with these mattes present. In order to avoid this problem, some animators make sure the film's sprocket holes are precisely threaded on the camera and projector's registration pins. Choosing the best fitting perforation out of the four per frame insures there will be no slippage from side to side or top to bottom, relative to the previous frame's position in the camera or projector.

What makes these rear-projection composites so revolutionary in animation work is that it allows an excellent image to be rendered (as long as certain control measures are in place to minimize any of the potential issues just discussed here) without any elaborate miniatures being fabricated. Another important advantage is that the original background plate projected on a rear (or process) screen has been reconstituted, along with the model, in the animation camera. Because this is an in-camera technique, there is no need for the optical printer to put the stop-motion together with the live-action. These specific points allow for static matte rear-projection composites to be yielded for substantially less money that Willis O'Brien's traditional protocol because they don't require expensive crews or optical work. Ray had practically reinvented the dimensional animation genre, for a great preponderance of subsequent features films which contain these visual effects were made adopting his methodology. Many other animators, including Jim Danforth, David Allen, Phil Tippett, Jim Aupperle and Randy Cook, have employed these process screen splits to craft wonderful dimensional animation effects as mainstays of their careers.

But at the time of *Beast*, the system was experimental and so had to be arrived at through trial and error; in the Ted Newsom article in *Cinefantastique* Volume 11 Number 4, Ray recalls just how this took place: "I rented a studio in Culver City. The first shooting I did, actually, was in 16mm for a test. Naturally, considering the budget of the picture, there was no way we could afford the glass shots and extensive miniatures of *King Kong*, so I devised a way of splitting the screen. My first test was with a 16mm color stock shot of a river, which I split to show the rhedosaurus rising from the water. That worked, and I knew it would work in 35mm as well" (35). Harryhausen had reached an agreement with Chester and Dietz in accepting the task of creating the feature's

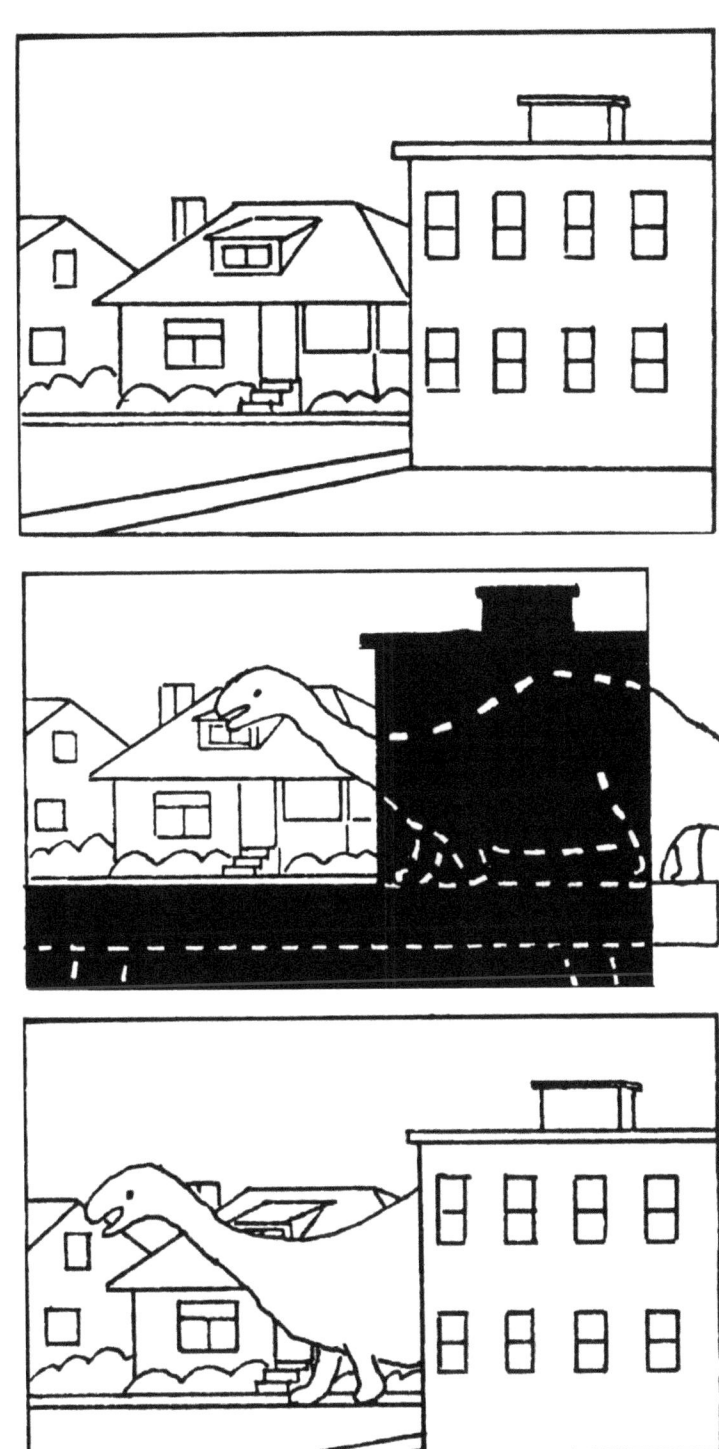

Static matte rear-projection composites can be used to make a dinosaur model go "behind" buildings and like objects in the background plate. A structure in the unaltered background plate (*top*) can be masked out by a matte with a model strategically placed in front of the rear projection screen (*middle*) to make this creature seem to be walking past its rear after the second pass yields the finished composite image (*bottom*). Illustrations by Douglas Klotz and used by permission of S.S. Wilson.

technical effects: For accomplishing this chore, he would receive remuneration (stated in a variety of sources as to range anywhere from $6,000 to $10,000; director Lourié had advised him to get the best deal possible from the "lean cow" producers) plus the equipment needed for the static matte rear-projection composite procedure. This included a 35mm Mitchell camera driven by a one-third horsepower motor connected by a rod for single frame exposure, and a rear projector custom-built by Harry Cunningham at RKO. In fact, the camera and process projector that were acquired had a venerable stop-motion pedigree, serving on *King Kong* and *Mighty Joe Young* respectively.

As could be anticipated, the prospect of being solely in charge of these visual effects for the first time through a procedure which had to be originated here must have been daunting. He relates this dread in *Land Beyond Beyond*: "Of course, I went through terrible pangs of 'Can I do it or can I not?' and I had to always prove it to myself first. I got into a state of mind that almost bordered on neurosis. I used to go into my little garage studio and do experiments in 16-mm before I would open my mouth and say I could do it" (83). An article appeared in *Midnight Marquee* #45 (Summer 1993) by Ralph Vincelli which uses Ray's confessed apprehension at its thesis statement, which is subtitled "Fear and Loathing in a L.A. Garage." But whatever anxiety Harryhausen felt churning inside in devising these proprietary static matte rear-projection composites was certainly alleviated by the film's content.

In hindsight, this turned out to be much more important than simply solving a problem in working on a specific motion picture; Ray came upon the means of insuring a career in feature films. He utilized these processes with only modest refinements for the next 30 years to realize the creature effects in a number of productions. To promote his technique of using splits to insert puppets into live action settings, and to avoid confusion with cartoon animation, the termed "Dynamation" was conceived several years after *Beast*. Coined by longtime producer Charles Schneer, the word is implicitly a combination of "dynamic" and "animation" but actually has a different genesis; Paul Mandell notes in *American Cinematographer* Vol. 73 No. 12 (December 1992) that Schneer "claims to have derived it from the Dynaflo insignia on his Buick" (80). It was heavily touted in advertising for *7th Voyage* to publicize these visuals, later evolving into "Superdynamation" and "Dynarama" for promoting subsequent productions. Although Dynamation has become a catch-all term for Harryhausen's effects, it technically only describes the static matte rear-projection composite method discussed here. The phrase "reality sandwich," which was dreamed up by Sam Calvin in the fanzine *FXRH*, is a colorful colloquialism that is synonymous with Dynamation.

As previously indicated, many of the scenes which include stop-motion of the rhedosaurus were not actually static matte rear-projection composites. These include examples where the figure was placed in a miniature set with no live-action elements ending up in the foreground. Lined up in front of the live-action objects on the rear-projection screen, the image is complete in the camera and therefore no second pass is required (Ray employed this method frequently in *One Million Years B.C.*). Although the use of such miniatures is extremely minimal when compared to *Mighty Joe Young*, there are several scaled-down prop buildings and related structures seen in the picture that needed to be built. Ted Newsom, in his *Cinefantastique* Volume 11 Number 4 article, writes "The few miniature streets necessary for the night shots of the beast were farmed out to a studio technician" (35). Needless to say, the small-scale lighthouse, building and roller coaster were fabricated for this purpose. However, there are sources that incorrectly credit their construction to George Lofgren (it was actually Willis Cook). Lofgren had also been on *Mighty Joe Young* and afterwards worked on several Harryhausen films, but the first of these projects was *Earth Vs. the Flying Saucers*. Besides the use of miniature sets in the foreground, some shots of the dinosaur puppet didn't require the use of mattes; these are the dolly shots of its head and neck when roaming in lower Manhattan. Taken together, these effects were crafted using rear-projection.

But not every shot in *Beast* depended exclusively upon the process screen in order to realize its image. Ray employed another technique, most notably on the lighthouse sequence, which is known as front-projection. As implied by its name, front-projection differs from rear-projection in that both the camera and projector are on the same side of the screen. The camera is aligned at a right angle of the projector (which is parallel to the plane of the screen) while it is shining on a semi-transparent mirror (also referred as a "half-silvered mirror," "two-way mirror" or "beam-splitter") positioned at a 45–degree angle with respect to the projector's beam. Since the mirror is semi-transparent, some of the projection is deflected onto the screen. Along the longitudinal axis of the light from the projector and on the opposite side of the mirror, the camera lens faces the screen perfectly lined up with this angled projection. If a model is situation before the screen, its shadow is concealed by the precise alignment of the camera. One advantage of front-projection: since the screen is highly reflective instead of translucent, the resulting image is sharper and brighter than rear-projection. This effectively serves to mask the part of the projection falling on the puppet by virtue of the screen image's much greater brightness.

However, this methodology wasn't employed for *Beast*. In his *Film Fantasy Scrapbook*, Harryhausen writes, "Many scenes in this film used a 'front-projection' technique, which, although not executed with the use of a 45–degree 60–40 glass and beaded screen, was nevertheless 'front-projection'" (21). Paul Mandell states in the *Starlog* publication *Dinosaur*, "When the long shot of the Beast decimating the lighthouse proved too wide for his rear screen, Harryhausen front-projected breaking surf over the miniature set — something he rarely did again" (68). Unlike normal front-projection, he apparently used a modified version only in conjunction with rear-projection; it served to complete the frame image in much the same way as a second pass does with his Dynamation procedure. To hold the front-projection in the foreground, reflective white cutouts precisely shaped to these elements are placed in front of the puppet. Besides the nighttime attack on the beacon, Ray hasn't divulged other instances of its use in this production; until he decides to list these particular set-ups, they may never be positively determined. He greatly preferred rear-projection over front-projection for creating visual effects and appears to have practically abandoned this alternate means of making a composite image following *Beast*.

Playing the part of Prof. Tom Nesbitt, Paul Hugo Hubschmid gives a wonderful performance and leads a very fine ensemble. Born in Schönenwerd, Aargau, Switzerland, on July 20, 1917, he had become the first real Swiss film star by the late 1930s; trained as a classical actor in Austria, his movie debut was in the 1938 picture *Füsilier Wipf*. Starring in several other Swiss and German films through the late 1940s, he traveled to Hollywood in 1948 and soon appeared opposite Maureen O'Hara in *Bagdad* (1949). He was credited here under the Hollywood-imposed surname of "Christian" (coming from Clark

Gable's Fletcher Christian, the first mate under Capt. Bligh in 1935's picture *Mutiny on the Bounty*) and in several other movies like *No Time for Flowers* (1952) and *Journey to the Lost City* (1959). In later years he was acclaimed for his acting on the Berlin stage, as Prof. Higgins in *My Fair Lady* and in the British spy film *Funeral in Berlin* (1966). A versatile international actor highly regarded for his talents and continental good looks, he can be seen in nearly 100 productions that were mostly European-based. Paul was cast in *Beast* by Hal Chester at the suggestion of Eugene Lourié, who noticed the tall handsome actor in *The Thief of Venice* (1950). Strangely enough, Harryhausen never saw Paul Hubschmid during the making of *Beast*, and finally met him only in September 2000. (That Spring, Paul was recorded on a video greeting "From one dinosaur to another" that was played for Ray at a party celebrating his eightieth birthday.) Paul died December 31, 2001.

As the female lead Lee Hunter, Paula Raymond projects an alluring yet very wholesome quality. Born Paula Ramona Wright in San Francisco in 1924, this pretty actress can be seen in over 25 films which include *Duchess of Idaho* (1950), *The Gun That Won the West* (1955) and *Hand of Death* (1962). She relates in *Filmfax* # 62 (August-September 1997) that her getting cast for *Beast* happened automatically; she was simply asked to do this project. Raymond later notes that she never had any contact with Ray Harryhausen during the making of this film.

Cecil Kellaway was superb as the mild-mannered, slightly eccentric Prof. Thurgood Elson. With over 100 productions to his credit, he can be seen in features like *Wuthering Heights* (1939), *The Postman Always Rings Twice* (1946) and *Hush ... Hush, Sweet Charlotte* (1964). Kenneth Tobey was known for several appearances in 1950s sci-fi offerings (including the lead in Harryhausen's next feature *It Came from Beneath the Sea*), usually as military or law-enforcement officers. His rugged, steely looks made him perfect for parts in *The Thing from Another World* (1951), *The Wings of Eagles* (1957) and *The Howling* (1980). He has a bit part in *Gremlins 2: The New Batch* (1990) as a projectionist, which featured a clip of the lone policeman being eaten by the rhedosaur watched by a couple of the titular critters. Ross Elliott, the unfortunate scientist George Ritchie killed in the Arctic, began his career in Orson Welles' Mercury Theater and performed in the famous 1938 "War of the Worlds" broadcast. He can be seen in *Tarantula* (1955), *D-Day, the Sixth of June* (1956) and *Kelly's Heroes* (1970).

Lee Van Cleef, famous for his many appearances in Westerns, portrayed the Army sharpshooter Cpl. Stone. He debuted in *High Noon* (1952) as one of Gary Cooper's would-be killers, and was subsequently cast in scores of film and TV productions. Other notable Van Cleef pictures include *The Man Who Shot Liberty Valance* (1962), *For a Few Dollars More* (1967) and *The Good, the Bad and the Ugly* (1967). Donald Woods, who played Capt. Phil Jackson, appeared in features like *The Lost Volcano* (1950) and *13 Ghosts* (1960). Jack Pennick, seen in *Mighty Joe Young* in a bit part, served here as mate Jacob Bowman. He made an appearance in virtually every sound picture directed by John Ford due to being part of his "troop of players." Some of these offerings include *3 Godfathers* (1948), *She Wore a Yellow Ribbon* (1949) and *The Searchers* (1956), which all starred John Wayne. King Donovan, who portrayed a rather laid-back Dr. Ingersoll, was married to comedienne Imogene Coca for many years. Some of his film credits include *The Magnetic Monster* (1953), *Invasion of the Body Snatchers* (1956) and *The Defiant Ones* (1958). A couple of the actors with very small parts in *Beast* are still worthy of note. Michael Fox, who was in the role of an ER doctor, is noted for being in a multitude of sci-fi and horror movies like *The Magnetic Monster, War of the Satellites* (1958) and *The Dunwich Horror* (1970). Fox also functioned as the production's dialogue director. Alvin Greenman, in a bit part as a radar man, was memorable as the young, heavy-set janitor at Macy's who lacked self-confidence in the holiday classic *Miracle on 34th Street* (1947). As an uncredited radio newscaster, a young Merv Griffin is heard by the recovering Nesbitt in his hospital room (Merv was under contract to Warner Bros. during the early 1950s).

Cecil Kellaway, Paula Raymond and Paul (Christian) Hubschmid.

During the course of principal photography, locations were used on both the East and West Coasts of the United States. Obviously, New York City was visited in order to shoot background plates for Ray to later insert his dinosaurian intruder. Most of the invasion takes place in Manhattan's lower end. Manhattan is one of five boroughs (the others being the Bronx, Brooklyn, Queens and Staten Island) making up the metropolitan area and certainly the most recognizable with its abundance of skyscrapers (such as the Chrysler and Empire State Buildings). In its lower section lies the Financial District (Wall Street) and a number of other neighborhoods which include Battery Park City, Greenwich Village and Tribeca ("Lower Manhattan" can refer to the extreme tip of Manhattan Island only).

Filming in New York was accomplished in only a couple of days and at a cost of just $5,000; this "junket" took place over a weekend in July 1952, headed by director Lourié and a skeleton crew. Since this was a whirlwind trip, the shooting schedule was both ambitious and carefully calculated to allow for rapid filming and then moving on to the next location. They met early Saturday morning at the Fulton Fish Market, the famed importer and distributor of fresh seafood, where plates of the pier and East River were photographed. A prominent feature in the background is the venerable Brooklyn Bridge, one of the city's oldest and most famous landmarks. Because some of the extras supposed to be impersonating stevedores looked too "puny," Lourié enlisted some real ones, which he felt worked out very well. On Sunday, the crew visited Wall Street and other sites in downtown Manhattan; it had to be that day because there was too much traffic the rest of the week. "Wall Street" is synonymous with finance, but the name actually owes to an enormous wooden fence built by the Dutch at what was then called "New Amsterdam" to keep out invaders. Now the deep canyons comprising Wall Street would be filmed to contain an extremely huge intruder. Although hampered by a limited number of extras (25) and automobiles, all went well and over 40 different set-ups in about 30 street locations were utilized. (Whether or not they were actually visited, the "Nassau" and "Pine" streets mentioned by the policeman on the phone exist in lower Manhattan.)

But not every "New York" exterior was really shot on the East Coast; a great number of scenes were filmed in California. These include the large panicked crowds fleeing the monster while the police bravely advance to meet it, and the nighttime shots of troops tracking and then becoming ill from the rhedosaur's blood. This all took place on a Friday in August 1952 at the New York Street set at Paramount in Hollywood. These scenes benefited from having about 400 extras available and a high crane for elevated camera angles. Edited together in the release print, the genuine and pretend New York streets blend together almost seamlessly.

A huge amusement area built along Brooklyn's waterfront, Coney Island saw its heyday during the early twentieth century; by the time of *Beast*'s making, it was already suffering a severe decline. For the picture's sensational finale, an amusement area in Long Beach was used quite credibly as the famous New York site. In *Cinefantastique* Volume 11 Number 4, Ted Newsom writes that "The full-size roller coaster track filmed at Pacific Ocean Park serves as background for the beast's action" (36); this was situated on a Santa Monica pier, slightly up the coast from Long Beach near downtown Los Angeles. All of *Beast*'s interiors were filmed at the Motion Picture Center on North Cahuenga Boulevard in Hollywood (this includes most of the "exterior" scenes in the Arctic region).

Scored music in film can be an incalculable benefit to the overall impact and success of a "creature feature" like *Beast*. Having been deeply affected by Max Steiner's pulsating *King Kong* score, he believes this legendary movie would not have been quite the overpowering picture without this accompaniment. The man who scored the first Harryhausen solo project was David Buttolph. Born James David Buttolph, Jr., in New York City in 1902, in his youth he studied piano at the Juilliard School of Music. After a period of working as songwriter and accompanist, he went to Europe to study opera in the mid–1920s. His affection for this art form led to a four-year stint overseas, learning from greats in both Vienna and Munich. While there, he supported himself by playing piano in a jazz ensemble at clubs and as an opera coach. After returning to America, he was based in New York State and worked in radio during the 1930s. Soon he worked in the film industry, moving to Hollywood after being hired by Fox in 1934. Buttolph stayed with the studio after it merged with 20th Century Pictures and served as musical director on many productions under Alfred Newman. During the 1940s he went briefly over to Paramount, then back to Fox, finally ending up at Warner Bros. It was during his stay at Warner where he turned out to be the most prolific, composing many dozens of scores throughout the 1950s.

Some of his best-known compositions across his lengthy career include *This Gun for Hire* (1942), *13 Rue Madeleine* (1946) and *The Horse Soldiers* (1959). Retiring in the 1960s, David and his wife traveled abroad extensively and settled in the San Diego area, living there until his death in the 1980s. His original music for *Beast* was actually not the first composed for this feature; producers Chester and Dietz had already provided a score when it was sold to Warner Bros. It was done by Michel Michelet, who wrote the music for a number of films like *The Hairy Ape* (1944) and *Captain Sindbad* (1963). According to Harryhausen, Michelet's discarded score was light classical music. The replacement score is generally praised; Paul Mandell states in *Cinemagic* #36 that "Buttolph's music created a dark, ominous mood underscoring key scenes in the tradition of Max Steiner" (60). Ray himself is more critical of his efforts, however, opining in *Animato!* #25 (Spring 1993), "When we sold *The Beast from 20,000 Fathoms* to Warner Brothers, I thought for one happy brief moment that Steiner might rescore it, because they didn't like the score that was done for $5,000; it was a dreadful score. It didn't do anything for the picture. Warner, when they bought the film outright, rescored it, but unfortunately Steiner was a first class musician and they wouldn't burden him with this film they'd just bought.... Buttolph did a competent score, but it slowed the picture down, it made it too lumbering. I would have loved to have had a Steiner score" (50). Steiner was in fact the head of the Warner Bros. music department at that time. Ray has admitted that he never made any attempt to contact the famous composer and personal hero in this regard.

Even though the animator's sentiments about the music's ponderous quality is justified, this "competent" score is indeed quite haunting and seems appropriate to the goings-on during the movie. Mandell adds, "Buttolph composed a descending four-note leitmotif for French horns and trombones, answered by bowed strings on a double bass" (60-61). There is no doubt that *Beast*'s musical accompaniment, orchestrated by Maurice de Packh and conducted by Ray Heindorf, stands as one of the better compositions mated with a Harryhausen project. It is available on a music CD collection titled *Monstrous Movie Music*.

Hal E. Chester and Jack Dietz were independent producers when setting about to make *Beast*. Their company, Mutual Pictures of California, was actually considering making three films when Lourié was hired but then quickly dropped the other two projects, with the monster movie remaining. This idea for a feature is believed to have originated with Chester, who functioned as the financial arm of Mutual Pictures. Dietz was apparently more the businessman type and also probably had more contact with Harryhausen than did Chester during the production of their feature. Chester was born in 1921 and most notably produced a series of "Joe Palooka" pictures from the late 1940s to the early 1950s. He also was executive producer on the Jacques Tourneur horror classic *Night of the Demon* (1957). Born in 1901, Dietz is credited with producing a number of the Leo Gorcey-Huntz Hall "East Side Kids" titles in the 1940s (Chester himself appeared in the earlier "Dead End Kids" series between 1938 and 1941 in several roles, credited there as "Hally Chester") and later would make *The Black Scorpion* with Willis O'Brien *The Black Scorpion* trailer includes a clip of the rhedosaurus next to a building; this footage is fascinating since it never appears in *Beast*. Frames from it can be seen on page 33 of Mark F. Berry's 2002 book *The Dinosaur Filmography*.

Eugene Lourié served as director but was really a production designer and art director up until this time, as *Beast* was his first directorial effort. A Frenchman who was born in Kharkov, Russia, in 1903 (some sources say 1905), Lourié began his career as an extra and scenery painter for the Paris stage. He would shortly become an art director in the French cinema, working with the legendary Jean Renoir on the classic World War I drama *The Grand Illusion* (1937). Following several other collaborations (including 1938's *The Human Beast*), he went to America with Renoir in 1941. In Hollywood, the pair teamed on such features as *The Diary of a Chambermaid* (1946) and *The River* (1951). Another notable feature on Lourié's list of art director credits is the Charlie Chaplin opus *Limelight* (1952), considered by many to be Chaplin's best "talkie." In later years, Lourié's talents were put to use on films like *Krakatoa, East of Java* (1969) and *Bronco Billy* (1980).

But in the 1950s, he was associated with the dinosaur genre as a result of *Beast*, his first time in the director's chair; he went on to direct others in this particular niche during that era which include *The Giant Behemoth* (1959) and *Gorgo* (1961). In his superb book *My Work in Films* (1985), Lourié talks about this unintended consequence: "In the eyes of prospective producers, I became identified with a specialized form of science fiction that dealt with prehistoric monsters" (241). The Frenchman regards Harryhausen highly, recalling, "Ray was a very agreeable person and fully dedicated, immersed in his work" (226). A very gifted artist and filmmaker, Lourié died in 1991. Another important principal involved in the making of this feature was Bernard Burton. Technically an associate producer at Mutual Pictures, Bernie previously served with Chester on the Palooka series but was best known as a film editor (which he served as for this production). He also accompanied Lourié on the weekend junket to New York for background plates.

Obviously, *Beast* was approached as a low-budget production but holds up very well in spite of the relatively small expenditure of capital. Since time is money, everything was done with a sense of urgency to try to keep the project within the allocated cost. All of the interiors were shot at the Motion Picture Center studios in Hollywood, where several stages had been rented for the purpose of completing them as quickly as possible. Filming these sets with the actors in place began the Monday after the New York Street scenes were photographed, with the snow set being tackled first. This occupied one of the large stages at the Center and happened to be shot during the hottest day of the summer, making those wearing parkas quite uncomfortable in the heat. The "snow" here was real crushed ice churned out by two machines running all day to replace that which was rapidly melting away. A layer of crushed ice, from one to three feet thick, was eventually built up deep enough for the snowmobile to ride upon. For falling snowflakes, corn flakes were used. They stuck to the actors' sweaty brows but looked quite natural adhering to their fur hoods.

Another large set was the paleontology museum and Elson's adjoining office space. Lourié had originally wanted to use a photographic enlargement of a mammoth skeleton on the back wall to represent one of the fossils there, but was reminded of a mounted dinosaur in the 1938 feature *Bringing Up Baby*. The papier mâché bones were found in an RKO warehouse and put back together. When completed, the reconstructed mount towered 16 feet and became a dominant set piece. Although the look of this "museum" and office area is quite spartan, it indeed serves its purpose for the movie. Other sets were built and rapidly taken down, keeping production on a very tight schedule; in his *My Work in Films*, Lourié notes, "Sometimes four sets were used in a day's shooting. A stone wall collapses on a group of frightened bystanders. The lighthouse keeper is crushed in the iron circular stairway of the shattered lighthouse. The fishing trawler advances through the foggy sea and is attacked and destroyed by the beast. And so on. Altogether we shot some twenty different sets, some of which used rear-projection backing" (237). To help keep the picture on budget and also to prevent the work from being edited in a way that altered his continuity, director Lourié dispensed with any additional shooting for protection. Paul Mandell states in his *Cinemagic* #36 article, "This was Roger Corman–type filmmaking, three years before Corman's advent" (58).

Besides Harryhausen's own contribution, Lourié's effects crew shot some miniatures in pre-production, like the cracking icebergs seen after the atomic blast and the bathysphere; he says it was "made on a dry, fogged-in stage, using underwater lighting effects" (234). This strongly contradicts Mandell's statements as to exactly how those scenes were created. It took only 12 days to complete the principal photography for *Beast* in California: nine days at the Motion Picture Center, two days (or nights more correctly) at the Long Beach amusement area and one day on the New York Street set. As a result of Lourié's Herculean efforts, his directorial debut stayed very close to his $200,000 estimated budget, but this was still an inflated dollar amount; the original figure for the feature was only a minuscule $150,000. Some of Harryhausen's output was required up front for the full-scale rear-projections, which was used for several shots. Whenever he finished a scene, it was immediately edited into the picture. In all, it took Ray somewhere around six to seven months to complete the animation for this production. Due to the manner of Ray's involvement, there isn't any physical connection between any of the film's principal characters and the monster. Practically every one of his subsequent projects has the human leads strongly interacting with the stop-motion creatures; this lack of contact lowers the dramatic qualities somewhat, but it reflects on how the film was made and not on any shortcomings which can be blamed on the animator.

Beast's storyline was in part based upon a Ray Bradbury short story published in *The Saturday Evening Post* the previous year, though its well-known association with the production is in reality more accidental than intentional. First printed in the magazine on June 23, 1951, "The Beast from 20,000 Fathoms" (an evocative title but entirely fictitious since 20,000 fathoms would equal about 23 miles, over three time deeper than anywhere in the ocean) is Bradbury's yarn of a prehistoric beast that rises out of the sea, beckoned to the foghorn of a lighthouse. It answers the sounds with plaintive cries, eventually approaching and destroying the beacon. It returns to the sea brokenhearted that the signal wasn't in fact another dinosaur. When the story was published in his *Golden Apples of the Sun* (1953) anthology, Bradbury retitled it "The Fog Horn."

This tale was unconsciously worked into a draft of the script for the project *The Monster from Beneath the Sea* when Ray Bradbury was called in by Chester to revise it. After reading it in the next room, the famous science fiction author informed Chester that there was a vague similarity to a story of his that was recently printed; Bradbury remembers the shocked expression of the producer's face upon hearing this revelation (Chester was clearly worried about a lawsuit). When Chester and Dietz obtained the *Saturday Evening Post* issue with his story and saw the evocative illustration by James R. Bingham showing a dinosaur climbing the side of a lighthouse, they decided to settle the matter; Bradbury was wired the next day for both the rights and title to his "Beast" story, and was paid a sum of around $2,000 but was never directly involved with the film. (Harryhausen remembers that the vignette in question was inspired by the *Saturday Evening Post* artwork instead of the Bradbury tale). Warner Bros. would later change *The Monster from Beneath the Sea* to match the purchased short story title.

When Lourié came on board in 1952, there was only a brief outline for the *Monster* project. With the assistance of a blacklisted screenwriter he doesn't name, they came up with about 80 percent of the first screenplay draft. Fred Freiberger and Lou Morheim were hired by the producers to polish the script and provide dialogue. Ray himself made several contributions to the story, which included the dispatching of the rhedosaurus from the roller coaster hill and runaway cars. These are aesthetically a big improvement over *Beast*'s original scripted finale; in the book *The Men Who Made the Monsters* (1996), writer Paul M. Jensen relates, "In the script's version of this climax, the beast dramatically, and pathetically, becomes tangled in the coaster's collapsing girders. When Nesbitt and a sharpshooter set out with the isotope, the sharpshooter is crushed by falling debris, so Nesbitt does the fatal deed himself. Meanwhile, a fire starts, and Colonel Evans rushes to Nesbitt's rescue" (104). Although it is a certainty that Harryhausen lorded over the visual effects and created many shots which weren't specified in the script, some proposed dinosaur scenes never got made. Jensen notes in his book, "Two incidents in the screenplay, however, do not appear in the film. In one, a young woman — 'partially dressed, evidently having just taken a shower'— is shocked when the beast's head appears at her window; in the other, the monster tears the Brooklyn Bridge apart" (104).

For a science fiction movie, *Beast* has a storyline which holds up extremely well. Obviously, the audience has to get past the supposition of a Mesozoic creature rapidly freezing and then surviving 100 million years in such a condition. The first glimpses of the Beast, strolling across the frozen Arctic landscape, is indeed a startling sight; many fans of this feature have scoffed at the possibility of a dinosaur surviving in a polar region. However, a prehistoric reptile re-energized by an atomic blast could have an accelerated metabolism, allowing for high activity levels even in such a cold climate. Its significant mass and dimensions would also prevent even such a "naked" animal from losing body heat very fast; with ever-expanding size, volume increases exponentially greater than surface area. There is never any explanation as to the mechanism the rhedosaur uses to navigate from "north of Baffin Bay" to the Hudson Submarine Canyons other than by "following the Arctic Current." Scientifically this migration would be quite impossible, since in 100 million years' time the continents have separated and drifted apart (plate tectonics), as well as the Earth's geomagnetism having shifted on a number of occasions. But on its own level, the journey of a reawakened Mesozoic monster heading down the Atlantic coast of North America to its presumed stomping grounds makes for a quite palatable concept.

Unlike the romances in many later Harryhausen features, the affection felt by Nesbitt and Lee builds in a realistic manner; there is little physical contact or passion expressed in the film, instead relying on amiable conversations and warm emotions. Another strong suit is the scientific discussions by the film's principals, never contrived or illegitimate. One excellent example of this is Prof. Nesbitt's response to Dr. Elson's assertion that the "empirical system of logic" might not sufficiently prove the rhedosaur's existence. He counters by saying, "It isn't a question of empirics. If a particle of the sun flew off into space, I wouldn't consider the man who brought that news to be insane. As a scientist, I would examine every facet of it." Nesbitt reinforces his position rationally by saying that if said solar fragment did fly away, the occurrence of such a phenomenon doesn't depend upon observation if it did in fact take place.

However, there are some plot elements which are at best hard to accept. For instance, the ability of pilot Bowman to even see (much less identify) a monster through the water-drenched window of the ketch's bridge in the gloom of night, is a stretch of credibility. Another reach is accepting that Dr. Elson can perceive his prehistoric subject clearly enough to give a detailed description; the only lighting there is available in the inky depths comes from the bathysphere. Another thing that detracts from the production is the narrative approach to explain "Operation Experiment" and the damage wrought by the rhedosaurus in New York. While the intent of these segments is understandable, to convey information to the audience, the monotone delivery along with the blatantly conspicuous stock footage gives them a turgid "newsreel" quality. But besides these flaws and perhaps a few other shortcomings, this motion picture concocts a competent progression that is abetted by agreeable characters and colorable conversations.

James R. Bingham's illustration for Ray Bradbury's short story "The Beast from 20,000 Fathoms," which ran in the June 23, 1951, issue of *The Saturday Evening Post*. This sea monster looks nothing like the rhedosaurus in the feature of the same name. Courtesy of Chris Endicott.

Included in the prehistoric stop-motin ensemble of *Planet of Dinosaurs* (aka *Planet of the Dinosaurs*; 1978), this saurian facing the large T. rex pays homage ot Harryhausen's *Beast from 20,000 Fathoms*. Photograph courtesy of Jim Aupperle.

An undercurrent in *Beast* is the consequences of Man's control over advanced technology, more specifically his handling of radioactive material. Within the first few minutes of the film, the groundwork for this premise is laid with the chronology immediately preceding the testing of an atomic device; after months of preparation, it explodes with a blinding flash that unleashes cataclysmic fury. Shortly after detonation inside the forward observation post, scientists Nesbitt and Ritchie have an exchange which touches upon the conflicting sentiments about the energy of the atom. While Ritchie expresses an unbridled optimism about its potential ("You know, every time one of these things goes off, I feel as if we were helping to write the first chapter of a new Genesis"), Nesbitt offers a more cautious point of view ("Let's hope we don't find ourselves writing the last chapter of the old one!"). Here is a point raised at other times during the film, the past versus the future; this wells up again during his visit to Lee's apartment. He foreshadows the aftermath of the detonation when talking to Col. Evans immediately following the test; when Evans says how eight weeks of preparation had ended in a second, Prof. Nesbitt waxes prophetic by countering with, "Jack, when energy of that magnitude is released, it's never over. What the cumulative effects of all these atomic explosions and tests will be, only time can tell." Then after Evans rebukes his statement ("You mean scientists can't tell, huh?"), the physicist addresses this remark by saying, "The world's been here for millions of years. Man's been walking upright for a comparatively short time. Mentally, we're still crawling." With his final statement, the scientist introduces a measure of doubt that humankind has enough wisdom or maturity to handle such advanced nuclear physics.

Although the Beast is a dinosaur, or at least a reptilian monster, it more broadly seems like a metaphor for undesirable or disastrous outcomes stemming from the manifestations of civilization. Just as dumped pollutants will inevitably wash up on a beach somewhere, the improper treatment of radioactive material will eventually come back to haunt mankind. However, the rhedosaur's death through an isotope shot does symbolically suggest that technology can also correct problems that were the upshot of previous human endeavors. In retrospect, *Beast* was the first motion picture linking radioactivity together with gigantic (and usually ill-natured) creatures, inventing an entire subgenre. Warner Bros. followed up on this theme with the 1954 release *Them!*, a movie about giant ants resulting from atomic tests; before the 1950s was over, the concept of ordinary animals (usually insects) mutated to gargantuan proportions via radiation became an overworked cliché. Another interesting aspect of *Beast* is the way in which radioactive substances are handled. Of course, it speaks to the general era but ironically tends to fulfill the predictions of Nesbitt right then and there. All the scientists and other are outside in full view of the detonation, wearing only goggles for protection from the blinding flash. A quick calculation (the plane passes over the outpost at approximately one minute before the blast, traveling at 350–360 miles per hour) shows that the farthest the device could have exploded from the outpost building was several miles.

It is a somewhat chilling reminder of the above-ground nuclear weapons testing in southern Nevada. Between 1951 and 1958, scores of mushroom clouds filled the skies over the Nevada Test Site (NTS), often with nearby troops equipped only with eye protection. Needless to say, many of these soldiers suffered premature deaths from cancer and related complications as a result. In addition, the handling of the radioactive isotope appears minimalistic at best; the truck bearing this material pulls in amongst all the military personnel, and the procedures taken with it in the possession of Prof.

Nesbitt and Stone seem slipshod by contemporary standards. So, in spite of the fatidic ideas aired here and it presaging a slew of thematically similar titles, this feature's depiction of radiation and nuclear detonations appears to be quite conventional for the era.

Coming in at a total cost of around $210,000, *Beast* was a triumph of quality moviemaking on a shoestring budget. In fact, it turned out so well that Dietz realized the feature was much too good for distribution through his regional distributors. So he decided upon finding a company for nation wide release of their production. Besides the inherent caliber of the project, another concern must have been the recent developments of CinemaScope, Technicolor and 3-D formats by filmmakers to combat the loss of theatergoers by 1953 to television; a limited availability B&W offering would probably have had difficulty being successful under these circumstances. Of course, the original negative cost for their proposed monster flick was $150,000, so the actual bottom line was something like $60,000 more than they had figured upon. Dietz approached Jack Warner about his studio releasing *Beast*, but the head of Warner Bros. was only interested in buying the feature outright. The studio offered $450,000 as a purchase price, based on production manager Tony Wright's opinion after being consulted by Mr. Warner as to what it would have cost them to make it; he estimated the production would have run a minimum of $1 million. So Dietz sold the property to Warner Bros. and netted a profit in excess of 100 percent.

Taking possession of its new title, the film company set about replacing the original score with the "louder, brassier" Buttolph score and added a stock footage shot of a ballet performance (which Lourié called "useless"). Spending around $200,000 on advertising in all forms of the popular media to promote it, Warners released *Beast* in June 1953 and it very quickly became a hit. It opened in 500 theaters, and 1,000 more screens were added a few weeks later. These first 500 prints were struck in "Glorious Sepia Tone," a fancy way for terming a brownish tint to the film (Harryhausen didn't particularly care for this alteration). Some of the larger markets also got to see the underwater scenes in a greenish hue. Benefiting from the promotional blitz as well as its superlative aspects, it became the fourth highest grossing movie of 1953 (behind *Peter Pan*, *The Robe* and *House of Wax*), earning about $5 million at the box office. Eugene Lourié remembers taking both Jean Renoir and his daughter to watch *Beast* right after it came out. In his book, Lourié states Renoir was delighted with it, but his six-year-old girl was quite upset and said, "You are bad, Daddy, bad. You killed the nice beast" (240). But on a more serious note, the revenue and acclaim that this production generated upon release was hardly pleasing to many of those involved. Lourié felt stereotyped by it, as was noted previously, and Jack Dietz became extremely jealous and livid over how much money Warner Bros. made off what he had sold them for a meager price.

Shortly following *Beast*'s release, Dietz hooked up with Harryhausen for another film project. Ray worked up two treatments as potential motion pictures, *The Giant Ymir* and *The Elementals*. Dietz was interested in the latter story idea and began work with the animator to develop it into a full-fledged motion picture. Set in Paris because Harryhausen wanted to travel to Europe, *The Elementals* is the story of alien creatures invading the world. In *Animato! #25*, he offers a synopsis of the proposed production: "Another planet had fired missiles — cocoons — down to Earth — we don't know what planet. These cocoons were like butterfly cocoons; they would hatch and the creatures would then go into caves. They were enormous, and they would metamorphise into these bat creatures, like a butterfly. This little boy discovers this, and by the time he alerts the adult world to all this, they've escaped from the cave and started nesting in the Eiffel Tower. They would attack cable cars going up the Alps. We had a scene I'd illustrated where they attack the cable car, the cable breaks, and six dozen fall out of the car as the bat creatures swoop down and grab them. We had various gimmicks like that: chasing people in wagons as they evacuate and so on. We wanted to make it quite spectacular" (46).

Unfortunately, the project never progressed beyond the preliminary phases before its dissolution. Lou Morheim was hired by Dietz to work on the treatment, and Lourié was again considered for the director's chair (Lourié in fact tried to launch a similar project years later). In addition to the outline, Harryhausen also created several sketches and even some animation tests with a monster he constructed. The achieved footage can be found on the Criterion *Jason and the Argonauts* laserdisc edition in B&W, and *The Ray Harryhausen Chronicles* in color. Playing himself as both a live-action and animated figure, Ray tries to defend himself against one of the flying monsters; he waves a stick as the hovering attacker relentlessly dives towards him. The animation stand-in is grabbed up in the winged terror's talons and then carried aloft. Even though these glimpses are all too brief, the stop-motion model made for these experiments represent the development of an important character type he would use over and over. Inspired by the bat-winged demons of Gustave Dore's engravings, the starring monstrosity of this film is somewhat humanoid in form though bearing an unmistakably reptilian visage. Its basic physiognomy imparts an apocalyptic feeling of doom through leathery wings with bat-like venation, clawed feet and scaly flesh; these qualities, with certain modifications, can be witnessed in the Harpies of *Jason* as well as the Homunculus of *The Golden Voyage of Sinbad*. Even the pterosaurs in both *One Million Years B.C.* and *Gwangi* were given bat-wings for dramatic purposes.

The Elementals was also contemplated as a 3-D film, with Ray performing tests to see if this was possible; in *Cinefantastique* Volume 11 Number 4, he states, "I made quite a number of shots to prove the feasibility of it, including some three-dimensional shots, because at that time everybody wanted to do 3-D projects. I also used the rhedosaurus in a 3-D test. But it just got so cumbersome. It would've taken an eternity to do the film in three dimensions. Not only do you have to set up so that the image is right in both cameras, you're limited in other ways. Regular process photography — the standard studio back-projection — renders only a two dimensional image" (36). Harryhausen has also divulged that a "beam splitter" (the semi-transparent mirror discussed earlier) was required for rendering the stereoscopic image, but indicated that it wasn't utilized in conjunction with front-projection. Dietz put up the money for these tests and otherwise tried to get it off the ground, but apparently his personal and financial woes put an end to *The Elementals*.

Although it isn't one of his dinosaur films, *It Came from Beneath the Sea* bears mentioning here due to its striking similarity to *Beast* in fundamental structure and storyline. This was the first project which Harryhausen teamed up with Charles H. Schneer, forming one of the most significant associations in fantasy filmmaking. Schneer had seen *Beast* and got in touch with the man behind the special effects to do a film about a giant octopus tearing pieces off the Golden Gate Bridge. *It Came* begins in the middle of the Pacific Ocean, when a strange, radioactive entity immobilizes a submarine, then disappears as quickly as it arrived. From a chunk of tissue lodged in the vessel, the attacker is identified as an enormous octopus. Because of the radioactivity, the cephalopod's normal prey can detect and avoid it, forcing the creature up to the surface for food. Before long, the leviathan sinks a freighter and ends up along the Oregon coast, killing a number of people. The Navy swings into full force, mining the ocean and making preparations for the colossal invertebrate. Eventually it is detected in the waters off San Francisco, where it heavily damages the aforementioned suspension bridge and other city landmarks. Using flamethrowers to repel its slithering tentacles, the authorities force the octopus back underseas. A specially designed torpedo is fired from the submarine into the monster but it doesn't detonate, so divers have to go out and trigger the explosion. They get the torpedo to successfully go off, destroying the cephalopod and saving humanity from yet another gargantuan menace.

It Came was made for even less money than *Beast* and it shows, never quite matching the caliber of the previous offering (it is believed to have cost between $100,000 and $150,000). To save both time and money, the octopus model was equipped with only six tentacles (Ray calls it a "sextopus"), but the omission of the other two arms is virtually unnoticeable. An oversized tentacle, about two and a half feet long, served for many close-ups of a suckered limb thrusting into the air. Nicely detailed miniatures make the creature's attack more palpable; these include a section of one of the Golden Gate's Bridge's looming supports, the Oakland Ferry Building and the clock tower. The bridge's destruction is definitely the highlight of the movie, showing the cephalopod scaling the suspension structure and crushing its supports with powerful arms. Harryhausen gave the tentacles crawling through the streets a "mind of their own," an interesting and dynamic way to give characterization to a mollusk. Glycerin made the skin of it look wet to offer a slimy, repulsive look. One shot, of the tip of an arm smashing the window of a store, was inspired by a scene in the 1925 *The Lost World* that Ray remembers from his early youth; this long-lost footage had the rampaging brontosaurus in London poking its head into a room.

As in *Beast*, the octopus rises up and seizes a ship at sea but here it is improved upon. Since the background plate contains breaking surf, the rolling action of these waves matches the commotion of the violently careening freighter under assault, as opposed to the rhedosaur's attack on the fishing ketch. In *Puppets & People*, S.S. Wilson expresses this opinion where he states, "The background plate is breaking surf, but through careful animation and editing, and with the addition of the spray effect (which helps to conceal the relatively sharp line of the static matte), Harryhausen makes the breaking waves appear to be caused by the octopus's violent wrenching of the model ship. In so doing, he improved this scene over a similar one in his previous film, *The Beast from 20,000 Fathoms*. The rhedosaurus sinks a ship in a background plate of rolling, open ocean; here the addition of the spray is only marginally helpful, since the sea is basically undisturbed all around the action" (113). While *It Came* is technically an improvement over *Beast* with better stop-motion effects and superior miniatures, overall the picture is an inferior product. Mainly, the leading characters are one-dimensional due to a script that only serves to move the story forward. Another weakness is the overabundance of stock footage, which even includes an unused cut of a fleeing crowd from *Beast*. Kenneth Tobey, Faith Domergue and Donald Curtis (who would later appear in *Earth Vs. the Flying Saucers*) play the major parts in the feature, which was directed by Robert Gordon.

Besides the inherent similarity of its storyline to that in *Beast*, another connection can be made between *It Came* and Harryhausen's saurians. Sometime after being used in the film, the octopus' six limbs were removed and later became "dinosaur tails" according to Ray. Even though he has a definite memory of this, it doesn't mean that all six of them became saurian posteriors in toto; most likely only pieces and portions from the lot were reused this way, with the remaining armature parts being fed into other characters.

Eugene Lourié directed two other dinosaur films, stemming from his reputation as a result of *Beast*. The first of these two is *The Giant Behemoth*, an Allied Artists feature that had unintentionally become a remake of the Harryhausen effort. Gene Evans and André Morell, whose appearance greatly helps the action along, star in this British-made picture. In the wake of atomic testing and the concentration of radioactivity in the marine food chain, huge piles of dead fish wash up along the English coast of Cornwall. Investigating this phenomenon, as well as the mysterious death of a fisherman covered with burns, are American scientist Steve Karnes (Evans), who was in London for an atomic research conference, and Prof. James Bickford (Morell). Arriving in Cornwall, they find no evidence of radiation on the beaches where the fish lie dead, but other evidence of something lurking in the sea begins turning up: A glowing radioactive mass is observed swimming underwater, a wrecked steamship drifts ashore and a farm is completely destroyed. Determining from a photo of a footprint that the monster may be prehistoric, Karnes and Bickford consult a paleontologist who informs them that their nemesis is a surviving dinosaur called a "paleosaurus." The fossil expert tells the pair that it can generate electricity like an eel, and believes it is heading for the shallow water of the Thames estuary to die.

The titanic octopus of *It Came from Beneath the Sea* capsizes a freighter. It is similar to the scene where the rhedosaurus in *Beast from 20,000 Fathoms* sinks a fishing ketch, but the rolling surf in the background plate makes the action here seem more realistic.

A ferry is soon attacked in London on this river, spurring the military to prepare for an invasion. Karnes, Bickford and others decide that the safest and quickest method of disposing of this highly radioactive creature is with a radium-tipped torpedo; this substance will serve to very rapidly accelerate its imminent death. Before long, the Behemoth rises out of the Thames and tromps through central London, killing scores of people and causing considerable property damage. Returning to its watery habitat, the dinosaur is tracked underwater by Karnes and a crewman in a mini-sub equipped with the special weapon. Detecting the paleosaurus, they fire the torpedo at it and score a direct hit, killing the titanic intruder and thereby putting an end to this menace. But just as Karnes and Bickford are leaving, a radio bulletin reports that mountains of dead fish are washing up along the American coast from Maine to Florida...

Behemoth turned out to be highly derivative of *Beast* though Lourié tried to avoid this from happening. He explains in *My Work in Films* that the original idea for this picture was an invisible "blob of expanding radiation" (241), but he was caught by his *Beast* reputation. The film's English producers wanted instead a tangible monster in a project patterned after *Beast*. Lourié took ten days, with a friend assisting, to rewrite a script producer David Diamond's writers were having trouble with. He was forced to plagiarize himself to finish it quickly, as Diamond had to show this to his associates in order to get the contract signed. Since there never were any changes made to this "'pro forma' document" (to Lourié's obvious dismay), the finished production bore a greater likeness to *Beast* than he would have liked.

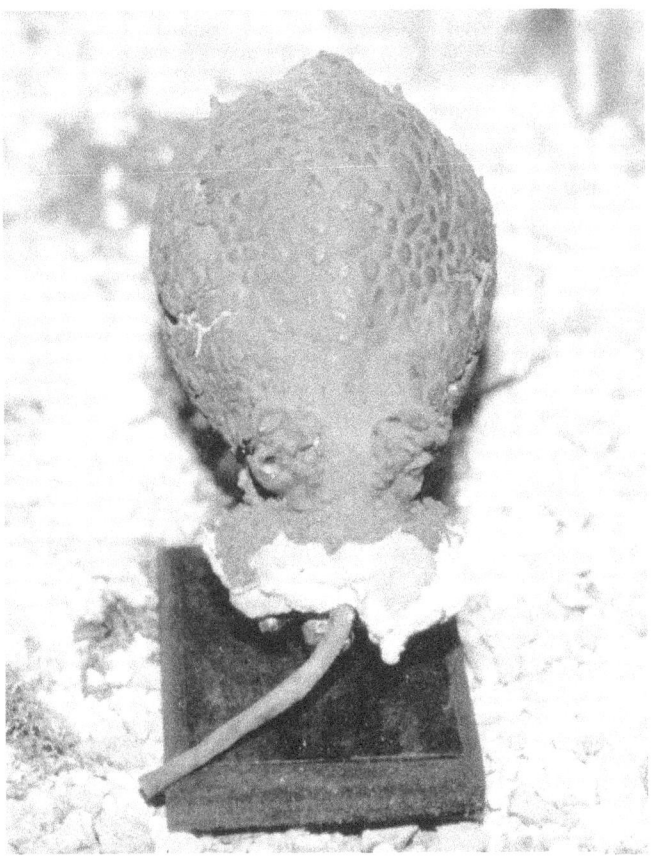

The head from *It Came from Beneath the Sea*'s titular cephalopod is all that survives of the model, on display in Babelsberg, Germany. Harryhausen used at least some of this figure's six tentacle armatures for dinosaur tails. Note the ball joint plainly visible near its base. Photograph by the author.

The basic story is greatly helped along by the performances of Evans and Morell; they act like believable people in pursuit of answers. But much of the sleuthing itself is handled in a less than satisfying manner. Besides most of the scientific investigation coming off as rather flimsy and superficial, there is never an adequate explanation of the Behemoth's origins. Has it survived continuously since the Mesozoic Era, and if so why hasn't it been previously observed? Also, how does the paleontologist know this creature is "electric" and that it would head for fresh water shallows where he somehow knows it was born? Compensated for these faults are the straightforward nature of the presentation and the generally good interaction of the principal characters. Another positive aspect is the location filming and the relative lack of stock footage, giving this modest picture at least a measure of originality even if lackluster in other ways.

Willis O'Brien and Pete Peterson (whose name is misspelled as "Petterson" in the opening titles) were responsible for the feature's stop-motion visuals. O'Brien, who was by now in his seventies and no longer animating, constructed the Behemoth model. The armature was tinkered together with parts cannibalized from other figures, then fleshed-out through the traditional "build-up" technique of modelmaking (just as Harryhausen did with his rhedosaurus puppet). Cast lizard skins were used as the monster's epidermis. Overall, the creature has a very good appearance but its composition isn't perfect, as seams are noticeable over the entire puppet. Peterson did the actual animation effects but suffered from a crippling illness (multiple sclerosis); to accommodate his physical condition, the miniature sets were only slightly off the floor so he could animate in a sitting position. In fact, this "studio" was really Peterson's Encino, California, garage, where they could keep costs down while working on low-budget projects.

Rampaging through the streets of London, the starring dinosaur in *The Giant Behemoth* is a highly radioactive creature. The exterior of this puppet came from cast lizard skins.

Even though the allotment for *Behemoth*'s effects budget was merely $20,000, the results show brilliant staging and characterization. A thrilling scene finds the marauding paleosaurus encountering high-tension wires at night (the electrical arcs were printed in later), a very dynamic and moody vignette that many animation fans list as a personal favorite. Also stunning is its after-dark sighting by the Houses of Parliament and Westminster Abbey, which were simply mounted photo cutouts but look quite realistic. Searchlights move across the Behemoth's body in an effect even more pronounced than that which was seen in *Beast*. Some other components used to facilitate the stop-motion include the miniature dockside cranes being made of malleable copper so they were soft enough to be trampled by the monster (made by Phil Kellison, who lived only two blocks away from Peterson). Matte painting on glass enhances a street that the Behemoth strolls down (marks on the sheet of glass make it visible over the puppet).

Unfortunately, there are numerous problems with the special effects content of *Behemoth*, enough so to seriously erode the quality of the product. One of these lapses include a faulty rear projector which didn't always advance the film to the next frame, so the running crowds in the background plates "freeze" at times in these cuts. Another problem is with the Behemoth mock-up in a water tank attacking the ferry; while this prop does look pretty decent, the lack of any movement besides its being pushed around makes these scenes practically comical (the base of the mock-up, which is the bottom of the neck, can be witnessed coming up out of the water when it tips over the model boat). It actually wasn't fabricated as an immobile representation but instead as a wire-operated model controlled by three actuating levers that moved the head, neck and jaws. But the mechanism was wrecked by rough working of the levers before ever being filmed in the tank, and unhappily it was required to be used in such a condition. There are other flaws here and there in the picture, but certainly the most fundamental deficiency is the blatant reuse of animation. Even someone watching the film for the first time would notice the shameless repetition of several shots, especially those of the dinosaur's head swaying as it moves through the city (the rear screen footage in these miniature projection cuts is also rather jerky, as if the camera was traveling over a bumpy road). This owes to the limited time and money O'Brien and Peterson had to work with (they were only given about six to eight weeks to do the stop-motion), so the amount of animation they yielded had to be extended. In addition to repeating certain shots "as is," others were optically zoomed in on and flopped to help disguise their reuse. Therefore, the paleosaurus really crushes just a single automobile underfoot instead of three, even though this is seen from differing perspectives.

Jack Rabin, Louis DeWitt and Irving Block were in charge of the effects for *Behemoth* and rendered all the optical work (which included the aforementioned padding) as well as other special effects which Obie and Peterson didn't achieve. Lourié wanted O'Brien to helm the movie's visual effects, but David Diamond doubted that they could pull it off with their limited facilities so he turned instead to Rabin to supervise the undertaking; under this arrangement, the two animators were subcontracted to him. Rabin & Company had realized this constituent for many "Saturday matinee" type flicks from the late 1940s through the 1950s. Some of these offerings include *The Invisible Boy* (1957), *Kronos* (1957) and *The Atomic Submarine* (1959). For *Behemoth*, the trio's creations include the "hypno-disc" swirl emitted by the Behemoth when projecting its radiation, the horribly charred victims of the creature and the water tank shooting. Rabin befriended O'Brien while he (Rabin) was doing optics for *The Beast of Hollow Mountain* (1956); the elder animator's only contribution to this production was its story. Since there is no much potential to be observed here, all the imperfections make this affair even more maddening; with only a little more money and attention to details, the feature could have rivaled or perhaps even surpassed *Beast* as a "creature feature."

Unlike the rhedosaurus, the paleosaurus stands on pillar-like legs and more closely resembles in form an authentic dinosaur. At first glance it looks like a brontosaur, but the longer front limbs belie the fact that the design was based upon a different genus of sauropod called a brachiosaur. Of course, it looks quite dragon-esque with the enlarged, toothy head and dorsal plates running down the middle of the neck and back.

Together with the darker mood than seen in *Beast*, *Behemoth* is a much more horrific picture that could have been an all-time classic with greater care taken in its making. However, the myriad shortcomings previously discussed seriously lowers its dramatic impact. Sadly, the paleosaurus model deteriorated soon after the animation was completed (it was even starting to fall apart during the stop-action photography; the bottom of its foot pulls away from the armature after stepping on the vehicle). *Behemoth* was released in England as *Behemoth, the Sea Monster* and given an "X" certificate (adults only). Besides Willis O'Brien and Eugene Lourié, there is another connection between this film and Ray Harryhausen: Desmond Davis, who later directed *Clash of the Titans*, was engaged as camera operator for this endeavor.

Willis O'Brien working on a sketch for *The Giant Behemoth*. It was one of Obie's last film projects before he died in 1962.

Lourié went on to direct one more dinosaur-related picture, the King Bros. production *Gorgo* (1961). Differing from both *Beast* and *Behemoth*, *Gorgo* was shot in color and employs a man in a rubber suit instead of stop-motion for the giant creature effects; there isn't any tie-in either to atomic testing or radioactivity either. Also, it features two dinosaurs rather than one: a baby about 30 feet tall (this is the size Lourié indicates; the movie says that it is 65 feet) and its mother standing over 200 feet high. In addition, the monsters are the victims here instead of mankind. Since the infant was captured and put on display in a London circus, the towering parent instinctively attacks the metropolis to reclaim her offspring. *Gorgo*'s use of realistic-looking London landmark miniatures and optical effects make these non-animation visuals come off quite marvelously. Strangely enough, the name "Gorgo" was not derived from gorgosaurus (the invalid name for albertosaurus, an early variety of tyrannosaur), even though it definitely looks like a theropod. Rather, the moniker is a slightly condensed version of gorgon, the creature of Greek mythology with snakes for hair "that the mere sight of it would turn a man to stone." Taken together, all three of Lourié's dinosaur pictures are often considered a "sea serpent" trilogy of sorts, with *Beast* and *Gorgo* at least usually thought of as being good in quality.

Reviews of *Beast* are almost universally favorable. Leonard Maltin states, "Good

Ray Harryhausen special effects, especially in amusement park finale." Critic Ed Naha lavishes great praise in his *Horrors: From Screen to Scream* (1975) by saying that it is "an amazing little tour de force by Ray Harryhausen" (18). Even more intriguing are the opinions of those directly involved with the project. Lourié wrote in his book, "Overall, I felt that the picture did not fail us. The action moved forward, the story progressed, the tempo was never lost. I think I caught the feeling of panic in the streets and the loneliness of the beast trapped in the deep walls of Wall Street or caught on the roller coaster. Moreover, I think the picture had a specific tone of its own. When all the shots were spliced together, the end sequence came as a surprise with the beast dying in the flaming ruins of the roller coaster. It was emotionally strong, like the finale of a tragic opera. The beast dies like an opera tenor" (240). In contrast to the director, Ray Bradbury is somewhat less complimentary about the movie. Though mentioning its significance, he thinks that it is "not a great film, not even a very good one, but the start of two careers that finally took his motion pictures, his beasts, and my books, into some of the farthest corners of the world." Indeed, it was an exceptional first solo venture for several reasons.

A bronze of the rhedosaurus, sculpted by Harryhausen, on exhibit in Babelsberg, Germany. Like the original stop-motion model, its underbelly has the distinctive skin pattern of a crocodilian hide. Photograph by the author.

Beast became a trend-setter in combining massive, monstrous life-forms with the advent of atomic energy, an original idea which quickly became an overworked cliché before the end of the decade. As a matter of fact, the entire "Godzilla" series owes its existence to this feature following the imitative Japanese-made *Gojira* (1954; released in the U.S. in English and with scenes of Raymond Burr two years later as *Godzilla, King of the Monsters!*). A sequel, *King Kong Vs. Godzilla* (1963), which was in reality the bastardization of Obie's unrealized *King Kong Vs. Frankenstein* project, seems to give a few nods to Harryhausen. Godzilla emerges from an iceberg and heads "on a predetermined course" for Japan. Later, the gigantic reptile is thought to be inhabiting waters "where the depths go to about 20,000 fathoms." More importantly, it helped sustain stop-motion animation as a viable means of crafting visual effects in full-length features through the development of a proprietary film process. Although it lacks a large measure of the artistry found in O'Brien's *King Kong* and *Mighty Joe Young*, the static matte rear-projection composite procedure economically places articulated models into background plates photographed prior to the animation. Besides proving that Harryhausen could simply operate under low-budget constraints, it instead demonstrates not only his ingenuity but also a fortuitous invention that allowed for a future in major productions. Willis O'Brien seems to have viewed *Beast* with a certain degree of apprehension however; according to his widow Darlyne as quoted in *Cinefantastique* Volume 11 Number 4, "Obie thought the animation was good, of course. But he was disappointed to see animation used in a low-budget film. He always felt the budget should be very big. Of course, he ended up doing low-budget films himself, like *The Black Scorpion*" (36).

Encapsulated in ***Beast from 20,000 Fathoms*** is the atmospheric Bradbury tale of a lonely prehistoric monster beckoned to a lighthouse, though its haunting romanticism is all but lost in the movie.

Released through Warner Home Video on VHS and laserdisc in 1991 (the outer jacket makes the wild claim that the rhedosaurus was "constructed at full scale, all 50 tons of it" for some inexplicable reason), *Beast* shows how a little bit of money can go a very long way. Good acting, decent production values and great special effects blend together into a successful film that can be genuinely called "revolutionary." Only a couple of years passed before Ray would cross paths with the dinosaur again; teaming up with his mentor O'Brien, his next cinematic involvement with them would be for a documentary about past and present fauna titled *The Animal World*.

3. The Animal World

After his Oscar-winning documentary *The Sea Around Us* (1951), Irwin Allen set about to make another nature-based motion picture which he hoped would garner the same success. *The Sea Around Us* was based on the best-selling book by Rachel Carson, a Pennsylvania-born woman who was an ecologist and scientist in addition to being a writer, and had been Editor-in-Chief for all U.S. Fish and Wildlife Service publications; her keen interest in marine biology is also expressed in other works such as *Under the Sea-Wind* (1941) and *The Edge of the Sea* (1955). Allen's feature was not an original production but rather a masterpiece of editing, culled from about 300 hours of underwater cinematography he acquired the rights to, and resulted in a montage of aquatic clips running just over an hour in length.

Narrated by Don Forbes and Theodore von Eltz, this movie was popular at the box office as well as being critically acclaimed and honored as Best Documentary at the 1952 Academy Awards. After forming Windsor Productions and moving to Warner Bros., he set about making a sequel about the development of terrestrial life forms, from simple single-celled organisms to dinosaurs and modern animal genera. There is some overlap with *The Sea Around Us*, since all life on Earth began in the ocean and thus there is some undersea footage near the feature's beginning. Again, Irwin got the necessary permissions to use film of living creatures in their native habitats and wrote the narrative for this subsequent picture, *The Animal World*.

Originally, the dinosaur sequence was not to have been done in stop-motion but rather through a series of dioramas with static models filmed as still-lifes. Allen was aware of Harryhausen's *Evolution* footage and approached the animator about creating the prehistoric content of his movie; Ray recalls this in the Steven Archer book *Willis O'Brien: Special Effects Genius* (1993), noting that Allen "wanted to buy some of my 16mm test footage from my defunked project *Evolution*. It was blown up into a 35mm color print. The quality was quite good, but unfortunately there was not enough of it" (82). So he convinced Irwin that animation effects would make this segment more memorable than through a series of stills in miniature sets. The filmmaker apparently was sold on the idea even if concerned about its cost, and decided to hire Ray. Willis O'Brien was brought aboard the project as the animation supervisor, in charge of working out the stop-motion vignettes and designing the dinosaur figures for the sequence. Harryhausen was responsible for the actual manipulation of the puppets to recapture a Mesozoic landscape teeming with these extinct monsters. Irwin's instructions were straightforward: achieve some decent special effects for his picture in as brief a production time frame as possible. Indeed, *Animal World* was the shortest engagement Ray ever had on a feature film, lasting only six to seven weeks in total duration.

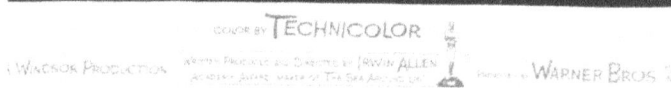

Since the dinosaur sequence is the only section of the movie Ray had anything to do with, the rest of it will not be discussed here. This part begins about 14 minutes into the film and runs nearly ten minutes in length. Instead of beginning with animation, this portion of the feature starts out with shots of fossilized tracks and then skeletal mounts in the American Museum of Natural History: Tyrannosaurus rex, allosaurus, triceratops, stegosaurus and brontosaurus (now apatosaurus). Moving in on the brontosaur's head and neck, the scene suddenly shifts backwards in time millions of years to the Jurassic period, with the head and neck now belonging to a living specimen; oddly, the narrator says, "Man had not yet been created, but if he had been..." just before the sauropod grabs a screaming caveman in its jaws. Next, the brontosaurus is seen grazing on the frond of a palm tree and ambles over to lay some eggs, squatting slightly so they don't drop too far to the ground. But this activity doesn't go unnoticed: an allosaurus observes the mother dinosaur and roars at her in anticipation of a meal. Leaving her clutch of eggs behind, the brontosaur moves off in haste as the allosaur seems to simply walk away and not pursue this beast. Warmed by the sun, one of these eggs eventually hatches and a chirping baby brontosaurus emerges, equipped with an egg tooth.

In another Jurassic setting, on a high plateau next to a deep river gorge, a stegosaurus peacefully nips at vegetation near the edge of the cliff when suddenly a ceratosaurus confronts the plated dinosaur. Launching an attack, it clamps on the dorsal plates on the stegosaur's back and neck and receives a piercing wound from the swishing spiked tail, but very quickly the ceratosaur kills its prey with a bite to the unprotected throat. Before it can consume the meal, another ceratosaurus rapidly approaches with a mighty leap and lands near the rightful owner of the stegosaur, resulting in a fierce battle for possession of this carcass. Savagely slashing and clawing each other with teeth and nails, the fight takes these two combatants dangerously close to the rim of the river canyon. When one lunges at the other at the edge of the precipice, they are carried over and plunge to their deaths in the raging current below.

The scene shifts to the very late Cretaceous, where a tricer-

A ceratosaurus challenges another of its kind that has killed a stegosaurus, leading to a fight to the death.

atops is foraging for food and pushes a palm tree over with its horned head to get at its delicate leaves. Hearing wails in the distance, the triceratops readies to face the creature—a Tyrannosaurus rex. Just as they square off, a nearby volcano erupts to mark the beginning of the dinosaurs' doom. Both immediately flee ahead of the flowing lava and fire but it is an exercise in futility; the triceratops is caught in a sticky quagmire and sinks below the surface, and the tyrannosaur falls into a fissure opened by an earthquake. Other dinosaurs try to escape but also succumb to the scorching upheaval. Thus the Age of Dinosaurs draws to a close.

The saurian puppets were fabricated by Arthur S. Rhoades and his crew in the Warner Bros. prop department (with the assistance of sculptors Pasqual Manuelli and Harold Wilson). They created the metallic armatures and cast the figures from molds. This technique, of injecting foam rubber into a mold holding the armature and then baking this mixture until it gels, is a much less time-consuming means of modelmaking than the traditional "build-up" method associated with O'Brien's longtime associate Marcel Delgado. Constructing models from the armature up can yield some wonderful results, but it takes longer and it is practically impossible to duplicate the physiognomy of an animated character if more than one is built for the stop-motion (sharp-eyed viewers of *King Kong* and *Mighty Joe Young* will notice at certain points that different gorilla puppets are used). Of course, a mold guarantees that the outward expression will remain consistent if multiple figures are made or a single one is re-cast. However, there are certain problems with the foam injection process. The foam latex might shrink when heated in the oven; Ray found that padding the armature by packing solid pieces of pre-shrunken foam rubber around it greatly reduced the chances of this taking place. From a personal standpoint, he preferred the build-up method over casting for aesthetic reasons, as his rhedosaurus model and all the dinosaurs in his earliest experiments and *Evolution* had been rendered this way. But he was to adopt this latter protocol for nearly every stop-motion character following this picture, mainly for the sake of expediency. (Notable exceptions are the skeleton figures seen in *7th Voyage, Jason and the Argonauts* and *First Men in the Moon*; they were built-up with cotton dipped in latex though their heads had been made of cast resin.)

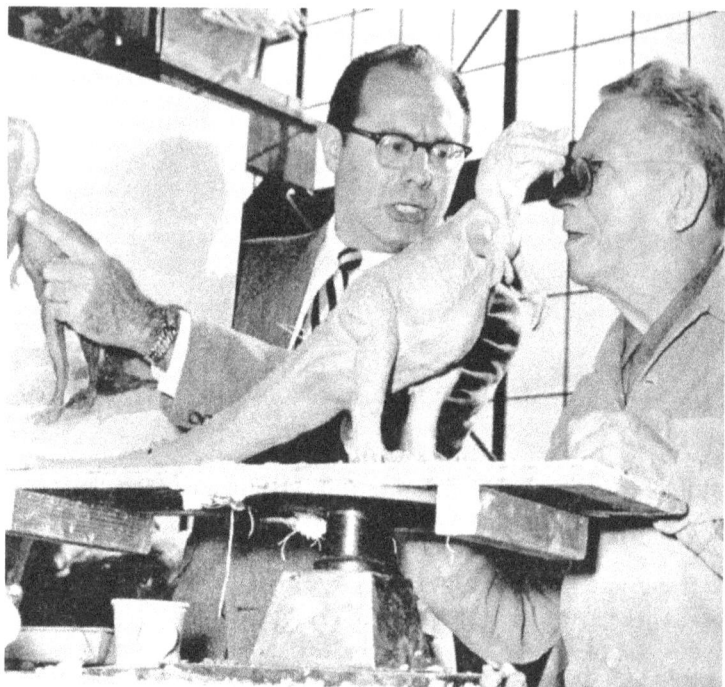

Naturally, the two ceratosaurs were cast from the same mold, though through some touching-up afterwards there was some variability in their appearance. One ceratosaurus saw extra duty serving as both the film's allosaurus and tyrannosaurus, sans the nasal horn to help disguise this fact. Another discernible difference in the ceratosaurs is that their front limbs are proportionally larger than those belonging to the allosaurus or tyrannosaurus here; while T. rex did indeed possess forelimbs that were quite small (and sported only two fingers on each hand), the allosaur seen here also has little ones as opposed to the more massive clawed limbs known from fossil remains. It therefore strongly suggests that the allosaurus is exactly the same as the tyrannosaurus and used without any attempt to

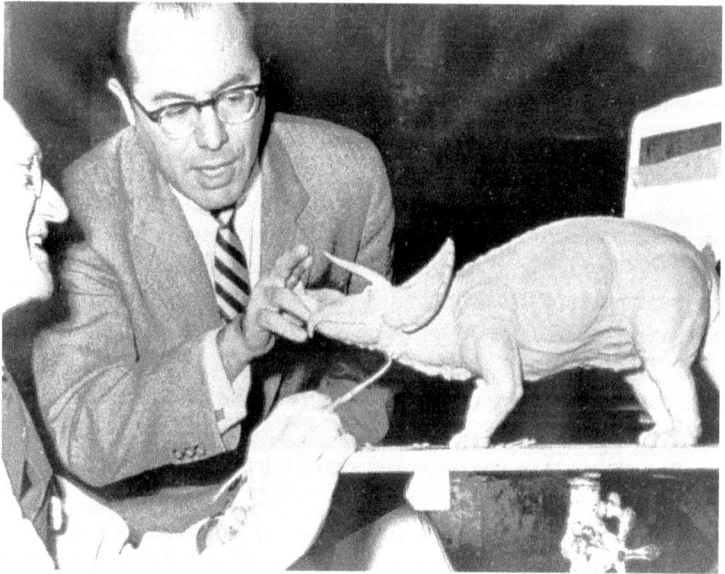

Irwin Allen inspecting models used for *The Animal World*. These were sculpted with at least an adequate amount of detail, even if they don't rival figures from other Harryhausen films.

alter its physiognomy. These dinosaur puppets were about the size that Harryhausen typically handled during animation; according to the *Animal World* pressbook, the approximate range of the measurements "are two to three feet in length" (9).

Further evidence of their stature can be judged from a series of stills of Ray posed with one of the ceratosaurs, looking by comparison to have stood about 14 to 16 inches high when rearing up to its full height. This would have made it roughly the same size as his later Gwangi model though not anywhere near as robust in the body. Besides the articulated stop-motion figures, a number of mechanical models corresponding to these but many times larger were constructed for close-ups. In the British magazine *Supernatural* #2 (1969), Ray gives a clear indication of their much greater dimensions: "The close-ups required detail that could only be incorporated in larger models. I remember our big ceratosaurus was about six feet tall" (42). Mainly consisting of only a head and torso, they were operated by wires so their mouths would open and close and the necks move around.

Unlike any of his solo feature film work, *Animal World*'s animation doesn't combine these characters with live-action elements photographed separately but combined in the same composite image à la Dynamation, instead using tabletop miniatures to recreate the prehistoric periods where they flourished. Manuelli and Wilson, who worked for the studio as staff effects men and whose sculptures served to create molds from which the models were cast, realized these small-scale landscapes that functioned to stage the saurians; they included a large number of palm trees on this otherwise barren terrain. Background paintings were used behind the miniature sets to give the feeling of great depth; they were done by Jack Shaw, who had worked before with Obie on the unrealized 1941–42 version of *Gwangi* and *Mighty Joe Young*. Glass shots designed by O'Brien probably functioned to conceal the edge of the tabletop with painted extensions of this antediluvian world. By virtue of the fact there was no rephotographing since every component of the image is present at or behind the tabletop stage, this allowed for the use of color film to record the frame-by-frame manipulation of the dinosaur thespians. Ray already had plenty of experience with color emulsions on his own, in projects such as *Evolution* and his Fairy Tale short subjects. But he had not combined their use with his innovative static matte rear-projection composite techniques at this point in time; he would be compelled to solve the myriad problems associated with the necessary duplicate printing to achieve the final composite image for his first full-color Dynamation feature, *The 7th Voyage of Sinbad*, as certain hues (such as greens) tended to degrade during this process. Using a new Kodak color stock (5253) helped to this end, as well as "flashing" the film with a low-level light in order to slightly fog it, serving to reduce contrast.

Another advantage with the simplistic tabletop set-ups to create the effects in *Animal World* was the absence of mattes, allowing for the use of two cameras at different angles to record a frame each of the animation in progress. This yielded twice as much footage as would be the case with in-camera methods to achieve a combined image from separately exposed components. However, there is no indication that the dual cameras were intended in any way to make the vignettes appear in 3-D; this craze had pretty much dissipated after a number of these pictures hit theaters during 1953, so it certainly wasn't a consideration in the filming of this segment. Harryhausen had previously made some tests for Jack Dietz and found that his static matte rear-projection composite procedures could be modified to give depth perception to his effects, though it would take him about three times as long to realize. Besides the utilization of more than one camera, he employed another means to obtain the maximum amount of stop-motion footage in a short amount of time. In Ted Newsom's *Cinefantastique* Volume 11 Number 4 article (1981), he says, "I double-framed certain parts, the slower-moving scenes where little movement is indicated, but for the most part it was simple, single-frame stop-motion" (39). This is also known as "shooting on twos," where a pair of frames are shot for each slight progressive movement made to make them seem nearly microscopic.

Harryhausen was given a secluded area for doing the animation, since he was accustomed to working alone and needed both the sense of privacy and calm afforded by such separation. Harold Wellman was the director of photography and lined up the shots according to O'Brien's plans; they were most likely in the form of storyboards, as this sequence had been storyboarded and therefore was not "invented" as they went along.

Overall, the animation in this sequence is very good even if fairly limited in scope and therefore hardly representative of Ray's finest achievements. Some aspects of it are definitely worthy of note. What introduces the audience to the Mesozoic Era is truly astonishing, (the completely fictitious supposition of Man co-existing with these long-extinct monsters) because there seems to be no logic to this idea whatsoever, the only impression it gives is that it was done for purely gratuitous reasons to elicit a response in the audience. Next, the brontosaurus nips at palm fronds up high in a tree; in a practically imperceptible manner, a tiny piece drops from the side of its mouth to the ground through a wire-supported effect. Then it continues across the open country (a shadow flickers several times here in the lower right part of the frame image; something encroached on the tabletop at several intervals while this stop-motion was being achieved).

The brontosaur is next observed laying an egg by squatting down in a somewhat ungainly manner. In the midst of this reproductive activity, the allosaurus (one of the largest theropods and probably top predator of its domain) makes its presence known with a roar. Both of these dinosaurs growl at each other in turn through their mechanical stand-ins, though a medium shot of the animated allosaur does a snapping vocalization to great effect. Making its retreat, the sauropod flees from her clutch of about ten eggs (the one seen laid was the first) lying on bare ground, and in the following shot of them it is obvious that some were destroyed out of careless trampling. The short encounter is not terribly exciting since these two dinosaurs are only viewed together through successive edits and not in the same frame image. Perhaps this was done just to keep things simple; perhaps the figures were not scaled with respect to one another (there is some strong photographic evidence that the brontosaurus model is much too small in relationship to the allosaurus, which couldn't be hidden on a miniature stage such as this). Jim Danforth was influenced by the hatching of the baby brontosaur and included a very similar scene within *When Dinosaurs Ruled the Earth* (1970).

Following this, the stegosaurus lumbers around near the edge of a plateau above a river gorge. A very familiar variety of late Jurassic saurian, it measured about 20 feet or so in length and was equipped with a single staggered row of bony dorsal plates (the issue of the arrangement of these structures along its back hasn't been completely resolved) and a tail terminating in four sharp spikes. Harryhausen had animated this type of plant-eating reptile in his early experiments, with a puppet Willis O'Brien made slightly infamous by saying it had legs that looked like "sausages," but he never included one of these well-known dinosaurs in any prehistoric-based feature that was realized subsequent to *Animal World*.

The stegosaur grazes on low-growing plants while slowly working its way along this elevated terrain. Its movements are so small that gentle breathing rhythms can be detected in the middle of the abdominal area (an

Irwin Allen in front of the larger mechanical dinosaurs employed for *Animal World*. Generally, they were much less effective than the animation puppets that they stood in for during close-ups. Photograph courtesy of Greg Kulon.

air bladder, inflated and deflated by an off-camera pump). Besides these regular tabletop shots, there are extremely long shots (showing the top of the stegosaur's back) looking upward at the cliff, most likely a smaller reproduction on a smaller version of the plateau; in these shots, its barely perceivable shuffling is definitely not stop-motion. Another cut, representing the view looking straight down from the very edge, shows the churning rapids running off the base of the stock footage waterfall. According to the pressbook, "These two sets were filmed in miniature on the backlot at the Warner studio, and with the aid of several boxes of soap flakes and an outboard motor, were made to resemble a most realistic cascade in all its full fury and breathtaking elegance" (10).

But soon this peaceful foraging is interrupted by a ceratosaurus bounding into the image, right next to the startled plant-eater. This horned, medium-sized bipedal carnivore is much larger than the fossil record indicates (much like the later incarnation in *One Million*); the narrator says it "stands 20 feet high and weighs eight tons." The stegosaurus is dispatched quickly but manages to impale the theropod with a blow to its hip, leaving a bloody wound where the spikes entered. A close-up of the mechanical ceratosaur biting a rubbery plate comes across as much less credible than its stop-motion equivalent. The dying throes of the stegosaur, toppled onto its side and frantically kicking the air for a few seconds, is both a vivid and unmistakable means of showing its defeat. However, before the flesh-eater has the opportunity to devour its meal, another ceratosaur arrives suddenly with a spectacular leap next to the killer and the slain stegosaur, then tackles the first ceratosaur after lunging rapidly and pushing it over with a well-placed bite. This piece of animation is the most dynamic moment of the entire dinosaur vignette and is dramatically effective as well. Reminded of a wire-supported maneuver from his earlier output, Ray decided he must include a similar entrance here as well; he relates in Jeff Rovin's *From the Land Beyond Beyond* (1977), "I had done that same shot with the test footage I had made for *Evolution*. In *Evolution*, I had the allosaur leap over the camera because I had used the music to *Firebird Suite*. And there was a key chord which, when I heard it, I said, 'I've just *got* to make an allosaur jump in to that music!'" (107).

After the first ceratosaurus gets back on its feet, a vicious altercation erupts between the two carnosaurs; with slashing teeth and claws, each receives bloody wounds as they fight. The employment of two camera angles is apparent as they grapple as close quarters, and it even looks like some of the same stop-motion is shown from each camera's perspective (during these shots, a palm leaf moves now and then; this is probably a case of being accidentally brushed by Harryhausen when reaching across the tabletop and not an attempt to simulate a breeze). Although the frame-by-frame filming of the battle excels, other shots edited in with these effects are detrimental to the impact of the battle. There are a couple more shots of the larger wire-operated heads going at it, which again doesn't fare well owing to their frenzied but rigid movements. Two more cuts are seen from an extreme distance below the cliff, which shows a pair of non-animation replicas moving unrealistically at the edge, knocking rocks lose and falling down the side that obviously have been slowed down by high-speed photography. After the squealing ceratosaurs topple off the plateau, the two following shots show plastic toys (probably what had been manipulated a moment earlier) plummeting.

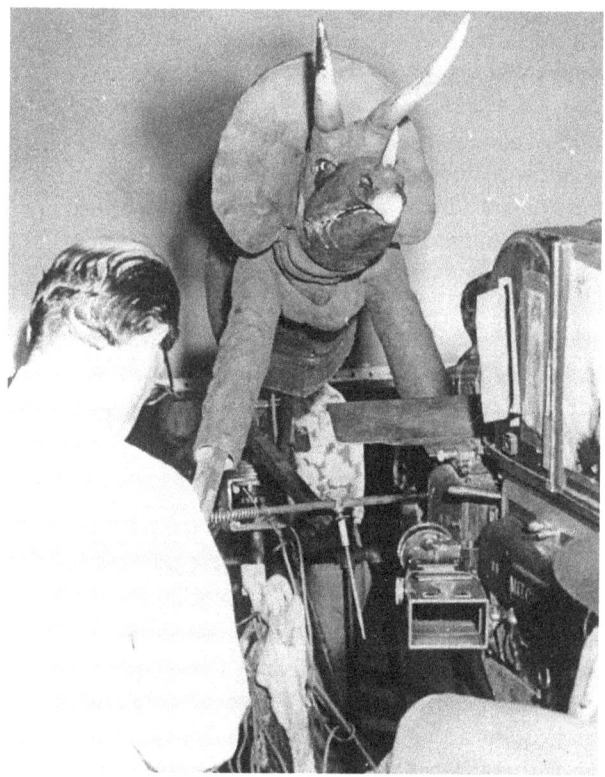

The large mechanical triceratops being set up for a shot. Note the number of connecting wires and that the legs end just above the knees. Photograph courtesy of Ronald V. Borst / Hollywood Movie Posters.

In the late Cretaceous, the triceratops (a three-horned quadrupedal vegetarian with a prominent shield on its head) wanders into an open expanse and growls. This audible is shown with the mechanical stand-in moving its mouth, the corners dripping with mucous-like saliva; it is actually better than its other close-up counterparts since it resembles the animation figure much more faithfully. Another shot employing the wire-operated larger head has it butting the palm tree over, also superior to those previously included to depict some kind of motion taking place up-close. While chewing on the fallen palm fronds, the animated horned dinosaur's sides expand and contract through an internal air bladder, which is even more pronounced than was observable within the stegosaurus in the preceding part. Hearing the wails of an approaching saurian, the ceratopsian quickly becomes alert and demonstrates a willingness to defend itself by pawing at the dirt; Ray later had his styracosaurus in *Gwangi* do this to signal aggression through this bull-like gesture. The high-pitched noise heard by the triceratops is interesting because it is the anguished cry issued by the rhedosaurus from *The Beast From 20,000 Fathoms*, a shrill sound that is in actuality the braying of a horse.

Striding into view towards the triceratops, the Tyrannosaurus rex faces its adversary. This enormous predator was one of the very few dinosaurs surviving right up to the end of the final Mesozoic period, along with the triceratops, and was truly the "tyrant king lizard" indicated by its moniker. Although the narrative indicates it is "50 feet in length, ten tons in weight," the T. rex was probably measured only a little better than 40 feet long and eight tons in weight. When glimpsed right next to its ceratopsian opponent, it is revealed that the tyrannosaur has three fingers on each hand instead of two (as mentioned, any dissimilarity between this model and the allosaurus is inconsequential). A volcano erupts (the same exploding mountaintop that was seen in 1951's *When Worlds Collide*), preempting what certainly would have been a contest of strength and agility. Now, with this cataclysmic event threatening to overwhelm them, the struggle has shifted to that of survival. With the onset of their extinction, the remainder of the sequence is saturated with a reddish tint to reflect the glowing lava and raging fire. For dramatic purposes, the Jurassic saurians were included to create a stampede of sorts though they obviously were not present at the K-T (Cretaceous—Tertiary) boundary. Some of the non-animation shots here are backed by footage of spewing volcanic fury. Miniature "lava" seen flowing at times in the foreground also contributes to the sense of overwhelming devastation.

There is some good characterization by Harryhausen during these scenes of chaos. A fine example is the tyrannosaur brushing against the triceratops while trying to escape from the molten rock; a deadly foe just before the eruption it is now totally forgotten in the face of greater peril. When the triceratops pauses at the bank of the sticky pool (probably a tar pit, as it is black and bubbles), it shows hesitation in sensing there is danger from the viscous liquid, but is forced to try to cross and so meets its fate. Helping the impact of these shots is a shimmering light, bouncing on trees in the foreground, to imitate the flickering from leaping flames. The tyrannosaurus is trapped by the upheaval as the ground cracks open to block its path, heaving and tossing about in a stop-motion process beneath this tormented creature, who eventually careens into the gap and is covered by lava spilling in. There is a rare close-up with one of the smaller puppets that has a ceratosaurus agonizingly roaring at the sky.

What makes the dinosaurs interesting, apart from the stop-motion animation itself, is how they are portrayed by the filmmakers in the sequence. Obviously, the view of these ruling reptiles was much different back in the 1950s so they therefore won't appear or behave like the dinosaurs in the *Jurassic Park* films or the excellent BBC series *Walking with Dinosaurs* (1999); it simply shows what was the prevailing conception held by scientists at that time. In his *Dinosaur Scrapbook* (1980), Don Glut states, "O'Brien, using Charles R. Knight illustrations as a basis and in consultation with Dr. Charles L. Camp, a paleontology professor from the University of California, designed the models to be animated by Harryhausen. The goal of the two special-effects geniuses was to re-create as authentically as possible the world as it was during the age of dinosaurs" (107). With respect to the multiple roles played by the ceratosaurus puppet, was this done with the approval of any of these three men or did Allen do this purely on his own for budgetary purposes? There was the hypothesis that the ceratosaurus was really the male counterpart of the female allosaurus, but this has been shown to be incorrect. These prehistoric monsters shuffle about in a fashion typically exhibited in the mid–twentieth century, with tails dragging on the ground behind them. More specifically, the bipedal meat-eaters stand very erect, their backs frequently rising higher than 45 degrees when not moving forward. This very upright position is not how they were disposed to carry themselves; they kept their spines horizontal and with raised tails stiffly serving as counterbalances for the weight in front of their hips. With a similar attitude at times to *The Lost World*'s carnivorous saurians, it has the unintentional effect of making them seem somewhat less monstrous through their human-like posture (this is especially true of the ceratosaurs, whose bigger arms and grappling toe-to-toe combat makes them seem to be engaging in something like a wrestling match).

The brontosaurus is also portrayed in a way that doesn't jibe with recent theories. For one thing, it was not the swamp-dweller that tradition would have, instead living in dry upland environments. Although it is depicted here on firm ground for the sake of animation, the narrator relegates the sauropod to an aquatic habitat: "engineered by nature in a freakish manner so that she was hardly able to support her massive weight on land, this huge monster spent most of her time wading in the waters of the world and came up on the land only to seek food or lay eggs." Regarding the awkwardness of the egg laying, Neil Pettigrew implies in his *Stop-Motion Filmography* (1999) that Ray said there was uncertainty as to how to approach it: "However, [Ray] did say the shot of the brontosaurus laying an egg was not the one originally filmed. The model was animated in a squatting position but this made it look more like it was constipated than laying eggs, so the sequence was refilmed" (40). In the excellent BBC series *Walking with Dinosaurs* (1999), this enigmatic activity of large sauropods is resolved by the use of an ovipositor, a muscular tube that female marine turtles employ to gently lower their brood into holes dug on the beach. Overall, these inaccuracies only demonstrate what was known about dinosaurs at that point in time and, therefore, shouldn't be considered flaws in the film.

Irwin Allen, the producer — director — writer of *Animal World*, is recognized today for his 1960s TV series rooted in science fiction and fantasy, as well as for a slew of 1970s feature films that earned him the nickname "The Master of Disaster." Born in New York City in 1916, Allen worked in myriad facets of the popular media by a fairly young age; he was a magazine editor, radio show producer for KLAC and wrote the syndicated column "Hollywood Merry-Go-Round." Irwin produced a 1940s television program also called *Hollywood Merry-Go-Round* which was the first celebrity panel show, bringing hundreds of film personalities into U.S. homes. After a brief stint as a literary agent, he went to RKO and produced several early-1950s films there, including *Where Danger Lives* (1950), *Double Dynamite* (1951) and *A Girl in Every Port* (1952). Some of his other memorable pictures from the 1950s are *The Story of Mankind* (1957) and *The Big Circus* (1959). *Mankind*, a comedic look at the history of civilization which includes a great preponderance of stock footage, was actually the third film of a trio preceded by *The Sea Around Us* and *Animal World*. Starring Groucho, Harpo and Chico Marx, *Mankind* was the final time that the famous brothers appeared in the same production though they were never all seen together in it. *Big Circus* was one of his first higher budgeted projects and seems a recapitulation of Cecil B. DeMille's opus *The Greatest Show on Earth* (1952). Moving to 20th Century–Fox in 1960 to do a remake of the 1925 silent classic *The Lost World*, Allen also made *Voyage to the Bottom of the Sea* (1961) and *Five Weeks in a Balloon* (1962) in the early part of the decade.

He returned to the small screen by making *Voyage to the Bottom of the Sea* a weekly program in 1964, and in the following year launched the highly successful *Lost in Space* TV series. Less viable though just as imaginative were two shorter running programs, *The Time Tunnel* and *Land of the Giants*, which endured for only one and two seasons respectively. By the early 1970s, Irwin went back to work on feature-length films beginning with *The Poseidon Adventure* (1972), about an ocean liner capsized by a giant wave. This star-studded, big-budget picture achieved impressive figures at the box office and was followed by *The Towering Inferno* (1974), dealing with a brand-new skyscraper catching fire. Having cemented his reputation as an impresario of mayhem, he went on to produce other "disastrous" offerings as *The Swarm* (1978), *Beyond the Poseidon Adventure* (1979) and *When Time Ran Out* (1980). Allen went into semi-retirement in the mid-1980s due to failing health, but continued to be involved in various projects up to his death in November 1991.

Paul Sawtell both composed and orchestrated the score for *Animal World*; he had written music for the aborted 1941–42 version of *Gwangi*. He worked, often uncredited, on literally hundreds on film and TV productions which include *The Black Scorpion* (1957), *The Fly* (1958) and Allen's *Lost World* remake. While the composition is melodic and blends with the stop-motion quite well, his sounds never really rise above the level of accompaniment to the excitement taking place on-screen, as opposed to many of the memorable scores from Ray's other features. John Storm and Theodore von Eltz provide the narrative descriptions throughout the title, giving a suitably detached sense of authority, lording over its vignettes by way of their fine speaking voices.

Some of the film's shortcomings have been touched upon already. While the effects Harryhausen realized in such a short-term engagement are very well-done (though there is ever the slightest hint of jerkiness at a couple of points), the stop-motion puppets themselves are not as archetypal as expected in a project of his. In his book *Cheap Tricks and Class Acts: Special Effects, Makeup and Stunts from the Films of the Fantastic Fifties* (1996), John "J.J." Johnson notes that "Ray was disappointed with the look of the models" (66). Ray thinks these puppets have a "rubbery" appearance, which is probably reflective of the comparatively modest amount of detailing in their exteriors.

Without going into specific details, Harryhausen has indicated his belief that Irwin Allen was hardly the best of producers, and this sentiment is extremely justifiable upon examination of his filmmaking practices. Reducing costs is the primary job of the producer, but Allen's zeal for keeping the expenses down to an absolute minimum seems totally inexplicable and consequently it only lowered the caliber of his productions. In the video retrospective *The Fantasy Worlds of Irwin Allen* (1995), personal assistant and costume designer Paul Zastupnevich candidly recalls that this penny-pinching became virtually a way of life on his productions, "Irwin used a lot of stock footage, that was one of his trademarks throughout. *Story of Mankind* actually was a picture that was built on outtakes and stock footage. I had to match up costumes and tie in things so that they would carry on through. Wherever he could beg, borrow or steal, he always did, that was one way of his cutting down the budget." He would also unabashedly recycle a monster from one of his TV series to be the nemesis in another.

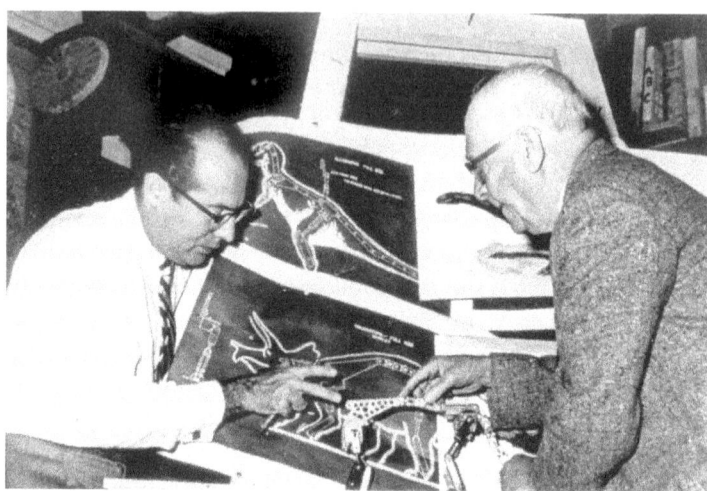

Willis O'Brien is holding part of the triceratops armature and conferring with Allen in front of drawing blueprints of the internal armature configurations for the feature's dinosaurs.

More specific to *Animal World*, the time-saving measures taken in showing the close-up mechanical dinosaurs and using toys to fall off the cliff create some horrendous shifts in continuity. Even worse than this, the structure and tone of the entire feature is uneven. Beginning with the creation of Earth, the progression is very logical in going from simple organisms to fish and higher on up the evolutionary ladder. But right after the dinosaur sequence has finished, the story moves straight to showing termites; like a train jumping its tracks, the remainder of the picture heads in directions nobody can possibly predict, becoming more or less a hodgepodge of nature clips. Besides this random splicing-together of disparate vignettes, the scope of the movie as a whole is oddly diffuse and non sequitur, with comedy, satire and social kitsch which is liberally mixed in for good (or bad) measure. Examples of this insipid blending include an aquarium conflict staged as a ludicrous "morality" play starring an octopus, moray eel and scores of fishes; a Japanese beetle caught in a Venus fly-trap that is screaming in a foreign language (hard to guess?) "Let me out of here" (displayed as a subtitle); and a chimpanzee cackling with a very annoying human laugh. Also strange, in light of the implicit nod to the evolutionary development of animals, is a strong infusion of the Old Testament as the impetus for how there came to be life on Earth, no doubt reflecting Irwin's religious beliefs. Even the opening moments of the film, showing a view of our planet from an outer space perspective, begs a question or two: The spherical body is covered with craters. Was this in fact a prop that had previously been a representation of the moon, thinly disguised for this picture?

First released in December 1955 for Academy Award consideration (it wasn't in wide distribution until the middle of 1956), *Animal World* came and went at the box office, then headed to obscurity. Unlike *The Sea Around Us*, which is a better known film and in fact still is broadcast fairly often on TV, it is never seen on the small screen. The movie also has the dubious distinction of being the only Harryhausen feature never released on a prerecorded video format, a situation that doesn't appear to be changing any time soon. Just why has *Animal World* failed to materialize as a home video offering? Its conspicuous absence from the market has to do with all the acquired stock footage of the fauna. Apparently, the legal rights to all this natural cinematography has either reverted back or still belongs to the original owners. Since there were so many sources for these clips constituting the bulk of the picture, it must be impossible to obtain the necessary permission for every one of them. "Bootleg" tapes of fairly decent quality (transfers from 16mm prints) are sold by a number of vendors.

Even though the feature itself has all but disappeared, its dinosaur scenes have been seen in at least two other venues. A significant portion of this stop-motion made its way into the movie *Trog* (1970), about a prehistoric cave dweller discovered in modern-day Great Britain and his problems coping with people when captured and moved to civilization for scientific research. Besides being a bad flick to begin with, it has gained some extra notoriety for being Joan Crawford's final film. Trog himself is a poorly realized character, with the mask from one of the earliest hominoids in *2001: A Space Odyssey* fitted on a much more normal human body (with only some extra hair added on the chest). The dinosaur sequence is seen as a Trog flashback when his memory is jogged by slides of dinosaur skeletal mounts (the same shots seen in the introduction of the vignette in *Animal World*) while hooked up to a battery of electronic equipment. Lasting around four minutes, these animation effects are heavily tinted blue and surrounded by a swirling border to signify they are being remembered by the troglodyte. It runs pretty much in the order seen originally, except that the hatching baby brontosaur here follows the battle of the ceratosaurs. When the cataclysmic eruption starts, the color shifts back to the crimson hue of the actual footage, which is a welcome improvement. An

One of the many posed stills of Harryhausen with a ceratosaurus puppet from *Animal World*.

interesting detail here is that the audio track was redubbed and now includes different sounds; the vocal confrontation between the titular allosaurus and styracosaurus in *Gwangi* is notable here, with the desperate roars issued by the close-up ceratosaurus during the devastation those of Gwangi. Also heard throughout is the distinctive dying bray of the rhedosaurus as it expires at the end of *Beast*. To end the recollection, a frozen wasteland is quickly glimpsed, probably representing a climate change that permitted Trog to exist in a state of dormancy until the present. An original animation sequence was planned for *Trog*, with models built and animated by Roger Dicken (who assisted Jim Danforth on *When Dinosaurs Ruled the Earth* 1970). The film produced was never used and is presumed lost, though shots from it appear on page 386 of Mark F. Berry's *The Dinosaur Filmography* (2002).

The *Animal World* dinosaurs are probably best known today for being a set of View-Master 3-D reels. These transparencies weren't taken from still frames of the actual sequence footage but instead photographed in a separate session, lasting about one week, after the main stop-motion effects had been achieved. Over the course of time, the title for this set of three stereoscopic discs has changed. When they first came out, these were called "Battle of the Monsters" though clearly tied-in to *Animal World* on the outer sleeve; by the 1960s, their label had become "Prehistoric Animals" *sans* any mention of the origin; and more recently they were simply titled "Dinosaurs" (sold in a nice gift box). But it is strange how (unlike many of Ray's figures which have been photographed on display numerous times after the animation was completed) the dinosaur puppets themselves have seemingly disappeared following their use in the movie.

Because the scenes were filmed with two cameras, there are of course unseen shots of the saurians which eventually ended up on the cutting room floor. There are also indications of scenes that are missing from the release print. Some negative comments about the violence and gore prompted Allen to edit some of the animation out of his production. In *From the Land Beyond Beyond*, Ray remembers, "We tried to make the sequence very gory at first, natural to animals. You saw many scenes in the rest of the picture where, for example, a tiger tore animals to pieces and quivering paws and legs all covered with blood were seen. We tried to do the dinosaur sequence in the same vein. When the stegosaur was killed, the ceratosaur, I believe it was, tore big hunks of dripping flesh from him and started chewing it. But when the picture was previewed, we received so many negative remarks about the bloodletting that a lot of it had to be removed in the final version" (106). Vestiges of this savage feasting can still be perceived in the film, which include the suddenly more bloody front end of the stegosaur carcass following an obvious sudden edit as the ceratosaur stands over the plated dinosaur. There seems to be other instances of some severe extricating of certain shots, judging from what is left in the finished product. One of these is the caveman being snatched up by the brontosaurus. After the sauropod has seized the screaming human in its jaws and hoisted him off the ground, the next cut very abruptly shows only the posterior end of the gigantic reptile strolling off with the fading cries of its victim still heard, with him not visible any more. Perhaps the critics complained about this implied killing of the caveman, probably dangling limp from the mouth of the brontosaur while it was making its way out of the frame image.

Aside from the feature itself, the View-Master slides offer possible evidence of stop-motion scenes missing from the movie. Even though the progression of photographs on these reels are highly analogous to corresponding scenes in the movie, they do not duplicate exactly the poses and positions which were utilized for the motion picture. Some of the figure placement in this View-Master set give an indication of the possibility of additional Harryhausen effects which didn't survive into the released film. Just as the eruption is beginning, the tyrannosaurus and triceratops clash in battle, with the latter managing to impale the former with one of its longer brow tines, leaving both a oozing puncture wound and a crimson-stained horn. There is no evidence that it was ever animated for *Animal World* as such. However, there might have been more there originally. Even though in the very clear *Trog* there doesn't appear to be any injury or stained tip, the triceratops does look like it has a bloodied left shoulder.

Neil Pettigrew notes in his *Stop-Motion Filmography*, "The pressbook for the film, which lists the running time as 82 minutes, contains three shots of a fight between the triceratops and the tyrannosaurus which did not feature in this print. Were they merely staged for the stills or

Two of the familiar View-Master slides featuring *The Animal World*'s very recognizable dinosaurs. Most of the images are highly analogous to what takes place in the film's stop-motion sequence. Note that the arm visible on the tyrannosaurus is proportionately larger here than those seen in the film.

did Harryhausen actually film this sequence? He vaguely remembered the encounter being longer, but again was unable to recall specific details" (40–41). These "three shots" (there are four in the pressbook) are not from the transparency discs but illustrate a similar goring and the eventual defeat of the predatory T. rex, lying in front of the horned herbivore. The tyrannosaur's head in three of the four stills (apparently those Pettigrew is referring to) appears much more elongated than seen either in the movie or the View-Master reels.

Tabletop shot of ceratosaurs fighting to the death over a stegosaurus carcass. Similar to, though different, from a View-Master slide, the battle in the motion picture ends up with these beasts going over a cliff instead. Photograph courtesy of Ronald V. Borst / Hollywood Movie Posters.

This relatively brief animation stint actually took place during a delay in the earliest pre-production phases of *Earth Vs. the Flying Saucers*; while this particular picture has no connection to these long-extinct reptilian types, the following *20 Million Miles to Earth* does have some connection to such prehistoric creatures. It was the third feature Ray made in conjunction with Charles Schneer and the first made under his longtime producer's Moringside Productions banner. The story came from a Harryhausen treatment called *The Giant Ymir*, which was writeen somewhere around 1952 along with an outline that never materialized as a feature, *The Elementals*. Charlotte Knight, a major influence in the development of young Harryhausen (she was his teacher and confidant at Los Angeles Community College and made scripting contributions to *Little Red Riding Hood* and other Fairy Tales), is credited for the story (as "Charlott Knight") instead of the animator; he chose not to receive acknowledgement as he felt the original outline had many flaws in it (and he also tended to be somewhat modest about his donation of story ideas at that time).

Along with the title change to *20 Million Miles to Earth*, all mention of the word "Ymir" was expunged from the screenplay. The term itself is the name of a giant from Norse mythology whose slain body created the known world; Schneer believed the word might be confused with "emir," an Islamic ruler or chieftain (and also may have unintentionally offended those of Middle Eastern descent). Ray notes in his *Scrapbook* that the concept of European locations for this proposed film stemmed from a feeling of restlessness and a longing to travel abroad; since he didn't have the money at the time to take a proper trip, designing a project so it would take him to Europe on someone else's bankroll was a shrewd and inexpensive way to get his holiday. Italy was the setting for the movie, with historic areas of Rome impressively providing the backdrop for the Ymir's destructive rampage.

20 Million was directed by Nathan Juran, who later did *7th Voyage* and *First Men in the Moon*, and stars William Hopper, Joan Taylor and Frank Puglia. It starts with the crash landing of a U.S. spacecraft into the Mediterranean Sea just off the coast of Sicily near some

An early Harryhausen concept of the Ymir, drawn as a sort of satyr-like troll. Photograph courtesy of Greg Kulon.

fishing boats. Witnessing the splashdown and the half-submerged rocket, one vessel heads over and rescues Col. Calder (Hopper) and a dying fellow astronaut. Though the crew member dies from a strange disease, Calder recovers in the care of Marisa Leonardo (Taylor) and sets about locating a cylinder containing a specimen from their space journey. Young Pepe, the son of the rescuing fisherman, has already found the tube, removed the gelatinous mass from inside of it and sold it to Marisa's grandfather, zoologist Dr. Leonardo (Puglia). By the time Calder locates the lad and discovers what has become of the special cargo, a small, extraordinary creature has been hatched. Dr. Leonardo finds the animal and puts it in an outdoor pen for the night; the next morning he discovers that it has at least doubled in size.

Deciding to take it to the Rome zoo for scientific study, he and his granddaughter travel up the road a distance, but by this time it has gotten big enough to break free. Enlisting the help of the police and Italian government, Calder meets up with Marisa and Dr. Leonardo and tracks after the still growing monster to a barn. Cornered, it turns violent and escapes from the assembled forces. Knowing that the beast subsists on sulfur, and that there are sulfur springs at the base of Mt. Etna, Calder and the military converge on the area and find the monster, and disable it with an electrified net. Hauled to the Rome zoo lab, it is kept under electrical anesthesia until an accident with the power equipment gives it a chance to free itself. While escaping the zoo, it battles an elephant; it later heads into the Eternal City. After much devastation and mayhem, it is finally trapped and shot off the top of the Coliseum in a spectacular (and very *King Kong*-like) finale.

An examination of the Ymir reveals that it is a combination of a number of different animal varieties. In the career article in *Cinefantastique* Volume 11 Number 4, Ray states, "In designing it, I tried to keep a basic humanoid form, in combination with a dinosaur" (42). Author Ted Newsom notes, "Owing a bit to the Creature from Jupiter with its upright stance and reptilian tail, the Ymir has a unique walrus-mustache appendage above its mouth, suggesting developed olfactory senses, a point that comes out in the script" (42). Perhaps this indicates the facial organ's function but not

The Venusian monster battles an elephant from the Rome Zoo in *20 Million Miles to Earth*. Ray chose to show the pachyderm both as a real and animated specimen, a gutsy maneuver that was pulled off quite well. Years later, the circus elephant in *The Valley of Gwangi* was seen only as a miniature.

the origin according to Harryhausen; in *Animato!* Issue 24 (1993), he responds to interviewer Stephen Bissette's question about the Venusian's "fleshy whisker," "That was something I got from some illustrations of fish which had similar features. I couldn't use it in *The War of the Worlds*, so I put them on the Ymir, as well as the Kraken [in *Clash of the Titans*] (44). In *The Men Who Made the Monsters* (1996), Paul M. Jensen opines, "Its face, less fierce than a dinosaur's, is sensitive and even vulnerable, with an almost feline quality owing to its whisker-like folds" (113). These protuberances above the lips give the monster a rather feline characteristic recognized by many; in *Films Illustrated* Vol. 7 No. 75 (1977), Charles Schneer describes the Ymir as "a strange reptilian creature, a cross between a cat and a dinosaur" (111). In addition, this alien organism is equipped with large arms, clawed three-fingered hands, a small crest and dorsal ridge running down its back (the artwork on the cover of the film's novelization in *Amazing Stories* has the Ymir sporting stegosaur-like plates instead) and a fork in the tip of its tail.

In *Land Beyond Beyond*, Jeff Rovin lists the unfortunate occurrences in this alien life-form's rather brief existence: "A pawn of human progress, not only was he snatched from the womb and brought to a strange world, but death came to him a mere few days after he had been born. And what a life! Crawling from his gelatinous incubator, Ymir is shocked with a harsh light, brusquely grabbed from a worktable and shoved into a cage, attacked by the dog, stabbed in the back by the farmer with a pitchfork, poked and pushed against a hay wagon, chased and electrocuted, locked in a zoo, tormented by an elephant, peppered with hand grenades, and shot with artillery. There was hardly a moment's respite for the poor creature!" (111–112). But even this recounting isn't complete; the Ymir was also whacked with a shovel, shot with small arms and blasted by a flame thrower. All of its retaliatory actions can be attributed to something that assails it and in so doing elicits a defensive posture; even its grabbing of Marisa (done with a live-action latex glove prop) and escape from Dr. Leonardo's pen was provoked by its growing uncomfortably large for the enclosure. What makes the Ymir a sympathetic character is not so much what it does but more a recognition of its being a "stranger in a strange land" and failing to cope, through no fault of its own, to the hostile environment.

Of course, the sophistication of this semi-human monster's characterization is a tribute to Harryhausen, who gave his fantastic creation a remarkable degree of variability in its facial movements to convey a range of emotions such as fear and anger; these displays are necessary for the audience to have any sentimental feelings towards such a grotesque creature, accepting even that what it suffers is basically undeserved. Helping round out its "personality" is a raucous, arboreal screech which sounds quite otherworldly. Ray was very gutsy in choosing to portray the combative elephant as both a live specimen and an animated puppet, and making a sharp substitution from the former to the latter (in *Gwangi*, he chose to depict the circus elephant entirely in miniature). The stop-motion zoo resident is effective (if not spectacular) as the Ymir's nemesis, made to look enormous by being juxtaposed next to a small actor. There were two different figures for the Venusian which were sculpted by George Lofgren, one about 14" high (whose armature was cannibalized for the second Cyclops in *7th Voyage*) and the other about six inches tall. *20 Million* nearly became the first color Dynamation film of the Schneer-Harryhausen team, but the animator insisted upon the use of a sharp B&W stock newly available from Kodak.

Only a few years following *20 Million*, Charles and Ray relocated to England and set about making *Mysterious Island*, a 1961 feature incorporating identifiable prehistoric animals. Originally, the script for this movie proposed actual dinosaurs inhabiting this isolated South Pacific island but the concept changed through several drafts of the screenplay. Columbia Pictures wanted to follow in the footsteps of the Disney blockbuster *20,000 Leagues Under the Sea* (1954), a wonderful yarn starring Kirk Douglas and James Mason (as the enigmatic Captain Nemo); written shortly after *20,000 League*'s box office success, Crane Wilbur's adapted version of the Jules Verne sequel was dug out of the files five years later for Schneer as a subsequent project for their "sleeper" hit *7th Voyage*. But since it had been decided that this property wasn't going to make the best use of Dynamation, it was necessary to rewrite the story from scratch. There were several revisions to the developing photoplay, written by John Prebble and Daniel Ullman, that supersede earlier ideas though the final version is somewhat a hodgepodge of unexplained vestiges from preceding drafts. The premise of an island populated by antediluvian creatures (giving it an undeniable *Kong*-like quality) gave way to more familiar but oversized animals bred by the reclusive Nemo to help solve the problems of world hunger. A couple of these "mutants" are long-extinct varieties with enough similarity to living organisms that they are usually mistaken as such.

Another concept persisting yet never elaborated upon are some undersea ruins lying just offshore (the area what is left from the lost continent of Atlantis, with Egyptian and Greco-Roman relics strewn about the ocean floor). But since nothing is ever explained beyond a very cursory mention of their being there (let alone what relevance they have to anything else in the story), they become artifacts of an abandoned conception of this region only. *Mysterious* was filmed in Spain along the same stretch of Costa Brava beaches as *7th Voyage* and *The 3 Worlds of Gulliver*; Ray was sent to the

Caribbean on a location scouting mission and had considered Trinidad, Tobago and the islands around Cuba. Director Cy Endfield is probably best known for his roles of director and screenwriter on the historical epic *Zulu* (1964). Michael Craig, Joan Greenwood, Michael Callan, Gary Merrill and Herbert Lom are very capable in their parts and lead a generally fine cast of Civil War era characters, with Lom's understated performance probably being the best of them all.

It starts off at a Confederate prison in 1865, during the siege of Richmond near the end of the war. Cptn Cyrus Harding (Craig), Herbert Brown (Callan) and several other Union soldiers plan an escape; they notice the top of an observation balloon close to their quarters. After Union war correspondent Gideon Spilett (Merrill) is put in confinement with them, they make good their escape and soon take the balloon by force. Flying away in a gale, Harding and the others get an extra member in the basket, a Confederate officer who tried to thwart the pilfering of this lighter-than-air vehicle. Rapidly drifting westward across America (never mind that the prevailing winds are west to east instead) for days, the damaged balloon finally loses altitude during a Pacific Ocean storm and just manages to reach an island.

Recovering and organizing themselves, they explore the area and find it to be uninhabited. The men are later joined by Lady Mary Fairchild (Greenwood) and her attractive niece, who were washed up on the shore after a shipwreck. The combined group occupies a rocky sanctuary called Granite House and soon encounters a strange and quite large bird. Following the arrival of a chest containing tools and weapons, they believe they have an unseen benefactor. After saving them from cutthroat pirates by sinking their vessel with a carefully-placed charge, Captain Nemo (Lom) finally reveals himself. When a nearby volcano threatens to erupt, Nemo and the castaways run a pipeline to its hull and fill this space with air (using the balloon envelope) to get it back to the surface. Fighting time and a giant cephalopod, they succeed, but Nemo is trapped aboard his submarine the *Nautilus* in a flooded grotto as the landmass is totally destroyed in an explosive fury. Sailing away, the castaways pledge themselves to carry on the legacy of the great man who had saved their lives.

The phororhacos is the first of two prehistoric creatures in the film's animated ensemble. This type of giant, flightless predatory bird, more correctly known today as "phorusrhacos," evolved during the early part of the Miocene epoch 25 million years ago. This group ranged anywhere from about five feet on up to the approximately nine foot-tall terror that pursues the settlers on this strange island. It follows war correspondent Spilett back to an enclosure full of goats. It leaps over the barricade, scratching Spilett's face, and assails Lady Fairchild, who swings the butt end of her rifle at it after the weapon jams. The makeshift club proves only to annoy the giant bird, who then goes after Lady Fairchild's niece and pins her under its foot. Spilett tries to ward the fowl off her by striking it with a long stick. Herbert Brown jumps on its back and stabs the downy neck with his knife; frantically hopping around to shake its tormentor, the phororhacos eventually smashes through the fence and drops dead on the ground.

The model is very well detailed and looks something like the usual illustrations of this earthbound genus of extinct birds, most notably with bright red plumage (and also some green feathers adorning the side of its face) on top of its impressively beaked head. However, the rest of this creature's body seems more like that of an oversized chicken and overall it has a clumsy quality reminding one of such a barnyard resident (most casual reviewers in fact take it for this common critter). Harryhausen obviously recognized the comedic elements of this sequence and gave his "menace" ungainly motions. Bernard Herrmann's score also reflects the lighter side of the attack and blends with the visuals quite effectively (the animator notes in the *Ray Harryhausen Chronicles* that Herrmann joked about using "Turkey in the Straw" for this vignette). Wires served to hold the phororhacos off the animation stage when jumping about; a live-action mock-up of the back and lower neck was used for close-ups where it is being punctured by the sharp blade. To lesser effect, the shadow from a "monster stick" cutout, looking extremely unrealistic, is waved over Spilett to help introduce the stop-motion episode. After serving for the feature, the phororhacos puppet was dismantled for its parts.

Ray's sketch of the invading phororhacos under attack by one of the men in *Mysterious Island*. Here the bird is dragging somebody who tossed a rope around its neck. Courtesy of Greg Kulon.

Later in the picture, during the underwater salvage operation to raise the pirate ship, a monstrous cephalopod appears to the divers and grabs the Confederate officer; Harding fires an electric gun at the mollusk, which squirts ink and recoils at the blasts, releasing its victim. While this tentacled aggressor is almost universally identified as a "nautiloid," this label is technically incorrect; the extinct squid-like organism is actually an ammonite (though the nautilus is closely related to them). Flourishing right up until the end of the Cretaceous period, these squid-like creatures are distinguished by prominent segmentation of their spiral shells to give them a ridged pattern (as opposed to the smooth exterior of their modern relative).

Ray has noted that the tentacles were moved as little as perhaps one-third of an inch to give them their delicate, drifting attribute as if they were underwater. In *Land Beyond Beyond*, Rovin states that the mollusk, like the cephalopod in *It Came from Beneath the Sea*, was "photographed through a distortion glass, both of which helped to simulate the look and resistance of water" (170). However, Harryhausen notes in his *Mysterious* laserdisc commentary that these "waves and distortions" were placed by the optical printer over the completed animation footage. Still in existence (though without its shell), the ammonite model has six arms like the titular octopus of *It Came* but is quite distinctive in configuration and so would never be confused with the earlier creature.

As mentioned previously, the *Mysterious* screenplay went through a series of revisions that all but obliterated the antediluvian content of this production. But there still remains one reference to the extremely distant past in this picture's spoken dialogue.

While exploring the elevated cavern they would soon occupy, the group discovers the remains of a man who, stranded on the island years earlier, eventually committed suicide; offering up a rather garish account of the man's unhappy final days, Spilett concludes his journalistic speech with "he hangs himself from the rafters of a prehistoric cave, the death of an ex-pirate." Also, the film's trailer describes the ammonite as a "prehistoric devilfish" though nothing is ever mentioned in the final version.

The other animated creatures in *Mysterious* are clearly quite modern sorts but nevertheless still effective as being formidable adversaries. A titanic crab (constructed with an armature inserted into the actual carapace of an edible crustacean from Harrod's) gives the men a fight before meeting its doom; likewise, an enormous bee seals two of the troupe inside a honeycomb; this was accomplished by running the stop-motion of the waxy barrier being chipped away in reverse, making it seem to be constructed by the apian giant instead.

Deleted concepts included a man-eating plant with poison-tipped tentacles and a "green man" who was unsavory to this carnivorous foliage through eating mushrooms though it changed the hue of his skin. He was going to be played by Nigel Green, remembered for his wonderful portrayal of a swaggering Hercules in *Jason and the Argonauts*, but the "colorful" Tom Ayerton is only depicted as a skeleton in Granite House. Besides the uniformly excellent Dynamation sequences (termed here as "Superdynamation"), some of the other special effects are also quite wonderful; these include the miniature *Nautilus* (about ten feet long) and observation balloon, both of which were made to look much larger through high-speed photography. Although most of Ray's fans consider this to be one of his best productions, there are several lackluster aspects which keep this feature from being a total success.

While the matte painting of a log bridge (included as an homage to *King Kong*) is fairly good, many other artistic creations are much less convincing, like those representing the Granite House and the island itself from an offshore perspective. Perhaps worst of all are the atrocious shifts in continuity during the concluding eruption scenes; the volcano itself ranges from live-action stock footage to a matte painting observed from the former pirate ship. (A six-foot high model was also used.) Crumbling rock miniatures look hopelessly inadequate and artificial. But by ignoring these relatively few lapses and shortcomings, the viewer will find *Mysterious Island* a satisfying adventure in the vein of "How to Survive on a Desert Island," with interesting human and non-human characters to inject excitement throughout the course of this motion picture.

For Ray Harryhausen, the roughly five year period beginning with *Animal World* and ending with *Mysterious Island* was one of his most prolific times with respect to film output; counting these two offerings, his effects are incorporated in six movies during this span, working out to about one per year. This steady stream of animated releases was primarily due to his partnering with Charles Schneer and the development of his proprietary static matte rear-projection composite techniques for *Beast*, insuring both a stable operating environment and an inexpensive means of executing dimensional animation effects. This young animator's star was rising steadily but the same cannot be said of Willis O'Brien; the senior technician's career was fraught with excruciatingly bad luck when trying to get personal ideas onto the silver screen, and had only been engaged on a handful of completed pictures by the time he came on *Animal World*.

Further hurting the opportunities available to O'Brien was the box office failure of *Mighty Joe Young*, which cost around $2 million to make in the late 1940s. His methodology demanded a retinue of artists and craftsmen to create miniature sets, glass paintings, etc. As a consequence, *Mighty Joe Young* became an albatross of sorts for puppet animation effects, causing many filmmakers to shy away from the process for its perceived exorbitance. But part of O'Brien's problem was of his own doing. In *Cinefex* #7 (1982), an issue devoted entirely to this creator of *Kong* and *Mighty Joe Young*, his philosophy was expressed: "Willis O'Brien had long upheld the view that stop-motion animation was an art form in its own right, and as such had no place in anything but a major film production. As a result, he was somewhat chagrined when the split-screen rear-projection system Ray Harryhausen devised to incorporate animated subjects into live-action background plates suddenly placed stop-motion work within the realm of the low-budget filmmaker" (62). O'Brien was inevitably forced to work on the very kind of pictures he had been loath to make, such as *The Black Scorpion* (1957) and *The Giant Behemoth* (1959); both of these flicks have some intriguing model manipulation to give life to their respective monsters but plainly suffer from the lack of anything approaching decent funding. It must have been a bitter pill of sorts for O'Brien to accept assignments on these somewhat less than stellar vehicles.

The ammonite on view in Babelsberg, German. Its spiral shell is not present in the display for some unknown reason. Photograph by the author.

Things never did improve any for Obie, though it seemed briefly like they would in 1960. Irwin Allen hired him for a remake of the silent classic *The Lost World*, an opportunity enthusiastically seized by the animator, who drew up a number of dinosaurian concepts for this production. Unfortunately, Allen had become leery of the stop-motion process ever since his *Animal World* experience and had never planned on using this device to resurrect the film's Mesozoic monsters, instead opting to go with photographically enlarged iguanas and other reptiles; apparently, his being brought aboard was solely for name value. Naturally, it was another setback for O'Brien, who never received another aesthetically satisfying project before his death from a heart attack in 1962. At the time of his passing, he was engaged by *Kong* associate Linwood Dunn to supervise a brief stop-motion sequence for *It's a Mad, Mad, Mad, Mad World* (1963; this film was animated by a young Jim Danforth and with miniature figures made by master modelmaker Marcel Delgado).

Harryhausen last worked with his mentor on *Animal World* and would only ever see him once or twice more; in fact, Ray found out about the passing of his personal hero some months after the fact (Ray was living in Europe by this time). So their final collaborative effort *The Animal World*, while not a masterpiece by any measure, stands as a tribute to the relationship between the two greatest animators in the field if nothing more.

Around a decade would pass before Harryhausen achieved bona fide dinosaurs in another feature, but when he did there were great improvements in staging and character design. These can be found within the Hammer films remake of the 1940 classic *One Million B.C.*, bearing the slightly lengthier title *One Million Years B.C.*

Even though *The Animal World* has a number of flaws, the excitement of the dinosaur sequence alone carries the rest of this otherwise unmemorable offering.

4. One Million Years B.C.

Starting work on a new project in 1965, Hammer Films decided to remake the seminal dinosaur movie *One Million B.C.* (1940). The original B&W picture is the tale of two lovers, one from the "Rock People" and the other from the "Shell People," fighting in order to remain together. They endure tribal power struggles, attack from many kinds of prehistoric monsters and a volcano that destroys the landscape through violent earthquakes and copious flows of searing lava. Victor Mature is cast as the young caveman Tumak. A brawny man with very classical facial features, he was perfectly suited to appear in Biblical pictures like *Samson and Delilah* (1949) and *The Robe* (1953). Carole Landis, who played the pretty and warm-hearted Loana, recreated her World War II USO performance in *Four Jills in a Jeep* (1944) and even wrote a book of the same name. Her promising career was cut very short when personal difficulties drove her to commit suicide in the summer of 1948. Lon Chaney, Jr., was Akhoba, the brutal Rock Tribe leader who suffers grievous wounds during a hunt and is mercilessly deposed as a result. Chaney became as famous as his acting father through roles in *Of Mice and Men* (1939) and *The Wolf Man* (1941).

One Million B.C. was produced and directed by Hal Roach; son Hal Roach, Jr., worked on the picture as director. D.W. Griffith came out of retirement to provide production assistance and had cast Mature and Landis in their parts, but didn't direct parts of the movie as had been rumored for years. The "dinosaurs" here are actually lizards that are photographically enlarged to pose as their enormous counterparts of long ago; some of them have fins and other accouterments attached to make them look somewhat less like the creatures they really are. Even a couple of small mammals are made to appear gigantic. Also seen in the film are dressed-up elephants serving as shoddy mammoths, a man in a tyrannosaurus suit, and even a pig placed inside a baby triceratops costume.

Erupting violently, the miniature volcano is one of the very best visuals of the entire production; Fred Knoth staged this sequence and was also responsible for creating the saurian outfits. Although *One Million B.C.* was nominated for two effects Academy Awards (sound and photography), the special effects became passé by the 1960s not only due to technological improvements in moviemaking but also from the frequent culling of clips from the movie. Many low-budget films of the 1950s incorporated stock footage of exploding mountaintops and Mesozoic reptiles; these include *Two Lost Worlds* (1950), *Jungle Manhunt* (1951) and *Teenage Caveman* (1958).

The remake, titled *One Million Years B.C.* begins with a hunt of the Rock Tribe, with one of the men flushing out a warthog that falls into a covered pit. Akhoba (Robert Brown), leader of this group, wants his son Sakana (Percy Herbert) to go down and finish off the quarry, but his other offspring Tumak (John Richardson) strongly objects and pleads for the opportunity to prove himself. His father agrees to this, so the young caveman leaps onto the boar-like creature and kills it after a brief struggle. Akhoba extracts one of its tusks with a mighty pull and hands the token over to Tumak, then moves him ahead of his brother in the procession back to the cave. This upsets and antagonizes the rival sibling. An infirm old man helping to carry the carcass slips and is injured in the open hole; he is left to die by the rest of the hunting group.

Arriving back at camp that stormy night, Tumak shows off the hunting trophy to his woman Nupondi (Martine Beswick). Inside the tribal cave, the beast is roasted over an open fire by Akhoba's mate Tohana (Malya Nappi); everyone is keenly interested in the feast cooking before their eyes. When the meal is ready, an all-out melee ensues, with the strongest getting the biggest portions. Not satisfied with his huge helping, Akhoba wrests Tumak's from him; angry, the son attacks his father but is no match for the elder man. The tribal chieftain backs Tumak out the cave with fierce swings of his staff, pushing him over the edge of a ledge in front of the entrance. Nupondi, watching in horror, is claimed by Sakana as a result of his brother's presumed demise. However, Tumak survived by plunging through one bush and landing in another; picking himself up the next morning, he sets out across the vast wilderness, turning his back on the only home he has ever known. Soon he encounters a large lizard that chases and nearly catches him with its tongue before escaping through a narrow fissure high on a rocky crag. Descending inside this hollow dome, he finds a large cavernous area with a pool of drinkable water and a coniferous, fruit-bearing tree. Tumak soon discovers that this oasis is actually the residence of some ape-like subhumans, so he makes a hasty exit before being detected. Climbing up through another opening, he sets out on his trek again.

Back in the Rock Tribe cave, Nupondi sneaks over to reclaim the prized tusk in the middle of the night but is caught by Akhoba. Sakana sees this take place and rises up to challenge his father, but backs down from a very determined stare. The son now nurses a bitter grudge.

The next morning, Tumak gets up and continues on his journey, finding a large set of tracks in the ground. Looking around, he sees a brontosaurus lumbering and decides to beat a hasty exit from the vicinity — nearly running into a gigantic tarantula trying to catch a meal!

Walking for many hours in the burning sun is taking its toll on the wanderer. Badly blistered and dehydrated, he slowly struggles onward with blurred vision until catching a glimpse of the sea and a sandy shoreline; taking a few more steps, the caveman passes out. However, he doesn't go unnoticed: the women of the nearby Shell Tribe are fishing on the beach, and one of them notices Tumak as he stirs slightly. Their leader, the beautiful Loana (Raquel Welch), climbs a hill to see the dark-haired stranger.

Just as Loana gets to Tumak, an enormous marine turtle appears on top of the ridge behind them, heading straight for the breaking surf. Calling with her conch shell to alert the men of her clan, she manages to drag Tumak out of the path of the marine turtle. Her tribesmen arrive with spears and battle the reptile, which eventually crawls into the water. One of the warriors, Ahot (Jean Wladon), notices Loana's preoccupation with this outsider and becomes jealous, even though he has the attention of the attractive Sura (Lisa Thomas). They all return to camp, carrying Tumak back with them and presenting him to Shell tribal leader Payto (William Lyon Brown), who gives his blessing for the weakened visitor to stay with them and recuperate.

Meanwhile, a Rock Tribe hunt is in progress; attempting to capture a goat, Akhoba climbs a steep cliff and, after losing his footing, hangs on precariously. He calls to his son Sakana for help, but Sakana pushes him off and he plummets off the cliff. The usurper makes the others in the hunt accept his new leadership role, which they do with some reluctance.

In the Shell camp, Tumak notices the more advanced culture of these people (making

necklaces out of clam shells, cave painting and spear making, among other activities). Loana offers him food which he greedily devours in Rock People fashion; the rest of the tribe are amused by the very crude behavior of this stranger. Back at the Rock Tribe, Sakana is presiding over a ritualistic ceremony when Tohana suddenly screams; the presumed deceased Akhoba appears at the cave opening and staggers in, badly scarred and crippled though still very much alive.

Loana gets Tumak to say his name and shows him rudimentary agriculture, apple picking (he climbs a tree and shakes a bunch of them down, to the amusement of some children) and fishing with a barbed spear. Trying his hand at catching a fish, he clumsily flails at his finned quarry but does happen to skewer one, much to the delight of the others. Before the laughter dies down, a hungry allosaurus suddenly invades the settlement. It kills a man trying to escape in the fishing pond and then heads over to the apple tree, where a small girl sits in its branches; frightened, the child falls to the ground and gets snapped at by the ferocious dinosaur. Tumak grabs one of the flint-tipped weapons and engages the creature, saving the girl's life. Joined by Ahot and two other Shell men, Tumak keeps fighting the allosaur with vigor though it manages to fatally wound one of the men caught underneath a collapsed thatch structure. His lance bitten away by the monster, Tumak grabs a large pointed stick from the thatch framework and impales the rapidly approaching allosaur's abdomen. It is hoisted to the height

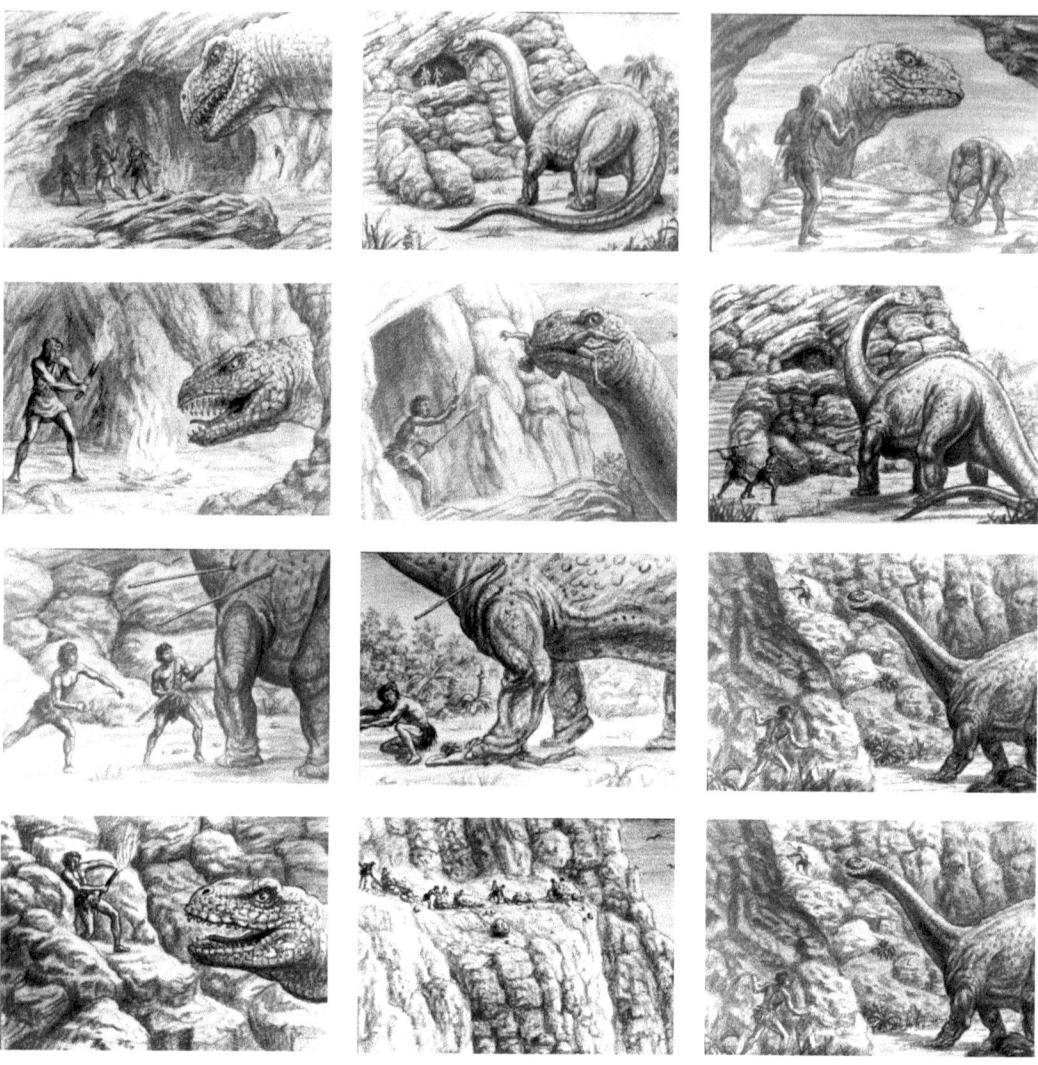

Harryhausen's concepts of an unfilmed climactic sequence in *One Million Years B.C.* in which a brontosaurus attacks the Rock encampment. Instead, the movie concludes with tribal warfare and a volcanic eruption. Courtesy of Simon Greetham.

of this stake by its own momentum, toppling on its side and convulsing in agony. Tumak delivers the coup de grace with a spear thrust in the throat.

Rivalry between Tumak and Ahot soon results in a savage fight and the banishment of Tumak. Loana decides to join Tumak on his trek over the open expanses.

After an encounter with the underground ape-men, Tumak and Loana stumble upon a huge triceratops. As it chases them towards the base of a low-rising bluff, a gigantic ceratosaurus suddenly steps into view on the crest. Tumak and Loana quickly duck inside a nearby cleft just before the towering dinosaur strides past their retreat to battle the horned saurian. Trapped inside as the titanic reptiles gyrate in front of the opening, Loana is able to squeeze through a small tunnel they excavated in the rear, but it fills in before her mate can follow. She flees the area but he must wait for the conflict to end. The ceratosaur is gored by the brow horns of the ceratopsian, being lifted off its feet and falling backwards to the ground. As the triceratops moves away, Tumak files past the gasping monster before it succumbs to its wounds.

Tumak calls to Loana, who is being accosted by Sakana and several other Rock men; she blows into her conch shell to signal for help, which brings her man running at full speed. Defeating the other men, he nearly kills his brother for the assault on Loana. They all go back to the Rock cave, where several of the group are happy to see Tumak again. But Tumak is much less than thrilled at seeing his now-disabled father, who ostracized him from the clan, and nearly runs him through with a spear. Nupondi brings the warthog tusk out to show her former mate but ends up fighting Loana when she tries to examine the trophy. After an altercation, Loana pins Nupondi and is called upon to smash her with a stone but Tumak intervenes and prevents this from happening. All of the drabber, darker women of the Rock Tribe show an interest in the gorgeous blonde visitor, who gives one of them her clamshell necklace.

Outside the Rock cave, a schism develops between its members as some are loyal to Tumak and Akhoba, while others think Sakana is the leader. They all now have the more advanced weaponry of the Shell Tribe, brought back to them by the traveling pair. The couple goes down to a small lake for recreation, joining others there. Loana leads the way by jumping in the water and coaxes those present to follow suit. But just after she gets ashore, a pteranodon suddenly swoops down and carries her away; following her cries for help, Tumak and another caveman give chase to the flying reptile as Nupondi smugly grins over her rival's fate. Dangled over two hungry hatchlings while clutched in the creature's talons, Loana seems doomed but another pterosaur flies up and starts attacking the mother pteranodon. Stunned by this brutal offensive, it drops the blonde girl into the sea near the nest as it grows weaker, finally falling from the sky when vanquished by the pterosaur. Loana climbs onto the beach and passes out while the raider wings over to the roost, devouring the infant pteranodons. Tumak sees the pterosaur and assumes his mate is dead, but she is actually lying only a few feet away.

Tumak finds his comrade, who has been injured, and heads back. Loana returns to her camp and gets Payto to agree to let the men search for her mate. As they proceed across the barren landscape, Tumak notices his woman with her people and calls to her; the lovers run to each other and are reunited. A young Rock man (Richard James) hurries over to them, after having escaped from Sakana's group in the dead of night, and relates that the brother is planning an attack on the Rock camp. Now informed of the plans of his sinister sibling, Tumak leads the others in a race back to the Rock cave. Sakana wakes up and finds the young man has fled so he orders his minions to rush over to commence the planned aggression. They ring the cave entrance and call out to Akhoba and the despised other son. Tumak, the Shell men and Loana arrive and launch an assault from the rear, catching Sakana and his cohorts off guard.

During the height of battle a nearly mountain explodes in volcanic fury, turning the warfare into a fight for survival. In spite of the mayhem created by the geologic occurrence, Tumak manages to kill his hated sibling with a spear in the belly. Members of both tribes scatter in a desperate effort to avoid the catastrophic effects of the eruption, but many die from falling rocks and earthquakes that tear the ground asunder in enormous cracks; Akhoba, Tohana and Nupondi all perish. Eventually these activities subside, and the weary and battered survivors crawl out of hiding to view their devastated world. Led by the lovers from different tribes, they make their way onto their bleak surroundings with the hope of making a better future.

Unlike the original feature, *One Million Years B.C.* uses stop-motion to realize most of the dinosaurs and other ancient creatures populating the prehistoric environment; however, it is not devoid of live reptiles photographed to pose as gigantic Mesozoic creatures. The first "monster" encountered by Tumak is not the expected Harryhausen-conceived nemesis but rather an iguana that was optically enlarged for its role; much of the sequence employs a split-screen technique achieved with the optical printer to combine the animal with the foreground image, making it seem massive. High-speed photography slowed its movements enough, when projected at the standard 24 frames per second, to convey this sense of significant bulk. Animation fans have expressed their disappointment over this lackluster substitution of having a lizard play the dinosaur instead of an articulated figure. Ray has noted that either two or three iguanas closely resembling each other were used.

There is a second magnified creature showing itself shortly after the conclusion of this vignette, a tarantula that has a proportionally large cricket in its clutches. Fortunately, the arachnid is only glimpsed for a scant few seconds, as it looks inferior even by comparison to the previous monumental yet too familiar living organism. Ray had tried to explain the presence of these prehistoric imposters in his *Film Fantasy Scrapbook*: "I have never favored using real lizards pretending to be dinosaurs, but in the remake of *One Million B.C.* we felt it might add to the realism if the first creature we saw was a living specimen" (94). Probably, the real reason for wrangling live animals under hot lighting had to do with the limited budget; these effects were less expensive to pull off than animation. In hindsight, the inclusion of these makes the remake seem to pay homage to these special effects prevalent within the earlier production, albeit an unintentional and collateral tribute.

It isn't long before an authentic stop-motion dinosaur is featured. Tumak comes across a set of huge tracks set in the gravel-strewn ground, then sees the immense creature responsible for them. A brontosaurus stalks off in the distance as it flanks the wanderer's position, trudging behind some large rocks while bellowing in low-frequency tones. This Jurassic variety of sauropod is presently known as apatosaurus, since the concurrent brontosaurus was based upon an incorrect skull (of a camarasaurus) and is, therefore, invalid with respect to scientific nomenclature. It is very closely related to the long-necked and more lightly built diplodocus though not as long, at around 70 feet vs. the diplodocus' nearly 90 feet. Since these facts were not known at that time, Harryhausen's colossal brontosaur was anatomically incorrect. The beast is briefly seen in two cuts: a long shot of it pausing to make a graceful arc of the neck when it notices Tumak, then an even longer shot as it swings this straight ahead again and proceeds on its way with Tumak in the bottom of the frame image. (It is now believed that these sauropods couldn't hold their necks this high.) Measuring some 36 inches in length and slightly more than a foot high, this model is one of the largest Harryhausen used in a movie; according to Neil Pettigrew's *The Stop-Motion Filmography* another sizable figure had been cannibalized to create it: "Built over the same basic armature that was used for the dragon in *The 7th Voyage of Sinbad*, it's an impressive model, wrinkles, warts and all, and it's a shame that it merely walks off" (520). Not only is this nicely textured puppet seen much too briefly, the lower section of body never even appears in the frame image as it is behind the foreground fraction of the static matte rear-projection composites.

A much larger role had been originally envisioned for the sauropod, a revamping of a sequence from *One Million B.C.*; the brontosaur was to assail the Rock cave, using its serpentine neck to reach into the opening while being repelled by the cavemen with fire and other means. The monster was to have grabbed a caveman and trampled another one. As mapped out in his storyboard sketches and identical to the antecedent version, the threatening monster is dispatched in a rockslide made by several cavemen positioned on a cliff directly above it. Owing to the fact this vignette would have consumed another two to three months of Harryhausen's time as well as more budgetary expense, it was replaced by the tribal warfare raging in the final act. There is a widely seen publicity still which now remains as a vestige of the unfilmed sequence, a Dynamation composite showing the brontosaur from top to bottom as it faces Tumak and another caveman (who looks like Ahot anyway). As it turns out, Ray was inadvertently far-sighted with his rendering of the "thunder lizard" by having it plodding along on a dry, upland environment; even the animator held the conventional belief that it was a "known swamp dweller" in his *Scrapbook* description.

The stop-motion brontosaurus model from *One Million Years B.C.* as seen on exhibit in Babelsberg, Germany. Photograph by the author.

Next of the stop-motion ensemble to make its way on-screen is the massive archelon. A very large marine turtle that lived during the Cretaceous period, this animal probably spent nearly all of its existence out in the open waters of the world. Depicted to be many times bigger here than the known 12-foot length, the initial glimpses show it crawling on flippered feet to rest on top of a berm directly above Loana and the unconscious Tumak before heading back to the sea. Loana cries out the actual scientific name of this prehistoric chelonian (a rather unusual move in choosing the tribal epithet for dialogue purposes). Apparently Michael Carreras, who adapted the original screenplay of *One Million B.C.* thought the word "archelon" was haunting and primitive enough to be shouted by the girl. Pulling itself along by the paddle-like appendages, the mariner can only locomote on dry land with great exertion, which Harryhausen conveys well in its smooth but straining surges when moving ahead. A threat because the supine Tumak happens to lie in its path, the animal climbs down the sandy hill towards him

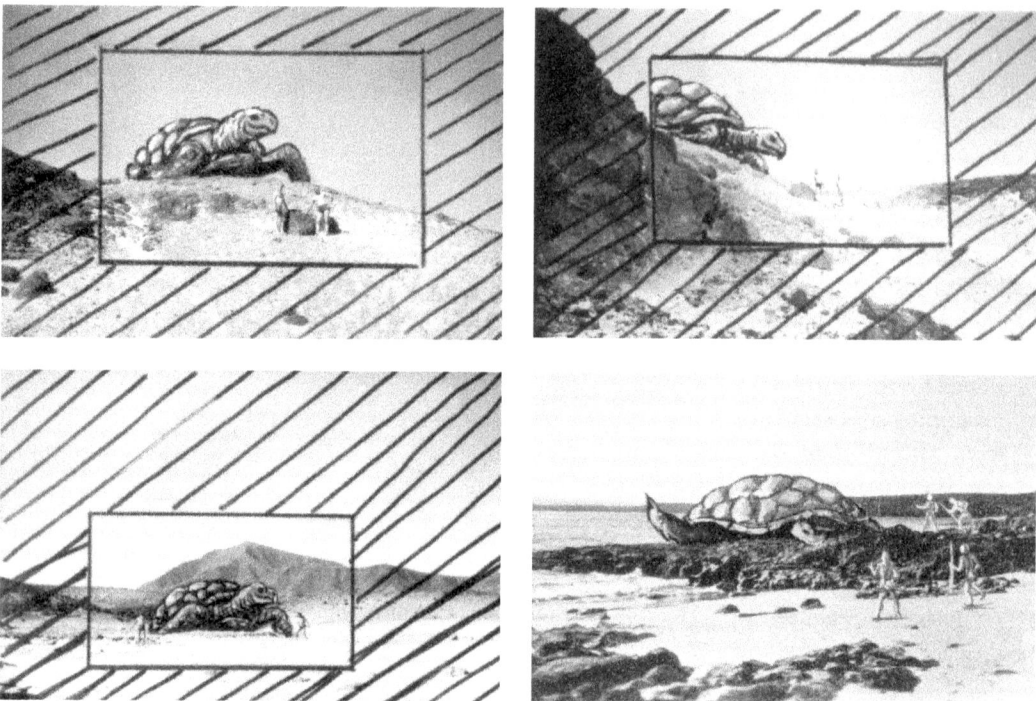

Photographic storyboards of the archelon crawling back to the sea. Here it is conceived as more violent than in the finished picture, with a man clutched in its jaws. Courtesy of Simon Greetham.

fast enough for Loana to have extreme difficulty in removing him from harm's way. There is an effective miniature rear-projection cut which is repeated a moment later, showing the turtle's lower front side while making its way forward with a sculling motion, growing steadily bigger within the frame. Several optical shots, where the blonde beauty drags the dark, handsome caveman clear of a flipper just in time, also prove to be very useful in communicating its enormity.

These shots greatly emphasize not only the immense bulk of this lethargic reptile but also that it can be dangerous simply owing to its huge size. When attacked by the summoned Shell men with spears and hurled stones, its snapping and growling is simply a defensive measurement as it instinctively plods towards a less hostile environment. A nice touch which greatly contributes to the sense of realism is that the hurled weapons apparently bounce off this creature, by substituting miniature animated props at the appropriate point when the real objects pass behind the model in front of the process screen. A floor inlay provides the substrata for solid contact with the ground and allows for these miniatures to end up falling at its feet. A traveling matte serves to place the comparatively tiny Shell men in front of the chelonian as they futilely thrust their lances. Harryhausen wisely avoids the problems of having it slide into the surf by making this occur behind a rock jutting out of the beach, using a static matte rear-projection composite set-up to conceal the bottom part of its body below the split. The entry into the sea is made more convincing by timing this action to a wave breaking on the sand just as it disappears from view. Aided by the sound of rushing surf, it gives the illusion of a great displacement of water caused by the turtle's considerable dimensions.

Actually a very nice model that measures 24 inches in length, nearly nine inches tall and 16 inches wide across the carapace, the archelon displays a host of characteristics that were masterfully budgeted into its outward expression. It is covered by many plate-like protuberances set in the skin; these fleshy sections appear in a regular pattern over its body. The reticulation on its flippers resembles that which is seen on the green sea turtle (Chelonia mydas) and it is likely that other sea turtles, like the loggerhead (Caretta caretta), had their specific features used to create the conglomerate physiognomy seen in this archaic genus. The archelon's shell, made from cast Fiberglass gives it a highly fortified visage but wasn't accurate with respect to known characteristics of the creature; instead of having a carapace composed of the typical horn-like material called keratin to form a protective dome over the back, it almost certainly had one made with thickened skin in the manner of the leatherback turtle (Dermochelys coriacea). Besides its familiar physical representation, this puppet could also perform in a fashion to help make it believable as a real, living organism. During the descent down the sandy slope when heading back to sea, the giant chelonian blinks while pausing near Tumak and Loana, a small reflex that makes it seem more authentic. Another minor movement is the occasional partial retraction of the neck under its carapace. A provision found within the armature itself to allow for such a motion, it mirrors all sea turtles' inability to pull the head in completely, a result of the specialization in their physiology to dwell there. Such an allowance, permitting it to draw its head back towards the shell, shows reactions to the cavemen more rapidly than does the general pace when crawling about; it imparts a responsiveness that might have been otherwise difficult to confer upon such a relatively slow-moving beast.

The archelon model, as seen in Babelsburg, Germany, is well-designed and clearly based upon modern marine turtles. Photograph by the author.

Owing to the excellence of this vignette in making the huge archelon nearly as realistic as it could possibly be, Ray had become a victim of his own success; in *From the Land Beyond Beyond* (1977), Jeff Rovin notes, "Ironically, reading newspaper critiques of the film, spawned by woefully ignorant reviewers, one was led to believe that Harryhausen had simply magnified a box turtle for the sequence" (213). But even when it was recognized as stop-motion and not a living entity, the similarity to existing animals was soundly criticized in some quarters. Tim Lucas' preview of *Clash of the Titans* in *Cinefantastique* Volume 11 Number 2 (1981) takes the animator to task for his perceived use of ordinary creatures in Dynamation: "In the former category, there is a rather dull giant vulture, which carries Andromeda's astral projection to the lair of Calibos each night. While it is as well-animated as one can expect, its design is hopelessly unimaginative. It's one of Harryhausen's eccentricities simply to enlarge normal animals whenever mythology runs out of bogeymen; a case in point would be *One Million Years B.C.*'s sluggish sea tortoise, which crawls on and offscreen before one has a chance to wonder why. One does wonder, in the vulture's case, why it wasn't made uglier, more fearsome" (51). While the archelon isn't the most scintillating of animated opponents, its purpose here is to introduce both the men and women of the Shell Tribe, quickly exposing the highly cooperative nature of their society, as well as their inherent bravery and heroic actions to save others.

Widely recognized as a dramatic and dynamic high point of the movie, the allosaurus sequence displays some superb examples of Harryhausen's wonderful dimensional animation techniques. This well-known dinosaur genus flourished in the late Jurassic and is generally regarded to have been the top predator in its domain, much like the lion is today on the African savanna. Known from the fossil record to have reached some 40 feet in length, the individual seen in *One Million Years B.C.* was scaled to only appear some nine feet tall. This episode is taken directly from the original *One Million B.C.* where a man inside a rubber costume portrayed the creature invading the Shell encampment. Ray has mentioned his impression of this nemesis, saying in *ImagiMovies* Volume 2 Number 3 (1995), "The first film had done this scene with a man in an awful tyrannosaurus suit, and it looked so dreadful they ended up keeping it hidden behind a bush. I felt we could do a little better than that" (25). Indeed, that Fred Knoth outfit was actually intended as a prototype for testing purposes, but Hal Roach saw it and decided this was adequate enough for his picture. Of course, the Harryhausen recapitulation is vastly superior on all levels of staging, dramatic impact and quality of the special effects. The relatively small size of the allosaur (it presumably is a juvenile specimen) allows for the possibility of its defeat at the hands of Tumak and the Shell men. Compared to the robust titular allosaurus in *The Valley of Gwangi*, the *One Million Years B.C.* incarnation is fairly gracile.

Modeled with a pebbly skin texture over its head, the creature's countenance is remarkably similar to that of the cobra, a deadly poisonous serpent which elicits terrified reactions in higher mammals. Coupled with its expressionless eyes and perennially toothy grimace, this meat-eater succeeds in coming off as the "villain" it is supposed to be. What makes this stop-motion figure especially striking, besides its malevolent appearance, is that its physiognomy is remarkably similar to an animation model Ray crafted back around 1940 for the *Evolution* project. Ray had a penchant for finding an archetypal design and sticking with it across a vast number of his articulated thespians; here is a good example of his ingenious reuse of bodily features that have worked out well in earlier puppets. Because of its very recognizable outer attributes, the allosaurus has become a "signature" character of his, almost as definitive as the Cyclops, Ymir or Medusa in its association with Harryhausen due to the proprietary nature of these physical details. Considering that it only stands about 10 to 11 inches high in its usual pose, this figure has an exceptional degree of exemplary sculpting packed into its rather modest stature.

There are many extraordinary components to this sequence in the film that make it one of Ray's most memorable. Upon entering the Shell camp, the allosaurus first approaches a man who dives into the fishing pool in his desperate attempt to escape but gets plucked out and lifted in the jaws of this marauding carnosaur. To effect this, the actor was hoisted up in a harness attached by a wire in the live action background plate and then mated with the animation figure to make it seem responsible for picking the hapless caveman up by his furry robe. In a nice touch, he then falls back into the water with a splash as he "slips" out of the maw of this intruder. A miniature version of this victim was substituted as he is seen firmly clasped in the mouth of the allosaurus, futilely flailing while being set down on dry land and then savagely torn asunder. These shots were done with the foreground entirely as a miniature, which not only allows for solid contact with the ground and shadows to be cast beneath a figure to achieve greater realism, but was also a time-saving move; there is no need to make mattes or backwind the film in the camera as would normally be done in the Dynamation process, since the matched process screen image and floor inlay creates the completed image when recorded together.

Next the allosaur approaches the treed little girl, who falls out of her perch when frightened and is saved by Tumak. Miniature rear-projection was used for several close-up cuts of this snapping beast, gnarling with its teeth exposed in a fierce display of animal rage. Although the model doesn't curl its lip as a facial expression, the loose skin on its throat does ripple while it growls in fury, probably animated with a wire support attached to the armature's neck area. Some fans have noticed that a prominent hair-like object ended up in these frame images just above its head. This occurred when the foreign filament was caught in the animation camera's film gate, a pair of steel plates that serve to hold the film within it flat behind the aperture. Although care is normally taken by filmmakers to inspect and keep the gate free of debris, there is always the chance something might end up in the front or back flanges of the gate; an unwanted fiber can therefore be situated on either side of the film to cause problems. It seems Ray had wanted to redo these shots after discovering this thick strand when he inspected this footage, but director Michael Carraras told him not to worry about it. There are other instances of debris in Harryhausen frames. One can be seen earlier in the vignette as the man plunges back into the pool; in *Gwangi*, a feather-like piece of material appears at the bottom of the frame in several medium shots of the allosaurus during the roping sequence. These cuts of the sneering carnosaur are well-conceived and vividly project its hostile disposition. They are intercut with some nice long shots of Tumak protecting the child by jabbing a spear at the constantly attacking allosaur in front of the apple tree, keeping it at bay long for Loana to rescue the young girl.

Joined by several men from the Shell Tribe, Tumak uses his weapon to repel the invader. There is a floor inlay below its feet as the four men are arrayed in front of this nemesis, thrusting spears to keep it several feet away from them. One of the men hurls his flint-tipped javelin and hits the neck of the allosaurus, causing it to hiss and recoil in pain. Here is an example of some nice trickery on the animator's part. Harryhausen substituted a miniature spear for the real one at the exact moment this missile passes behind the model placed in front of the process screen; he shrewdly avoided any problems posed by the tossed spear remaining in the background plate as it passes behind the dinosaur by having this puppet lurch backward a few frames ahead of the impact to cover up the right periphery of the image. So the real lance passes completely out of sight, concealed by the model as it is momentarily situated over this bordering area in the live-action footage.

The allosaur then rushes at the three remaining cavemen and forces two underneath the thatch roof. The monster yanks at palm fronds and the structure collapses with them inside. When one of the Shell men is slow to extricate himself from the pile, the monster rapidly steps up and picks him up with its teeth. Several key components contribute greatly to the effectiveness of these scenes. Ray carefully matched miniature palm fronds to the rear-projection image for his stop-motion allosaurus to bite on; this is well-synchronized with the physical effect of the falling thatched structure (rigged to something pulling on it off-camera). A nice close-up of the head shows its leering expression while bending over, an eye cast forward in anticipation of catching an easy meal. Lifted out of the strewn palm leaves, the unfortunate man becomes an animated puppet (probably the same one seen earlier by the fishing pool) while held in powerful jaws. Tumak stabs its abdomen with his spear, causing it to release his comrade; both the dropped palm fronds and jointed caveman were supported by invisible wires and incrementally moved to the stage.

Tumak and Ahot force it to backpedal by jabbing it with their lances. There isn't a floor insert below the model as it begins to back up; since actor Richardson steps across the frame image as it disappears from sight, a matte would have been impossible in that area. This leads into a nice medium tracking shot of reverse motion as it defiantly snaps at the warriors' armaments. But the reversal halts when the beast nips the end of Tumak's spear and twists its body, yanking the weapon from his grasp. Now facing the dinosaur alone, Ahot throws his flint tip into the throat. The allosaurus rocks backward just before impact to conceal the peripheral area of the image. Its reaction to the stinging wound is to squirm and paw in order to rid itself of the dangling stick.

All of this builds to an electrifying conclusion, a wondrous visual that is one of Harryhausen's most memorable. While Ahot is dealing with the dinosaur by himself, Tumak falls back to the wrecked thatched structure and tries to free a large wooden pole with a sharpened end; the allosaur is striding quickly towards him. This shot, with Tumak superimposed in front of its rapidly oncoming lower body, is a traveling matte. Tumak falls backwards and holds the pointed end of the pole at the ferocious intruder. What happens next is truly spectacular, as the allosaurus becomes impaled on the stick as it tilts to a vertical position, pivoted upwards by the considerable momentum of its forward progress. Now skewered on top of an impromptu stake held in place by Tumak directly below, the kicking saurian's weight drives the end deeper into its abdomen. Rolling out from beneath his precariously balanced antagonist, the courageous Tumak escapes just before it topples over to the ground. Retrieving his hurled weapon, he rushes over to the convulsing, screaming allosaurus and smites it with a mighty blow to the throat. Its raspy and labored breathing soon stops, bringing to an end the brief reign of terror over the Shell camp.

In *From the Land Beyond Beyond*, Jeff Rovin offers a detailed explanation of just how this famous visual was rendered: "Like the props in the aforementioned effects, the bulk of the pole was a full-scale set piece, while the portion imbedded in the stop-motion dinosaur was a complimentary miniature. Thus, to have Tumak fall back with the allosaur thrashing wildly at the end of the spike, Ray raised the monster with an

The exciting allosaurus sequence was realized very close to what was proposed in these pre-production sketches.

aerial brace, always keeping the miniature section of the stake in careful juxtaposition with its life-size counterpart" (213). This account is not completely correct. In fact, the entire pole was a prop scaled to the size of the puppet so as to make the effect completely seamless, with Tumak's right arm a miniature (which obviously wouldn't be necessary if the live-action version was employed) attached to the base, aligned to the prone Richardson's upper torso. Besides making a more unbroken connection between man and beast, this depiction was also required because the whole foreground in a floor insert just below the actor's body. To create the simulated breathing action of the dying marauder, this model was equipped with an air bladder located in the chest cavity, inflated and deflated through the use of an air pump in incremental steps. An added touch is the end of the prop stick moving in cadence with the final respiratory rhythms; it protrudes above the monster's midsection. Again, the ground beneath and in front of the allosaurus is a miniature stage, which serves not only for solid connection but also eliminates the possibility of a mismatch between different elements in such a composite image.

On an emotional level, this vignette is by far the film's most thrilling, with hardly any let-up until this menace has drawn its last breath. Unlike the passing of Gwangi, there isn't a single tear shed here over the killing of such a relentless aggressor; there can be no feelings of sympathy over something so monstrous and frightening. The wonderful Harryhausen effects build to such an exciting climax, this can be counted among only a few other scenes as being a "show-stopper" of utterly sensational animation.

Harryhausen's allosaurus model as it currently appears. The model shows an incredible amount of detail in its sculpting.

In *One Million B.C.* a dwarf alligator, with a rubbery fin attached to its back to appear as a dimetrodon, battles with a tegu lizard as Tumak and Loana are caught between the two reptiles. Jumping into a fissure to avoid the conflict, they watch the photographically enlarged reptiles clamp onto each other and twist violently over the opening straight above them. After a very energetic tussle, the dwarf alligator crawls off, leaving the tegu lizard on its back, bleeding profusely from a neck wound and twitching. Fortunately, this barbaric treatment of living creatures is now expressly forbidden (at least in Hollywood), thanks to groups like the Society for the Prevention of Cruelty to Animals. At least this isn't a worry when working with stop-motion figures.

In the remake, the couple happen upon a triceratops facing the opposite direction in a patchy field of grass. The triceratops is an extremely popular dinosaur, a quadruped with the quite recognizable frill and three horns adorning its head. Two of the horns are longer and point forward from over the eyes, and a shorter one is right at the end of its snout. One of a closely-related group of horned saurians which evolved during the Cretaceous, it flourished at the very end of the period, one of the last genera roaming the Earth before the Age of Reptiles came to an end. Harryhausen had previously animated this particular type in *Evolution* and *Animal World*. As first glimpsed by Tumak and Loana, the ceratopsian is grazing on the sparse vegetation, momentarily oblivious to the humans who happened to have stumbled upon it. This set-up is very nice, with the model on a realistic floor inlay that is barely discernible to the eye. Other touches which makes its initial sighting very realistic include the subtle but noticeable expansion and contraction of its midsection to imitate breathing, and chewing with a grinding, sideways action; the triceratops was equipped with batteries of massive molars to deal with tough vegetation, so this nuance probably shows the actual manner in which it masticated food. Hearing the pair encroaching upon its territory, the startled beast wheels around and lets out a roar, lifting a front leg to signal that it is going to react to the situation. Getting a profile view of the saurian exposes more clearly its elephan-

Photographic storyboards showing the appearance of the triceratops. In the completed film, this dinosaur was found in a more open landscape. Courtesy of Simon Greetham.

tine limbs, hide (covered with tubercle-like bumps) and the characteristic beak seen in ceratopsians.

Ray was disappointed with the overall appearance of this model; apparently, the body section was cast from a separate mold and had shrunk too much, making the head seem disproportionately large and thus giving the figure an artificial look in his opinion. Even though there are steps that can be taken during molding to help prevent the foam rubber mixture from not gelling properly during baking, such as packing cut pieces of pre-shrunk foam around the armature, it can still "fall" in cooking (much like a cake).

Charging after the wandering twosome, the triceratops moves in an amble with a shuffling motion to its feet. Though this imparts a slightly awkward, ungainly quality to the locomotion of this animal, the movement seems natural enough considering its thick body type; an effective close-up shot reinforces this impression, with the ceratopsian stomping heavily across the frame image. In long shot, it trots after Tumak and Loana as they head towards an outcropping of rock but all stop dead in their tracks as another dinosaur steps into view at the crest of the bluff. This creature is a ceratosaurus, a theropod similar to the allosaurus though a completely different genus; characterized by a more elongated skull with a small horn above the nasal cavity, it was once believed to be the male counterpart to the "female" allosaur. A contemporary of the allosaurus during the late Jurassic, ceratosaurus was actually a more primitive and less common carnivorous variety which still happened to exist at that time. Unlike the model Harryhausen animated, it didn't possess three-fingered hands but instead had four fingers. But for the most part, this figure represents a good estimation of its appearance with the long cranium, horned nose and row of small bony plates that run

Cast of the triceratops figure from the same mold. Note that the midsection of this replica is slightly larger than the stop-motion version's foam rubber body, which shrunk when cooked in an oven. Photograph by the author.

dorsally from the back of the head to the tip of the tail. Other aspects of the exterior that distinguish it from the allosaurus are relatively smooth skin and a drab olive coloration. Since all the other animated dinosaurs appear as some shade of brown or gray in the feature, the ceratosaur's pigmentation helps to set it apart.

The pair duck into a narrow crevasse under the ceratosaur as it snaps at them and the horned opponent directly beyond. When it strides down the slope to take on the formidable ceratopsian, the extreme size of this reptile becomes obvious while passing the humans cowering in the rocks, as only the feet, lower legs and very end of the tail are visible going past the makeshift hideout. Ray obviously took dramatic license in his rendering of the ceratosaurus, scaling it to reach approximately the proportions of a large T. rex when it actually was only a medium-size saurian. Paleontologist Gregory S. Paul, in his 1988 book *Predatory Dinosaurs of the World*, suggests the possibility of a huge ceratosaur from remains found in East Africa; the fragmentary evidence is based on teeth. Stepping in front of the triceratops, the horned theropod weaves and swishes while facing its opponent, conveying some trepidation about the matter even though unwilling to retreat from the formidable defenses projecting from the massive lowered head. It is interesting to note that placing these two particular genera together represents an anachronism nearly as great as having Homo sapiens exist during the Mesozoic Era; nearly 60 million years separate the time ranges each was known to have thrived in. Playing the role of the T. rex for a classic conflict, Harryhausen once again incorporated his favorite dinosaurian variety, the lightly built allosaurus / ceratosaurus type carnosaur, as a stop-motion character. It is no coincidence either that the ceratosaur had the largest presence by far of all the prehistoric monsters in *The Animal World* of a decade earlier.

Stalking to gain an advantage on its foe, the ceratosaurus circles around the ceratopsian with a wide arc though the maneuver is countered adequately; now squaring off while facing the opposite direction, the predator lunges at its quarry but is repulsed by the pointed armaments adorning the head, causing the attacker to rapidly backpedal to avoid being stabbed by them. The ceratosaur, more nimble and fleet-footed, follows this initial thrust by rapidly pivoting around the front of the slowly charging triceratops and clamping onto its frill, placing a foot upon the brow horns in an attempt to impede the progress of the torpid but more sizable opponent. Ray didn't include an insert beneath the fighting dinosaurs in these extreme long shots from a perspective across the open countryside, making them basic Dynamation composites; this was probably done in the interest of saving time and money. Much of the battle is seen from the vantage point of the couple stuck inside the narrow fissure of rock, with the altercation taking place just outside the opening. This was achieved by filming John Richardson and Raquel Welch back in England in an appropriate set to simulate the inside of the crevasse, the pair being superimposed over miniature projection footage of the stop-motion combatants seemingly right outside the entrance in these traveling matte cuts. Rather like the close-up grappling in *One Million B.C.*, these scenes feel somewhat helter-skelter. Most of the action is a partial view of the dinosaurs shuffling around each other, making this feel much more frenetic and capricious than would be otherwise.

While Tumak and Loana are trying to tunnel through the rear of their hideout, another long shot shows the ceratosaurus attacking the front end of the triceratops by pouncing on its head. After getting tossed off by a powerful body twist, the bipedal creature makes a quick dash at the ceratopsian and ends up getting flipped across its forward-pointing cluster of weapons. Next is a shot from inside the rocky gap of the prone ceratosaurus kicking frantically to right itself before its horned adversary can inflict any damage. After Loana manages to escape out the back way, Tumak tries to slip past the battling monsters but is held at bay by the end of the ceratosaur's swishing tail. Harryhausen designed these miniature projection cuts just

Not the original model but a cast from the same mold, the ceratosaurus stands on display in Babelsburg, Germany. Photograph by the author.

like the shot of the theropod stepping by here earlier, to place emphasis on the magnitude of these prehistoric beasts. Again, he made a floor inlay serve entirely as the foreground in order to allow shadows beneath its tail and save time in the animation process. Tumak gets forced back into the narrow refuge; the next shot is another from the inside looking out of the continuing fight. It is interesting because the gyrations differ greatly from what have been witnessed from here previously. The ceratosaurus steps into view facing the opposite way, sweeping its lengthy posterior in graceful curves along the dirt, in anticipation of a charge from the triceratops positioned right in front of it. This smooth, snaking movement is reminiscent of the *King Kong* T. rex after knocking the titular gorilla on its back. Once again, the more agile ceratosaur avoids the lance-like projections of the ceratopsian with relative ease. Another distinct shot of the truculent dinosaurs follows; as Loana climbs the bluff to escape, she turns and briefly watches the action before leaving the area for good. Ray inserted a cut from an overhead vantage point that was achieved using miniature rear-projection, making the hostilities appear from a safe yet uncomfortably close distance.

Seen once again from an extreme long shot over an expanse of terrain, the ceratosaurus is picking itself off the ground immediately in front of the ceratopsian. Seizing this opportunity to defeat the enemy, the triceratops coils with an arch in the back and gores the biped, lifting it clean off the turf through the force of the initial thrust;

it then continues to push the off-balance ceratosaur backwards at the end of the lethal horns and finally topples the shrieking creature over onto its back. As the dying theropod's labored breathing continues for a moment, the victorious three-horned dinosaur roars and retreats from the battleground. The caveman cautiously emerges from the crevasse and crawls up the ridge alongside the recumbent monster just as it expires from the wounds. Harryhausen made the conclusion to this battle extremely vivid through some superb staging and animation. The ceratosaurus model was suspended in mid-air with a wire support instead of by the triceratops' brow horns, but the tips did actually pierce into the latex of the belly region to achieve this effect, with some "blood" oozing out to further enhance this visual. An extreme close-up of the ceratosaur's head (accompanied by a high-pitched scream) is inserted at the peak of the reverse motion to emphasize its agony.

Two cuts of the triceratops follow. One is done with miniature rear-projection, with the ends of its paired weapons glistening with crimson stains, issuing a loud bellow; the other is the last traveling matte seen from inside the fissure, as Tumak watches the growling ceratopsian back away from its defeated adversary. As his character did in *One Million B.C.* with the tegu lizard, Tumak wallks past the body of the prone ceratosaurus, immobile except for the expansion and contraction of the belly region. Although this utilization of an air bladder is technically just as competent as that in the allosaurus sequence finale, the close similarity of this situation to the fate suffered by the allosaur greatly lessens the originality and emotional impact of these shots.

Neil Pettigrew (*Stop-Motion Filmography*) tells how he feels this vignette compares to the preceding one: "The allosaurus sequence begs the question: Why aren't all of Harryhausen's episodes so well designed? For example, the next stop-motion sequence in *One Million Years B.C.*, a battle between a triceratops and a ceratosaurus, is a major disappointment. Although the animation is as complex as in the allosaurus battle, the scene has little dramatic context, serving merely to delay Tumak and Loana. There is little interaction between puppets and actors, and the struggle between the dinosaurs is repetitious, lacking the careful pace of the allosaurus scene" (524). While there is plenty of truth in this statement, the fight is actually pretty decent but happens to follow a more exciting encounter. It proves a colorful episode

The ceratosaurus vs. triceratops battle is an exciting episode in *One Million Years B.C.*

even though it really only serves to temporarily separate the pair of wanderers. Sound effects greatly help make these creatures seem real; the triceratops' vocalizations came from an elephant, while those of the ceratosaur were from a mountain lion or puma. The ceratopsian figure was around 18 inches long and some nine inches in height, while the ceratosaurus stood about 12 inches tall in its typical pose. Neither model now exists; the triceratops figure was stripped down and, with a new head attached, became the styracosaurus in *Gwangi*, and the ceratosaur was also taken apart for use somewhere else. Ray says that this bipedal figure wasn't incorporated into his subsequent Gwangi model, even though these two dinosaurs are physically similar.

All that survives of the triceratops puppet animated in *One Millions Years B.C.* The body was stripped for its armature, which was fed into the styracosaurus of *The Valley of Gwangi*.

Concluding the stop-motion sequences in *One Million Years B.C.*, the encounter with flying reptiles provides some genuine thrills. These creatures were not actually dinosaurs but instead a different order of reptiles which adapted themselves for a life of flying and gliding; like the "terrible lizards" themselves, this group of Mesozoic animals steadily evolved and diversified throughout this period, thriving right up until the very end of the Cretaceous. The first one observed in the film is probably the most familiar of all, the crested pteranodon. This creature flourished during the late Cretaceous period, a toothless type of pterosaur whose crest probably served to counterbalance the lengthy beak. It was one of the largest due to its nearly 30-foot wingspan. Its entrance is very impressive and startling (much like the initial glimpse of the allosaurus) during a lighter moment in the life of prehistoric Man trying to scratch out an existence in the harsh environment. While several members of the Rock Tribe, along with the leading couple, immerse themselves in a small lake with black sandy shores, a large pteranodon swoops down upon Loana. Harryhausen depicts this first sighting quite dramatically, showing an extreme close-up from Loana's perspective of the monster rapidly descending monster from the sky. There are a number of subsequent cuts showing the entire flying pteranodon model from a fairly great distance (animated against a large process screen), ascending and descending over Loana and the others as it attempts to snare a meal with its talons.

The pteranodon's representation seems to jibe with the standard countenance of this animal with only a few differences. Since this creature is portrayed as an active flier through the beating of powerful wings, these membranous flaps attach to the body as

Ray's conceptual artwork of the pterosaur sequence. These sketches are interesting since Loana is shown feeding, and not being fed to, the hatchling fliers. Also, the roles of the pteranodon and rhamphorhynchus are reversed from what is seen in the film. Courtesy of Simon Greetham.

opposed to being connected to the legs. Another significant departure is the inclusion of "bat-wings" in its design. The spoke-like structure makes the wings seem more substantial, unlike the thin sheet of tissue usually seen stretched out along the elongated fourth finger; the bat evolved to support its flying apparatus with all of its fingers instead of a single digit. Because this creature's wings look more reinforced through the addition of struts in the detailing, it helps to facilitate the pteranodon as an active flier.

But a less obvious purpose for the pattern has to do with Ray's fascination with Gustave Doré. Doré composed numerous illustrations of winged demons for *Dante's Inferno* (1861) and several other books; they have a bat-like shape and texture in these bodily parts. Ray incorporated this inspired guise within several previous stop-motion characters (the unmade *Elementals* test footage, the Harpies of *Jason*), and later in *Golden Voyage of Sinbad*'s tiny Homunculus. Like the vividly animated harpy sequence before, the sight of a bat-winged monster hovering over its victims instinctively gives the feeling of it being a "Black Angel" of Death, fulfilling an apocalyptic destiny over which the unwitting have no control.

Held aloft by invisible wires, the pteranodon dives at several humans before snatching up Loana. To create this effect, Raquel Welch reacted to the unseen terror which

Harryhausen would later insert directly over her head; she then threw herself into a hole out of view as the flying reptile settles upon her, and flies off with a tiny animated Loana. Next is a nice tracking shot of the abductor flapping vigorously to gain some altitude. Wilkie Cooper made the effective camera pan to follow the flight of the creature going in one direction, then banking and reversing its route, with the miniature Loana kicking and struggling convincingly. Tumak throws a spear as it starts heading off with his mate (the missile is seen in the background plate barely missing both her and the pteranodon), then gives chase with another Rock Tribe member in tow.

By the time they climb the first steep hill in pursuit, the airborne monster has already returned to its nest where two babies are waiting to be fed. In a long shot, the mother hovers over the roost while the chicks strain to reach the dangling meal; the nest is sitting upon a rocky outcropping along the seashore. The formation that this aerie rests upon was matted into the scene over some other pinnacles of stone, probably to conceal what was being used to support the nest in front of the rear-projection screen. Following this is a famous shot of the live-action Loana shown clutched precariously over the snapping baby pteranodons; Ms. Welch was held up by a pair of prop claws in front of a blue screen, which would later be a miniature projection image of the nestlings trying to reach her, with the foam-strewn surf rolling in beneath the roost. These well-animated chicks appear excellent in close-up, as they are the same models seen in long shot and scaled to the size of the adult, each one being only a few inches tall. Except for the silkiness of Raquel's hair causing problems in these composites, the traveling matte shots of Loana grasped in the talons are very well done. A discarded pre-production concept shows the blonde on top of a cliff actually feeding these infants by hand; apparently some lighter scenes had been considered to introduce the babies.

Another flying reptile swoops in and starts attacking the mother viciously. Noticeably different from the pteranodon, the other flier lacks the crested head and has a mouth full of sharp teeth, is dark-gray to charcoal in color instead of being tan-brown, and actually has a tail of some length. However, this creature is about the mother's size and also sports the bat-wing design of the three other pterosaur puppets. Even though it is labeled in Don Glut's *The Dinosaur Scrapbook* (1980) and other reference books as a rhamphorhynchus, this second flapping monster is not quite identical to well-preserved remains found in the Solnhofen limestones of Germany; these animals had an even longer tail ending in a diamond-shaped flap of skin which served as a rudder. Since they only had a wingspan of perhaps three feet, the rhamphorhynchus was (like the ceratosaurus) greatly magnified for dramatic purposes.

After a long shot of the rhamphorhynchus flying up to the mother, it begins biting the throat of the pteranodon with its sharp teeth. Several cuts rendered via miniature rear-projection show the assault quite strikingly, with their pulsating wing beats flicking around the frame image at such close range to impart a very frenzied feel to these proceedings. Moving out over the sea, the rather one-sided battle continues in a series of long shots interspersed with close-ups of bites to the mother reptile's neck and Tumak racing towards the nest. Weakened by the offensive, the pteranodon loses its grip on Loana. Welch slips out of the prop claws; her animated version falls smoothly below the combatants on a wire, and finally hits the water in live-action. The injured Loana struggles to shore while the rhamphorhynchus presses on with its barrage in a number of long shots from varying distances. The pteranodon soon drops from the air with barely a flutter to slow its descent.

Like he did with the archelon sliding into the surf, Harryhausen wisely avoided the problems of splashdown by having it fall behind a jut of rock extending some distance into the water; this peninsula was masked out and reinserted after the drop was filmed so the figure disappears below the split within this static matte rear-projection composite set-up. One slight problem here is that the point seems further away than the relative size of the model against the sky, so this gives the impression of it seemingly dropping beyond the horizon itself instead of merely past the peninsula. This happens while the Shell woman makes it to shore and staggers along the beach; when she faints from her experience and crumples behind a small sand dune, the victor shows no interest in her but rather in the nearby nest.

Appearing even more ominous than the mother pterosaur, the rhamphorhynchus flaps over and lights upon the edge of the roost with a demonic flourish, as the terrified babies instinctively react by laying down. Making this scene more chilling and macabre is the implicit doom of the offspring, which is unmistakable when glimpsing the dark flier entering the frame image with them. Tumak arrives only after all this has transpired and witnesses the rhamphorhynchus tearing off and swallowing flesh from the infant pteranodons, shown from his vantage point below as it is perched on top of the rocky pinnacle adjoining the shoreline. The sequence concludes with the caveman sullenly walking off, thinking Loana has been devoured when she is actually nearby. Harryhausen's work here is wonderful to behold, with dramatic values that approach those seen in the allosaurus sequence.

Perhaps the most obvious flaw in the animation, endemic of the traditional stop-motion process, is the "strobing" effect seen in the flapping cycles of the pteranodon and rhamphorhynchus; since each frame shows the rapidly moving wings in a sharply defined pose, there isn't the natural "blur" that would occur from such fast movements, giving these fliers a somewhat phantasmic countenance while maneuvering on-screen. These two adult puppets are approximately the same size, though the pteranodon was slightly larger (if accepting that the version reworked for *Gwangi* does possesses the same dimensions as before) at 13½ inches tall and 28 inches from wingtip to wingtip (the rhamphorhynchus was 11 inches high with a 24-inch wingspan). A common misconception regarding the construction of these flapping monsters, stemming from a Mark Wolf article in FXRH #4 (1974) concerning aerial braces, is that "the winged reptiles of *Years B.C.* were fabricated around the Harpy armatures, which explains the similarities in structure of the wings" (23). Dr. Rolf Giesen notes that Ray instead dismantled only a single harpy model and, along with one of his seven skeleton puppets from *Jason*, tried to assemble the Homunculus of *Golden Voyage* out of these components but didn't succeed; he had to eventually build that figure from scratch. After its use in the movie, this crested pterosaur figure was completed remodeled and reconstructed for *Gwangi*, as indicated above.

There was a second, smaller model of the mother pteranodon used during this sequence, with the wingspan of this particular puppet somewhere in the area of 18 inches when fully extended. (The larger figure appears in all of the battle scenes with the rhamphorhynchus because of the scale between them.) There was also another, smaller wire-armatured figure of Loana other than the five-inch version previously mentioned.

It took Ray nine months to complete all his visual effects. But even the most scintillating stop-motion possible within an evocative sequence will be muted if the caliber of the models aren't quite up to par. Throughout his career, Harryhausen had collaborated with others skilled in areas like sculpture and taxidermy to achieve many of the spectacular creatures which grace his motion pictures.

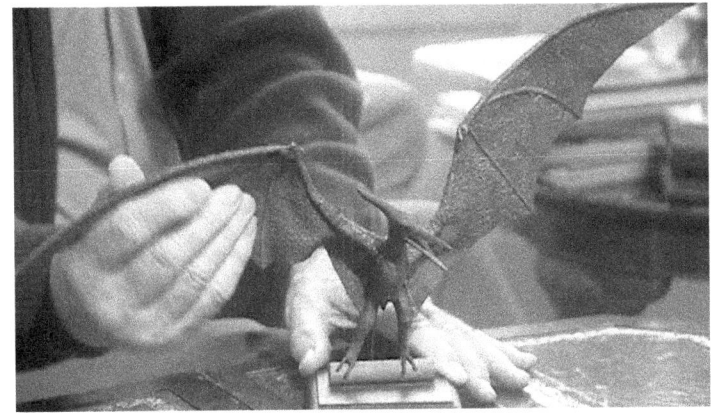

The pteranodon figure grasped by its animator is the smaller of two such crested flying reptiles utilized for the movie.

George Lofgren assisted Ray on *7th Voyage*, fabricating the outward features of the "Snake Woman" (with boa constrictor skin) and the two-headed roc puppets (with feathers and duck down). Lofgren developed a process for "rubberizing" the fur which was used on the *Mighty Joe Young* gorillas, making their hair resilient to the touch. The legendary animator also worked with Janet Stevens, a studio sculptress whose unforgettable figures include the Wooden Figurehead in *Golden Voyage* and Medusa in *Clash*, and Tony McVey, whose sculpture can be seen in *Sinbad and the Eye of the Tiger*.

When Charles Schneer and Ray relocated to England in 1959 to take advantage of European locations, lower costs and a newly developed "sodium-backing" traveling matte process, they employed the talents of Arthur Hayward. Hayward, an exhibits preparator at London's British Museum of Natural History, assisted Harryhausen with his puppets on a number of releases beginning with *3 Worlds of Gulliver*. For *One Million Years B.C.*, he crafted an assemblage of Mesozoic animals through his shaping of sculpting clay. His association with the museum allowed him to closely examine the fossil material on hand to render very accurate (for the time) reconstructions of the numerous extinct genera depicted, even though the overall morphology is based largely upon Ray's concepts. According to *Hammer Films: An Exhaustive Filmography* (1996) by Tom Johnson and Deborah Del Vecchio, Ray also intensively researched these creatures' designs: "He began collecting photographs from the Museum of Natural History in New York and based his model armatures on the skeletons in the British Natural History Museum. Eight models were eventually built" (273). Compared to *The Animal World* of a decade earlier, the paleontological correctness of these is remarkably superior. This high standard of artistry carried over into *Valley of Gwangi* with its own blend of presumed long-deceased fauna populating a "forbidden" valley in Mexico.

Since Ray was quite adept at modelmaking and could have definitively rendered the outward expressions of his characters (at least the ones not requiring taxidermy to complete), why did he farm so much of this work out? He explains the rationale in his *Film Fantasy Scrapbook*: "In the past I have modeled most of the creatures we use myself. Although I still construct all of the final animation figures it becomes necessary, in the interest of shortening production days, to have other people do the time-consuming

This model from ***One Million Years B.C.*** is usually referred to as a rhamphorhynchus even though it lacks the elongated tail characteristic of these pterosaurs. Photographs courtesy of Rolf Giesen.

modeling in clay as well as plaster molds" (94). Harryhausen always did the casting of the foam latex puppets himself, since he retained possession of the armatures which eventually became their chassis, but would sometimes turn them over to outside agencies for the addition of external details, as noted before.

Practically all of the volcanic destruction was achieved by using miniatures, from the pyrotechnically spewing mountaintop to the splitting plains and rocky slabs thrusting through the ground. Although some physical effects can be noticed behind the scurrying actors (small explosions, plumes of smoke drifting towards the sky, etc.), most of the devastation is combined with the actors through traveling matte. These visuals run anywhere from very good to rather mediocre; the lack on consistency and continuity within this vignette considerably weakens its impact. An example where it works well is several cavemen seen buried under rubble shaken loose from a cliff high above. The timing of this optical is excellent, with the falling stones seeming to cover them at the cliff base; as the actors performed in front of the blue screen, which would later be replaced by footage of miniature debris, they dropped to the floor and were then concealed by dirt and rocks which were also shot before a blue screen and then printed over them.

However, there are similar instances of this which look much inferior, such as when Akhoba perishes inside the Rock Tribe cave. Additionally, several cuts showing the ground giving way under the feet of cavemen look woefully contrived; these are certainly piles of earth or gravel optically placed over natural irregularities in the terrain, which "appear" as this loose material drops down. Some victims of the disaster, like Nupondi, are killed when the collapsing landscape was actually staged in front of the blue screen and mated to scenes of upheaval that later completed the composite image. Flames (superimposed in the newly formed openings) and a miniature shot of molten lava surging through a distant rock formation helps support the feeling that these events were triggered by the exploding volcano.

Ray created the visual effects for this tumultuous conclusion (George Blackwell also contributed). The sequence is adequate but no improvement over those in *One Million B.C.* But there is a notable vignette with technical effects which Harryhausen had nothing to do with. At the beginning of the movie, a montage of shots show the creation of Earth from out of the cosmic void. Les Bowie, a veteran special effects man who was long associated with Hammer Films and noted for his work in miniatures and matte paintings, crafted this introductory sequence. Bowie also collaborated with Ray on *Jason, First Men in the Moon* and *Eye of the Tiger*. It took only six days for Bowie to concoct the film's prologue (which he proudly noted in comparison with the Biblical account of these events) and he required a very modest sum of money; in *House of Hammer* #14, John Brosnan notes, "He succeeded by using such economic short-cuts as porridge to represent lava and water running out of taps to represent a vast prehistoric deluge" (28). Boiling furiously behind the credits, this porridge-lava was probably made to look "hot" by having dry ice immersed into it. The gaseous billows drifting across the frame image at the prologue's onset were probably dyes dropped into tanks of water and photographed dispersing throughout the clear liquid.

What exactly is a traveling matte and how is one achieved? Basically, it is a method of superimposing an actor over a completely separate film element to make these two components appear realistically together in a composite shot. Some uses of this technique are quite obvious, such as having a character (in a medium shot) dangling 1,000 feet above the ground at the end of a rope or streaking through the air under his own power à la Superman. It was mentioned here as being used to "bury" several cavemen under a pile of rubble. Even some close-ups of Tumak and Loana during their trek across the wilderness employed traveling matte in order to better show their faces than was possible on location. But certainly the biggest need for this technical procedure in a Harryhausen film was to place the live humans over the stop-motion models; in static matte rear-projection composites, putting the articulated puppet in front of real people is simple, but doing the reverse is impossible. So an altogether different methodology is needed to realize these desired images.

Traveling matte effects can be achieved in more than one way, but one very common procedure involves the use of a large blue screen for the actor(s) to perform in front of, to get the footage to be seen later superimposed over the background in the release print (hence the origin of the term "blue backing"; green screen effects have become popular recently for their being more "digital-friendly"). The film which serves as the rear portion of the frame image in a finished composite shot is called the background plate. Many steps are necessary to place an actor or actors over this separately photographed stock, beginning with the performance before the blue screen in a studio setting. From these recorded actions two pieces of film, a matte and a counter-matte, are struck from the original footage; high-contrast black-and-white film captures the silhouette of all in front of the screen when the blue is converted to black by way of a red filter. Similar to a lock and key, the matte / counter-matte are complimentary though completely opposite, with the matte showing the outline of the actor(s) in black against a clear background and the counter-matte showing a clear outline upon a black background.

There are four strips of film in total: the blue-screen footage, the background plate, and the matte / counter-matte (which can also be properly referred to as a "matte

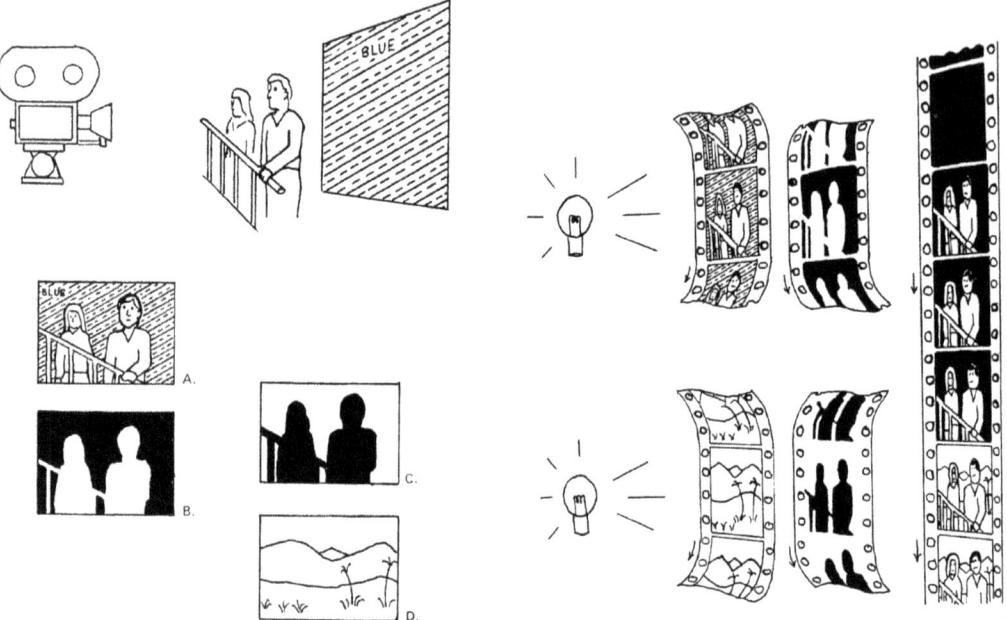

How a traveling matte composite is achieved. Actors are photographed in front of a blue screen to yield film with a blue background (A). Mattes and counter-mattes of the actors' outlines (B & C) are made to use for printing with a background plate (D). In the printing phase, the top two film strips (original blue and matte) are run through the optical printer to place the actors' images onto raw stock. In the second phase through the printer, the bottom two film strips (background plate and counter-matte) then serve to place the background plate around the previously printed outlines to create the composite image. Note that original blue screen and background plate film strips would be negative but are drawn as positives to avoid confusion. Illustrations by Douglas Klotz and used by permission of S.S. Wilson.

/ reverse-matte"). Now having rendered these pieces of film, the final composite image can be realized with the use of an optical printer. To achieve this, the matte is layered over the background plate (termed "bi-packing"; they are placed together inside the film gate) to form an unexposed area corresponding exactly to the silhouette(s), and exposed on a raw piece of film. Next, this new film is backwound and rephotographed with the reverse matte and original blue screen film now bi-packed and also printed onto this new emulsion. With these steps completed, the newly created negative will be used to eventually produce the traveling matte seen in the release print. Sometimes the matte is referred to as the "holdout" matte, and at times the counter-matte is called a "window" matte. Even though this explanation is very basic and doesn't take into account numerous considerations which may arise and cause technical difficulties, the procedure itself is fundamentally quite easy to understand: A matte and counter-matte are formed by filtering the blue screen film, then each of these high-contrast strips is bi-packed in the above noted manner with either the blue screen footage or the background plate in the optical printer, and recorded onto raw stock to achieve the negative.

"Blue screen" traveling matte composites sometimes belie the fact that the superimposed actors do not actually "belong" with the rear portion of the frame image. Raquel Welch's fine hair strands were not completely transposed onto the optical printer negative when she was placed in the prop pteranodon claws in front of the blue screen; this problem is typical in the process with anything that is so delicate. Sometimes there is a blue fringe surrounding the outline of those who stood before that deeply hued backdrop; this is not caused by "spill" (blue from the screen reflecting onto the actor[s]), but instead by the tendency for these high contrast mattes to shrink a very slight but perceptible amount during the procedure. If the reverse matte's clear silhouette is slightly larger than the matte, the blue from the screen itself can seep in around the outline of the matte and end up on the negative, resulting in the "halo" periodically observable within these composites (though the "color-difference" process, developed by Petros Vlahos, resolved the problem of blue fringing in these composites by the early 1960s). Also, if the person to be superimposed wears something that has the same saturated blue as the screen, a "hole" in him/her will later appear where this article is.

It was stated earlier that the negative created by the optical printer will "eventually" yield the traveling matte to be seen in the release print. No, this negative isn't merely rendered and then spliced into the rest of the movie; many steps are necessary to prepare the raw image imprinted on the negative to make it suitable for the release print. To generalize these stages quite a bit, the original negative from the optical printer is first exposed onto low-contrast, orange-base interpositive stock ("IP"), then color correction is made and printed onto dupe negative stock. This negative ends up within the cut work picture (edited version of movie) at the appropriate point, and the "feature cut negative" is color corrected, and test prints ("answer prints") are made until the chroma is approved. Finally, this cut negative is printed with those adjusted hue settings onto a feature interpositive, which is then printed on a feature internegative ("IN") from which are the release prints are struck.

To summarize, a series of stages are needed to create a master negative, with color correction and without physical splices, to generate positive prints of the movie on high-speed printers. Another important point to note about traveling matte is that it only represents a very small component of the optical work in feature films; split-screens, superimposed rain or smoke, the titles placed over a background, dissolves, etc., are examples of things which are also conceived through the use of an optical printer.

Besides the blue screen, there are other techniques to achieve traveling matte shots. It has been mentioned that Harryhausen moved overseas in part to make use of a new sodium backing ("yellow backing") process to do these particular composites; sodium backing was employed for *Gulliver*, *Mysterious Island* and *Jason* to realize these films' virtually flawless optical shots. This procedure for making traveling matte effects is entirely different, necessitating equipment very different from that employed in blue backing. Sodium vapor lamps give off a yellow light to illuminate the yellow screen the actor(s) perform in front of; the image is captured by a split-beam camera running two films through the gate at the same time. One film, through filters, produces the opaque matte while the other captures (via didymium lights used to nullify any monochromatic yellow shining on the cast) the detail of the action before the screen. The advantage here is that an instantaneous matte is created, thereby saving several steps and thus allowing for a much lower probability of error. Also, no exclusion of a particular color is necessary. Unfortunately, the yellow backing means of superimposing a person on a background plate wasn't available for *One Million Years B.C.*; since the prism of this specialized camera fell into disrepair and was not fixed, these opticals were impossible to realize at that time.

Raquel Welch was actually in several movies (along with some guest TV spots) before appearing in *One Million Years B.C.* A stunning actress usually considered as one of the sexist women in cinematic history, she was born Jo Raquel Tejada on September 5, 1940, in Chicago. Growing up and attending high school in California, the teenager won winning several beauty competitions in the 1950s. After graduating from La Jolla High, she married her school sweetheart James Welch in 1959 and shortly afterwards had a couple of children. In the early 1960s Raquel relocated from Dallas to Hollywood, where she worked as a waitress and model; within days of arriving she had a manager, Patrick Curtis, who would become her second husband. Her first movie role was a bit part in the Elvis Presley film *Roustabout* (1964), and soon she appeared in *A House Is Not a Home* (1964) and *A Swingin' Summer* (1965). By the time she was working on *Fantastic Voyage* (1966), Ms. Welch was a contract player for 20th Century–Fox, which loaned her out to Hammer Films for the vehicle that made her a star.

Often criticized for her acting abilities and behavior considered rude and unprofessional by her peers, Welch actually does fairly well in the role of Loana though admittedly the limitations make it hard to fail. According to *The House That Hammer Built* #5, her voice was later dubbed by Nicolette McKenzie (289). This is borne out by the contemporaneous *Fantastic Voyage*, where she does have a different, much softer speaking voice. If not especially praised for her work throughout the 1960s, Welch received some measure of critical acclaim for her subsequent acting in productions such as *The Four Musketeers* (1974) and the TV movie *Right to Die* (1987), in which her character suffers from a terminal illness.

In a 2002 interview, Raquel talked about her feelings on *One Million Years B.C.* and how she came involved with the project. Having just made *Fantastic Voyage* and being loaned to Hammer Films by Richard Zanuck for a dinosaur film, she felt that her career would be stuck in some kind of "sci-fi hell" as a result. But the next issue of *Time* magazine changed her mind, since it was entirely about London's "swinging" cultural revolution and Carnaby Street; she thought to make the best out of a trip over to England, and that this "turkey" would be quickly forgotten anyway. But she instead ended up in the Canary Islands, which Welch remembers as being extremely cold that time of year, especially when wearing a scanty costume (she got tonsillitis as a result). Raquel noted that she tried to add some "subtleties" to the Loana character which the director strongly discouraged, but in hindsight feels that due to her lack of experience this lack of development was probably for the best. An aspect of acting that she did find satisfying was the fight with actress Martine Beswick in the cave; her training in dance served her well for the movements. By the time she returned to London she had already become a sex symbol. Raquel concluded the conversation by conveying that even though she is still uncomfortable about her *One Million Years B.C.* role, she has come to terms with it, and overall is glad to have been involved in the production.

John Richardson, a handsome English actor who previously was in the remake of *She* (1965) with Ursula Andress, played Tumak in the picture. Born in 1934, he also appeared in *Pirates of Tortuga* (1961), *Execution* (1968) and *On a Clear Day You Can See Forever* (1970). *One Million Years B.C.* was originally to have been a re-pairing of Richardson and Andress, but she declined the role and so Ms. Welch was tapped to appear opposite him; this leading man was also in *The Vengeance of She* (1968), a sequel to the 1965 film which also did not feature his former co-star. According to director Peter Hunt of *On Her Majesty's Secret Service* (1969), Richardson was briefly considered for the role of James Bond, which eventually went to the one-film 007 George Lazenby. In the aforementioned interview, Ms. Welch notes that Richardson was a

Raquel Welch and John Richardson.

"wonderfully good-looking, beautiful beautiful man" whom she thought was also a good actor though he really didn't seem to care at all doing his part. She also divulges that he was a "camera bug," seeming to prefer this over acting.

Martine Beswick, a Jamaican by birth and former Miss Jamaica, was the savage but sensual Nupondi. She can be found in other Hammer productions such as *Dr. Jekyll and Sister Hyde* (1971) and *Prehistoric Women* (1967), in which she got the lead directly as a result of *One Million Years B.C.* Martine was also a "Bond Girl," seen in *From Russia with Love* (1963) and *Thunderball* (1966), and appears in vehicles such as *Seizure* (1974) which promoted her "femme fatale" image. Robert Brown (Tumak's father Akhoba) was a veteran of numerous films. He notably was an admiral in *The Spy Who Loved Me* (1977) and had a recurring part as "M" in four 1980s James Bond titles. Brown was also cast in *Billy Budd* (1962) and *Operation Crossbow* (1965). Percy Herbert (Tumak's sinister sibling) had worked earlier with Harryhausen on *Mysterious Island*. Herbert's competent though rather pedestrian acting style can be seen in *Mutiny on the Bounty* (1962) and *The Viking Queen* (1967). Other actors who made up this predominantly British ensemble are Jean Wladon, William Lyon Brown, Lisa Thomas, Malya Nappi, Richard James, Frank Hayden, Terence Maidment, Micky de Rauch and Yvonne Horner.

A great benefit to *One Million Years B.C.* are the beautiful locations used to portray the world in its primordial phase. It was filmed on the Canary Islands off the western coast of Africa for its barren yet captivating exterior vistas. The Canaries comprise an eastern Atlantic archipelago of seven larger and several smaller land masses; volcanic in nature, they cover an area of about 2000 square miles. Two of the major islands, Tenerife and Lanzarote, were visited for location shooting beginning in October 1965. Tenerife is the largest of the Canary Islands and also extremely mountainous, with the highest elevation of the entire archipelago at over 12,000 feet. Las Canadas National Park (used for much of the filming here) is a large caldera many miles across and containing the tallest mountain of this island group, Pico de Teide. Many scenes of Tumak just after he leaves the Rock Tribe showcase the natural wonders of this park and Tenerife in general. Teide can be spotted several times during the film, as can the craggy and eroded Los Roques de Garcia. Seen in the background when Tumak spits in disgust towards his former abode, the Roques are framed in the shot with a smoldering Teide off at a great distance; this great peak was not active at the time so a plume of smoke was optically printed over the summit.

Raquel Welch as seen in a 2002 interview.

Lanzarote is much flatter than Tenerife but is also very desolate in appearance, having seen geologic activity which covered significant areas in lava fields and ash back in the eighteenth and ninteenth centuries. The western coast area of El Golfo is the site of Lago Verde, the greenish, saline lagoon adjoining the ocean where the pteranodon swoops down on Tumak, Loana and others (it is also featured in the 1985 movie *Enemy Mine*). Papagayo, a region on the lower end of the island, known for its fine sandy beaches, was seen as a fishing area for the Shell women and also as background plates for the archelon heading back to sea. The volcanic field making up the National Park of Timanfaya can be observed here as well. Two other main Canary Islands, Gran Canaria and Fuerteventura, have been indicated as locations but it isn't clear whether they were used; they *were* later tapped for Hammer's saurian opus *When Dinosaurs Ruled the Earth* (1970).

In all, the Canary Islands contribute a wonderful look to the production. Clouds wrapping around the mountain tops like a thick fog are just as breathtaking to witness as they are otherworldly. Some of the impressive visuals during the opening moments were lifted and reused in two subsequent Hammer films, *When the Dinosaurs Ruled the Earth* and *The Lost Continent* (1968).

Although it would seem filming in the Canary Islands would have been an arduous experience, Ray notes in *Land Beyond Beyond* that the visit was fairly comfortable: "Actually, we lived in a hotel, we didn't bivouac on the peaks of the lava flows. We had very pleasant quarters in a Spanish Parador hotel" (209). This is located very close to where much of *One Million Years B.C.* was filmed on Tenerife. A fascinating fact about the film is that Iceland, a geologically active island situated in the northern part of the Atlantic, was considered first by producer Michael Carreras. All of the interior sets were built in England at the Associated British Picture Corporation's Elstree Studios; these include the caves of the Rock Tribe, Shell Tribe and subhumans, the oasis-like Shell camp where the allosaurus attacked, and the area just outside the Rock cavern. Principal photography in the Canaries and England was completed by January 1966. Even though the raw look imparted by fields of igneous rock is effective in creating a prehistoric world, one has to wonder how such an ecosystem could support all the large herbivorous dinosaurs roaming about.

Mario Nascimbene composed the film's score. Born in Milan, Italy, in 1913, he became established in Italian film before coming to the attention of Joseph L. Mankiewicz, who had Mario score his *The Barefoot Contessa* (1954), starring Humphrey Bogart and Ava Gardner; stemming from this movie's success, the composer was hired by other Hollywood producers for their projects. His list of notable pictures includes *Alexander the Great* (1956), *The Vikings* (1958), *Solomon and Sheba* (1959) and *Barabbas* (1962). However, after the early 1960s his worked in these Hollywood costumers waned, and his later compositions ended up in many science fiction–fantasy films, beginning with *One Million Years B.C.* Before he scored this, Nascimbene had been engaged as the musical director for *Jason*, working under the great composer Bernard Herrmann.

The music is not a typical arrangement but rather highly percussive in nature (in fact, there was an entire percussion section to make these sounds). In his book *Hammer, House of Horror: Behind the Screams* (1996), Howard Maxford writes that this atmospheric score "made excellent use of weird percussive sound effects, including rocks, bell sticks and the jawbone of an ass" (88) to superbly concoct its aural qualities. This is put to good use within a number of scenes to invoke just the right mood. For example, the sounds heard during much of the Rock Tribe's presence is quite harsh and visceral, indicative of the group's comparatively savage nature; during several key vignettes, these raspy, clicking noises increase in rapidity to an almost feverish pitch as a violent act is unfolding. By contrast, the music composed for the appearance of the Shell people is far more melodic, with the idyllic qualities of wind instruments filling the air in a mesmerizing fashion. Another distinct sound can be perceived when the subhumans are present. Loud, low-pitched crescendos blare out suddenly during these scenes, an extremely harsh audible that is emblematic of these even more primitive hominoids. (A very similar noise can be heard during the titles of *Barabbas*.)

Ray feels that Mario Nascimbene's work in *One Million Years B.C.* is appropriate for the movie, saying in an *Animato!* #25 (1993), "A lot of people didn't like it, but I thought it had that primitive ring to it. I thought it was most impressive. It's not a score you would go out humming in the lobby, though you might go out *grunting* it! It was suitable for the subject matter, and I think anything other than that would have been like the original *One Million B.C.*, which had a melodic theme that was very unsuitable. I think Nascimbene's score had that wonderful primitive ring to it" (50). But as Harryhausen mentioned, the arrangement also has plenty of detractors; critic Ed Naha utterly panned it in his *Horrors: From Screen to Scream* (1975): " Annoying background music, as melodic as the sound of chalk squeaking on a blackboard, concocted by Mario Nascimbene adds to the general cacophonous aura generated by the film" (224).

Besides the composition, other sounds are strategically employed to conjure up the desired mood in various scenes. Several of the dinosaur sequences feature a low-frequency "rumble" as a background noise to heighten the tension of the unfolding action. Every step taken by the allosaurus is in sync with a barely audible kettle drum banging amidst this rumbling threshold; it is a subliminal way of making these vignettes even more intense. In all, the score fits the prehistoric mood of the picture, an aboriginal theme that blends harmoniously with the savage people and landscape of long ago. It is available on a CD that includes Nascimbene's other Hammer Films prehistoric compositions, *When Dinosaurs Ruled the Earth* and *Creatures the World Forgot* (1971).

Long associated with the horror and science-fiction genres, Hammer Films was a independent company with a long string of successful 1950s–60s movies. It was formed out of a partnership between Enrique Carreras and Will Hinds in the 1930s. Carreras was a Spaniard who relocated to England and became the owner of a chain of cinemas, eventually forming his own distribution company (Exclusive Films) during the late 1920s to maximize the profits from his theaters. Hinds was a failed vaudevillian actor whose stage name was "Hammer" and who had owned several businesses. After they joined forces in 1932, the very first release under the Hammer banner was *The Public Life of Henry the Ninth* (1935). Shutting down in the late 1930s because of the advent of World War II, the company began making pictures again shortly after the mid–1940s. During this period, sons James Carreras and Anthony Hinds joined their fathers' company and became very important figures in its administration. To keep costs low, the fledgling film company was located in a small country estate known as Down Place and staged their productions there. This came to be called Bray Studios when serving as Hammer's base of operations, with the neighboring Oakley Court used for their many horror features with a Gothic flavor.

It wasn't long before Hammer started turning out a number of horror pictures, beginning with *The Quatermass Xperiment* (1955); this was followed by *The Curse of Frankenstein* (1957), *Dracula* (1958) and *The Mummy* (1959), the latter two are remakes of classic Universal features of the 1930s. But around the mid-1960s the winds of change were blowing at Hammer; the Bray Studios were abandoned as it was proving too small for their larger productions and, thematically, the movies were more science fiction and fantasy than horror. Several of these include the remake of *She*, *Quatermass and the Pit* (1967) and *The Lost Continent*. *One Million Years B.C.* was only their second foray into fantasy (after *She*).

Kenneth Hyman of Seven Arts had originally suggested them. Hyman, who ran this company started by father Elliot Hyman in the late 1950s, had a long association with Hammer through their financial backing of a number of projects. Although Kenneth Hyman's contributions to Hammer went unbilled (except as producer on 1961's *The Terror of the Tongs*), he is credited with producing the well-known features *What Ever Happened to Baby Jane?* (1962), *The Hill* (1965) and *The Dirty Dozen* (1967). He served as a silent co-producer with Michael Carreras on *One Million Years B.C.* in addition to being responsible for the idea of this successful production. The rights were purchased from Hal Roach, who made the original *One Million B.C.* and was given credit as associate producer along with Aida Young, who also produced the follow-up *When Dinosaurs Ruled the Earth*. Because *One Million Years B.C.* was touted as the hundredth Hammer production (though in reality this milestone had already been passed), it benefited from a higher budget than would have normally been the case.

As noted previously, Michael Carreras was the producer of this film. He joined the company started by his grandfather while still a teenager, working in various departments at Exclusive during the war and shortly afterward, then returning after his Grenadier Guards stint in 1948 and soon becoming a casting director and assistant to the producer. He joined the board of directors in 1950 while in his early twenties, filling the vacancy created by the unexpected passing of grandfather Enrique. Receiving his first producer credit the following year, Michael was in charge of *Prehistoric Women, Lost Continent, Moon Zero Two* (1969) and others and was executive producer on scores of other releases. In addition, he took on directing and scripting roles for many 1960s projects; he adapted the Mickell Novak–George Baker–Joseph Frickert screenplay of the original *One Million B.C.* Gaining control of Hammer in 1972 after buying all his father's shares in the company (after James Carreras tried to sell it to an outside agency that would have deposed his son), Michael headed Hammer in its waning days, even putting his own money up for financing right before the end came in the late 1970s. This third generation studio head died in 1994 at the age of 66.

Carl Toms' conceptual drawings of the costumes for the Rock and Shell people. Courtesy of Simon Greetham.

At Hammer, Ray Harryhausen probably didn't enjoy the same degree of artistic expression as was customary under the aegis of Charles Schneer, but he nevertheless found the experience to be quite satisfactory. Due to the failure of *First Men in the Moon*, Charles went on to make non-fantasy pictures like *You Must Be Joking!* (1965) for a period around the mid-1960s, so Ray was available when approached by Hammer. But because of his licensing arrangement with Schneer, the term "Dynamation" could not be used for any advertising or promotion in conjunction with *One Million Years B.C.* The compositing techniques used to combine the dinosaurs and live actors in the same frames were basically the same as before. Harryhausen had to convince Carreras not to make this movie in an Anamorphic (widescreen) format, since his static matte rear-projection composite methods were not readily adaptable to this different aspect ratio. Since his previous *First Men* was filmed in Panavision, Ray was forced to rely heavily upon the use of traveling matte to combine the miniature elements with the live-action footage.

Don Chaffey, the director of *One Million Years B.C.*, was hired at the request of Harryhausen, who worked alongside Chaffey on *Jason*. Known for wringing good performances out of actors and also moving them quickly through their scenes, Chaffey did a very competent job. Born in England in 1917, Don also helmed *The Prince and the Pauper* (1962), *A Twist of Sand* (1968) and *Pete's Dragon* (1977) along with many episodes of TV's *The Prisoner*, *Charlie's Angels* and *MacGyver*. He stayed busy right up until his passing in 1990 at age 73. For Hammer Films he also served as director on *The Viking Queen* (1967) and *Creatures the World Forgot*.

Wilkie Cooper (who also had been brought aboard this endeavor by Ray) had served earlier as cinematographer for Charles Schneer and Ray on every venture of theirs from *7th Voyage* to *First Men*. As usual, his camera captured many magnificent sights, showcasing the natural wonders of the Canary Islands.

In sharp contrast to the Rock Tribe, the Shell Tribe is a peaceful society that practices a much higher degree of interpersonal cooperation. For example, their tribal elder Payto is a relatively frail man who could easily be vanquished by any one of the younger tribesmen; obviously, they revere experience and wisdom much more than any display of power. Along with exhibiting more refined behavior, the Shell people also possess a more advanced culture, with many of its manifestations completely unknown to the Rock Tribe. These include flint-tipped spears, rudimentary agriculture, cave painting and costume jewelry. What makes these differences most intriguing is that they seem to tacitly indicate the Shell Tribe is comparatively Cro-Magnon to the Rock Tribe's Neanderthal lifestyle; they're a more developed race that should eventually replace these brutish cavemen of the rocky landscape. Even though there are no sloping foreheads or bony eyebrows, the Rock Tribe's inferiority is conveyed by their generally thicker body types, black hair and darker complexion.

It is easy to overlook the third group of hominoids, the subhuman ape-men Tumak encounters in an spacious cavern lying far below the surface (they are referred to as both "Gorilla people" and "Gorilla men" in the film's pressbook). They are an evolutionary throwback to even more ancient times; Australopithecus types who lack any sort of developed skills and even the ability to speak beyond grunts.

Since the film is a remake of *One Million B.C.*, many of the dramatic elements are virtually the same but not a shot-for-shot recapitulation of the original version. Like the first film, the remake is bereft of English dialogue, instead depending upon a limited vocabulary consisting of words such as "akeeta" and "neetcha" strung together with very rudimentary syntax to pose as a crude language. This is carried even further in the follow-up *When Dinosaurs Ruled the Earth*, which has its cave people using 27 identifiable words in varying combinations to communicate ideas to each other, if not to the audience. The characters in *One Million Years B.C.* also utilize gestures to get the message across, but these pantomimes border on hyperbole at times. Tumak in particular displays exaggerated reactions to various situations, such as when he asks his father to be allowed to kill the warthog, and also when he walks practically on top of the brontosaurus tracks before being startled by them. Two of Harryhausen's stop-motion sequences, the allosaurus and the ceratosaurus vs. triceratops fight, are quite similar to vignettes in the 1940 film but are much more visually impressive. The beginning of the allosaurus sequence, with the girl stuck in an apple tree as the ferocious invader approaches, seems to come straight out of the Book of Genesis. All of the Biblical elements present in the Garden of Eden story are recognizable in this scene: the evil reptilian, the apple tree and the innocent girl. Carrying this a bit further, Tumak and Loana seem representative of the first couple, Adam and Eve.

John Richardson and Raquel Welch are physically more appealing in their reprisal of the lead roles than Victor Mature and Carole Landis, even if the acting isn't quite

Raquel Welch combing her hair before shooting for *One Million Years B.C.* Note that the person holding the mirror is wearing a heavy jacket. Photograph courtesy of Ted A. Bohus.

up to the level previously achieved. Welch was intimidated in the presence of the very handsome Richardson, saying in the *Imagi-Movies* career article, "I thought, 'He's the pretty one — those blue eyes and that face! I look butch next to him!'" (25). But it was her visage that Hammer and Carreras were counting on to sell movie tickets, more than Harryhausen's prehistoric monsters. She was costumed in a stunning and skimpy doeskin bikini (usually referred to as a "fur bikini") designed by Carl Toms and fabricated by Monty Berman (uncredited), and supplied with false eyelashes and make up to maximize her physical appeal. One photograph of Welch in wardrobe has become an indelible image of the 1960s. A mesmerizing still (taken by Pierre Luigi) of Welch gazing off towards the distance with hands held away from her sides, poised to react suddenly, it was used profusely on advertisements and posters and thus turned into an enduring cultural icon for this turbulent decade. Still very recognizable years later, it has a significant presence in the feature *The Shawshank Redemption* (1994), serving as screenwriter-director Frank Darabont's homage to Ray.

But even if there is no doubt the remake is visually leagues beyond the 1940 offering, it lacks the "heart and soul" of the preceding epic. Victor Mature and Carole Landis' Tumak and Loana exude a warmth and chemistry which is completely absent in the subsequent film, and the savagery is balanced out by a number of lighter moments to lend an overall poignancy to the production. *One Million Years B.C.* has only a few scenes of relative mirth but they are muted if not actually out of place. While *One Million B.C.* has a happy ending, the latter film is quite ambiguous about the fate of these people in the wake of volcanic chaos. Several shots following the cataclysm are in black-and-white to emphasize the utter bleakness and devastation. One proposed ending would have shown the survivors walking towards a mushroom-shaped cloud on the horizon, a strange juxtaposing of that horrific Atomic Age vision with the antediluvian past. It more than likely was to have been mated to a concluding piece of narration to explain the nuclear apparition, it is quoted in *The Hammer Story* (1997) by Marcus Hearn and Alan Barnes: "How lucky we are. We can create such destructions and disasters without any help from Nature at all. Goodnight children ... everywhere" (105).

After *One Million Years B.C.* proved financially successful, Hammer followed with *When Dinosaurs Ruled the Earth* and *Creatures the World Forgot*. *When Dinosaurs* starred Victoria Vetri and Robin Hawdon as the lovers Sanna and Tara, struggling against both prehistoric creatures and those who seek to make Sanna a human sacrifice (she avoided that fate during a ritual ceremony at the film's start).

Since Harryhausen was working with Charles Schneer on *Valley of Gwangi* and thus unavailable for the special effects, 28-year-old Jim Danforth was hired to do the animation for this dinosaur epic. The ensemble of Mesozoic animalia here consists of a plesiosaurus, chasmosaurus, rhamphorhynchus (with the complete tail), mosasaurus, giant crabs and quadrupedal mother and baby saurians; contradicting the movie's title, there is only one bona fide dinosaur present, the horned chasmosaur (a ceratopsian variety related to the triceratops and styracosaurus). With a row of dorsal spines down the middle of its back, the mother reptile closely resembles Ray's *Beast from 20,000 Fathoms*, but the similarity was totally unintentional. *Creatures the World Forgot* is completely forgettable since it lacks any saurians and is only slightly salvaged by Norwegian Julie Ege's presence.

Recently, the British version of *One Million Years B.C.* has become quite well known to audiences in the U.S., virtually replacing the theatrical release. The British version runs nine minutes longer (100 min. vs. 91 min.) and contains significantly more dimensional animation as well as plenty of additional non-effects scenes. The longer incarnation includes more footage of the archelon, allosaurus, pteranodon and rhamphorhynchus.

The archelon sequence runs about 40 seconds longer. The turtle crawls up next to a sandy knoll on the beach; four men are confronting the creature while another climbs upon this hillock and attacks from the side, swinging his spear like a bat to strike its carapace, then following with a thrust of the spear tip. Noticing the lateral offensive, the chelonian wheels around surprisingly fast and snaps at this tormentor, and then whips forward to again repel the cavemen arrayed before it. Since the man on the small mound is in front of the archelon, the end of his lance passes slightly over the shell for a few frames during the jab; more than likely, either a miniature prop aligned to the real lance in the background plate or glass painting was used to replace what the model concealed when inserted into this shot. There are also a couple more traveling matte cuts of these relatively small warriors superimposed over the turtle as it aggressively defends itself.

The plesiosaur being tied down in *When Dinosaurs Ruled the Earth*. Jim Danforth's effects are the highlight of this feature.

In the allosaurus raid on the Shell camp, there are two additional clips with a combined running time of 30 seconds. The first one (about ten seconds long) shows the dinosaur's reaction upon seeing the girl stuck in the tree; it displays some surprise seeing her on the branch by seeming slightly off-balance, then leans under a protruding limb and bites at the terrified child. Between the two shots is one of Tumak trying to wrest Ahot's spear from him. Lasting just a bit over 20 seconds, the second clip shows Tumak working his way around behind the tree to draw the monster away from the girl, then rapidly backing away as the creature lunges at him. This animation is very dynamic. Also seen is another close-up of the allosaurus's head nipping at the tip of Tumak's spear.

There is also much more footage of the pteranodon flapping above the lake (about 50 seconds). A neat miniature rear-projection screen cut shows another close-up glimpse of the aerial antagonist from directly beneath, moving straight up and down. Another excerpt runs a little over ten seconds and shows what happened to Loana when the monster lifts her out of the basin. The flying reptile soars behind a rise in the extreme distance (which probably employed both the smaller mother pteranodon and Loana figures). Later in the sequence are two very brief clips of extra animation. The first is a few seconds of the pterosaurs fighting while the dropped Loana is battered by heavy surf; the other is a few extra seconds of the rhamphorhynchus perched at the nest, feasting on the chick pteranodons.

Other previously missing footage:

• While the warthog is cooking on the open fire, a wizened old man is struck in the forehead by a rock hurled by Akhoba's mate Tohana, presumably to thwart his feeble attempt to purloin a piece of meat. He falls to the floor and is seen whimpering from a bloody wound.

• More shots of the tribe as they dine on morsels of flesh, nestled in various pigeonholes along the cave wall, with two elderly males wrestling over a bone tossed away by their leader.

• Tumak in the Shell camp examining their cultural advancements. He inspects a pigment for wall painting by tasting and rubbing it on his arm, and touches a pool of water (heated by underground geological activity) that makes him recoil.

• During the climactic cataclysm, some extra bits can be spotted: a traveling matte shot of Nupondi and others running away in a panic, superimposed over falling miniature stones; several cavemen perishing in massive rifts seen from a fairly distant perspective; and a Shell man rolling down an embankment like a log. A much longer inclusion is seen as Tumak starts his journey. He is seen for a full minute strolling and then stopping to look at a glowing (tinted) red area lying across a great expanse of terrain; pulling himself up a steep incline and using an end of his furry cape to wipe off his face; and walking past a dinosaur skeleton miniature (looking like the mooncalf's remains in *First Men*) matted into the foreground of this composite shot. Also, during the Rock Tribe's ritualistic ceremony, additional footage reveals it to be some sort of fertility rite. Nupondi leaps and dances about in front of Sakana and the younger men, who are sexually aroused by the provocative performance of the raven-haired beauty. Strung together in a series of very brief shots with a rapidly pulsating Nascimbene score, the frenzied motions in these images grow into a feverish pitch of animalistic lust, with Nupondi collapsing from exhaustion at its climax. She is carried and placed on a flat slab of stone, presumably to consummate the intended procreative action, but before anything else happens, Akhoba appears.

More "new" footage is seen when Tumak and Loana hide in the tree to avoid the fight between the subhumans. There is much more of this pitched battle as two of them savagely go at it, with one being horrifically defeated in a very severe beating; the weaker one is slammed against the cavern wall, his cranium bashed on a rock and body pummeled with fists. Eventually, the unfortunate subhuman is killed and has his head severed from the body and impaled upon a stick as a macabre trophy. This explains what Tumak saw during his first visit to the grotto: several ape-like skulls displayed upon sticks, which is glimpsed in the U.S. version but left completely unexplained due to the deletion of these subsequent scenes. There are even differences in the opening

The chasmosaurus, as seen in 1994 at Forrest J Ackerman's home, is the only actual dinosaur in *When Dinosaur's Ruled the Earth*. Unfortunately, this nicely detailed miniature has suffered quite extensive deterioration over the years. Photograph by the author.

credits between the two; the U.K. edition starts out with "Associated British-Pathe Limited presents" followed by "A Hammer Film Production" while its American counterpart opens with "A Seven Arts-Hammer Film Production." Another discrepancy which is less obvious is that while the American version gives an associate producer credit to Hal Roach, he is not listed in the other. Overall, the British version is more kinetic, brutal, even logical than what was released in America (not to mention all the extra Harryhausen animation). A thorough discussion of these missing scenes is found in Stephen Bissette's *Video Watchdog* #40 (1997) review.

One Million Years B.C. was released in the U.K. near the end of December 1966; its U.S. release wasn't until February 1967. Following many years of televised showings (it was first broadcast on the ABC-TV network in the fall of 1970), this movie finally became available as a licensed VHS prerecord in 1994, one of 20th Century-Fox's video "Selections." While this was the familiar American theatrical edition, it came out on laserdisc as the British version in late 1996, almost exactly 30 years after its initial debut. The British cut has come out as a Region 2 DVD for the European market but still hasn't been released yet in North America.

The author of this book played a direct role in the recent popularizing of this incarnation of *One Million Years B.C.* Having heard of its existence from dinosaur enthusiast Richard Mirissis, a VHS prerecord in PAL format was purchased on a trip to London

Together on display but never together in the movie, the miniature Loana and allosaurus. Photograph courtesy of Rolf Giesen.

in 1992 and later converted to NTSC on another tape. A friend, John Ballentine, was shown this video and then endeavored to see that the laserdisc release would indeed be the longer version. He wrote a letter to Image Entertainment to inform them of a "British" version and how it would behoove them to obtain a print; they called him back within a few days and inquired "scene by scene" what was missing from the familiar copies of this feature. Image then apparently went to work to obtain the lengthier edition, postponing the street date for around six months as they set about obtaining a complete print to transfer onto lasersdisc.

Although it is far superior to the prerecorded VHS tape in color and clarity (inherent in this format), as well as the heretofore unseen footage, this "widescreen" laserdisc suffers a bit from being matted; there are black bars on the top and bottom of the frame image to impart an aspect ratio here of 1.78:1, approximating that which was supposed to have been originally 1.85:1, but was achieved through some loss in the upper section of the film itself to give a letterboxed look (for example, the prominent "hair" seen during the allosaurus sequence is completely cropped out of the laser). It is likely that the true aspect ratio may have been 1.66:1 or even lower. Following its emergence, the British incarnation of *One Million Years B.C.* has quickly gained recognition and even replaced the U.S. theatrical version as the standard TV print, frequently shown on cable and satellite purveyors like American Movie Classics (AMC).

The film was extremely profitable in its initial screenings, earning around $9,000,000 in revenue worldwide within a few years, many times the roughly $1,000,000 it cost to produce; owing to the very respectable finances generated by the film, it became the most successful Hammer production.

Wishing to follow in the wake of this box office hit, Hammer explored the possibility of remaking the 1933 classic *King Kong*, again employing the talents of Harryhausen for the dimensional animation effects. Ray was personally somewhat ambivalent about the prospect of such a filmic revisitation, especially since it would have been a color feature, but decided that if there was going to be one he wanted to be the person handling the stop-motion. Sad to say, this prospective *King Kong* never got off the ground as the rights to a remake couldn't be secured; RKO at that time would only authorize a continuation of the story but not a reworking of the same. What exactly would have come out of this second Hammer-Harryhausen pairing is now of course entirely speculative, but without a doubt he would have infused great measures of loving care on the gigantic ape and dinosaurs. Unfortunately, the remake that was eventually made wasn't by Ray or even has any stop-motion therein. In the 1970s, after the copyright on the 1932 novelization of the film was inadvertently allowed to lapse into the public domain (which effectively permitted remakes to be produced), Dino De Laurentiis come out with his utterly abysmal version of *King Kong* (1976). Although the Rick Baker gorilla costume is reasonably competent, the movie is an abomination and totally dispenses with the poignancy and mythos which made the 1933 movie an all-time classic.

The profitability and success of *One Million Years B.C.* may now have seemed like a stroke of pure luck, but there are actually many elements which contributed to the great recognition this production has earned. Obviously, the copious virtues of Raquel Welch were made out to be the paragon of feminine beauty; she and handsome John Richardson represented the "beautiful people" who lived and loved countless ages before other attractive types. While all this is surely complete fiction in that early Homo sapiens were neither quite this appealing physically nor wore alluring garments or make up, the look positively captivates the senses and imagination. Perhaps it is the placement of scantily dressed youth in outdoor settings that explains such a subconscious inclination towards this material. Then there is Raquel's famous pose in a fur bikini, which has become an iconoclastic image representative of the entire 1960s. The film spawned two Hammer follow-ups and also the subgenre of women in primordial settings wardrobed in minimalistic native styles, for the benefit of the audience more than their male counterparts. Some films have even parodied *One Million Years B.C.*, like *Caveman* (1981) and *Dinosaur Valley Girls* (1997), with situations far more funny and absurd than were ever seen in their inspiration.

But from a historical perspective, the Harryhausen-animated dinosaurs and other prehistoric reptiles are every bit as important as the "cheesecake" component, even if they cannot be credited as much for the film's immediate success. Certainly, these effect sequences are leaps and bounds beyond *Animal World* of some ten years earlier, with Mesozoic creatures that are not simply designed and constructed better but also show some measure of revolutionary thinking through their gyrations. Except for the archelon, all the stop-motion monsters move about with a dynamism not seen in the previous film; the bipedal dinosaurs stride with tails held off the ground and positioned less vertically, and the flying reptiles are facilitated as active, flapping aviators instead of gliders. Reviews have been generally favorable. Leonard Maltin says this "Hammer remake of 1939 prehistoric adventure boosted fur-bikinied Welch to stardom; watchable saga with spectacular Ray Harryhausen dinosaurs...."

It seems reasonable to pin the excellence of the feature on the overall combination of multitudinous facets of production, more than merely the presence of Raquel amongst antediluvian creatures; good direction, locations and music also serve wonderfully to create a special ambience to these proceedings as well. However, the marvelous sights and sounds make the product completely sensory, as there isn't any real theme or message being imparted to the viewer, and as mentioned lacks the warmth and poignancy of *One Million B.C.* Taken at face value as it should be, *One Million Years B.C.* has precisely the right blending of parts to make it both entertaining and extraordinary.

Harryhausen's next film also features dinosaurs and is the only one made in conjunction with his longtime associate Charles Schneer. Dusting off a project Willis O'Brien was to have made about 25 years prior but failed to materialize, they went on their ninth joint production, released just several years after *One Million Years B.C.* as *The Valley of Gwangi*.

5. The Valley of Gwangi

Ray Harryhausen's final film to include dinosaurs (the only one in association with producer Charles H. Schneer) is *The Valley of Gwangi*, released in 1969 by Warner Bros.—Seven Arts. The movie's inspiration and impetus was a project begun back in 1941 by Willis O'Brien and John Speaks of Colonial Pictures. It began when Speaks, who had formed the independent film company, approached O'Brien about a possible collaborative effort which resulted in a proposed RKO feature when the jointly worked-out idea was accepted by the studio. With financing secured through RKO President George Schaefer, who gave it an impressive $552,000, the co-producers proceeded to work on their *Gwangi*, which was to have been the story of cowboys vs. dinosaurs set in the Grand Canyon of Arizona.

A group of cowboys from a traveling Wild West show ride into a remote section pursuing a herd of miniature horses (only about two feet tall) to catch one to put on display. But after tracking these small creatures and winding up in a hidden valley, they discover there are larger and more ferocious creatures inhabiting the area. A pteranodon grabs one of the men off his mount and carries him away but he is rescued by his companions, attracting the attention of Gwangi, a large allosaurus. After a series of skirmishes with this monster, a triceratops appears on the scene and does battle with Gwangi. Defeating the horned reptile in a fight to the death, it gives chase to the horsemen until a rockslide renders it unconscious. Captured, it is hauled back to civilization to be placed on exhibit in a circus. During a performance, several escaping lions assail the caged dinosaur, who breaks free in an enraged state. Soon attacking people, buildings and a bus, Gwangi makes its way out of town and is finally forced off a cliff by a truck.

Unfortunately for O'Brien, wartime constraints and a shake-up in RKO's studio executive structure brought about the cancellation of *Gwangi*, which never left the early development stages (though slightly over $50,000 was spent on it before the plug was pulled). While *Gwangi* itself failed to materialize, elements from it ended up in several subsequent features. In *Mighty Joe Young*, the ideas of cowboys roping a sizable adversary and battling with lions were used. *The Beast of Hollow Mountain* (1956), made by the Nassour brothers, is a thematically similar movie which gives Obie an on-screen credit in the title for the treatment he wrote, and whose displacement animation dinosaur model had the armature from the original puppet intended for *Gwangi*. Also, *Dinosaurus!* (1960) has a revived tyrannosaurus attacking a bus and getting pushed over a cliff by a steam shovel. It took more than two decades for O'Brien's concept to finally appear on the screen, with a large segment very faithful to what had been conceived back in the 1940s.

5. The Valley of Gwangi

Before the dissolution of this 1941–42 *Gwangi*, its principal players were cast and a Paul Sawtell score composed. The screenplay was written by Harold Lamb and Emily Barrye, based on the concept by O'Brien, who had also done a number of drawings serving to storyboard the effects scenes. In addition, some of the articles needed to create this special effects content had also been fabricated before the demise of this film project. Ray had kept in touch with his mentor since the first visit to the RKO — Culver City studios in the late 1930s, during preproduction of *War Eagles*, stopping by again while Obie was working on this proposed picture.

In Steve Archer's *Willis O'Brien: Special Effects Genius* (1993), Harryhausen recalls what he had observed of the unmade *Gwangi*: "I do not know if any footage was photographed. O'Brien had many glass paintings made during preproduction. I saw six of them in his office. Marcel Delgado had made a beautifully articulated allosaurus for the film. I remember it had a wonderful skin texture, but it had not been painted" (44). He also remembers seeing several oil paintings by Jack Shaw (who would later work as a matte artist on *Mighty Joe Young* and do background landscapes for the tabletop sets of *Animal World*) hanging in Obie's office in addition to this puppet and the Juan Larrinaga artwork on glass. There were also numerous cardboard cutouts made into miniature sets.

After *Gwangi*'s collapse in early 1942, O'Brien gave his young protégé a copy of the script and storyboards, which he filed away for many years. While rummaging through his garage, Harryhausen came across this material and brought them to the attention of Charles Schneer for consideration as a future undertaking. It took several months to locate the current owner of the property and obtain the rights; RKO had apparently sold *Gwangi* after it reverted back to the studio, following Colonial Pictures' failure to exercise an option to pick it up for the sum of $30,000. The rights to *Gwangi* were eventually sold in 1966 to Forest Park Productions, from whom Schneer purchased them soon afterwards. Paul Mandell notes in the *Starlog* publication *Dinosaur* (1993) that this took place "during a time when Harryhausen had considered revamping *War Eagles*" (70).

William E. Bast was called in to write a script for this developing production, working with Ray on the story. (Most likely it incorporates elements from the unmade *Valley of the Mist*, which probably includes the "Lope" character; additional material for the screenplay is credited to Julian More). Instead of its being a contemporary story as was the original, *The Valley of Gwangi* was pushed back to the early part of the twentieth century to avoid a clichéd ending in which the dinosaur is dispatched by military means. Many people have noticed the absence of O'Brien from the opening credits. Harryhausen has said the reason for this is that since his name had never been associated with *Gwangi*'s screenplay, Obie couldn't be given recognition for the story though it is widely known to be his. (The basic storyline and buildup within *The Valley of Gwangi* are seminal to *The Lost World* and *King Kong*.)

Set in 1912 Mexico (the year isn't precisely indicated in the film; the subtitle reads "At the turn of the Century"), the story starts out at a deliberate pace. Arriving in a small town south of the border, Tuck Kirby (James Franciscus) watches a parade promoting the Breckenridge Wild West Show that is about to open. He then befriends the small yet savvy orphan boy Lope (Curtis Arden), who is trying to hustle some money from him.

After watching a staged battle between cowboys and Indians, Tuck sees the owner of this traveling circus, Teresa Juanita (T.J.) Breckenridge (Gila Golan), performing a dive from off a high platform into a water tank on horseback. Tuck is a former lover and business partner of this attractive woman. He is met with a very cool reception by T.J. and her manager Champ Conners (Richard Carlson). It is revealed that he came to buy her trick horse Omar for rival Buffalo Bill. Not surprisingly, the opportunistic Tuck's offer is completely rebuffed.

Lope introduces Tuck to a British paleontologist who is digging for fossils in the vicinity, the cheerful and mildly eccentric Prof. Horace Bromley (Laurence Naismith). Bromley shows Tuck and

Lope an interesting find he made nearby, a track from a small creature set next to a fossilized leg bone of a humanoid. Back at the bullring, Tuck again meets up with T.J., but their conversation is suddenly interrupted when he rushes out and saves Lope from a charging bull. After treating the slightly injured Tuck, T.J. begins warming up to him and lets him in on a secret: She has obtained from Carlos dos Orsos (Gustavo Rojo) a wonderful miniature horse that is only about a foot tall and is being trained to perform. Carlos had obtained "El Diablo" in a burlap bag from his dying brother Miguel while being cursed by the blind old gypsy witch Tia Zorina (Freda Jackson) for this deed. Tuck, remembering the Professor's unique find, lets the scientist view the diminutive equine, which he recognizes as the early evolutionary ancestor called an eohippus.

Carlos becomes enraged when questioned about the tiny horse and refuses to tell Tuck or Bromley anything about its origins. Enlisting Lope, they search for and find the band of gypsies led by Tia Zorina. After refusing to tell them where the eohippus came from, Bromley slyly decides to tell Zorina its present whereabouts, knowing she will have her people steal and return the horse to its natural environment, Forbidden Valley.

Hiding nearby when the gypsies arrive at night and take El Diablo, the Professor and Lope tail the fleeing abductors. Carlos decides to put the blame on Tuck for the theft.

T.J., Champ and Carlos set out for Forbidden Valley with troupe members Rowdy (Dennis Kilbane) and Bean (Mario de Barros) in tow, also figuring that is where the gypsies are returning the miniature creature. Tuck, following them, discovers the Professor with Lope in the desert. He rebukes the paleontologist for his role in the tiny horse's abduction but agrees to join up with them nevertheless, listening to the explanation that they may discover many more eohippi at the end of the trail. Camping that night near the mysterious realm, they hear a loud flutter of wings and discover that a mule is missing, with blood-stained rocks as evidence of a vicious attack.

Tuck, Bromley and Lope meet up with T.J., Champ and the others the next day, at the site where the little equine was released. As they argue with Tuck about the robbery, the prancing pony appears before the assembled group. As they chase it around the desert, it slips through a narrow rocky crevasse and escapes for good. Champ explores this opening and discovers that if one boulder is removed, they can ride through into a valley beyond the rocks.

Pulling the stone away, they file through it and are awestruck by magnificent and unusual rock formations. Soon they encounter a pteranodon that takes Lope and carries him a short distance. Carlos wrestles the flying reptile and kills it by twisting the neck. Meanwhile, Tuck and Champ glimpse a small ornithomimus on a rock and attempt to lasso it for the show, but are cut short in their efforts as Gwangi the allosaurus steps out and grabs the fleeing dinosaur in his jaws. Tuck and Champ rejoin T.J., the injured Lope and Bromley as they retreat from the gigantic allosaur. The fascinated scientist refuses to leave the site of the pteranodon corpse so he is left to his fate. They encounter a large horned styracosaurus in a narrow ravine and flee. Gwangi finds the dead pteranodon and the Professor but is interrupted by the styracosaur, who emerges from the rocks. They roar threats at one another before each goes its own way, with Gwangi taking the slain flier in its mouth.

Tuck, T.J. and the others find refuge in a cave opening in a cliff and settle down for the evening. Lope admits that the Professor had been responsible for the eohippus's theft. Champ flares up at Carlos for his falsehood.

Making weapons out of sharpened sticks and covering up an open pit near their encampment, they all call it a night except for Tuck and T.J., who stay up and discuss a possible future together. Their conversation is cut short by a rustling sound in the darkness. It is Bromley, falling through the strewn branches and into the hole where he is discovered by the troupe.

Early the next morning, Tuck goes out to get some water and suddenly faces Gwangi when it strides out from a gorge. It chases Tuck back to the campsite and is met with spears thrown by the others. The cowboys lasso Gwangi just as the styracosaurus reappears, and the allosaurus frees itself of the lariats as the horned reptile approaches. Gwangi defeats the styracosaur after a spectacular fight and chases the band back to the crevasse leading into Forbidden Valley, killing Carlos along the way. Trying to force its way through this narrow passage, Gwangi causes a landslide that dislodges tons of rocks that knocks it unconscious.

Secured in a cart and hauled back to the Mexican town, the allosaur growls with displeasure en route. Before long they meet up with Zorina and a dwarf gypsy (Jose

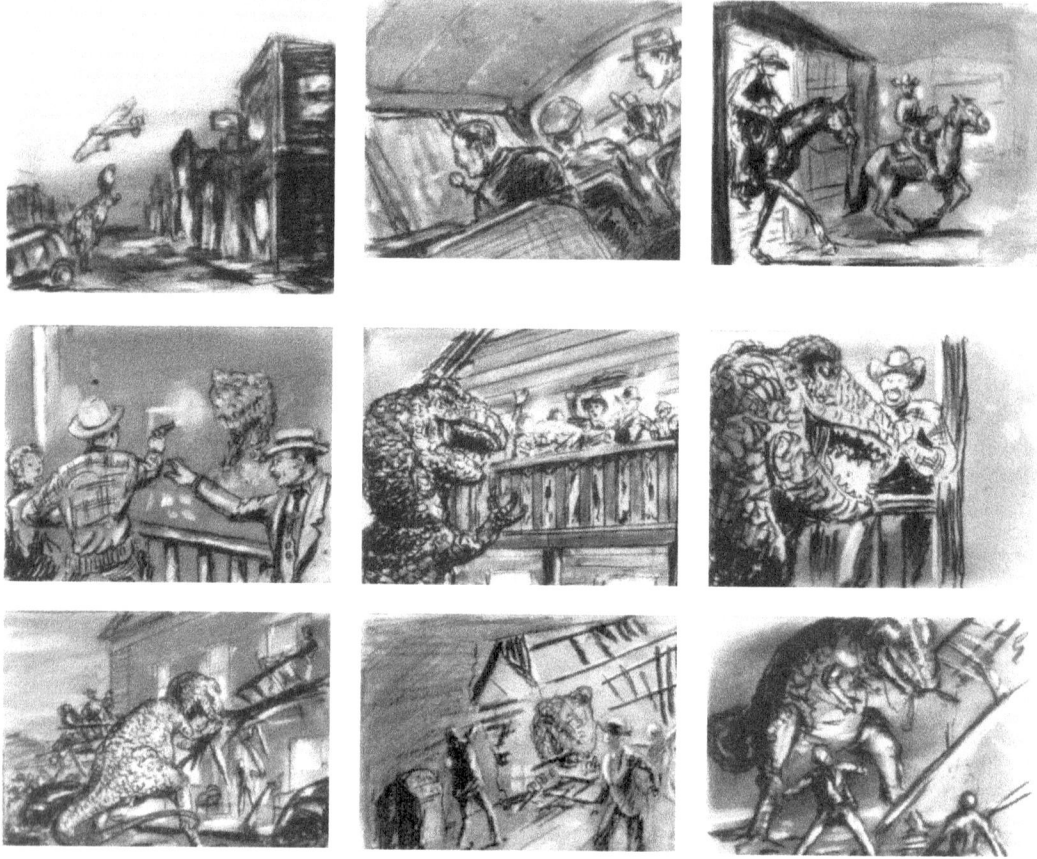

O'Brien's storyboards for the 1941–42 version of *Gwangi* showing the titular dinosaur's rampage in a town. Courtesy of Greg Kulon.

Burgos). The blind witch issues a harsh warning to all involved for taking the legendary Gwangi from its home; she is met with scorn and ridicule, especially from Prof. Bromley. However, all are surprised by her knowledge of Carlos' death. Tension starts to build between the main characters after returning to civilization. Bromley has become incensed at the thought of the dinosaur being crassly exploited in T.J.'s show instead of being used for scientific research. Tuck is shocked by the ambition expressed by T.J. now that she has a huge attraction for her struggling show, since she had talked of selling it off and raising a family.

The arena fills to capacity for the premiere of "Gwangi the Great." At the bidding of Zorina (to bring about her prophesy), the dwarf gypsy removes bolts that holds the allosaur's cage together and is killed for his efforts. When the curtain is rising and Champ is announcing the new act, Gwangi starts to push the walls of the steel pen apart, panicking the townspeople into a hasty exit from the arena. Zorina is trampled to death in the corridors and Bromley is crushed by a section of cage as he rushes toward the escaping monster. Battling and killing a circus elephant, Gwangi exits the arena and heads into town, following the running masses.

Gwangi breaks into a cathedral after nearly the whole population has fled through it, with only Tuck, T.J. and Lope left inside. The dinosaur traps T.J. and Lope under an organ loft but both are saved by Tuck. As they head for the door with Gwangi on their heels, Tuck throws a lighted brazier at the beast, starting a fire. Tipping another one over with its tail, the allosaur is now trapped inside a raging inferno. Its suffering is cut short as the structure collapses all around and it is struck by a huge chunk falling from an upper section. The principal characters and local citizenry watch in silence as the anguished shrieks of Gwangi rise over the flames and the cathedral is completely consumed.

For the first time since the latter part of the 1950s, Harryhausen rendered a film with a central animated character. The storyline is quite reminiscent of *The Beast from 20,000 Fathoms*, *It Came from Beneath the Sea* and *20 Million Miles to Earth* in that it has a "monster-on-the-loose" motif in the final scenes. Ray had abandoned this genre when shifting from B&W to color for every feature commencing with *7th Voyage of Sinbad* and only returned to it here. The star of the movie is obviously the titular allosaurus, who is first glimpsed just past the mid-point and soon dominates the proceedings in a manner paralleling *King Kong*. Gwangi is approximately 15 feet tall (the *Gwangi* pressbook states that its height is 14 feet instead) as inserted within the live-action background plate; in the outstanding book *Puppets & People* (1980) by S.S. Wilson, there are several pictures of the "monster stick" used as a reference for the actors to help visualize this creature during the principal photography stage of production.

The thick-bodied, massive allosaurus was designed with many T. rex attributes incorporated within and has been frequently mistaken as the famed Cretaceous hunter. In *The House That Hammer Built* #15 (2001), Ray says, "Gwangi was supposed to be a bigger character, sort of a Tyrannosaurus rather than an Allosaurus" (360). Even though the three-fingered hands should make it easy to distinguish from the two-fingered tyrannosaurs, it must be pointed out that *King Kong*'s T. rex sports three digits also. Another noticeable aspect of this dinosaur is the disproportionally large head. Dr. Rolf Giesen uses the term "overdimensional" to describe this comparative hugeness of the cranium. This combining of physical properties from different genera was nothing new to Harryhausen; his rhedosaurus model in *Beast* was configured as a blending of parts from unrelated saurians to make the composite monster unique but still recognizable as dinosaurian. Gwangi, therefore, isn't simply an allosaur by virtue of these additions, but in reality represents some sort of hybrid. Perhaps for this reason and to keep Gwangi enigmatic, the word "allosaurus" is not used in the dialogue to identify this creature though it appeared profusely in advertising. (For that matter, "dinosaur" is never spoken here either, just as it wasn't anytime during *Beast*.) As a result, Gwangi is described with epithets such as "big lizard," "two-ton lizard" and "living wonder of the prehistoric era," whereas the other antediluvian survivors are given more scientifically accurate names. The exception is the ornithomimus, which is called a "plucked ostrich" by Rowdy.

Characterization is of paramount importance when basing a feature around a lead that will be realized by dimensional animation. A means of defining an animated character is to construct the model on a larger scale, allowing for better texturing, additional detailing and greater fluidity of motion. This allosaurus is completely different from the *One Million Years B.C.* incarnation, with a smoother skin surface decorated with circular indentations and some sulcating of its underbelly and tail. Bigger than both of the theropods that were employed in the preceding feature film, the size of the Gwangi puppet allows it to stand up under the intense visual scrutiny resulting from numerous close-up shots during the roping and other sequences. During these cuts, it is clear that the teeth are well defined, an improvement over the peg-like dentition observed in the *One Million* bipeds. Because this robust animal is several times bigger than its counterpart which menaced the Shell Camp in *One Million*, it is a more formidable adversary. The actual model is still in existence and measures about 12 inches high in a leaning pose. If it stands fully upright, it would be significantly taller with a measurement of around 14 to 16 inches. Since there was only one Gwangi figure constructed for all the animation effects, it required regular maintenance from all the manipulation received to reposition it before the process screen, which included having the tension that decreases from repetitious handling taken up on its ball joints. Gwangi's armature was fabricated entirely new for this film.

Besides the expression of external characteristics, included through the given puppet's design, there must be internal provisions budgeted in as well to make it convincing as a living entity, especially when placed in a demanding role as the main stop-motion figure. There are over 300 animation cuts throughout *Gwangi*, a record number for a Harryhausen feature; they required nearly a year and a half to finish all its effects content. This huge amount of effects dictates the need for the allosaurus to be as realistic as possible, since it appears in a great preponderance of them. In *L'Incroyable Cinema* #5 (1971), Ray said, "*Gwangi* had to be able to snarl, bleed, blink and do many more things in front of the cameras because he was seen throughout the film" (22). It is important that major stop-motion characters, as can be observed in the Ymir and Mighty Joe Young models going through their paces, have a greater degree of individuality when compared to others with a minor presence, especially with regard to versatility of facial movements. Many of these distinguishing traits are readily observable during the roping

Frontal view of the Gwangi model. Photograph courtesy of Rolf Giesen.

sequence; the robust allosaurus is seen nictitating and effecting an angry curl of the upper lip as the lassos tighten around its neck in several close-up cuts. Levered wires attached directly to the metal armature allow for these naturalistic actions.

Sound effects also imbue the model with personality displayed through a wide range of emotions; curiosity, anger, bewilderment, pain and even fear are conveyed by the vocalizations of Gwangi during many dramatic moments in the feature. The slobbering of camels was dubbed to become the guttural noises that gurgle forth from the dinosaur, but it made a host of other sounds which serve to show its disposition at any given point. Roars that sometimes trail off into breathy hisses and a vociferous screech while in extreme distress help accomplish this characterization.

Close-up of Gwangi's head. Note the wire that can be seen where the lip is missing. Photograph courtesy of Rolf Giesen.

The animator has divulged that the gnashing of teeth often heard on the heels of a growl came courtesy of "metallic clapping like a bear trap." Combined in an almost infinite variability, these audibles convey the sophistication of the dinosaur's nature and even lend it an intelligence of sorts. But one thing this model couldn't do was breathe. Although the respiratory rhythms of both the allosaurus and ceratosaurus in *One Million* are used dramatically by Harryhausen to indicate the dying last gasps of these monsters, he didn't feel the effect was particularly noticed in his work so this puppet wasn't furnished with an air bladder. Yet there are a few seconds where the styracosaurus and circus elephant can be seen inhaling and exhaling as their life-forces ebb away, so the special effects wizard didn't completely abandon this technique. Taking all these steps is therefore critical in order to make a more rounded stop-motion thespian, necessary when in a starring role.

Infused with a plethora of identifiable traits, Gwangi is referred to by the human cast with the pronouns "he" and "him" quite frequently. Perhaps it isn't conclusive proof that this allosaurus is a male specimen (actually, a mature female would be much more massive than a full-grown male), but rather is indicative of the refinements which make it about as anthropomorphic as any dinosaur can possibly be, at least in this straightforward of a presentation anyway. While it is obviously a credit to Ray's abilities that Gwangi can emote so well, the necessity of such a high degree of characterization should be apparent with only a little bit of thought. Without any qualities for the audience to relate to, the creature becomes completely monstrous and loses any sympathetic connection, even if the plight suffered by it is basically unfair. Unlike that which is seen briefly in *One Million*, a ferocious animal with no redeeming value and whose demise is often met with applause by those watching, this allosaurus must instead meet its unavoidable fate somewhat apologetically, due to being an intrinsic element of the storyline. Without the possibility of any sentimental feelings or remorse over its passing, Gwangi would lack any depth and thus fail as the film's marquee attraction.

Even though they play only supporting roles, the other stop-motion characters in *Gwangi* nevertheless greatly enhance the visual effects by contributing their own aesthetic qualities. The first creature seen in *Gwangi* is the tiny "dawn horse" eohippus. Now known properly (if less evocatively) by the name hyracotherium, the eohippus evolved about 50 million years ago, during the early Eocene epoch, and is believed to be the ancestor of the modern horse. Extremely small by comparison to its present-day descendants, this prehistoric mammal stood only about eight inches high at the shoulder and was around two feet in length. Besides growing many times in size during the course of equine evolution, the horse has a hoof that began as a multi-toed foot, which can be plainly seen in the fossil record. One of these digits steadily increased in size over countless millennia to become the familiar pedal extremity of the present-day animal. Shown with a tawny hide covering its unmistakable horse-like attributes, the eohippus is presented here in a fairly accurate fashion though there is one piece of information passed along by Prof. Bromley that is slightly in error; he says it has three toes with "four on its hind feet," which is exactly opposite of the established four on the front foot and three on the rear.

An illicit prize carried away from Forbidden Valley, the diminutive equine exhibits some charming characteristics from the moment it is first seen in the movie. Poking its head out of a tiny stable at the cue of a playing music box, the animal emerges and trots around a small corral with graceful, measured paces and is heard to gently whinny with the appropriate softness for its bulk. This scene is almost magical to behold, with the dainty colt trotting about to these musical chimes in the fenced-in enclosure situated on a tabletop inside a dimly lit room. This animation is some of the smoothest of the film, with barely a hair disturbed in the process, and works with other aspects that greatly contribute to the effectiveness of the vignette. These include the small equine's mannerisms, through the twitching of ears and swinging head to foster a sense of awareness with its surroundings. Also, there is a miniature surface for the puppet to both cast shadows and seem in solid contact with the floor of the corral, as it moves about behind the correspondingly tiny wooden fence rails. Later on, it is rediscovered near Forbidden Valley, a lighthearted chase ensues before it escapes for good through a crack in the rock wall. The musical score accentuates this pursuing after the galloping eohippus, which gets away from T.J. by pulling the young woman off her feet with a mighty tug as it rears up on its back legs after being lassoed (the figure was supported by a wire when its front end was lifted; it also had to be so held up while running, with all feet up in mid-air) and then let go by Tuck after her angry demand that he keep his "thieving hands off" it. Interestingly, a living quadruped was used in one shot just before T.J. ropes it but is fairly hidden in the distance (prancing in between clumps of brush). In *The Dinosaur Filmography* (2002), Ray notes that a small goat served as the thrashing creature when confined in a burlap bag.

Even if this stop-motion seems second-nature, Ray was actually quite pensive when approaching these scenes for the movie; he relates in his *Film Fantasy Scrapbook* that the dread of doing these familiar equine locomotions made him put it off until last but he did achieve these scenes in only two weeks. If he had a "horse phobia," this must have cured it, for he later animated mythological creatures with a strong resemblance to the horse: the cyclopean Centaur in *Golden Voyage of Sinbad* and the winged Pegasus in *Clash of the Titans*. Of course, the inclusion of the eohippus comes from the idea that dwarf ponies were to be included in the original *Gwangi* concept, but its existing in Forbidden Valley seems somewhat incongruous, as it didn't flourish in the Mesozoic Era and therefore never inhabited the world

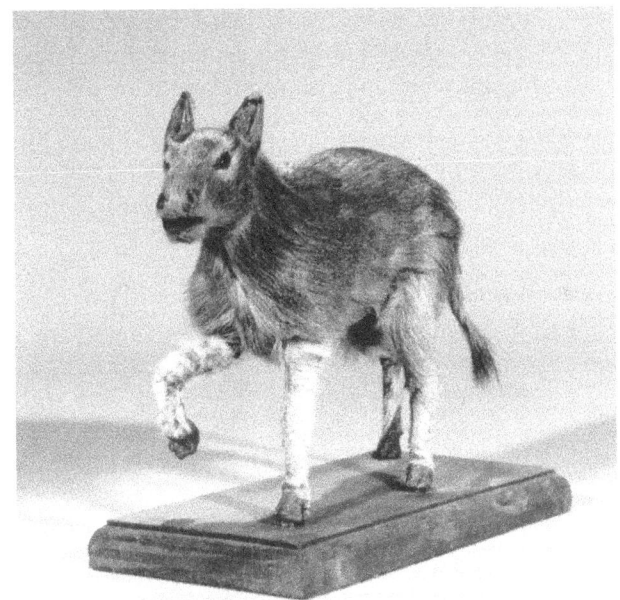

The very horse-like eohippus figure. Photograph courtesy of Rolf Giesen.

with dinosaurs. Measuring eight inches tall also, this model is remarkably close in size to the ancestral mammal, though it undeniably resembles a tiny modern horse closer than the actual forebear.

Next to show itself in the feature is the pteranodon, the first prehistoric creature seen after the troupe enters the mysterious realm beyond the narrow fissure. The same variety of crested aviator that abducted Loana in *One Million* in a memorable sequence, it appears over the heads of T.J., Prof. Bromley, Carlos and Lope. Weaving over the group while diving vertically to grab at the riders, the pteranodon finally latches onto Lope and starts flapping skyward with the boy in its clutches. Certainly, this suddenness and rapacity sounds quite familiar to those who saw Raquel Welch abducted in *One Million*. Lope is lifted with a foot gripping each shoulder and his legs dangling freely below, kicking furiously to wrench himself from the clawed grasp. Although the concept of a man being plucked from his horse by the shoulders had come from Willis O'Brien's storyboards, Harryhausen took care to see that this episode doesn't seem like a reenactment of his previous feature film.

Indeed, the entire incident is unique in its presentation and only reminds the spectator of *One Million* in that the same kind of winged monster is used again. Mark Wolf wrote in *FXRH* #4 (1974), in an article on Ray's aerial braces, that there is a difference in the effects between the two in that "The cycles of the winged creatures in *One Million Years B.C.* are basically 9 frames, the same cycle of the Harpies (although there is a fluctuation of the cycle of the Harpies). The reptile in *Gwangi*, however, uses a 12 frame cycle prior to picking up the boy, and when it gets the boy in its clutches, the movements appear to be slower, indicating more frames per cycle. This change produces the effect of the creature laboring to keep aloft with its burden" (24). To achieve this illusion, actor Curtis Arden was hoisted by a crane during live-action filming and later the pteranodon was aligned to make it seem to be responsible for this elevation. He was replaced by an animation figure only a few inches high for several long tracking shots with the flier, but remained himself in medium shots. For these live-action cuts, he was equipped with a prop resembling the lower part of the flier's body while suspended above the ground, which probably concealed the rigging connected to the harness worn under his clothes.

The pteranodon puppet used in *The Valley of Gwangi*. This model was redesigned to differ slightly from the one which appeared in *One Million Years B.C.* Photographs courtesy of Rolf Giesen.

After a brief flight, the pterosaur flutters to the ground with Lope still held in its talons. Carlo's fight with the pteranodon is well executed. The puppet was carefully matched with Gustavo Rojo frame-by-frame in long shots during the struggle, with miniature hands substituted over the actor's upon the model to impart a sense of tactile directness between the contestants. A full-size mock-up of the crested flier served for close-ups, looking reasonably like the puppet and moved with Rojo on its back in a physical effect that is at least satisfactory. With a hand on either end of the beak and crest, Carlos kills the reptilian nemesis by twisting its neck, ending this exciting encounter.

There is a slight blur of the wingtips at times throughout this vignette;

Neil Pettigrew notes in *The Stop-Motion Filmograpy: A Critical Guide to 297 Features Using Puppet Animation* (1999) that "Harryhausen achieved this by gently flicking the wings so that their natural tension would cause them to vibrate during camera exposure" (730). Its dimensions offered as that of the larger *One Million* model (approximately 13½" tall with a 28" wingspan), this pteranodon isn't actually the same one observed in the preceding feature but instead had been

Harryhausen preproduction concept showing a cowboy's abduction by the crested flying reptile.

redesigned for *Gwangi* and shows differences in color (purplish blue) and shape of the head. However, the wings retained the ubiquitous venation of a bat, inspired by the engravings of Gustave Doré (a Harryhausen trademark over the years).

Based upon an unused vignette from *One Million* and not out of the original version, the ornithomimus provides some lighter moments as the vehicle to the startling, sudden introduction of the titular character. The ornithomimus was a lightly built, bipedal creature that had both an elongated neck and legs resembling an ostrich (or a "plucked ostrich" within the film) but with relatively large hands and arms instead of wings; closely related to the gallimimus (of *Jurassic Park* fame) and struthiomimus, they typically were about six feet in height and 12 feet in length, existing along with much larger dinosaurs towards the end of the Cretaceous period. Proposed in conceptual art drawn by Ray for his earlier saurian epic, a prehistoric bird kept penned within the Shell camp was to have provided for the startling and sudden appearance of the allosaurus from behind a rock. It seems that this flightless bird was to have been a female kept for egg-laying purposes inside an enclosure and, according to the animator, escapes when Loana was going to feed it. (In his concepts it appears to be hit with a stick, apparently disciplined for some unacceptable behavior and seeming to spur it to flee). While fleeing the camp with a caveman giving chase, the huge poultry is caught not by the pursuer but instead by the allosaurus as it pounces upon its unlucky victim. While he refers to this extinct bird as a "phororachos," as was included in *Mysterious Island*, it definitely bears a likeness to the diatryma, a gigantic variety from the early Eocene. Since this sequence was ultimately cut out of *One Million*, it allowed the basic premise to be recycled into *Gwangi* to visually announce the film's main saurian character.

Observing a small two-legged dinosaur grazing on a rock, Tuck and the others decide it might be a nice attraction for the Wild West Show and pursue with lassos at the ready. Racing after the fleet-footed animal, the riders try to get close enough to toss a rope around its slender neck but, before they can effect a capture, Gwangi rushes

Harryhausen sketches for *One Million Years B.C.* (an unused vignette involving a large flightless bird). This incident was recycled into *The Valley of Gwangi* featuring an ornithomimus. Courtesy of Simon Greetham.

out from behind a rocky outcropping and snags the ornithomimus in its jaws. Convulsing and squealing in the allosaur's grasp, the hapless quarry quickly goes limp and silent, then is set down and stripped of flesh by Gwangi's razor-sharp teeth. This vignette starts out like the eohippus chase in its being a lighthearted affair, but unlike the amiable outcome in that the little horse slips away, the "ostrich mimic" meets a completely opposite fate. The suddenness of the ambush instantly destroys the cheery mood prevalent in the scenes leading up to this creature's killing.

There were two models used for this sequence, a large and a much smaller version of the ornithomimus, which is quite unusual for such a brief episode in the movie; Ray had employed more than one puppet of the Cyclops, Ymir, Pegasus and the baboon among others, but these had much larger parts. However, the depiction of the birdlike saurian from vastly differing perspectives demanded there be two of diverse scale. The larger figure allows for intense scrutiny when placed against the miniature rear-projection image for a couple of medium cuts of it running; this particular incarnation of the dinosaur is also shown grazing on a rock while spotted by Tuck and the others. To imply great distance from the camera's point of view, the smaller one was animated in front of the large process screen while being chased by the horsemen in several long shots. Although not very flexible by comparison, this version is still effective since it only needs to sprint and make broad movements while squirming in the clenched maw of the Gwangi puppet. Standing around 16 inches high, the bigger ornithomimus is fairly sizable; the little one is only a few inches tall but measures six inches in its vertical pose.

As the only dinosaur proportioned enough to be a significant threat, the styracosaurus is a very formidable challenger to the huge allosaur's implicit dominance. Related to both the triceratops and centrosaurus, though smaller than triceratops at no more than about 20 feet in length, styracosaurus was a genus that flourished during the latter part of the Cretaceous. A well-known saurian variety, it was characterized by six long spikes of bone projecting along the top

The larger ornithomimus figure as viewed at a convention. Photograph by the author.

of its frill; these developed over many millions of years from small nodules, called epoccipitals, which grace the edge of many ceratopsians' frills. Although these backward pointing horny spikes would seem to function in defense like a protective dog collar, recent scientific thinking suggests their real purpose was for sexual display and mating. Styracosaurs had a prominent nasal horn but lacked the lance-like brow horns seen in triceratops, which would have proved more than satisfactory to protect it from predatory dinosaurs if this in fact was its evolutionary purpose. While it did indeed flourish late in the last Mesozoic age, it lived several million years before Tyrannosaurus rex emerged so they were not contemporaries, in spite of numerous illustrations to that effect.

It was conceived as a triceratops in the original version, but Harryhausen converted Gwangi's primary opponent into this closely related genus since he had included a three-horned type in *One Million*; he had a penchant for avoiding repetition from a previous picture. The first sighting of the styracosaurus is in a narrow canyon. It comes into view as seen from adjacent to the hindquarters in a miniature projection set-up, stepping forward towards the cowboys and shaking its massive head as Champ fires a round with his rifle. The ceratopsian later reappears before Gwangi, foretelling their inevitable battle to come later on in the feature. More observable here than in the earlier scene, the exterior of the horned creature is relatively smooth compared to *One Million*'s triceratops, having a lateral ridge of skin running midway down the dark gray hide. Also dissimilar are the styracosaur's front legs, rotated outward to give a slightly sprawling stance, as opposed to the elephantine posture seen before.

Along with a number of medium shots throughout, these monsters are seen from

Harryhausen conceptual drawing of Gwangi's battle to the death with the styracosaurus.

across a great expanse in a pair of wonderfully pulled-back cuts, with the figures looking tiny against a giant, well-lit background image. Issuing threatening growls with their defiant gestures, the reptilian antagonists dare one another to attack. Both retreat after the brief face-off and go their separate ways for the time being. There are those who feel that the styracosaurus puppet is something of a letdown, believing its design to be uninspired when held up against Ray's pre-production sketch, but the character is at least acceptable in its role if no more than that.

An interesting bit of information about this figure is that the armature came courtesy of the aforementioned triceratops, stripped down to be recycled and fitted with a new head bearing the multi-spiked frill. Of course, many stop-motion characters are disarticulated and pieces fed into other figures, but here is one of only a few instances where a direct substitution of the metallic chassis had been made between two structurally alike models; the Ymir was changed into the second Cyclops of *7th Voyage* and the troglodyte of *Sinbad and the Eye of the Tiger* was converted into Calibos of *Clash*. About a foot and a half long, Ray's original styracosaurus in kept in London but the one on display isn't a copy from the same mold; it is a separate piece commissioned expressly for this purpose. Portrayed as an aggressive dinosaur, this creature is very worthwhile as Gwangi's major nemesis and provides the challenge to be resolved in an exciting fight.

In order to battle the stop-motion allosaurus, Harryhausen depicted the circus elephant with an articulated figure. Reenacting the familiar movements of a living organism in miniature is a very gutsy move on the part of any animator, requiring a knowledge of anatomy and physiology to grasp the structural basis of motion. Larger animals are especially troublesome, since they walk with superficial ripples and undulations of loose tissue lying beneath their epidermis. So if such a creature is rendered via dimensional animation effects, it will certainly not be 100 percent successful. Ray had previously utilized an elephant model in *20 Million Miles to Earth*, battling the Ymir as it escapes from the Rome Zoo laboratory. After the elephant rushes to attack the Venusian creature, Ray abruptly substituted a jointed manifestation of the pachyderm seen heretofore as the real thing. He had wanted to do pretty much the same in *Gwangi* but couldn't obtain an 11–foot-tall elephant necessary for the fight with the allosaur, so this performing beast is depicted completely in stop-motion. However, there was a smaller specimen in the Breckenridge Wild West Show parade earlier in the movie. A completely new model, since the one in *20 Million* had long before been dismantled to feed its armature into other puppets, the circus elephant is a pretty good facsimile of the actual animal. In *Photon* #18 (1969), Bill Warren offers praise for Ray's decision: "Harryhausen very cannily uses exclusively an animated elephant even prior to its fight with the allosaurus. This makes the actual fight more realistic for most audiences, as they will not be aware of a sharp distinction between a real and an animated elephant, as occured in *20,000,000 Miles*" (17).

The styracosaurus model on exhibit in Babelsberg, Germany. This is neither the original model nor a cast made from the same mold, but instead a separately commissioned replica. Photograph by the author.

Never really a serious threat, the pachyderm confronts Gwangi mostly out of fear and in a quite defensive manner. It trumpets nervously in scenes leading up to their conflict as it detects the presence of the captive dinosaur; since these plaintive wails sound unnatural, it erodes the character's believability somewhat. Some of the battle is filmed from an overhead camera angle as the two figures are repositioned inside a miniature arena floor to great effect, casting stark shadows on the stage as if from bright sunlight. Not everybody cared for this replacement with a stand-in. In *A Pictorial History of Science Fiction Films* (1975), Jeff Rovin criticizes the substitution: "It is strange that the battle between the Ymir and the elephant in *Twenty Million Miles to Earth* far surpasses a similar sequence in Harryhausen's 1969 film, *Valley of Gwangi*, wherein an elephant is engaged in combat by an allosaurus. The elephant in *Valley of Gwangi* is far from realistic—one of the flaws that haunts that film" (239). Rovin's point has some validity but condemns the artificial pachyderm too thoroughly since it does very much resemble and move about like one in a show. Perhaps Ray didn't succeed here to the degree he had with the eohippus or even the archelon of *One Million*, extinct genera which bear a strong similarity to modern-day analogs and thus would have more recognizable gaits. But all in all, the animation of the tusked performer indeed proves acceptable even though it admittedly wouldn't fool even a young child. Nearly a foot tall at the shoulder, the model must be convincing enough in its outward expression, since some local TV station airings edit the fight for its perceived "cruelty to animals" in the elephant's brutal slaying.

Thrust onto the screen right at the midpoint of the picture, Gwangi instantly becomes the focus of attention and remains so for the duration of this drama. So it is important that the introductory scenes quickly establish its behavioral complexity, qualities hinted at (and actually expected) from the very first spoken lines. After the sudden snaring of the ornithomimus in its teeth halfway into the film, the robust allosaur dominates everything taking place from there on, like the giant gorilla after its heralded debut in *King Kong*. Bolting down pieces off the slain bird-like reptile, the sight of this enormous bipedal carnivore prompts Tuck, Champ and Rowdy to turn back but Rowdy stops and fires two rounds at Gwangi, who until now had been oblivious to their presence. Grunting loudly, the surprised dinosaur shifts its weight when spotting the horseman, who is puzzled that his rifle doesn't appear to be inflicting any injury upon the target (Rowdy is unaware that his weapon is loaded with blanks); he rides off in a hurry as it now rushes forward to catch another meal. This interrupted feasting on the ornithomimus quickly helps to develop the character of Gwangi; reacting to the report of the rifle by trying to determine the direction the loud noise came from by cocking its head, the allosaur displays a marked alertness to the aural stimulus. It also expresses a reflexive response as it notices Rowdy by simultaneously leaning over and vocally snapping at him, further defining the sophistication of this creature. Ray also tweaks the credibility here by having his allosaurus puppet in shade to match the rock's shadow, then step forward into bright light.

Carlos mutters "Gwangi" as he identifies the legendary creature. Soon the whole group reunites at the point when the pteranodon was killed and decide to depart before the oncoming allosaurus arrives. But Bromley would rather stay and examine the carcass. Right after leaving him behind, the professor sees the reason for their haste as the monster bursts into view; he seeks refuge in a nearby rock cavity. The allosaur arrives and discovers the dead created reptile, standing over this bounty while growling and swaying its huge cranium. Tripping over some stones at the shelter's entrance, Bromley accidentally makes himself known to the dinosaur, who stalks over and snaps at the cowering man just as the styracosaurus approaches. After an exchange of boisterous growls, both back away and soon disappear. Gwangi picks up the pterosaur in its teeth and struts off.

These scenes further augment the character of the central saurian, demonstrating to the audience that it is more an intelligent animal than an overgrown lizard, insofar as a dinosaur can be considered to be able to reason. When it gazes at the flying reptile's body with lateral head movements and growling, which includes nudging with the tip of its nose and mouthing this potential food source during the examination, there is the unmistakable feeling that a thought process is going on. Accompanied with a thumping of the tail when situated by the carcass, seemingly agitated in sensing there is something lurking nearby, these nuances give the vital characterization needed to individualize a non-anthropomorphic figure in such a primary role. Although the stop-motion here is fairly straightforward, a couple of things are worthy of note. A sharp eye can perceive that Harryhausen reused a clip of Gwangi next to the dead flier after returning to this particular location following its encountering the styracosaur (a bit disguised by being split into two cuts the second time around); he had done this in *One Million* while the ceratosaurus and triceratops battle, as seen from the fissure, the rhedosaurus behind the electrified barricade in *Beast* and other films. Actually, the earlier insertion is the repeated shot, as the model is slightly out of place compared to those immediately before and after. There is nothing wrong with this cost-saving device as long at it doesn't call attention to itself, as is the case in *The Giant Behemoth* (1959).

Also, the allosaurus puppet's joints had enough tensile strength to hold up both the ornithomimus and the pteranodon without fear of slippage, so there was no need for wires to assist in their support.

The centerpiece of the production, the roping sequence and subsequent fight with the styracosaurus, provide plenty of excitement through some truly amazing dimensional animation effects. Running about ten minutes, this segment of the movie, from Gwangi's reappearance in a gorge to when it is knocked out by falling rocks in a narrow cleft, is by far the most dynamic of the entire film with regard to the staging and execution of the creature effects. Unlike the first encounter, wherein the robust allosaur's emergence was completely a surprise, this time there is a clue something is going to happen right before it is spotted by Tuck in the canyon; his horse becomes very nervous and neighs as it senses the proximity of this prehistoric beast. A medium tracking shot shows that it is following behind Tuck after he quickly gets back on his ride and races back to the others. He tries to climb the path to their cavernous base but slips off his mount and tumbles down to end up directly beneath this elevated shelter. The allosaurus arrives and confronts the humans (armed with makeshift spears) assembled on a terrace just outside the grotto, while Tuck crouches below. Shown with a couple of Dynamation cuts seen from inside the cave, and medium (non-matte) as well as static matte rear-projection composite long shots from the outside, the vignette is thrilling since it is the first time there is direct contact between Gwangi and the human cast.

Smaller ornithomimus figure from the film in Babelsberg, Germany. Photograph by the author.

While the eyelines aren't perfect here (it is obvious at times that the actors are jabbing at thin air), there are nice touches to offset this and thus helps convince that the confrontation is really taking place. One marvelous detail is when Carlos waves a blanket to shoo it away and gets yanked off the ledge when the flapping end is seized in the allosaur's mouth. Done in live-action, with the model mated to the physical effect of the abruptly pulled bedding, it is strongly reminiscent of the harpy attack on blind Phineas in *Jason and the Argonauts* where he loses a ribbon-like piece of his attire. Also, when rushing out to save Carlos from the hostile visitor, Tuck grabs up a hurled torch and waves it frantically at his nemesis, a wonderful bit in that both man and monster interact as if they were actually together.

Throwing the burning stick at Gwangi and running, Tuck is chased by the allosaurus until scampering up a slope and hiding behind a rock shaped like a stalagmite; seeing the immediate peril Tuck is in, the others race over to where he is being pinned down. There are some long shots of Gwangi biting at the cowboy behind the stone, and a neat Dynamation cut from the viewpoint behind his shoulder of the snapping dinosaur's head seen just slightly below (the rock was matted out, as its snout disappears behind this). It is remarkably similar to the unfortunate sailor in *King Kong* being treed by the brontosaurus, trying to avoid the vicious jaws of this fearsome sauropod. As Gwangi wheels around, Carlos manages to get a lasso over the snout and momentarily secures the creature. Ray did very well on these shots, which shows his puppet in long shot straining against the braided line by leaning back with its upper body, perfectly matching those of the tugging horse and rider on the other end. A trio of miniature rear-projection cuts display the allosaur's toothy grimace, pulling and snarling in close-up with its mouth held closed. Lurching forward after the rope slips off, Carlos falls and hits the dirt. Tuck latches upon this opportunity and flees from the rocky knob, jumping aboard his comrade's retreating transport and takes off. Gwangi follows with a sudden burst of speed rather than heading over to Carlos, thereby saving him, and runs smack into several men on horseback. It suddenly stops and views this pack with a swiveling neck, then pivots to chase one of them who is traveling past. Here again, the allosaur's intellectual capacity is expressed during these gyrations, reinforcing its portrayal as a creature with at least some ability to reason. The shifting of attention among the swarming humans tacitly suggests that a calculatory procedure results from its sensory input. Taken together, these scenes are rendered quite well, with only a slight mismatch in color to belie the use of floor inlays beneath his animated figure.

Running after one of the cowboys, Gwangi turns about as Tuck ensnares its foot with his lariat. Toppled over by a heave on the rope, the allosaurus struggles with one leg immobilized and receives another lasso over its head. But soon the foot lariat slips off, and the other line is let go as the saurian stands upright. A couple of pulled-in shots completely in miniature details the rope encircling Gwangi's foot and the subsequent slipping from it. In *Jason*, Harryhausen used animated prosthetics to magnify Talos' hand and foot for dramatic purposes, but the one in these cuts belongs to the model seen throughout (the tie-down hole on the bottom can be detected, though it appears an attempt was made to cover it up). The rest of this segment is shown in several long shots, with the lower body contorting to get free. Getting back on its feet, the allosaurus plucks the lariat off and roars triumphantly; Rowdy comes and tosses another around its neck but is slapped from his mount with a powerful swish of the tail. Throwing dust at the oncoming carnivore, the cowboy is saved by Champ taking up the slack after picking up the loose end of rope. Tuck rides up and flings his lasso around its neck, then Bean gets a line on it also; so now there are three ropes around Gwangi's throat. A sudden tug from the reptile knocks Bean off his horse, and T.J. rides up to retrieve the unmanned rope in an alert reaction to this. Rowdy flings a fourth line over its head and secures the thrashing dinosaur, but only for a short time. These scenes are extremely well-staged and provide plenty of thrills; edited briskly and with a musical accompaniment that blends perfectly with its high adventure mood, the sequence is a great synergy of stop-motion and live-action elements. All the shots of the braided loops falling around Gwangi's neck were done with a miniature rear-projection image behind the puppet and stop-motion wires as the restraints.

5. *The Valley of Gwangi*

Storyboards for the 1941–42 *Gwangi* depicting cowboys' encounter with the huge allosaurus. Courtesy of Greg Kulon.

Of course, there is the danger of appearing repetitious in doing a series of similar shots but Ray manages to keep things fresh through a variety of camera angles and movements. Along with a range of facial expressions, the model is shown from both a medium low-angle view showing the upper half of its body (a frightening visage from the troupe's point of view) and only from the neck up. Even the lariats themselves drop over the allosaur's neck in differing ways; Bean's wraps around with a slinging motion and is unlike the other ones which more or less fall over the head. The animation in these close-up shots is uniformly smooth, with the wire lassos moving like actual hemp cord. Throughout are long shots that feature the jointed figure in the midst of the cowboys, tethered by lines running among them. During the principal photography, a Jeep with a 15-foot pole attached stood in for the titular allosaurus and was roped by the actors in this footage (a sharp eye can spot a tire track in the ground during these frolics). Just how was the vehicle hidden when the model was inserted into the frame? This was achieved by the use of the optical printer to meld separately shot left and right halves of the frame image together, removing the Jeep but leaving the horsemen and lariats intact. Ray then animated the Gwangi puppet in front of this modified film, carefully aligning the wires to the stretched lines remaining in the rear screen projection. When the styracosaurus encroaches upon their attempt to subdue it, the tied-up dinosaur becomes quite aroused at the sight of its foe and begins wildly exerting against the bonds. As the ceratopsian gets closer, the allosaurus begins to slash the ropes with its teeth while careening to remove these restraints running from all sides. Again, Harryhausen excelled by clearly demonstrating the enraged condition through the leering mouth and growing hostility as this mortal enemy is now coming straight towards it. He has indicated the roping sequence took five months to complete, and the results show it was time well spent.

As the styracosaur reappears in front of Carlos, it lets out a roar and proceeds towards him and the others who are busily trying to tie down the allosaur. In close up, the horned dinosaur approaches over a miniature stage and rustles a small bush as its legs swipe over the top, a nice touch to enhance the sense of realism. Following Carlos when he retreats to the raised area in front of the cave, the shuffling styracosaurus attacks from below by rearing up at the ledge. These were rendered both by several long shots, with one of them including a floor inlay in place where the creature contacts the area underneath the rocky porch. There are also two medium shots from the interior like Gwangi was seen earlier, as its beaked snout snaps upward while the cowboy waves a burning brand in self-defense. The styracosaurus backs down when the fire stick is thrown into brush. It ignores the burning vegetation and fixes upon the lashed dinosaur in the distance, pawing the ground like a bull and proceeding straight ahead towards the adversary. Done as a small refinement to the quadrupedal saurian's character, the foot-scraping indicates an aggressive temperament and willingness to charge, which was seen in *The Animal World*'s triceratops.

After stopping in front of the allosaurus while it frantically bites the ropes away, the ceratopsian goes forward to engage its adversary. Circling each other, the theropod lunges and is repelled by the spiked reptile, then rushes over and pins it with teeth sunk into the back. This cut was achieved with miniature projection and shows the bite being inflicted from the perspective of only a few feet away. As the battle progresses, Gwangi partially upends the styracosaur by clamping onto its hind leg, then latches onto the nasal horn in its vise-like jaws, with a gut-wrenching noise of enamel scratching into the horny sheath. Thwarting this advance, the tide now turns in favor of the horned dinosaur when it flips the biped backwards to the ground and proceeds to gore its supine enemy; the allosaurus is also lifted skyward, after getting back onto its feet, by the formidable nose horn of the oncoming ceratopsian. Again, the sound effects demonstrate the extreme anguish suffered here by Gwangi with high-pitched shrieks.

Ray's dynamic rendering of Gwangi leaping at a horseman who is riding away furiously.

To do this hoisting into the air, the model was wire-supported and held suspended by such means at spike's end. Just when the battle is starting to shift in favor of its two-legged adversary, Carlos grabs a spear and drives into the side of the styracosaurus. Harryhausen created a wondrous visual when it is impaled in the midst of combat by closely connecting man and monster in a shot. During the live-action filming, a real lance was thrust into what the animator remembers to be a bale of hay at the appropriate height to serve as a backstop, with the puppet carefully posed much later to make the sharpened stick seem to enter its flank. A miniature spear replaces it in the next animation cut, working loose and dropping to the ground next to the grappling dinosaurs. For the rest of the conflict, it is obvious the styracosaur is being overwhelmed by Gwangi's relentless onslaught, which is characterized by its frantic working of the mouth and nervous flicking of the tail.

The roping sequence is a highlight of *The Valley of Gwangi*. It took Harryhausen five months to achieve this sequence in the film.

Finally, as the humans flee past on their horses, the writhing dinosaur squeals as the allosaurus begins devouring it, bolting down chunks of flesh in single gulps; this cruel action illustrates the terrible price of defeat in the saurian world. Although Ray had largely moved away from the use of air bladders, the bloody ceratopsian is obviously breathing as the victor moves away, but it should be remembered that there was one within the previous manifestation of this figure so it therefore would have already been in place. Ray keeps this vignette from becoming a rehash of *One Million* through differing parries and thrusts, though unavoidably there is a degree of similarity to the ceratosaurus-triceratops fight. Spliced together with brief cuts for a frenzied feeling, and with participants more equally matched in size this time, the bout is an exciting culmination of the foreshadowed aggression and is dramatically worthy following on the heels of the roping sequence.

Riding furiously to distance themselves from the allosaur, the group makes a beeline for the portal to escape Forbidden Valley. Carlos lags behind the others and actually seems to wait for Gwangi to approach, keeping a large, flat rock between them until it comes precariously close, then racing off as the dinosaur takes several seconds to navigate around the obstacle. However, this delay proves fatal to Carlos and thereby fulfills a prophecy made by Tia Zorina in the opening sequence. The legendary monster catches him and yanks him clear off his horse, then picks up the screaming human in its dagger-like teeth. To realize this wonderful interaction, a stuntman was pulled abruptly off his mount when a wire running to his harness stretched tight formed the live element, to be mated with the model to make it seem responsible for this action. A miniature figure of Carlos was substituted when held in the puppet's mouth, as was the case with Lope being carried off by the pteranodon.

Gwangi gets to the narrow gap and tries to squeeze through while the others watch anxiously on the opposite side, in several static matte rear-projection composite cuts. After breaking through but being clobbered by falling boulders from above, it lies before them in an unconscious state. To lash the mouth shut, a mock-up of the head served for the purpose of having actor James Franciscus wrap a rope around it in closeup; the prop is adequate in both looks and function, like the preceding flying reptile, with a blinking eyelid to heighten the realism.

Gwangi's fight with the styracosaurus is a very dramatic stop-motion episode as realized by Harryhausen.

Subsequently, the massive allosaur is towed back to town in a horse-drawn cart, lashed to the side rails by thick braided cords. The stop-motion of Gwangi confined within the carriage is pretty decent, with the beast making its displeasure known throughout by not going quietly. The next time the creature is seen is within a steel cage. Shown in long shots after the curtain goes up, it is amazing to see the allosaurus animated within such a miniature (this pen was actually an enclosed circle and not two distinct pieces "joined" by the camera's perspective). In the *Stop-Motion Filmography*, Neil Pettigrew mulls over the possibilities: "He may have manipulated the puppet from below, reaching up into the cage; or it may be that the rear of the cage was part of the live-action set, allowing him to access the puppet from behind; or it may be that he removed and replaced the front part of the cage for each frame of film. The last of these is the most likely" (741). But his last statement doesn't appear valid because the escaping dinosaur pushes the front panel of the enclosure ajar. Could it have been easily replaced frame by frame? To facilitate this seemingly enigmatic set-up, Harryhausen combined the cage with the platform upon which it seems to rest with static matte rear-projection composites. Ray accessed the model from the area below it, as the cage was designed with a false floor. He sat beneath the staging area and removed the bottom to animate Gwangi, then replaced it with the model for each exposure in such a precise way that it didn't give away this dropping out of the floor. The cage floor was visible in earlier interior shots when the captive allosaur is viewed by the dwarf gypsy; the cage is not shown as a whole and only a partial section was certainly employed for these cuts. (The bars in the foreground would have likely been painted on a sheet of glass or otherwise superimposed over this miniature set through a matte.)

Some other noteworthy aspects of the premiere of "Gwangi the Great" include the animated elephant's performance. Ray has the pachyderm stand on its head at the handler's cue in a nice bit. Another one is the killing of the small gypsy in the allosaur's maw, done as before with a jointed version of the person (but this is obviously a different figure than was used before). This sequence imparts the feeling that something terrible is about to occur; the sight of the pins being removed from the cage panel and the loud protests of the circus elephant foretell that there is a catastrophe brewing.

Pushing against the loose panel, Gwangi begins to make its escape in front of a packed arena and causes mass hysteria as many hundreds run towards the corridors leading outside. Here again, the barrage of quick cuts of the star attraction freeing itself interspersed with the fleeing masses both inside and outside the bullring accentuates the panic and disorder of the crowd. This seems to actually play out longer than in real time, similar to the Odessa steps sequence in the classic silent film *The Battleship Potemkin* (1925), since most of the main characters are included at points amongst the shots of escaping local residents. Finally pushing the loose steel grating far enough out so that it falls to the arena floor (and right on top of Bromley), the allosaur leaps quite dramatically and lands on the ground, facing the approaching elephant. The cuts of Gwangi just before attaining its freedom, butting against the enclosure panel as Prof. Bromley rushes over without regard for his own safety, shows only the extreme edge of the pen and platform so this would have avoided the previous difficulties. For the dynamic jump off the platform, the puppet was obviously wire-supported.

Gwangi sets upon the somewhat reluctant pachyderm and is clearly too much for the lumbering mammal. Besides the interesting mid-air perspective above these fighting creatures, there are also several long and medium shots showcasing the vicious dinosaurian offensive and its bloody, overmatched recipient. Constantly biting the weakened circus performer, the allosaurus clamps upon its throat to administer the coup de grace. Letting out a feeble trumpet and then going limp on its side, it succumbs to the attacking allosaurus, who roars with a loud flourish with a foot upon the mortally wounded elephant that is still breathing but otherwise not moving, like its counterpart in *20 Million*. These shots of the circus animal's final defeat were static matte rear-projection composites, looking out into the central area from just inside one of the corridors.

Rushing after the last of the fleeing patrons, Gwangi grabs a man just outside the facility; this is a slightly macabre image, with the hapless human lifted up to be seen under a "Gwangi the Great" banner across the road. Setting down the puppet at its feet (probably the "Carlos" figure in different garb), the rampaging saurian heads towards the heart of civilization.

The next sighting is at the vaulted archway leading into the center of town. Stopping in front of the portal and snapping at something (small birds can be seen in the rear screen image), the dinosaur enters through this stone structure. Met by Tuck, T.J., Champ and the others brandishing rifles with real bullets, it faces those who were present in Forbidden Valley. Some aspects of this plaza area encounter are well conceived by Harryhausen. For example, Gwangi becomes quite agitated as depicted by the swiping of his tail along the ground (this is matched to an abrasive sound of leathery flesh scraping along the hard surface when he focuses on Tuck, who has fallen off his horse near the middle of the court). Another instance is where the allosaurus is closer to the front of the imposing cathedral that dominates the plaza. Feeling the sting of flying lead, the marauding saurian winces while being shot. This takes place with the shadow from the roofline of a building falling across the prehistoric beast. To further increase the realism, this shadow moves up and down in harmony with its taking strides forward and back, corresponding to the shaded location within the background plate.

Although one could quibble that Ray didn't have his puppet throw a shadow in kind beyond the roof's edge on the ground, this definitely helps to make it seem to really be involved in the scene. Also, as the allosaur pursues the receding mass of humanity towards the sanctuary, it stands at the base of the stairway up to the doors when a couple of people tumble down the steps close by. Here is additional reinforcement of the premise that the titular dinosaur can reason somewhat, as it obviously shifts its focus between this pair and the greater number racing up the stairs of the edifice.

The circus elephant is no match for Gwangi's slashing teeth.

Standing outside the doors of the cathedral, Gwangi is prevented from entering momentarily when Tuck and some locals barricade this portal while it presses hard from the outside. The scene is extremely reminiscent of and unequivocally inspired by *King Kong*'s mighty gorilla forcing its way through the colossal entrance into the native village. Gwangi is partially visible between the ajar doors, looking out from behind the men straining to fully close them, oscillating in its efforts to get through. When viewed from the exterior, it is perched upon the stairs running up to the entry. The top several steps were actually a floor inlay beneath the model in this Dynamation composite, used to further augment the look of realism in these cuts. Soon the massive allosaurus uses its superior size and strength to shove open the doors and strides into the sanctuary after the last of the retreating crowd. Now within this medieval structure, the specter of a (presumed) long extinct creature juxtaposed with the barely illuminated Gothic edifice evokes an eerie reaction to these scenes. A dinosaur strutting about to the sounds of its fleshy footpads slapping the stone floor while issuing throaty gurgles, reverberating throughout the cavernous walls, helps concoct a quite haunting mood to this unusual situation.

There are many fine components to the film's denouement. One of these is a marvelous Dynamation cut in which Gwangi walks into the frame and passes behind a support column of the cathedral as Tuck quickly slides around to the opposite side to avoid detection. Mike Natale took it to task in his thorough effects critique of *Gwangi* in *FXRH* #1 (1970): "The only flaw that I can think of in this sequence (up to the fire) is found in one shot in which Franciscus ducks behind a pillar (toward the camera) to hide from Gwangi, the outline of the edge of the pillar 'ghosts' over Franciscus' body as he passes the pillar" (19–20). This is an artifact of the Dynamation process from having the column masked out when photographing the model, then exposing in another pass through the camera; the "ghosting" he describes happens when Tuck crosses from one element of the composite image into the other.

Another wonderful shot is the allosaur's fight with Franciscus at the organ loft. Much like the impaling of the *One Million* allosaurus, an unbroken connection can be made from the clamped jaws of the title character holding a spear tip and Franciscus at the other end trying not to let go. Harryhausen precisely aligned the figure's mouth with the real flagged weapon in his hands to craft a seamless effect. Following this brief tug-of-war, the pointed end of the flagstaff slips out of the allosaur's clenched jaws, sending Tuck backwards onto the pipe organ. Startled by a loud blast from the instrument, Gwangi backs off, a nice bit of characterization expertly pulled off to show emotion in the reptilian star. The flag becomes a miniature when hurled into the head of the dinosaur, who growls in pain while pawing at this protruding projectile that leaves a bloody wound.

The fiery climax inside this great sanctuary features colorful and dazzling visuals that send a chill down the viewer's spine. Substituting a stage with miniature pews trampled by the anguished monster to increase the feeling of authenticity, these composites were most likely created by Ray himself, through an in-camera method that double-printed flames around its feet via the process screen. The fire had originated from the brazier hurled by Tuck at the oncoming dinosaur, forming part of the barrier that leads to its immolation. Together with the raging inferno seen behind the puppet in the rear-projection image, started when Gwangi tips over another brazier with its tail, this blocks any escape by completely surrounding the allosaur in a curtain of fire. As Gwangi screams shrilly in torment at the ceiling, a stained glass window explodes from the heat just above its head, and non-animated miniature pieces of the edifice drop from high above. Several exterior shots of the burning cathedral sandwich a miniature upper layer over the real bottom of the building (a split probably made with the optical printer); although they don't perfectly match up, the combination is quite satisfactory. Gwangi's suffering is mercifully cut short when falling chunks of the structure kill it, with rigged prop debris done in stop-motion.

By having it meet a painful end, Harryhausen definitely succeeds in giving a touch of pathos to his dinosaur lead. While the searing fate might seem too cruel, this extreme demise is necessary to both evoke pity and highlight the unfairness of its plight. Like King Kong and the Ymir, it dies after being transported by Man to completely unfamiliar surroundings and so is a "victim of circumstance." If its passing does not garner any feelings of sympathy, Gwangi would utterly fail as a tragic hero and largely defeat the purpose of even being in the movie's central role.

Other types of effects also vastly contribute to the wonderful sights within the feature. Matte painting on glass is a relatively inexpensive means of extending and enhancing a real landscape into something more fantastic (obviously much more economical than constructing full-scale sets). Ray made plenty of use of this methodology in previous films. The treasure trove inside the base of Talos' pedestal seen in *Jason and the Argonauts* and the *King Kong*–inspired log bridge in *Mysterious Island* are striking examples of this artistry. There is only one matte painting in *Gwangi*, the incredible vista seen by several of the group entering Forbidden Valley. An extremely large archway in an eroded rock formation looms in the distance, with several towering pinnacles much further beyond the vaulted structure. Traveling matte, explained in the *One Million* section, is a type of optical shot used primarily to place an actor or actors over the animation plate (film used for the background plate which was made through the Dynamation process) by having them perform in front of a blue screen and then striking a series of mattes and counter-mattes from this performance to create spaces that correspond exactly frame by frame with the outline of the actor(s) to allow their images from before the blue screen to perfectly occupy each of these "slots." In the perfect fit manner a key is precisely matched to the lock it can open, this "keyhole" is an area matted out on the background plate (lock) to allow the actor(s) image (key) to fill this gap when it is printed.

There are relatively few of these composite shots to be found in *Gwangi* but those employed here are very effective. It was used for the shot where Carlos is circling around in front of the allosaurus with lariat in hand to save Tuck, who is cowering behind the rock. The riders on their bucking mounts are superimposed over the battling Gwangi and styracosaurus in one cut, and some extras scramble over the lower body of the allosaur as it exits the arena through a tunnel with low clearance, crouching in the miniature set as it snaps at the people flitting just ahead. A highly evocative scene is the titular dinosaur forcing its way through the cathedral doors as Tuck and several locals are straining on keep them closed on the other side. The dimensional animation of the shifting allosaurus is inserted into the open space of this entrance. Even the nighttime shots of Tuck and Bromley gazing toward the mountainous peaks ringing Forbidden Valley include the use of traveling matte.

Harryhausen made use of a transparent color wheel to create a flickering effect upon his Gwangi puppet during the conflagration at the end of the picture. When a beam is shined through, it will filter this light, illuminating the model in different hues when this disc is rotated between exposures. Probably best remembered during the climactic encounter with Medusa in *Clash of the Titans* as she prowls around her subterranean lair, it rendered a fire-lit countenance of the allosaurus while thrashing about in the inferno. The same type of flashing was utilized in the live-action filming of those assembled to watch the magnificent structure being destroyed by flames. It represents the brilliance of the holocaust as seen shimmering upon the faces of those gathered around. To combine the large "Gwangi" balloon with the cage in live-action, a miniature of the float was lined up with the pen to make them seem joined. This technique is a common cinematic ploy known as "forced perspective," where the camera's two-dimensional view can be strategically made to meld disparate things into a single unit or place distant objects together; it was broadly employed in *3 Worlds of Gulliver* for the effects in many scenes.

Once again responsible for sculpting the dinosaurs in a Harryhausen feature, Arthur Hayward crafted a new assortment of these prehistoric ruling reptiles that are wonderfully detailed. He never received any credit in the titles of the half-dozen films on which he collaborated with Ray, though this relationship is widely known by fans of the animator (Arthur is listed as a special effects consultant for the Hammer movie *The Lost Continent* [1968]). In particular, his Gwangi figure was crafted with great attention to external characteristics and texturing, making it perhaps the most exemplary of his creations which was turned into a stop-motion model.

Most certainly owing to this association of about ten years, Hayward seemed intrigued enough to try his own hand at dimensional animation. In the August 1969 issue of *Animals*, he relates the travails encountered in making a 20–minute educational film called *The Age of the Dinosaurs*. This article, titled "Making Fossils Live," is a personal essay describing his approach to all the essential steps of modelmaking and staging the actual frame-by-frame manipulation. As one would expect, he had few problems in sculpting and casting the figures for his short subject, but the process of filming the incremental moves to create their illusionary locomotions proved to be extremely difficult. He wrote that his first attempt went abysmally: "At last the first 50 feet of film came back. Now I would see my dinosaur walk, eat, and look around for possible enemies. The screen lit up, but the dinosaur did not walk across it with a measured stride. It slithered and jerked about all over the place, its legs and neck flying in all directions; and the trees jumped up and down together with the rest of the scenery. To anyone who had not spent uncounted hours on its production it would have been funny, but I could only weep with disappointment" (151–152). "Lightning flashes" in the finished product were the unwanted result of voltage fluctuations. Noting that his project took two years to complete and was done on a shoestring budget, Hayward gives the impression that the results justified all the experimentation and hard work.

To the average reader, there is nothing especially noteworthy about the essay, but it would raise the eyebrows of anybody aware of his affiliation with Ray; strangely, there is never a mention of the man with whom he has associated for the past decade, and the only stop-motion picture even referred to is the 1925 *Lost World*. Perhaps Arthur didn't want to implicate him in what he felt was ultimately an amateur exercise in these special effects. But even more obvious in the article are the photos of unmistakable saurian figures from Harryhausen features. There is a photograph of the *One Million* triceratops at the end of the piece, and on the cover is a two-fingered maquette or alternate version of the titular allosaurus in *Gwangi*. As it turned out, their association suddenly ended at about the time this periodical came out. Is there a connection between these events? Possibly, but Ray won't elaborate (and rightly so) upon the details of what brought about the end of their collaboration. In *Cinefantastique* Volume 31 Number 1/2 (1999), Ted Newsom pinned the blame on the *Animals* article and another article regarding Arthur: "Clearly, Hayward created duplicate models, then foolishly claimed to have 'invented' the technique of stop-motion. When Harryhausen saw the articles, he must have felt betrayed" (69). Such a conclusion is hardly proven here and even seems illogical, since the sculptor would not have been competition for Ray's wizardry and apparently didn't employ these identifiable reproductions for any animation.

But it should be noted there were other places where the familiar menagerie of prehistoric creatures can be seen besides *Animals*: in at least two British paleontology-based books with his being credited for these illustrations. If this was at the center of their parting of ways, it may have been a case of poor judgment or breach of a signed agreement rather than outright "betrayal." Whatever the actual cause, the cessation of the Harryhausen-Hayward partnership is quite lamentable, for this teaming of two talented artists helped bring to the screen many genuine-looking dinosaurs and fantastic monsters in a number of wonderful feature films.

Undeniably, the cooperative achievements of Ray and Arthur realized the finest Mesozoic reptiles to have graced any motion picture up to that time, in both *One Million* and *Gwangi*. These models remained paragons of reconstructive accuracy for many years after their release. The appearance of these prehistoric animals holds up very well with the most up-to-date interpretations. For one thing, most current depictions of dinosaurs are very lean and muscular, as opposed to the bloated, balloon-like beasts seen in *Fantasia* (1940) and many cartoon short subjects of that era; while Ray's are not exactly as trim as those currently illustrated, they much more closely resemble these than the fat-laden monsters of older cel-animated works. Not only are the puppets' visages much more agreeable with the latest knowledge, his stop-motion characterization of them also expresses some very forward thinking which has become scientifically accepted. An excellent example of this is the bipedal theropods holding their tails aloft when moving about, keeping them off the ground to counterbalance the front half of their bodies when

Cover of the *Animals* issue with the Arthur Hayward article. This version of Gwangi is somewhat different from the stop-motion puppet, (notice that it has only two digits per hand).

taking strides; although there are instances where Gwangi and the *One Million* carnosaurs drag their tails behind them, for the most part they are held high enough not to touch the terrain they walk across (implicitly, though the lower part of its body is never observed, the *One Million* brontosaurus would not have lifted its tail off the ground when ambling over the landscape, as there is clearly a trail left from it being dragged behind, running between the footprints that were observed by Tumak).

But Ray found the current perception of carnosaurs in the 1990s to be somewhat jarring, expressing he was uncomfortable with recent theories about them. In the January 27, 1998, *L.A. Life* section in the *Los Angeles Daily News*, he says, "Now scientists believe they walked with their tails up. Who knows how a dinosaur walked? I think they look a little vulgar with their tails in the air" (8). Obviously he thought this contemporary view, with backs held horizontally and their stiffened posterior appendages extending like a continuation of the spine, is a radical departure from what he had been accustomed to his entire life. Another farsighted representation, mentioned in the *One Million* section, is making the pterosaurs active fliers through the rapid flapping of their wings, as opposed to the traditional images of them gliding on thermal updrafts. Most likely they used both means to travel across the skies, but Harryhausen's vigorous flying reptiles seem better suited to fit the most recent revelations about these creatures.

Of course, a rather significant amount of his dinosaurs' dispositions lie squarely in the past school of thought. In particular, his theropods have a habit of leaning back and propping themselves up on their tails for support. This can be seen when Tumak battles the *One Million* allosaurus and also as Gwangi strains against the tightening lassos, making them seem like reptilian kangaroos of sorts. However, his dynamic interpretation of these long-extinct animals holds up very well many years later and is definitely at least intermediary between the current and older wisdoms about them. Apart from his portrayal through the actual stop-motion, Ray doesn't necessarily believe that cavemen and dinosaurs could not have existed at the same time. Indeed, this philosophy is the premise of *One Million* and even manifests itself in Bromley's fossil find, of a very ancient human tibia alongside the impression of an eohippus' foot. He takes up this viewpoint in his *Scrapbook*, noting that "New discoveries keep pushing the age of *Homo Sapiens* further back in time. It may yet be proven that man did live nearer the age of the great beasts than has been assumed all these years" (93). One could conclude that he leaves himself open to the possibility they flourished together but would need some evidence before fully embracing this idea.

James Franciscus has the starring role in a cast of generally good actors. Born in Clayton, Missouri, in 1934, and later a Yale graduate, he worked primarily in TV during the early part of the 1960s and was the original choice for the lead role in *Dr. Kildare* which went to Richard Chamberlain. He appeared in a number of features during this era including *Marooned* (1969), *Beneath the Planet of the Apes* (1970) and *Hell Boats* (1970). James returned to the small screen in *Longstreet*, a 1971 series about a New Orleans insurance investigator turned detective after being blinded by a blast. Franciscus was also featured in the TV movie *The 500 Pound Jerk* (1972), *The Greek Tycoon* (1978) and *When Time Ran Out* (1980). His genteel good looks, toothy grin and energetic mannerisms made him successful in many parts.

Polish-born Gila Golan, who was abandoned as a child on the streets of Krakow at the end of World War II, co-starred in *Gwangi*. She was adopted by a family and sent off to a French boarding school, but ended up being raised on a kibbutz in Ramat Hadar, Israel. A beautiful woman whose looks helped garner the Miss Israel crown and become a Miss World runner-up, she can also be seen in *Ship of Fools* (1965), *Catch As Catch Can* (1967) and *Our Man Flint* (1965), with her real first name for the character. ("Gila Golan" was actually her stage name, adopted after the 1961 Miss Israel contest; she had been raised as "Miriam Goldenburg".) She got into the film industry after meeting Columbia Pictures executive William Cohan and his wife in London during the Miss World competition; both of them looked upon the beauty contestant as a foster daughter and would help her relocate to Hollywood. Since she had only learned English in recent years after moving to America and spoke with a conspicuous accent, all of her lines therefore had to be dubbed, which probably accounts for the fact *Gwangi* was one of her final movie appearances.

Richard Carlson was a veteran of 1950s sci-fi motion pictures like *The Magnetic Monster* (1953), and *It Came from Outer Space* (1953) and *Creature from the Black Lagoon* (1954). Suffering health problems while working on the production, his somewhat haggard look reflects the condition he was in. This was one of his last performances in a theatrical release. British character actor Laurence Naismith, a favorite of Harryhausen's who played Argo in *Jason*, had a distinguished and lengthy career. His many movies include *A Night to Remember* (1958), *Sink the Bismarck!* (1960) and *Scrooge* (1970). He made Prof. Horace Bromley an excellent supporting role with his affectionate portrayal of the mild-mannered scientist whose misdeeds never bore any malice. Freda Jackson also worked twice with Ray, later playing a Stygian Witch in *Clash*. She had previously been in *Brides of Dracula* (1960). In addition to Dennis Kilbane and Curtis Arden, several Spaniards who round out the ensemble include Gustavo Rojo, Mario de Barros and Jose Burgos. Rojo is perhaps the most notable of these, having appeared in numerous European film and TV productions (including Charles Schneer's 1969 *Land Raiders*).

This entire feature was filmed in Spain during a six-week period that likely took place in the early part of 1968 (Ray remembers that it had taken place somewhere around this period); it doubled very well for "Somewhere South of the Rio Grande" as is noted after the opening credits. It was very familiar territory for Schneer and Harryhausen; previously they shot *7th Voyage of Sinbad*, *The 3 Worlds of Gulliver* and *Mysterious Island* along the same beaches on the Costa Brava, and used the caves of Arta and other locales on the island of Majorca for *7th Voyage* and, later, *Golden Voyage*. The city of Cuenca, situated east of Madrid, is the site of the splendid medieval cathedral wherein the allosaurus stalks Tuck, T.J. and Lope. Schneer notes that this town, now home to a colony of Spanish artists, is a very historic settlement, dating back to the Middle Ages. Near Cuenca is a wonderful natural attraction which was exploited very well for *Gwangi*: Consisting of unusual wind-eroded rock formations resembling giant mushrooms (and other objects with a little imagination), the Ciudad Encantada (Enchanted City) served for the first glimpses the group marvels at upon entering Forbidden Valley. But the southern area of Spain was the most exploited part of the country, providing the preponderance of locations.

Almeria, found on the Mediterranean shoreline of the Andalucia region, was where the "plaza de toros" was rented for the arena of Gwangi's disastrous debut. Because shooting delayed the bullfighting season there for two weeks, the residents became rather upset (the bullfighting season starts around March to April in Spain, which gives the approximate period when principal photography took place). Within driving distance of

Gila Golan and James Franciscus.

Almeria were many other places used as backdrops. The *Gwangi* pressbook declares, "The forbidding Mountains of Tabernas on the southeastern tip of Spain serves as the film's fascinating setting" (2). Tabernas was the setting for countless European Westerns due to its similarity to the American Southwest. In the *Starlog* publication *Dinosaur*, Paul Mandell wrote, "A modernized script set in Mexico was developed by Bill Blast (sic), action plates were filmed in Antecuera, Spain and Harryhausen plunged into the animation" (70). Antecuera (Antequera), which lies west of Almeria in this southern tract, is likely where the roping sequence was staged with the Jeep and attached pole, as well as being the site of the troupe's cavernous shelter. No doubt there were other spots around Almeria which were utilized for their rugged features and wonderful vistas.

Jerome Moross composed and conducted the wonderful *Gwangi* score, which is comparable to others done for Schneer and Harryhausen. Moross, born in 1913 in New York, was musically gifted as a child, composing on the piano by age eight. He graduated at 18 from New York University School of Music, where during his senior year he concurrently held a Juilliard conducting fellowship. His first film credit as a composer was when he was in his mid-30s for *Close-Up* (1948), but he had already accomplished quite a bit musically; Jerome had previously written concert pieces, ballets and musicals, and worked as orchestrator on *Our Town* (1940), *The Bishop's Wife* (1947) and other '40s films. Renowned for his quintessentially American sound, through his love of folk and other indigenous styles of music, he has become especially identified with these native motifs in his film scores. It is probably best exemplified in the composition for *The Big Country* (1958), often considered one of the most famous "Western" themes and earning him an Academy Award nomination. He traces its influence to a bus trip taken from Chicago to Hollywood in the 1930s, where the awe-inspiring vistas near Albuquerque affected him in a way he likened to a religious experience. Some of his other film composing credits include *The Proud Rebel* (1958) and *The Jayhawkers!* (1959); for television he wrote music for *Have Gun Will Travel* and *Gunsmoke*, among others.

The exquisite *Gwangi* score is rich and vibrant, with the orchestrations accompanying the title sequence and journey into Forbidden Valley being perhaps the finest of all. While its bold and exuberant sounds conjure up the flavor of a sweeping Western, the softer sections are appropriate when the story slows down by imparting a melodic poignancy to the parts showcasing the love interest. Moross composed *Gwangi* along with *Rachel, Rachel* (1968) and *Hail, Hero!* (1969) in the late 1960s in order to pay cash for his apartment which was going co-op. He didn't want to take out a mortgage since composing wasn't steady work, so he called around and got three pictures in a row, with *Gwangi* the second of the lot. After scoring this trio, Moross quit the film industry since he had earned enough money for his housing and so was "through with Hollywood." Truly an American original, Jerome Moross passed away in 1983 at age 79.

Naturally, since Moross worked for the "fantastic duo," it invites people to compare his efforts to works others have composed for them, mainly the great Bernard Herrmann. Herrmann, most famous for collaborating with Alfred Hitchcock over eight movies such as *Vertigo* (1958), *North by Northwest* (1959) and *Psycho* (1960), and for others like *Citizen Kane* (1940), scored the four consecutive Schneer-Harryhausen features starting with *7th Voyage* and ending with *Jason*. Jerome and Bernard were friends ever since high school, knowing each other decades before their common bond here. In a 1979 interview by John Caps, Moross indicates that he wasn't hired by Charles Schneer specifically for his own brand of music: "No, they wanted exactly the opposite. They had done a whole series of fantasy pictures with Bernard Herrmann. Benny had done marvellous things for him but that's not my style. And I just wrote my style and he was startled. And I said, 'Well, if you wanted that other, you shouldn't have hired me'" (6). He maintained Herrmann had nothing to do with his getting to do *Gwangi*. In *Photon* #18, Bill Warren relates a critical comparison between these two fine composers: "Although I am not especially aware of music in films, Jon Berg (who is) assures me that Jerome Moross' score for *The Valley of Gwangi* was outstanding; he muttered to himself several times, 'Herrmann couldn't have done better'" (17). Available in a music CD collection of Moross' work, the score has just the right blend of adventure, drama and fantasy, and flush with enough memorable interludes to make it a masterpiece in its own right.

It is amazing to see the great degree of faithfulness Harryhausen's Forbidden Valley section in *Gwangi* has to the vignettes put forward for the unmade Willis O'Brien movie. This was his unmistakable intent when designing these sequences, for he wanted to largely preserve the 1941–42 project here as an homage to the stop-motion animator whose *King Kong* proved so pivotal to his professional calling. Many of the large charcoal preproduction sketches Ray rendered of scenes in this hidden realm are nearly exact duplicates of the storyboards Obie made some 25 years earlier. A cowboy lifted off his saddle by a pteranodon's claws, Gwangi lying prone with a loop around its foot as it flails about to stand upright, and the allosaurus leaping at the heels of a horseman going flat out are examples of this faithful reproduction. The opening credits are in fact adorned with close-up details from Ray's concepts which are heavily tinted, forming a very artistic wallpaper for the names to be placed over. However, Charles Schneer seemed somewhat less than happy about their use as titles here. In *FXRH* #4 (1974), when comparing them to *Golden Voyage*, he says that "Yes, they were poor. I guess they were done after the money ran out. I think that they even used Ray's sketches as background. Ray and I have worked out the titles for the new film — I think you'll like them" (28). It is interesting to see that his drawn bipedal dinosaur looks much more like his quintessential *One Million* allosaur than the sculpted version for the stop-motion. Harryhausen also manages to pay tribute to *Kong* as Gwangi emerges out of a canyon and scratches the side of its head like the T. rex appearing near Ann Darrow when she was stuck in a tree.

But there are also some differences between the two. As mentioned before, the triceratops becomes a styracosaur and a small ornithomimus is a new addition to the prehistoric population of the lost valley. Some of the action shots are slightly transformed when held up against the previous version of *Gwangi*; O'Brien had his allosaur fall into the covered pit in front of the cave-like campsite and the rider tumbles from his mount upon spearing the triceratops, neither of which happen in Ray's incarnation. Also, it is hauled back to civilization behind a motorized tow vehicle as opposed to the team of hitched horses seen in the realized picture.

The similarities vastly outweigh the differences, with many cuts virtually identical to those numerous drawings outlining the animation of the unmade feature. It is obvious from close examination of these storyboards where many of Harryhausen's animation cuts in the roping sequence were culled; the tail of Gwangi lashing and knocking a horse over, and a cowboy taking cover behind a jutting rock, look precisely like what had been mapped out for the one never produced. Of course, the rest of *Gwangi* is a vast departure from the earlier concept, becoming a period piece like every other film he made since *7th Voyage*. Even though his *First Men in the Moon* is actually set in modern times, most of it takes place in the Victorian era since the aged Bedford recalls that he had actually visited the Moon long before several astronauts who have just arrived there. While it is a shame the early 1940s O'Brien project dissipated during the earliest phases of production, the fact of the matter is that it would have been highly unlikely Harryhausen would have remade a film realized by his mentor, so only one version would have been in existence anyway.

Reunited with his primary producer after a one-film hiatus, *Gwangi* turned out to be the only Schneer-Harryhausen offering to have included dinosaurs in the ensemble of animated characters. Although *Mysterious Island* and *Sinbad and the Eye of the Tiger* both feature recognizable prehistoric creatures, and *20 Million*'s Ymir is partially based upon a theropodal saurian, not one of these is a bona fide "terrible lizard" of the Mesozoic Era. Out of their aggregate body of collaborations, the two men are best remembered for the *Sinbad* trilogy and the Greek mythology adaptations *Jason* and *Clash*. Charles H. Schneer is much less well-known than Ray, preferring to stay in the background and allowing his partner to bask in the limelight, though he rightfully deserves much of the credit for Harryhausen's prolific and celebrated career. Schneer, who was born in Norfolk, Virginia, and grew up in New York, served in the Signal Corps during World War II. After being briefly employed by Universal, he went over to Columbia in 1946. A mutual Army friend named Lou Eppleton contacted Ray about ann eager young producer (Schneer) who wished to talk to him about doing the effects for a movie similar to *Beast from 20,000 Fathoms*. This resulted in *It Came from Beneath the Sea*, and initiated one of the most significant associations in fantasy filmmaking, jointly responsible for a total of 12 productions over more than a quarter of a century. Both *It Came* and *Earth Vs. the Flying Saucers* were made when Charles was working at Columbia in a low-budget unit under executive producer Sam Katzman. They were made inexpensively by tapping into the studio's pool of contract players, technicians and stock music. Forming Morningside Productions in 1957 to be more in control of his future endeavors, he remained affiliated with Columbia, which allowed him greater autonomy in choosing and procuring the content of his films.

This partnership is certainly one of the biggest factors contributing to the animator's successful, heralded career; lacking such a stable environment for his artistry in which to operate relatively unfettered, Ray probably would have become a visual effects "gun for hire," plying his craft for a number of producers with wildly fluctuating results. Evidence to back up this assertion can be found in the two dinosaurian titles he made outside the aegis of Schneer, *One Million* and *Animal World*. While *One Million*'s production values compare favorably to those observed in his longtime associate's typical undertakings, the same cannot be said about the substandard quality of *Animal World*, where Ray performed but little more than the actual stop-motion. Schneer has often praised Harryhausen's professionalism and skillfulness while plugging away on their movies. Speaking in the Midwich Entertainment video *Aliens, Dragons, Monsters & Me* (1991), he opines, "It's been a great pleasure of mine to see Ray at

Harryhausen's roping sequence is very faithful to what Obie had proposed a quarter-century earlier. Courtesy of Greg Kulon.

work. That power of concentration, his area of creative design, and his ability to do what today crews of 70 or 80 men are doing is certainly unmatched in cinematic history." Demonstrative of this high regard, as well as indicating his myriad contributions in the planning and development of these productions, Harryhausen is officially credited on *Gwangi* as "Associate Producer and Creator of Visual Effects." While it is basically how he had been acknowledged for several previous color pictures, it reflects an elevation in status from the cursory "technical effects" credit given for his 1950s B&W films. Likewise, he consistently praises Schneer and their "very happy association which has lasted for over 20 years" (25), as noted in the *Film Fantasy Scrapbook*.

Critics have not been particularly kind when reviewing *Gwangi*. Most have offered considerable praise for Harryhausen's stop-motion animation but have panned most of the other facets of moviemaking comprising the completed feature film. These mixed reviews have shown some similarity; Leonard Maltin wrote, "Standard reworking of King Kong theme.... Script and production have holes, but film is sparked by Ray Harryhausen special effects." Ed Naha more thoroughly nixed it, writing in *Horrors: From Screen to Scream* (1975), "Cowboys battle monsters in the lost world of a forbidden valley. Not a bad idea, eh? No, providing the script is as good as the publicity blurbs. It's not the case here. The superficiality of the story line (if there, indeed, is one) coupled with the super-slick Ray Harryhausen dinosaur antics makes for a helter-skelter motion picture experience" (289).

Such unevenness is inherent when producing this sort of effects-laden offering, because the story has to wrap itself around and be subservient to the visuals serving as the focal points of the film. But *Gwangi* seems to play like two separate movies loosely stitched together, giving the final edit a disjointed, awkward quality. Some of this can be attributed to British director James O'Connolly. Apparently O'Connolly approached the project as he would any other, which would be fine for a more conventional picture but not one than has been carefully planned to keep the Dynamation scenes from going over budget. Ray would typically direct the scenes where the film would be used as the background plate, knowing that precise camera positions will save time and money later on in the animation studio. Jim could therefore exert little influence over much of *Gwangi*. He did work on script alterations and probably tried to put more of a personal stamp upon the dramatic components that move the plot along.

However, the result of such tailoring only makes the stop-motion more obvious since it doesn't blend too well with the live-action footage, which should serve in a complimentary role. Harryhausen has stressed how important it is for directors to understand the nature of these productions, for they are not the kind where such moviemakers can enjoy their usual expression. Noting this in Jeff Rovin's *From the Land Beyond Beyond* (1977), Ray says, "They feel that I'm taking their power away from them, which I dislike to do. I certainly don't do it purposefully. Unfortunately, we're out to make a picture, a product, and we have to work this way. Because you can use up enormous sums of money by having a director say, 'I *insist* that this camera be placed here,' whereas if he moved it and changed his concept a little bit — which wouldn't sell another ticket, if I may say so — it could make the difference between being able to do the sequence for a reasonable amount of money or a vast amount of money" (251).

The Gwangi model used for animation, on display in Babelsberg, Germany. Photograph by the author.

However, the director cannot be held liable for all the fundamental story problems in *Gwangi*. As noted, the plot portents are a secondary consideration when making a movie with fantastic elements and should function to move things along and connect the vignettes containing such wizardry. But the storyline itself has to stand up to some degree of scrutiny and seem plausible, given the suspension of disbelief necessary for the premise that is put forth. One big problem here is a lack of character development with regard to the dramatis personae of the photoplay. The "dubious" morality of Tuck Kirby is clearly stated in the opening acts upon his arrival in town, through the admonishments of T.J. Breckenridge and Champ Conners, but no negative characteristics besides his slightly arrogant attitude ever manifest themselves later on. In fact, Tuck goes out of his way to rescue Lope from the bull, put Bromley onto the rare eohippus and generally assist the other principals as he sees fit. In addition, the obligatory love interest between Tuck and T.J. is somewhat ineffective. Even though James Franciscus and Gila Golan are attractive physically, their passionate interactions don't generate much heat and even seem heavy-handed at times in spite of their genuine approach to these scenes. Their reconciliation is shown in a long shot that hardly helps the bland nature of this affair. There is also Champ, whose interest in T.J. seems to be more than playing a father figure and looking out for her best interests; his jealousy of both Tuck and Carlos is apparent when they come near her, but his underlying feelings and motivations are never dealt with in the script.

Carlos' relationship with the gypsies is poorly defined, as he is first seen searching for his brother Miguel in the introductory sequence before the credits in customary gypsy attire, but is afterwards always seen wearing more traditional cowboy clothing. Does this change in wardrobe represent his being ostracized by Tia Zorina or rather him choosing to disassociate from these nomadic people? Again, there is nothing spoken to indicate exactly how he stands with them, though there are signs he is staying some distance away. Another shortcoming is with the representation of the legendary allosaur. The aforementioned sequence, where Carlos finds his dying sibling (and a small animal struggling inside a burlap bag) provides a feeling of mystery and foreboding about "Gwangi the evil one" that is never completely attained in the remainder of the feature. There is no mythology other than a handful of veiled threats by witch Zorina, so the viewer has no further insight about the creature. Is Gwangi an individual of extreme longevity, or is it descended from a lineage of dinosaurs bearing this mantra?

Some of the situations, even though they are highly theatric, fall short from a logical standpoint. Why does Zorina want to risk hundreds of human lives by having Gwangi released in the middle of a performance? Perhaps an alternative would have been freeing the beast under cover of dark; it could still wreak plenty of havoc at night and surprise a congregation in the cathedral during a service. It also seems odd that Tuck lashes Gwangi's powerful jaws closed yet it is snapping at the riders in the following scenes while being brought to town. Wouldn't it be safer to wait until arrival to allow its mandible to open at will? The fires raging in Forbidden Valley and the cathedral burn so rapidly as to be totally unbelievable, even if accepted as contrivances necessary to advance the plot. Albeit, it might be impossible to adequately explain or elucidate upon every particular of the story, but *Gwangi*'s deficiencies in this regard are far greater than they should be.

Due to the extraordinary amount of special effects in the picture, some are not of the caliber that is expected out of the usually very competent Harryhausen. The first stop-motion shot in *Gwangi* is a trick horse diving off a 20-foot platform into a water tank; it serves the purpose of showing the mounted T.J. taking the plunge but is very rigid, probably because the model is not articulated. Another, more obvious instance where this occurs is the allosaurus trying to squeeze through the narrow crevasse serving as the boundary between the hidden valley and the outside world. Gwangi is animated inside the fissure in the normal manner, pushing hard as it becomes stuck halfway through, but then a static model is substituted as it breaks past the rocky cleft and brings tons of stone down upon it. Of course, this was done to solve the problems associated with the falling rock and flying dust along with saving time but remains a flawed visual; the lifeless rubber figure made from the same mold just doesn't pass muster, since this prop suddenly replaces the dynamic puppet. An unrealistic looking traveling matte of the troupe gazing at the comatose dinosaur further damages the effectiveness of these scenes. Also, a life-size cutout stiffly doubles as the allosaur from a great distance as this creature gets carted back to the Mexican town (a road running parallel to the caravan is barely visible in the foreground).

Although it is a high point of the film, the roping sequence does contain imperfections. Some of the real ropes can be spotted here and there in the background plate which weren't concealed by the miniature lines on the Gwangi puppet. The greatest degree of misalignment takes place in a couple of long shots near the end as the styracosaurus encroaches on the attempted capture; several glimpses of the live-action lassos going slack are visible beside the squirming allosaur. In addition, a very sharp eye can detect other artifacts in the background plate, which includes the edge of the Jeep at one point during the roping sequence and the hay used for the spearing of the styracosaurus by Carlos (seen beneath this dinosaur). Many have noticed that Gwangi has a peculiar habit of changing color, especially during this portion of the movie. It shifts between a robin's egg blue, an earthen brown and a slate gray, in a completely arbitrary manner that is often taking place with rapid succession. Jim Aupperle, who also faced this chromatic problem when making *Planet of Dinosaurs* (aka *Planet of the Dinosaurs*; 1978), offers an explanation for the anomaly. He says it stems from the color timing of the release print; this lab process is employed to correct the color shifts in the rear projected dupe shots so they match the original photography when edited together. Since the stop-motion puppet is really a separate element within the composite image, the laboratory procedure serves not only to rectify the background component but also alters the hue of the model, changing its tint towards the color correction that was used on the background.

Ray holding the original styracosaurus model from the film in his London home. Photograph courtesy of Richard Mirissis.

Bill Warren found the static matte rear-projection composites to be objectionable, stating in *Photon* #18 (1969), "Also due to poor processing, almost every effects shot is foreshadowed by the appearance of grain, or a sudden loss of resolution" (17). There are scenes where there is a big difference between animated and non-animated shots, such as when Tuck and Bromley gaze at the eohippus moving around in its corral. Also, as the pteranodon settles to the ground under the weight of Lope, the grain of the process screen is quite noticeable. However, these problems aren't really as severe as he suggests in the article. Besides the unnatural swiftness of the cathedral's destruction by fire, *Gwangi*'s finale is overblown in its interior and exterior images by the sheer magnitude of both the leaping flames and collapsing masonry. Even the very last glimpse of the dead allosaurus can be faulted, because it is now clearly unencumbered by the fallen section of edifice which killed it just a moment earlier. But all these noted shortcomings are relatively minor in an absolute sense and have to be considered along with the huge number of animation set-ups, and the alacrity required on Harryhausen's part to finish them on time and remain within the allocated cost.

Gwangi was a commercial failure upon its original release in 1969. How could such a feature not realize a profit? The answer lies mainly in a series of events that took place while it was being made. Due to earlier box office failures and a higher proposed budget,* Columbia backed away from this prospective feature. It was then picked up by the newly created Warner Bros.—Seven Arts. This merged company resulted when Jack Warner, the last of the brothers to have a stake in the studio, sold off his remaining interest in the family business to Canadian film producer and distributor Seven Arts, Ltd. Seven Arts was run by Kenneth Hyman and owned by his father Elliot, who knew that dinosaurs were a viable commodity, since Ken had been an uncredited co-producer of the successful *One Million* by way of Seven Arts' relationship with Hammer Films. However, in the time it took Schneer and Harryhausen to complete *Gwangi*, the debt-laden studio was sold for $400 million to Steven Ross' Kinney National Services, Inc., a New York–based conglomerate with holdings such as parking lots, funeral parlors and DC Comics in 1969. Showing little interest in their inherited property, the new management ignominiously dumped *Gwangi* on the market with poor advertising and distribution; it occupied the lower half of double bills with exploitative R-rated features. This seems very strange now, since it was rated G and probably missed younger viewers by being placed alongside such adult-oriented material.

Ray was naturally very unhappy about the abysmal treatment of his film and seriously considered retirement as an outcome of this ordeal. Even when first broadcast on network TV, it never debuted in prime-time but rather became a fixture on *The CBS Late Movie* during the early 1970s. There were other factors at work which also doomed *Gwangi* at the theater. In 1969, the nation was undergoing many social upheavals from the Vietnam War and changing cultural mores; these newly-discovered preferences of the public were espoused in films like *Midnight Cowboy* and *Easy Rider*, making straightforward science fiction offerings seem ineffectual and out of place. Ray believes that *Gwangi* should have been able to recoup its initial investment if a proper advertising campaign had been launched, especially with an unrecognizable word in the title (it had been filmed under the working name *The Valley Where Time Stood Still*). A "What is Gwangi?" series of ads might have tickled the curiosity of the public and helped boost receipts at the box office. This name for the allosaurus comes from a Native American term for reptile, so it is a legitimate moniker and not something that had been dreamed up by Willis O'Brien decades before. Harryhausen opines that his version was five years too late and would have done much better in the less cynical and tumultuous first half of the 1960s.

Arriving at movie theaters in June 1969 with a running time of 95 minutes and with little publicity, *Gwangi* has become a favorite of dimensional animation buffs over the years. This latter-day popularity is greatly deserved for both the quality and quantity of its visual effects. Erwin Hillier, who replaced Wilkie Cooper as cinematographer, captures the Spanish landscape very well with numerous panoramas. What really helps make it palatable is that there is never any heavy-handed "message" being foisted upon the viewer; it may have hurt the success of *Gwangi* back in 1969 but certainly the lack thereof now benefits the feature greatly.

The opus is quite underrated when compared to Ray's other, more highly touted

---

*Charles Schneer remembers the gross amount to be no more than $1.5 million; it doesn't sound like much by today's standards but 7th Voyage, for example, was made for only $650,000 a decade earlier.

Sinbad and mythological features. It is almost as good as *7th Voyage* and *Mysterious*, and is only clearly outdone by *Jason* when examined from all facets of production in a comparative manner. Expressing much the same sentiment, Bill Warren declares in *Photon* #18 that, in comparison to *7th Voyage*, "*The Valley of Gwangi* is simply a better-made movie." He adds, "I think that *The Valley of Gwangi* is the best film Ray Harryhausen has had anything to do with since *Mighty Joe Young*" (17). Some just don't seem to appreciate the virtues of this film. In *The Men Who Made the Monsters* (1996), Paul M. Jensen found little to praise and summarily dismisses it: "Owing to the mixed emotions of the climax and the rather unpleasant human characters, *The Valley of Gwangi* leaves the viewer uncomfortable. In a way, Harryhausen had created his own antiheroes, and the public did not want them" (140). In spite of scathing criticisms like this, it is still an impressive tour de force teeming with stop-motion animation that eclipses even his own *One Million*, earning a reputation as being "the" dinosaur movie for nearly a quarter of a century; not until the revolutionary computer-generated saurians of *Jurassic Park* (1993) came along did Ray finally get surpassed.

Released through Warner Home Video on VHS and laserdisc in 1991, *Gwangi* is enjoyed not only by Harryhausen fans but also those liking adventure, Western or fantasy films; the straightforward presentation mated with spellbinding stop-motion photography produces escapist fare which has broad appeal to an abundance of viewer sensibilities.

6. The 1970s and Beyond

It is safe to say that the final months of 1969 were not the best of times for Harryhausen, owing to the treatment of *Valley of Gwangi* by Warner Bros.' new management. *One Million Years B.C.* was a financial success but the last three Schneer-Harryhausen offerings were box office disappointments. In order for these men to survive in the industry, they needed a picture that would do well at the theater; it was decided to return to the formula which proved to be their greatest hit, the Arabian Nights–type fantasy found in *7th Voyage of Sinbad*. Deciding to send the famed sailor out on another adventure, Schneer was able to get the funding for this follow-up feature in 1970. Released in 1974 as *The Golden Voyage of Sinbad*, it turned out to be a very profitable movie for Columbia Pictures.

Although it has basic elements in common with *7th Voyage*, such as an ocean voyage and battles with fanciful mythological creatures, there are some significant differences. One of these is a strong infusion of mysticism and the occult, along with other intangible forces (such as telekinesis) at work which have an effect on both man and monster in the film. There is some of this in *7th Voyage* also, where Sokurah the magician casts spells to help attain his diabolical goals, but it completely predominates the proceedings in *Golden Voyage*. In fact, this feature's mood is very dark in comparison to the 1958 release and has characters, both live-action and animated, which by their outward expression alone are symbolic of Good and Evil. Another aspect of *Golden Voyage* which separates it from its predecessor is the strong presence of East Indian mythology (the preliminary title was actually *Sinbad Goes to India*). The six-armed goddess Kali, a force of destruction in Indian folklore, provides a formidable challenge for Sinbad and his men. They also have to deal with other animated monstrosities like a living wooden Figurehead and cyclopean Centaur. Filmed in Spain (as was *7th Voyage*), this subsequent Sinbad outing even revisits some of the earlier film's locations, including the caves of Arta and remote Torrentes de Paries on the island of Majorca. Directed by Gordon Hessler, *Golden Voyage* stars John Phillip Law as the legendary sailor, Caroline Munro, and Tom Baker as the splendidly sinister Koura. Miklós Rózsa composed the movie's wonderfully exotic score.

Even though it is not a saurian film in any way, there are a couple of attributes that somewhat relate to Ray's endeavors in this area. For one thing, the faraway destination of Sinbad in this movie is Lemuria, a "lost continent" which was to have served as the backdrop for an unrealized project dating back to the late 1930s. Harryhausen refers to this mythical landmass as being "pre–Atlantean," since it supposedly had flourished back even before Atlantis. Additionally, the bat-winged Homunculus (actually there were two identical specimens) is another quintessential Harryhausen creation in the Doré tradition, like the Elementals, Harpies (of *Jason and the Argonauts* but were originally envisioned for *7th Voyage*) and flapping pterosaurs. Although the diminutive being is quite effective in its role, some fans have complained that the scene where this creature is brought to life plays too much like the discovery of the newly hatched Ymir; both scamper across a tabletop in front of a much larger human. Although there is certainly a degree of validity to the comment, the dissimilarities are much greater between them than any measure of incidental likeness. The golden Gryphon (griffin), which is diametrically opposite the Centaur as a representative of Good, has the same shrill screech as is heard from the rhamphorhynchus in *One Million*.

Due to the great theatrical success of *Golden Voyage*, Columbia wanted Schneer and Harryhausen to send Sinbad on another voyage. Beginning to work on this newest adventure while the second film of the series was still in release, they proposed an even more ambitious (if somewhat less plausible) installment which again features the stalwart captain and a number of animated grotesqueries. Unlike either of the two previous productions, there are a number of recognizable prehistoric creatures present in the stop-motion ensemble. Filmed under the working title *Sinbad at the World's End*, the third Sinbad feature stars Patrick Wayne (the son of legendary actor John Wayne), Taryn Power (daughter of Tyrone Power), Margaret Whiting, Jane Seymour and Patrick Troughton (who had earlier played the blind and harpy-plagued Phineas in *Jason*). Directed by Sam Wanamaker (a Shakespearean actor-director who had been instrumental in getting the Globe Theater restored in London), this picture was released in 1977 titled *Sinbad and the Eye of the Tiger*.

The film begins with Sinbad (Wayne) arriving at the walled city of Charak, which is under curfew and suffering from an evil influence; shortly before coming here, a mysterious tragedy befell the crown prince at the moment he was being coronated as caliph. The person responsible is Zenobia (Whiting), a witch and the stepmother to the prince and his sister Princess Farah (Seymour). Zenobia had cast a spell on the prince that transformed him into a baboon, since she wants her own son to become caliph instead. Both the witch and her equally wicked child try to kill Sinbad and his men with poisoned wine and three weapon-wielding ghouls conjured up through her witchcraft. With Princess Farah and her transfigured brother aboard ship, Sinbad decides to seek out a Greek wise man who lives on the remote island of Casgar, off the coast of Phyrgia. He comes to their aid out of a sense of duty to the prince (for having previously saved his life) and for love of his sister whom he'd like to marry. However, it is decreed that the prince must be coronated within the passing of seven moons or will forever lose his right to be caliph; a voyage to discover how to get him back to human form must proceed at once.

Hearing of their plans to locate the legendary Greek, Zenobia creates a giant bronze creature possessing the head of a bull on a man's body as an assistant. This mechanical henchman, called Minaton, does the rowing chores of six men on her metallic vessel as Zenobia and son pursue Sinbad's ship. Getting to Casgar before their demonic pursuers do, Sinbad and his men head inland with Farah and the prince-baboon. They come across a magnificent pillared building carved out of solid rock and are pelted by stones thrown by men standing on high cliffs. They are saved by a pretty but aloof girl named Dione (Power), who turns out to be the daughter of the man they have been seeking, the Greek philosopher Melanthius (Troughton). By way of his telepathic progeny, Melanthius knows the captain's name and the reason they came. Examining the caged simian in his laboratory, the scientist ascertains that the baboon is indeed not a genuine anthropoid since it weeps when shown its reflection in a mirror, instead of displaying aggression.

Melanthius tells Sinbad that an ancient race of people, the Arimaspi, had knowledge which could change the prince back to human form. Found in the world's northernmost reaches (Hyperborea), they built a shrine to the four elements (earth, fire, air and water) with powers that allowed for a temperate climate in the midst of this polar region. The Greek shows Sinbad old scrolls giving directions there, a map, and a key for them to enter the Arimaspi structure if they survive the extremely perilous voyage through ice-covered seas.

While Sinbad heads north towards the Celtic Islands with Princess Farah, Melanthius and Dione, the sailor's route puzzles his malevolent pursuers. Using a magic potion to change herself into a seagull, Zenobia flies over to the craft they are following to find out. As Zenobia sneaks around in tiny human form, the prince-baboon discovers her and alerts all to her presence. Captured, placed in a jar, and interrogated by Melanthius, the witch still manages to gather some information about their expedition and escapes through the help of a wasp enlarged by a fluid in a locket she was carrying. However, after returning to her barge as a bird, there isn't enough of the potion left to completely convert her back, so as a result Zenobia permanently possesses the right foot of a seagull.

Sinbad and his passengers soon enter frigid waters full of icebergs. They see a passage in a wall of ice that would lead them straight to Hyperborea, but their ship is much too large to take it. Traveling as far through the waters as they dare push the ship, the group disembarks and goes the rest of the way on foot. Fighting bitter cold and blowing snow, they face a giant walrus that surfaces through a sheet of ice. Although the creature is quite torpid, it kills a couple of Sinbad's men before diving back through the frozen hole from which it came. They soon arrive at the mild oasis in the middle of the Arctic latitudes and observe a shimmering aurora borealis in the sky above it. They notice that the transformed prince is now becoming carnivorous; this worries Melanthius, who had warned the others that the longer he remains a baboon, the greater the chance that he will permanently adopt the behavior of such a primate.

While Princess Farah and Dione sun themselves after bathing in a stream, they are surprised by a fierce-looking troglodyte. Sinbad and his men face the monster, which turns out to be basically friendly and can be communicated with via the prince. Shown a drawing in the dirt of the portal leading to the Arimaspi shrine, the prehistoric man points the way to it. Meanwhile, Zenobia and her son find the tunnel shortcut and take it (their vessel is small enough to fit through the opening). Seemingly drawn inward by the power of the shrine, both see what appears to be human remains of the Arimaspi. Sinbad, Melanthius, Trog and the others come upon and open the huge gate leading to the pyramidal shrine. But Zenobia reaches the structure before them and, lacking a key, makes an opening through a potion and the strength of Minaton to remove a giant stone. However, the creature of bronze is crushed as the block slips and falls on top of it.

Shortly afterwards, Sinbad and company arrive and notice the gaping hole in the pyramid's side; Melanthius is stunned and warns that this breach will destroy the shrine's powers. Inside they observe the shrine itself, a towering shaft of shimmering light extending up from a vortex on top of an enormous staircase. Seeing a suspended basket attached to a chain designed for winching somebody inside into the beam, Sinbad tests this apparatus and finds it is in working order. But before the prince-baboon can be restored, Zenobia and her son confront the group. Instructing her evil offspring to slay the Greek, he is instead killed as the prince pounces on him and they both tumble down the steps, with the youth suffering a broken neck. Zenobia screams in grief, but she is forgotten as Sinbad and all those present witness the shrine's powers begin to rapidly deteriorate, and quickly set about hoisting the prince up within the basket before it completely fails. The prince changes back to his recognizable old self.

Seething, Zenobia transfers her essence into the nearby frozen guardian of the shrine, a saber-tooth tiger. Breaking free of the ice the saber-tooth attacks Trog, who has just entered the shrine, and viciously kills the caveman. The cat turns on Sinbad and his men while the others flee, killing one of the crew with a swipe of its paw. Sinbad kills the saber-tooth (and Zenobia) by impaling the feline on Minaton's weapon. All the survivors leave Hyperborea in haste as the climate quickly shifts towards one that is typical of the Arctic region. Back in Charak by the seventh moon, the prince is crowned caliph in front of Sinbad, Princess Farah, Melanthius and Dione, who are all in a happy and festive mood.

Eye of the Tiger has two unmistakable prehistoric creatures in its stop-motion cast of characters, the friendly troglodyte and the fierce saber-tooth tiger. Trog, who is much larger than a normal human being, joins up with the protagonists of the movie and helps them by pointing the way to the gate leading to the shrine and using his considerable strength to open this entryway. He also displays advanced behavioral traits, like loyalty and compassion, by coming to their aid when the saber-tooth cat threatens even though he lacks the ability to speak. By practically all aesthetic standards, the troglodyte's appearance is extremely hideous: a thick, hairy Neanderthal body type, leathery grayish skin and a large horn sprouting from the top of his head (similar to that of the *7th Voyage* Cyclops). It is a credit to Harryhausen that this repulsive early hominoid comes across as very sympathetic; his passing is a tragic occurrence.

By contrast, the saber-tooth tiger is entirely monstrous. The antagonistic feline shows all the characteristics of the genus Smilodon, a group of saber-toothed cats which flourished from about 2.5 million to 10,000 years ago. (The commonly applied term "tiger" is technically incorrect since their huge canines were flattened, unlike the rounded fangs of real tigers.) Also contributing to the very convincing performance here are its stealthful movements, twitching ears and menacing growls. Ray animated the figure carefully so that barely a single strand of its fur seems to be disturbed; he had manipulated the saber-tooth tiger model on the side away from the camera and used hairspray to minimize the visible ruffling of hair like the *One Million* allosaur. Ray even dispatches the stocky tiger the way he did that allosaur: by having it skewered in the midsection at the end of a pole. The death of this ferocious cat is dramatic due to the absence of any merciful or redeeming qualities. Even though it is designed and animated very well, one thing which noticeably detracts from the scenes of the tiger are close-ups of its face; because cats are such familiar animals to most viewers, the slightly artificial expression is magnified by these tighter shots.

Another creature in the film is identified as being prehistoric though it isn't obvi-

The models of Trog (*left*) and the saber-toothed tiger (*above*) as seen on exhibit in Babelsberg, Germany. This troglodyte is not the original one but instead a reproduction, as it was cannibalized for the Calibos figure used in *Clash of the Titans*. Photographs by the author.

ous as being anything of the sort. This organism is the huge walrus, which is given the scientific-sounding name "Walrus giganticus" by Melanthius after it slips back under the ice, but by all appearances in merely a titanic specimen of this familiar tusked variety of pinniped. Something like the archelon in *One Million*, the marine mammal poses a threat to Sinbad and his fellow adventurers simply by crossing their path. As it moves along through blowing snow, fans can certainly be reminded of the first glimpses of the rhedosaur in *Beast from 20,000 Fathoms*.

There was an authentic type of long-extinct mammal though which was proposed for *Eye of the Tiger* but never materialized in the completed feature: the horned arsinoitherium. A massive, rhino-like ungulate from the early Oligocene epoch of around 25–35 million years ago, it was the subject of an early Harryhausen sculpture and was also planned for O'Brien's unrealized *Creation* (1931). As illustrated in several of Ray's preproduction concepts this massive quadrupedal mammal, with two prominent horns jutting forward from its skull, charges at Trog and appears to defeat its two-legged adversary, but then somehow gets mired in a pool of tar or quicksand and presumably perishes there.

The movie belies the addition of components recycled from features which profoundly influenced the animator in his formative years, namely *King Kong* (1933) and *She* (1935). There isn't any doubt that the portal to the shrine, with its colossal doors and large bolt, was inspired by *Kong*. Much of the shrine's interior is taken from *She* (which also takes place in a mild area in the northern latitudes) including the shimmering light and vortex, enormous staircase and saber-tooth tiger frozen in ice (though it never comes to life in the 1935 picture). Harryhausen had earlier worked in some of the design from this personal favorite of his into *First Men in the Moon*, particularly the impressive room with many steps leading up to the throne of the Grand Lunar.

Ray's conceptual artwork for *Sinbad and the Eye of the Tiger* depicting a battle between an arsinoitherium and the troglodyte. This prehistoric rhino-like ungulate never made it into the completed film. Courtesy of Greg Kulon.

With good cause, critics have not been very favorable to *Eye of the Tiger*. Leonard Maltin opines that it has an "unusually hackneyed script (even for this kind of film), disappointing Ray Harryhausen effects, and goes on forever. For patient kids only." "Dreary" is perhaps too strong of a critical term for it, but there are definitely major problems with this third Sinbad title, which is undeniably several rungs in quality below the first two series entries. Indeed, *Eye of the Tiger* is by far the weakest color feature that was ever made by Schneer and Harryhausen, plagued with enough problems to make even the shortcomings of *Gwangi* seem trivial by comparison. Though Patrick Wayne does make an honorable attempt in the role, his portrayal of the Arabian seafarer is the least effective out of the three actors who played him in Ray's productions. As noted by Maltin, the storyline becomes trite by its overuse of names and words of a historical context, becoming a jumble of ideas rather than something following along with a fairly logical progression. Certainly, the concluding section of *Eye of the Tiger*, with Sinbad and his companions sailing past icebergs and then traversing a frozen wasteland, is a rather jarring juxtaposition of widely differing elements. The spectacle of a pyramid with an aurora borealis hovering directly above it is also quite bizarre.

Some of the stop-motion content here isn't as captivating as that found in nearly every other Harryhausen release, which only further detracts from its impact since these visual effects don't really offset the other lapses. For example, the three ghouls that rise from the fire and attack Sinbad and his men look very much like the skeleton warriors from *Jason and the Argonauts* (with mummified flesh shriveled up on their bones) and with heads very much like the Selenites of *First Men*. Also, the Minaton is a very limited character which lacks the ability to express itself (a bronze robot with immutable facial features); it is mostly seen repetitiously rowing Zenobia's vessel. The enlarged wasp fluttering about in the ship's cabin is barely memorable. Some of the other special effects here are also not quite up to snuff either; many of the film's traveling matte composites were so poorly executed that they become woefully obvious as separate elements being thrust together, and the transformation of Zenobia into a seagull is so bad that it is truly laughable. Additionally, some of the movie's scripted occurrences and dialogue don't make complete sense. If the prince-baboon retains most of his human intellect, why is there the need to confine him at the start of the voyage? Another thing is Zenobia's reaction when Minaton is crushed under the stone block: Why does she dismiss the event so matter-of-factly, since there is now no apparent means of getting home? These plot deficiencies undermine the quality of the adventure unfolding onscreen, which is already below average. Also hurting matters is the thinly disguised use of stand-ins for the main actors in a number of scenes (like at the rock city of Petra, Jordan), visible only in long shot or from behind their backs, with the genuine leads clearly having been superimposed over background plates to place them here. Finally, the music (composed by Roy Budd) is extremely nondescript. What little is actually cognitional seems more like incidental sounds rather than a legitimate accompaniment.

In spite of all the problems, a few things do shine through. Most of Harryhausen's animation is quite engaging, and (like every other picture he has labored on) it carries everything else along with it to a major extent. The realistic stop-motion effects of the baboon are so convincing that, like the *One Million* archelon, many people thought that a living specimen was used rather than a miniature moved frame-by-frame. Another high point is the pitched battle between the troglodyte and the saber-tooth tiger. An improvement upon the fight between the cyclopean Centaur and golden Gryphon of *Golden Voyage*, the action here is more intense and even crueler, with the cat mercilessly raking Trog's body with its claws and biting with sharp teeth. With respect to the non-animation constituents of the film, the performances of Troughton and Whiting stand out from the rest of the cast. Melanthius is a temperamental but basically good-natured eccentric who is a pleasure to watch, and the sinister Zenobia hams it up enough to make the character a delightful villainess. So while *Eye of the Tiger* is a comparatively substandard Sinbad adventure, there are enough appealing ingredients to save it from total disaster.

Ray never made a feature film after the 1960s which included dinosaurs, but a great number of fans don't realize that the animator actually tried to get them in some of the many projects that didn't get off the ground in the 1970s and 1980s. Some of these were continuations of his financially successful Sinbad series, with several different ideas considered as the premise for a fourth feature. Out of these, the one that seems to have progressed the furthest before its eventual abandonment was *Sinbad Goes to Mars*, which was scripted at least to a significant extent but was dropped when certain story problems couldn't be solved (the means of getting him to Mars had apparently been resolved, however). Another potential but unrealized entry in this category was *Sinbad and the Seven Wonders of the World*. Dr. Rolf Giesen indicates that there was a Sinbad project, circa the 1970s, that was to have included a styracosaurus, ceratosaurus and a fight between an unidentified dinosaur and giant snake. He adds that there are drawings in the animator's possession showing the styracosaurus attacking a camp with a man getting thrown over its back and this horned ceratopsian battling the ceratosaurus. It also seems that Harryhausen briefly considered doing his own version of *War Eagles*; in *Wonder #5* (1991), he divulges this when asked about this aborted O'Brien film of the late 1930s: "We tried to revive that project. After Charles Schneer and I made *Clash of the Titans* in 1981, we got the scripts for *War Eagles* from MGM. None of the artwork was left, unfortunately" (33).

Behind-the-scenes preparation work being done on the cast of the allosaurus model. Photograph courtesy of Rolf Giesen.

Yet another unrealized motion picture which would have included saurians was *People of the Mist*. This prospective feature was based upon the 1894 H. Rider Haggard novel of the same name. Haggard is widely credited for having practically developed the "lost race" genre throughout his collective works, which include well-known titles like *King Solomon's Mines* (1885) and *She* (1887), the latter being the basis of the 1935 film. *People of the Mist* is set in Africa, like many of his other books, and deals with a still-inhabited ancient city located deep within this mysterious continent. In *Starlog* #127 (1987), Ray gives a quick synopsis of the book: "It was an adventure story about finding a lost Greco/Egyptian civilization in Africa" (65). In the version that was going to be filmed, a number of Mesozoic reptiles were envisioned for inclusion; according to Giesen, several of these prehistoric creatures would have included a "pterodactyl," stegosaurus and plesiosaurus. Giesen further indicates that artwork rendered by Harryhausen for this unrealized undertaking depicts the "pterodactyl" carrying off a girl, an armored stegosaurus being attacked with a horse in the foreground, and a "giant statue with dinosaurs." He also relates that gigantic birds that land in a city (one of which also attacks a man) were sketched as planned key components.

People wasn't originally conceived by Harryhausen as a possible movie idea but rather brought to him by Michael Winner back in the early 1970s (this would have been made outside of the relationship with Schneer). Winner, who lives in the same Kensington neighborhood where the animator makes his home, is a producer and director who was most notably involved in the Charles Bronson *Death Wish* series. He also directed such offerings as Charles Schneer's comedy *You Must Be Joking!* (1965), *Serpico* (1973) and *The Big Sleep* (1978). A person with strong political views and also considered "a brash and aggressive person" by many, Winner apparently got along well with Harryhausen during the preliminary phases of this collaborative project. At least two scripts were written for *People*, the original draft dated 1970 and revised versions dated 1983, but apparently what had been penned wasn't completely satisfactory. Ray opines in *Starlog* # 127, "I think it would have made an interesting film, if we could have gotten the right script together" (65). This, and the inability of Winner to secure finances for production, prevented this Haggard adaptation from ever reaching the screen.

The author of this book fortunately has had the privilege of scrutinizing several illustrations from the aforementioned unmade movies. Like scores of the stop-motion animator's other preproduction renderings, these are of impeccable artistic quality and they detail what was imagined to take place at pivotal moments in the picture. The first of the drawings is for the Sinbad film and shows the match between the unrecognizable saurian and the giant snake. They are in front of two towering rock formations to make them appear to be within a valley, and several people are in the lower foreground obviously scrambling to get away. Looking like a quadruped though rearing up on its hind legs here, the saurian has long clawed forelimbs and back legs with rounded feet like a pachyderm. Its flattened head, mouth with blunted teeth and squat body identify this monster as a herbivore, which strongly resembles a late Permian mammal-like (therapsid) reptile which flourished about 250 million years known as moschops. Wrapped once around its belly is the serpent, with a long forked tongue and fangs in its agape mouth, seemingly attempting to squeeze the life out of its foe.

There are three concepts from *People* which can be described here, the first of these being a pteranodon (this "pterodactyl" has the defining crested head) flying away with a girl in its clutches, held by the midriffs in the fashion observed in *King Kong* and *One Million Years B.C.* Below and in front of the flying reptile are two men tied back-to-back to a pole that has a skull propped on top of it, representing some kind of altar as all of this is situated upon a small mound. Scurrying around the two captives are a number of native tribesmen, equipped with Zulu-like spears and shields, clearly reacting to the girl's abduction.

The next sketch is quite elaborate. With a volcano spewing smoke in the distance, an enormous stadium-like shrine is seen in the foreground. In the center is a square pool of turbulent water. There is a long-necked monster sitting on a rock out in the middle of the water, looking like a plesiosaurus except that it has feet instead of flippers (it could have been intended as an actual type of ancestral marine reptile from the Triassic Period that collectively are known as nothosaurs). Flanking this pool are bleachers full of people, and on the opposite end is a colossal statue of some kind of grotesque deity. The stone idol is in a squatting position, with its forearms resting palms up on the knees. It is obvious that this giant figure is at least partially hollow, since there is an opening in the upper right arm just above the elbow joint for passage to the upturned palm of its hand; several individuals are standing on the statue's arm and palm, and there is a soldier or sentry in the left palm though that opening isn't visible. Its open mouth (also populated) bears sharp fangs, with the tongue hanging down to the chin in a very bizarre expression. Directly beneath this, between the stone god's feet and next to the pool of water, is a large metallic gong on a small platform. Looking at this wonderfully conceived drawing, it is difficult to ascertain what is going on here until a couple of minute details emerge which help to explain things. Although it is rather hard to see, there is a body falling towards the water that obviously dropped out of the mouth, and in the pool right below this unfortunate person is another creature that resides here in addition to the plesiosaur-like animal. This other inhabitant is a mosasaurus-like marine reptile, with its jaws thrust up out of the water in obvious anticipation of a meal. These particulars strongly point to what this conceptual drawing is all about: a huge gathering of people witnessing human sacrifice to their towering deity of stone — victims being fed to reptilian monsters lurking in waters next to the idol's feet.

The last of the three sketches has nothing to do with prehistoric creatures. It shows a man and woman inside a cave by a sizable urn filled with round objects, presumably jewels, coins or something else of value. Both are looking back towards the entrance of the cavern with surprised expressions on their faces at what they are seeing, a ten-foot-tall wizard-like being staring intently at them. The looming man has a beard extending down to his chest and is dressed in a long robe, holding a very long staff in his right hand and a short cylindrical object in the left that looks like a scroll. A radiant aura appears to emanate from his body, which seems to light the entrance of the cave with

Top and above: Miniaturist Holger Delfs putting final touches on the Harryhausen displays at the Filmmuseum Berlin, Sony Center. Photographs courtesy of Rolf Giesen.

a soft glow. However, his face and front of his body are quite shaded in appearance.

For a number of years, Harryhausen kept his entire collection of models, including his menagerie of dinosaurs and other prehistoric animals, with him at his home* (A quantity of related memorabilia was stored in Forrest Ackerman's residence for some time.) Starting some time around the early 1980s though, many figures from the animator's stop-motion collection traveled around on exhibit in many cities for fans to see close-up. There was a 1981 display at New York's Metropolitan Museum of Art, and a showing at London's Museum of the Moving Image (MOMI) about a decade later. The latter exhibition, titled "Creatures of Fantasy," ran from October 19, 1989, until March 31, 1990, and is featured in the Midwich Entertainment video *Aliens, Dragons, Monsters & Me* (1991). *Monsters & Me* originally came out in the mid–1980s as a retrospective on the special effects wizard's life and career; this revamped version makes

---

A 1969 article about Ray in Supernatural *#2 is titled "Dinosaurs on the Hall Cupboard," indicating the upstairs display case in his house.*

a videotaped tour of the MOMI the central component of the show (filmclips and interviews from the antecedent edition now play "supporting roles"). Walking through the very colorful displays with host Eric Boardman, Ray discusses his productions at a number of stops as they wind their way through it. While standing next to the Gwangi model, he recalls how a non-animation version became a favorite plaything of his then young daughter Vanessa, who was pushing the dinosaur around in her baby buggy while in Harrod's with her mother Diana Harryhausen.

Though at a quick glance this looks like modern-day falconry, it is actually Holger Delfs and pterosaur from *One Million Years B.C.* Photograph courtesy of Rolf Giesen.

When two old women at the fish counter pulled back the blanket to inspect the cute little girl's "doll," they were horrified and proceeded to chastise Ray's wife for giving her child such an inappropriate toy. (This very funny story is also recounted in *From the Land Beyond Beyond*). The *Monsters & Me* laserdisc also includes some extra pulled in shots of puppets from *One Million* and *Gwangi* such as the archelon, eohippus and miniature incarnations of Loana and Lope.

Most Harryhausen devotees are aware of this British exhibit thanks to the video, but fewer fans realize that these animation figures have been in Germany for the majority of the past 20 years. This began in 1983, during the "Fantastival" retrospective of his films, with a small display accompanying his event. There was another exhibit in 1985 at the Berlin Film Fest, where dozens of Ray's puppets were set up in "Wertheim," a department store located at Kurfurstendamm. Berlin had no film museum back then, so the fifth floor of that building was employed for the display instead. In 1988 Frankfurt then hosted an exhibit at its new filmmuseum, which allowed for a show entirely devoted to the man's lifetime achievements: "Sagenhafte Welten" (Legendary Worlds). From 1992–93, this personal animation collection was at the BavariaFilmPark at Bottrop-Kirchhellen, just outside of Düsseldorf in the Ruhr district. His memorabilia then traveled in 1993 to the Babelsberg StudioTour, situated on the lot of the old UFA studios on the outskirts of Berlin. The author of this book visited the exhibit (called "Cinefantastic") during this stint, and much of the *Harryhausen Chronicles* was taped during its lengthy engagement here, lasting until 1999. Finally, the stop-motion models (as well as items from the collections of Forry Ackerman, Gregory Jein, Phil Tippett, Craig Barron and various others) were transferred to the "Artificial Worlds" section of what is now their permanent home that opened in September 2000 at the Filmmuseum Berlin, Sony Center, Berlin, Potsdamer Platz. Some may remember that a Criterion *Jason* laserdisc supplement indicates that something different was to happen to these figures. It states that, in the context of Forry Ackerman's memorabilia, "A target date of 1995 has been set for the establishment of his collection at the $42 million Hotel Esplanade in Berlin which is currently being renovated into a motion picture museum. His collection will be joined by Ray Harryhausen's 62 dinosaur and animation models." The remainders of the Hotel Esplanade are now incorporated within the huge Sony Center. What kept this from happening was the reunification of West Germany and East Germany into a single nation back in the 1990s, which created a shortfall of money and thus prevented such a depository from materializing at that time.

Responsible for this significant group of stop-motion figures and movie artifacts is Dr. Rolf Giesen. Born July 4, 1953, in Moers, Rolf studied at Freie Universität Berlin (Free University Berlin) and received a doctorate in philosophy in 1979 with a thesis on the subject of "Der phantastische Film " (Fantastic Films). Dr. Giesen has been involved in the motion picture industry and television for years in a number of productions, serving as a special effects consultant on films like Roland Emmerich's *Joey* (a.k.a. *Making Contact*; 1985) and, with Albert Whitlock, on *The NeverEnding Story II* (1990). He has also functioned in the role of writer-producer for animated features such as *Asterix and the Big Fight* (1989) and the TV series *The NeverEnding Story* (1996). A member of the Visual Effects Society, Giesen has written extensively about filmic special effects, publishing about four dozen books in this respect. Several of these German-language titles include *Lexikon des Phantastischen Films: Horror, Science Fiction, Fantasy* (1984), *Sagenhafte Welten: der Trickspezialist Ray Harryhausen* (1988), *Cinfantastic: Babelsberg StudioTour* (1994) and *Lexikon der Special Effects* (2001). He has also written the English-language book *Nazi Propaganda Films* (2003) for McFarland & Company. While growing up in a small town in the Rhine Valley, young Rolf was first exposed to Harryhausen when he caught the trailer for *7th Voyage*, impelling the lad to see the entire picture. It had a profound influence upon him. It would be another 25 years before he would get to meet Ray in person. Since that time (1983), Dr. Giesen has had a close working as well as a personal relationship with Ray that only a handful of fans have been lucky enough to enjoy, even staying with the animator in London when he visits.

Rolf finds Harryhausen to have a boyish sense of fascination, a charismatic personality and a great sense of humor e.g. talking about Laurel & Hardy (he has adopted the well-known Oliver Hardy expression "I have nothing to say!" when politely not wanting to answer a specific question). Both he and Ray Bradbury once talked about making a pilgrimage to Stan Laurel's home but unfortunately nothing ever came of it. Another instance where the old effects master had shown these qualities, according to Rolf, took place on a boat tour on Frankfurt's River Main that he found extraordinarily boring. Ray quipped that what was needed here was a good animatronic dinosaur popping its head up out of the water, demonstrating this idea with his hand and arm as the swiveling head and neck of a surfacing saurian. Dr. Giesen suggested that Harryhausen design a replica of Kong that could be made into a "life-size" reproduction, and both settled on the gorilla's escape from the theater for this purpose. Artists of the Bavaria Studios in Munich made this miniature into an 18-foot-tall colossus, much to the creator's satisfaction. (This was later sold by Dark Horse as a model kit). He earlier made a similar model of *King Kong* as seen atop the Empire State Building which, along with a few model reproductions, is at the MOMI in London (it can be seen in the *Monsters & Me* video). His German associate also was instrumental in getting him together with Paul Hubschmid, star of *Beast from 20,000 Fathoms*, in Berlin at the Filmmuseum's opening in September 2000 (the two never met before). To display Harryhausen's animation figures in their new home, Rolf joined forces with miniaturist Holger Delfs to construct exciting dioramas for this assortment of dinosaurs and other unusual creatures. Together with artifacts coming from other, more current special effects features, Ray's memorabilia is an intrinsic part of what is known as the Rolf Giesen Collection in the Filmmuseum, which will be sure to fascinate and awe those who come and see this treasure trove of movie paraphernalia. Dr. Giesen opines that "it is a shame how careless Americans themselves sometimes regard film history, and for many years nothing similar happened in Hollywood itself, although several people tried their best."

With the advent of pre-recorded video formats, every one of Ray's full-length features except for *Animal World* has been available on VHS and laserdisc, and the vast majority of these have subsequently been released on DVD as well. This accessibility has made these titles much more familiar and has allowed a wider viewing public that random airings on television would permit. Harryhausen has also been the subject of two productions on his life and career that have been frequently mentioned in this book, *Monsters & Me* and *Harryhausen Chronicles*, and was featured in a number of other programs pertaining to cinematic effects. He has also been in several videos and documentary programs which are based upon dinosaurs, like the Walter Cronkite–hosted television series *Dinosaur!* (1991), Don Glut's two-tape video *Dinosaur Movies* (1993), an episode of the Bravo Network series *Opening Shot* dealing with saurians (this is extremely interesting, since a documentary clip of Arthur Hayward working on his stop-motion amateur film project is also shown) and the Discovery Channel *Movie Magic* installment titled "Dinomania" (1996). In addition, the filmography included on the *Chronicles* DVD lists Ted Newsom's *100 Years of Horrors: Giants and Dinosaurs* (1996) where Ray appears as himself. He also includes a 1999 program whose name (*Working with Dinosaurs*) is obviously a play on the superb BBC series.

Besides being seen via the electronic medium, the animator has been a guest of honor at many science fiction and modelmaking conventions over the past 20 years in the United States and many other countries. Many of these appearances have been for special screenings of his films. There have been hundreds of magazine articles about Harryhausen ever since the April 1941 *Popular Mechanics* feature, though most of it has been written since 1975. Some of the more outstanding publications include the early 1970s fanzine *FXRH* that endured for four issues, the three-part *Cinefantastique / Imagi-Movies* series by Ted Newsom (though there is at times some unnecessary negativity present) and *Cinefex* #5 (1981). Among the books about this subject: Jeff Rovin's *From the Land Beyond Beyond* (1977) and Ray's own *Film Fantasy Scrapbook*, of which four editions have been in print. His next tome (with associate Tony Dalton) promises to be both lavishly illustrated with previously unpublished photographs and expose any remaining filmmaking "secrets" which he has still managed to keep up his sleeves.

Obviously, this intensive barrage in the popular media has made his name familiar as a pioneering figure in the field of animation. The timing must have been somewhat bittersweet for him; by the time this increased awareness took place, Hollywood was of the mind that a "better" method than conventional dimensional stop-motion needed to be used in films. This was borne out in the 1980s first through "go-motion," a variation of the time-honored process which used a computer-controlled mechanism to create a "blur" by moving the model during exposures, and later in the decade the advent of computer-generated images (CGI).

Although Ray announced his retirement from moviemaking during the latter part of the 1980s (after several potential film projects never made it past the early preproduction phases), his lifestyle has been anything but sedentary. Travel is something that Ray and Diana both enjoy doing, spending a significant part of the year at their seaside home in Spain and out in California. Of course, conventions and special screenings also allowed them to visit faraway places that they might not otherwise have seen. Another activity in his golden years is crafting exquisite sculptures which are cast in bronze. These renderings of his animated characters are extremely limited, museum-quality pieces that would cost several thousand dollars at least (some are more expensive than others). He has produced something like a dozen or so bronzes over recent years, permanently preserving the forms of many models that have either decomposed or were stripped down to feed the armature into another puppet.

Pertaining to dinosaurs, Ray has crafted two different bronze versions of the rhedosaurus: one in a quadrupedal pose with a front leg raised in the air, and a larger figure rearing up and attacking a replica of the lighthouse. (A small photograph of the latter can be seen in the 1995 *SFX* article about him.) In addition, he did a scene ("Prehistoric Challenge") showing a ceratosaurus fighting a caveman holding a spear, with a female lying next to the monster's feet. This, like Dark Horse's King Kong, has been released as a model kit by the Janus Company. The ceratosaur looks nothing like the creatures in either *One Million* or *Animal World*, but is instead a unique Harryhausen interpretation of this saurian in the vein of the Kong kit. Also, the animator has created bronzes of the semi-dinosaurian Ymir and the memorable *King Kong* battle between the ape and T. rex. This very large casting of the highlight from the classic film was fashioned in 1983 for the fiftieth anniversary celebration of the movie at Mann's (formerly Grauman's) Chinese Theatre. Dr. Giesen notes that there are three of these bronzes in existence. One was bought at this event by John Landis, a second was purchased by "an unnamed pop singer" and the third is at the Filmmuseum in Berlin.

For this anniversary occasion, Jim Danforth and others recreated the large moving bust of Kong that was in the forecourt during its original release; though it had been hurriedly constructed, Ray thought the bust was quite good. The 1933 opus was shown at the Chinese Theatre, followed by a gathering across the street at the historic Roosevelt Hotel that included Harryhausen, Fay Wray, Darlyne O'Brien, Linwood Dunn, Orville Goldner, Terry Moore and Ray Bradbury. The animator continues to demonstrate his affection and affinity towards *King Kong* even in retirement. Not only has he attended numerous celebratory events and other such *Kong*-related happenings, the very accomplished devotee even went on a personal pilgrimage to the Nias Islands near Sumatra somewhere around the early 1990s (they were mentioned in *King Kong*, in the context of the language spoken by the natives). Even though he never saw the giant wall, legendary ape or dinosaurs there, the journey was undoubtedly a moving and fulfilling experience for someone whose life has been so thoroughly shaped by its overwhelming sights and sounds and majestic beauty.

Ray was never nominated for an Academy Award during his entire professional career. True, he did most of the animation which helped Willis O'Brien garner one for *Mighty Joe Young*, but even Jim Danforth received a nomination for the 1970 movie

When Dinosaurs Ruled the Earth owing to his distinctive style of stop-motion effects. Many fans had long felt that Harryhausen was unjustly deprived of such an honor. He was finally awarded a long-overdue statuette on March 7, 1992 (the ceremony was videotaped but only a brief clip was televised), as part of the 64th Academy Awards shown on March 30. Presented during a Scientific and Technical Awards dinner, the Oscar he was given was the ninth Gordon E. Sawyer Award, a lifetime achievement Oscar handed out to recognize "an individual in the motion picture whose technological contributions have brought credit to the industry." Much of the credit for Ray being bestowed with this great award goes to fan Arnold Kunert, who contacted Ray Bradbury and precipitated a chain of events which included letters of support written by many important Hollywood names that helped make this happen.

Sculpted by Ray himself as a bronze rendering, this model kit of a ceratosaurus versus a caveman and fallen female is named "Prehistoric Challenge." Courtesy of the Janus Company.

Actor Tom Hanks served as the master of ceremonies that night, but it was lifelong friend Bradbury who actually presented Harryhausen with the Oscar. Speaking at the podium with Ray, Diana and Vanessa Harryhausen at the front table, the famed science-fiction writer gave a moving speech recalling their youthful ambitions, stating, "It's rare, in the history of motion pictures or any other art form, that two young men meet and promise themselves a lifelong friendship plus an enduring love for dinosaurs — how to bring them to life, how to put them on the screen. And in 1938, just out of high school, Ray Harryhausen came into my life. I went to visit his garage, where he built and animated prehistoric beasts on 16mm film. Good Lord, what a friend to have! Someone just as crazy as I was about primeval monsters and how to get them into theaters and keep them there forever. We made a pact, promising to grow old but never grow up, and keep the pterodactyl and the Tyrannosaurus rex forever in our hearts. And lo, it happened!" When Harryhausen came up on stage and accepted his richly deserved statuette, the two Rays embraced and so expressed both their happiness with this honor and affirmation of two lives sent in pursuit of the dinosaur.

What exactly is Harryhausen's legacy with respect to dinosaurs and other prehistoric creatures? This would be very difficult to precisely define, but it is safe to say his wizardry has created some quite compelling moving images of these long-extinct animals. His stop-motion animation breathed life into many types of saurians whose movements are very close to being entirely believable rather than merely passible. Not only was his model manipulation done so masterfully as to be almost completely realistic, the figures themselves were built-up or sculpted with so much attention to detail that they even look like a viewer's expectation of a living prehistoric. These wonderful monsters, whether or not based on actual fossilized genera, come alive so convincingly that they always seem to steal the show through their expository nature. His dinosaurian efforts have proved inspirational to two generations of technicians within the film industry, and serve as a bridge between Willis O'Brien's early productions and dazzling computer-generated images in features like *Jurassic Park* (1993) and others by those influenced by him.

But there is also the man behind the magic. Growing up with a love for extinct creatures of all shapes and sizes, young Ray was forever transformed by *King Kong* and in it saw the means for bringing his vivid imagination into a tangible form. Toiling unheralded for many years at home, his skill and artistry steadily improved through his commitment, which was abetted by the likes of O'Brien, Bradbury and many other people. Even after becoming a revered icon in the realm of special effects, the boyhood fascination with these colossal beasts remains, and he has avidly kept up an interest in paleontology through reading books, visiting museums and participating on at least one bone dig.

With the preservation of both his feature-length and amateur films, Ray Harryhausen's dinosaurs will continue coming to life for future generations to enjoy. Though they certainly won't be considered "state-of-the-art" then, many will still be entertained and appreciate the work of one of the most original pioneers in cinematic history.

Ray Harryhausen in front of a case full of dinosaurian and other models in his London home. His lifelong achievements have expressed an abiding love for these long-extinct reptiles.

Ray Harryhausen Dinosaur Filmography

This is a list of dinosaur and dinosaur-related films for which Ray Harryhausen did or was to do the animation effects. Asterisk indicates an unrealized production.

AMATEUR PROJECTS

Early experiments (1938–40): Existing footage includes a cave bear, triceratops, allosaurus, agathaumas, brontosaurus, pteranodon and Jupiterian in varying combinations. Animated at 16 FPS (one clip is at 24 FPS). B&W

Lemuria* (circa 1939): Only a single sketch (a brontosaurus attacking a distant city on the lost continent of Lemuria) for this proposed film was rendered.

"Creature from Jupiter" film project* (circa 1939): Test shows Jupiterian grabbing a spaceship model. Animated at 16 FPS. B&W

Evolution* (1940–1941): Intended as a feature-length documentary for educational purposes. Completed footage includes a brontosaurus, allosaurus, tyrannosaurus, triceratops, hadrosaur, lemur/monkey and a caveman. Color

Mammoth vs. Jupiterian, and the Tyrannosaurus (circa 1940): Brief tests using static mattes and rear projection which isn't bona fide *Evolution* footage. Color

PROFESSIONAL PROJECTS

Valley of the Mist* (1949-50): An unmade Willis O'Brien project on which Ray was to have been chief animator à la *Mighty Joe Young*. Proposed saurians include a triceratops, two allosaurs and a pteranodon. Harryhausen prints of conceptual artwork for it have been commercially available.

The Great Adventure* (?) (circa 1950): According to Paul Mandell, another unrealized O'Brien-Harryhausen undertaking in conjunction with Merian C. Cooper which was to have included "prehistoric monsters."

The Beast from 20,000 Fathoms (1953): Features fictitious dinosaur called a "rhedosaurus," based on a combination of real saurians and present-day lizards. Skin pattern on its underbelly came from authentic crocodilian hide.

The Elementals* (1952–53): An original 1952 treatment by Ray which was going to be developed into a feature film by *Beast from 20,000 Fathoms* producer Jack Dietz. Features bat-winged, reptilian aliens. Test footage (color and B&W) and pre-production sketches exist.

The Animal World (1955): O'Brien-Harryhausen effects in this motion picture's dinosaur sequence, which includes adult and infant brontosaurs, an allosaurus, stegosaurus, two ceratosaurs, a triceratops and tyrannosaurus.

20 Million Miles to Earth (1957): Developed from a 1952 story outline titled *The Giant Ymir*. The Venusian monster in this film is a composite animal partially based on a bipedal dinosaur.

Mysterious Island (1961): Prehistoric creatures include a phororhacos and ammonite / nautiloid cephalopod. In an early version of the script, actual dinosaurs were proposed for this movie.

One Million Years B.C. (1966): Mesozoic reptiles here include a brontosaurus, archelon, allosaurus, triceratops, ceratosaurus, mother and two baby pteranodons, and a pterosaur / rhamphorhynchus. A remake of the 1940 feature *One Million B.C.*

King Kong* (circa 1967): After *One Million Years B.C.*, Hammer Films wanted Ray to do the animation in a remake of the 1933 classic, but the planned film was cancelled.

The Valley of Gwangi (1969): The antediluvian creatures dwelling in "Forbidden Valley" include an eohippus, pteranodon, ornithomimus, styracosaurus and allosaurus (Gwangi). A revival of O'Brien's aborted 1941-42 feature *Gwangi*.

Sinbad and the Eye of the Tiger (1977): Prehistoric creatures include a troglodyte and saber-toothed tiger, with a "Walrus giganticus" supposedly being one of these as well. An arsinoitherium was proposed during pre-production.

Unnamed Sinbad project* (circa 1970s): Ideas for this unrealized Sinbad installment included a fight between a moschops-like saurian and snake, and a styracosaurus attacking a camp and fighting a ceratosaurus. Conceptual artwork is in Harryhausen's possession.

War Eagles* (1981): Charles Schneer and Ray Harryhausen explored resurrecting this abandoned O'Brien production after *Clash of the Titans*. (According to Paul Mandell, Ray had already considered "revamping" it in the mid-1960s.) The original movie was to have included a brontosaurus and several allosaurs. Ray has three different scripts for *War Eagles*, all dated 1939.

People of the Mist* (1983): Adaptation of H. Rider Haggard's "lost race" novel was to have featured a stegosaurus, pteranodon, plesiosaur / nothosaur and another marine reptile. This film project was first brought to Ray in the early 1970s by Michael Winner; the original script is dated 1970. Conceptual artwork is in Harryhausen's possession.

Casts and Credits

The Beast from 20,000 Fathoms

Cast: Professor Tom Nesbitt: Paul Hubschmid (as Paul Christian); Miss Lee Hunter: Paula Raymond; Professor Thurgood Elson: Cecil Kellaway; Colonel Jack Evans: Kenneth Tobey; Captain Phil Jackson: Donald Woods; Corporal Stone: Lee Van Cleef; Sergeant Loomis: Steve Brodie; Professor George Ritchie: Ross Elliott; Jacob Bowman: Jack Pennick; Sergeant Willistead: Ray Hyke; Miss Nelson: Mary Hill; ER Doctor: Michael Fox; 1st Radar Man: Alvin Greenman; Dr. Morton: Frank Ferguson; Dr. Ingersoll: King Donovan; Radar Man: James Best; Radio Operator: Fred Aldrich (uncredited); Lighthouse Keeper: Ed Clark (uncredited); Deckhand: Robert Easton (uncredited); Major Evans: Roy Engel (uncredited); Ballet-Goer: Franklyn Farnum (uncredited); Ballet-Goer: Bess Flowers (uncredited); Longshoreman: Joe Gray (uncredited); Voice of Off-Screen Radio Announcer: Merv Griffin (uncredited); Cop with Rifle: Kenner G. Kemp (uncredited); Cop: Lee Phelps (uncredited); Doctor: Hugh Prosser (uncredited); Radio Announcer: William Woodson (uncredited).

Credits: Production Company: Mutual Pictures of California; Distributed by: Warner Bros.; B&W (500 prints were originally in "Glorious Sepia Tone"); Running Time: 80 minutes; Released: June 13, 1953 (U.S.); Directed by: Eugene Lourié; Produced by: Hal Chester and Jack Dietz; Music by: David Buttolph; Music Conducted by: Ray Heindorf (uncredited); Associate Producer: Bernard W. Burton; Technical Effects Created by: Ray Harryhausen; Screenplay by: Lou Morheim and Fred Freiberger, Eugene Lourié (uncredited), Robert Smith (uncredited); Suggested by: *The Saturday Evening Post* Story by Ray Bradbury; Director of Photography: Jack Russell, A.S.C.; Assistant Art Director: Hal Waller; Film Editor: Bernard W. Burton, A.C.E.; Sound by: Max Hutchinson, George Groves (uncredited); Special Effects by: Willis Cook; Eugene Lourié (uncredited); Production Design: Eugene Lourié (uncredited); Set Decorator: Edward Boyle; Dialogue Director: Michael Fox; Costumes by: Berman's of Hollywood; Makeup Artist: Louis Phillippi; Assistant Director: Horace Hough; Orchestrations: Maurice de Packh.

The Animal World

Credits: Production Company: Windsor Productions; Distributed by: Warner Bros.; Color by: Technicolor; Running time: 82 minutes; Released: December 1955 (not in wide distribution until June 1956); Written, Produced and Directed by: Irwin Allen; Production Associate: George E. Swink; Music Composed and Conducted by:

Paul Sawtell; Photographed by: Harold Wellman A.S.C. and naturalist photographers throughout the world; Art Director: Bert Tuttle; Film Editors: Gene Palmer and Robert A. Belcher; Sound Effects Editors: Henry L. DeMond, M.P.S.E., Walter Elliott, M.P.S.E. and Bert Schoenfeld, M.P.S.E.; Music Editor: Richard Harris; Supervising Animator: Willis O'Brien; Animation by: Ray Harryhausen; Special Effects by: Arthur S. Rhoades; Narrated by: Theodore von Eltz (as Theodor von Eltz) and John Storm; Sculptures: Pasqual Manuelli (uncredited) and Harold Wilson (uncredited).

One Million Years B.C.

Cast: Loana: Raquel Welch; Tumak: John Richardson; Sakana: Percy Herbert; Akhoba: Robert Brown; Nupondi: Martine Beswick; Ahot: Jean Wladon; Sura: Lisa Thomas; Tohana: Malya Nappi; Young Rock Man: Richard James; Payto: William Lyon Brown; 1st Rock Man: Frank Hayden; 1st Shell Man: Terence Maidment; 1st Shell Girl: Micky de Rauch; Ullah: Yvonne Horner.

Credits: Production Companies: Hammer Film Productions Limited, Seven Arts Productions (U.S. version only); Distributed by: Warner-Pathe Distributors Limited (U.K.) and 20th Century–Fox Film Corporation (U.S.); Color by: Technicolor (U.K.) and De Luxe (U.S.); Running Time: 100 minutes (U.K.) and 91 minutes (U.S.); Released: December 30, 1966 (U.K.) and February 21, 1967 (U.S.); Directed by: Don Chaffey; Produced by: Michael Carreras and Kenneth Hyman (uncredited); Associate Producers: Hal E. Roach Sr. (U.S. version only) and Aida Young; Screenplay by: Michael Carreras; Adapted from an Original Screenplay by: Mickell Novak, George Baker and Joseph Frickert; Special Visual Effects Created by: Ray Harryhausen; Music and Special Musical Effects Composed by: Mario Nascimbene; Musical Supervisor: Philip Martell; Art Director: Robert Jones; Supervising Editor: James Needs; Costume Designer: Carl Toms; Costumes: Monty Berman (uncredited); Director of Photography: Wilkie Cooper; Production Manager: John Wilcox; Editor: Tom Simpson; Assistant Director: Denis Bertera; Camera Operator: David Harcourt; Continuity: Gladys Goldsmith and Marjory Lavelly; Second Unit Cameraman: Jack Mills; Assistant Art Director: Kenneth McCallum Tait; Special Effects: George Blackwell; Sound Editor: Roy Baker and Alfred Cox; Sound Mixers: Len Shilton and Bill Rowe; Make-up Supervisor: Wally Schneiderman; Hairdressing Supervisor: Olga Angelinetta; Wardrobe Mistress: Ivy Baker; Prologue Designed by: Les Bowie; Recording Director: A.W. Lumkin; Narrator: David Kossoff (uncredited); Still Photographer: Pierre Luigi (uncredited); Sculptures: Arthur Hayward (uncredited).

The Valley of Gwangi

Cast: Tuck Kirby: James Franciscus; Teresa Juanita (T.J.) Breckenridge: Gila Golan; Champ Conners: Richard Carlson; Professor Horace Bromley: Laurence Naismith; Tia Zorina: Freda Jackson; Carlos dos Orsos: Gustavo Rojo; Rowdy: Dennis Kilbane; Bean: Mario de Barros; Lope: Curtis Arden; The Dwarf: Jose Burgos (uncredited).

Credits: Production Company: Morningside Productions; Distributed by: Warner

Bros.— Seven Arts, Inc.; Color by: Technicolor; Running Time: 95 minutes; Released: June 1969; Directed by: James O'Connolly; Produced by: Charles H. Schneer; Screenplay by: William E. Bast; Additional Material by: Julian More; Story by: Willis O'Brien (uncredited); Associate Producer and Creator of Visual Effects: Ray Harryhausen; Music Composed and Conducted by: Jerome Moross; Director of Photography: Erwin Hillier B.S.C.; Art Director: Gil Parrondo; Editor: Henry Richardson G.B.F.E.; Production Manager: Miguel Gil; Production Supervisor: Luis Roberts; Assistant Director: Pedro Vidal and Carlos Gil (uncredited); Camera Operator: Alec Mills; Continuity: Gladys Goldsmith; Sound: Malcolm Steward and Bill Creed (uncredited); Dubbing Editors: Philip Bottomley and Selwyn Petterson; Wardrobe Designer: John Furness; Wardrobe Supervisor: Antonio Pueo; Title Designer: Antonio Saura; Horse Master: Juan Majan; Sculptures: Arthur Hayward (uncredited).

Bibliography

BOOKS

Archer, Steve. *Willis O'Brien: Special Effects Genius*. Jefferson NC: McFarland, 1993.
Bakker, Robert T. *The Dinosaur Heresies*. New York: William Morrow, 1986.
Berry, Mark F. *The Dinosaur Filmography*. Jefferson NC: McFarland, 2002.
Bradbury, Ray. *Dinosaur Tales*. New York: Bantam Books, 1983.
Desmond, Adrian J. *The Hot-Blooded Dinosaurs: A Revolution in Palaeontology*. New York: Warner Books, 1977.
Dixon, Dougal, *et al. The Macmillan Illustrated Encyclopedia of Dinosaurs and Prehistoric Animals: A Visual Who's Who of Prehistoric Life*. New York: Macmillan, 1988.
Glut, Donald F. *The Dinosaur Dictionary*. New York: Bonanza Books, 1984.
_____. *The Dinosaur Scrapbook*. Secaucus NJ: Citadel, 1980.
Goodenough, Simon. *Purnell's Book of Dinosaurs and Prehistoric Animals*. Paulton, Bristol (UK): Purnell Books, 1977.
Harryhausen, Ray. *Film Fantasy Scrapbook* 4th ed. London: Titan Books, 1989.
Hearn, Marcus, and Alan Barnes. *The Hammer Story*. London: Titan Books, 1997.
Hutchison, David. *Film Magic: The Art and Science of Special Effects*. New York: Prentice Hall, 1987.
Jensen, Paul M. *The Men Who Made the Monsters*. New York: Twayne Publishers, 1996.
Johnson, John. *Cheap Tricks and Class Acts: Special Effects, Makeup, and Stunts from the Films of the Fantastic Fifties*. Jefferson NC: McFarland, 1996.
Johnson, Tom, and Deborah Del Vecchio. *Hammer Films: An Exhaustive Filmography*. Jefferson NC: McFarland, 1996.
Lourie, Eugene. *My Work in Films*. San Diego: Harcourt Brace Jovanovich, 1985.
McLoughlin, John C. *Synapsida: A New Look Into the Origin of Mammals*. New York: Viking, 1980.
Maltin, Leonard, ed. *Leonard Maltin's Movie & Video Guide 2001*. New York: New American Library, 2000.
Maxford, Howard. *Hammer, House Of Horror: Behind the Screams*. Woodstock NY: Overlook Press, 1996.
Naha, Ed. *Horrors: From Screen to Scream*. New York: Avon Books, 1975.
Norman, David. *The Illustrated Encyclopedia of Dinosaurs: An Original and Compelling Insight Into Life in the Dinosaur Kingdom*. New York: Crescent Books, 1985.
Paul, Gregory S. *Predatory Dinosaurs of the World: A Complete Illustrated Guide*. New York: Simon and Schuster, 1988.
Pettigrew, Neil. *The Stop-Motion Filmography: A Critical Guide to 297 Features Using Puppet Animation*. Jefferson NC: McFarland, 1999.
Rovin, Jeff. *The Encyclopedia of Monsters*. New York: Facts on File, 1989.
_____. *From the Land Beyond Beyond*. New York: Berkley, 1977.
_____. *A Pictoral History of Science Fiction Films*. Secaucus NJ: Citadel, 1975.
Svehla, Gary J., and Susan Svehla, eds. *Guilty Pleasures of the Horror Film*. Baltimore: Midnight Marquee Press, 1996.

Swinton, William Elgin. *The Wonderful World of Prehistoric Animals.* Garden City NY: Doubleday, 1969.
Wilson, S.S. *Puppets & People: Large-Scale Animation in the Cinema.* San Diego: A.S. Barnes, 1980.

PERIODICALS

Bennett, Rod, *et al.* "A Conversation with Ray Harryhausen." *Wonder* 5, 1991.
Bissette, Stephen R. "From Creator to Artist: Part two of an interview with Ray Harryhausen." *Animato!* 25, Spring 1993.
_____. "Laserdiscs: One Million Years B.C." *Video Watchdog* No. 40, 1997.
_____. "Ray Harryhausen: ...From Creator to Artist." *Animato!* 24, Winter 1993.
Bohus, Ted A. "An Interview with Effects Wizard Ray Harryhausen." *SPFX* 3, 1995.
Bradley, Matthew R. "Ray Harryhausen: Now and Then." *Filmfax* 52, Sept./Oct. 1995.
Brosnan, John. "*One Million Years B.C.*" *The House of Hammer* 14 (Vol. 2 No. 2), Nov. 1977.
"Cashing in on a Fantasy." *Popular Mechanics* Vol. 75 4, April 1941.
Cox, Vic. "Ray Harryhausen — Acting Without the Lumps." *Cinefex* 5, July 1981.
Delson, James. "Ray Harryhausen, Master of the Art of Stop-Motion Model Animation." *Fantastic Films* Vol. 1 No. 4, Oct. 1978.
Feilberger, Dan. "Harryhausen Props on Display in the Ackermansion." *Cinefantastique* Vol. 31 No. 1 / 2, Feb. 1998.
_____. "Harryhausen Retirement." *Cinefantastique* Vol. 31 No. 1 / 2, Feb. 1998.
Golder, David. " The SFX Interview: Ray Harryhausen." SFX 6, Nov. 1995.
Hankin, Mike. "Ray Harryhausen." *Dark Terrors* Issue 8, Apr. 1994.
_____. "The 7th Voyage of Sinbad." *Colossa* Vol. 1 No. 2, 1995.
Harris, Ernest. "A Conversation with Ray Harryhausen." *The Late Show* 3, 1976.
"The Harryhausen Sketchbook." *The House of Hammer* #17, Feb. 1978.
Hayward, Arthur. "Making Fossils Live." *Animals* Vol. 12 No. 4, Aug. 1969.
Johnson, Daniel Bryan. "*The Valley of Gwangi.*" *Monster Memories* #5 (1997 *Scary Monsters* Yearbook), Jan. 1997.
Kinsey, Wayne. "Hammer — The Special Effects Part 2: Ray Harryhausen." *The House That Hammer Built* # 15, Feb. 2001.
_____. "*One Million Years B.C.*" *The House That Hammer Built* # 5, Oct. 1997.
_____. "When Dinosaurs Ruled the Earth." *The House That Hammer Built* #6, Dec. 1997.
Lucas, Tim. "Reviews: *Clash of the Titans.*" *Cinefantastique* Vol. 11 No. 2, Fall 1981.
MacQueen, Scott. "Classic Restoration: The Lost World — Found!" *Cinefex* 70, June 1997.
_____. "Effects Scene: Cinematic Archaeology." Cinefex # 55, Aug. 1993.
_____. "Ray Harryhausen: From Fan to Technician..." *Animato!* # 24, Winter 1993.
McRobie, David. "One Million Years B.C." *Xenorama* 4, Halloween 1993.
Main, Jim. "*The Prehistoric Times* Interview: Ray Harryhausen." *The Prehistoric Times* # 18, May / June 1996.
_____. "Ray Harryhausen: Master of Movie Magic." *Collectible Toys & Values* # 16, Feb. 1993.
Mandell, Paul. "Animation Archive: *The Beast from 20,000 Fathoms.*" *Cinemagic* # 36 (Vol. 7 No. 6), Autumn 1987.
_____. "Of Genies and Dragons: The Career of Ray Harryhausen." *American Cinematographer* Vol. 73 No. 12, Dec. 1992.
_____. "The Giant Behemoth." SPFX No. 4, 1996.
_____. "Harryhausen's Dinosaurs." *Dinosaur* (*Starlog*), 1993.
_____. "It's a Wonderful Life." *Starlog Spectacular* No. 6, Jan. 1993.
_____. "The Remarkable Mr. Harryhausen." *Cinemagic* No. 30 (Vol. 6 No. 4), Summer 1985.
_____. "Split-Screen 'Dynamation' Technique." *Cinemagic* No. 27 (Vol. 6 No. 1), Autumn 1984.
Massaro, David M. "I Was a Teenage Harryhausen." FXRH (Special Visual Effects created by Ray Harryhausen) Vol. 1 No. 4, Spring 1974.

Murphy, Mike and Dan Gale. "One Million Years B.C." *Dark Terrors* # 8, Apr. 1994.
Murray, Will. "Ray Bradbury's Dinosaur Chronicles." *Dinosaur (Starlog)*, 1993.
Nadler, Harry, and Dave Trengove. "Talking to ... Ray Harryhausen." *L'Incroyable Cinema* # 5, Autumn 1971.
Natale, Mike. *The Valley of Gwangi*: A Critique on the Special Visual Effects." FXRH (special visual effects created by Ray Harryhausen) Vol. 1 No. 1, Winter 1970.
Newsom, Ted. "King of Dynamation: Ray Harryhausen." *Imagi-Movies* Vol. 2 No. 3, Spring 1995.
_____. "Ray Harryhausen: Stop-Motion Magician." *Cinefantastique* Vol. 31 No. 1 / 2, Feb. 1998.
_____. "The Ray Harryhausen Story: The Early Years 1920-1958." *Cinefantastique* Vol. 11 No. 4, Dec. 1981.
_____. "Sorcerer's Apprentice: Arthur Hayward." *Cinefantastique* Vol. 31 No. 1 / 2, Feb. 1998.
O'Neill, Kevin. "Harryhausen, Master of Motion." *Just Imagine* No. 2, 1977.
"*One Million Years B.C.*" *Image Laserdisc Preview* # 27, Apr. 1996.
"*One Million Years B.C.*: *Mania* Movie Review." *Monster Mania* # 2, Jan. 1967.
"*One Million Years B.C.*: Told in full, in dramatic action artwork ... the 1966 Hammer film." *The House of Hammer* No. 14 (Vol. 2 No. 2), Nov. 1977.
Parla, Paul, and Donna Parla. "Beauty & the Beast from 20,000 Fathoms: An Interview with Paula Raymond." *Filmfax* # 62, Aug. / Sept. 1997.
Reardon, Craig. "Charles Schneer...Speaks his mind." FXRH (Special Visual Effects created by Ray Harryhausen) Vol. 1 No. 4, Spring 1974.
Rigby, Jonathan. "Hammer's Other Worlds." *Starburst* # 266 (Vol. 25 No. 1), Oct. 2000.
Schneer, Charles. "The sky is not the limit: Charles Schneer on filming fantasy." *Films Illustrated* Vol. 7 No. 75, Nov. 1977.
Shay, Don. "Willis O'Brien—Creator of the Impossible." *Cinefex* # 7, Jan. 1982.
Skotak, Robert and Dennis Skotak. "Special Effects Designed and Created by: Jack Rabin & Irving Block." *Fantascene* Vol. 1 No. 2, Summer 1976.
Stockler, Bruce. "Ray Harryhausen: The Godfather of Visual Effects." *VISFX*, June 1998.
Stout, Tim. "Dinosaurs on the Hall Cupboard." *Supernatural* # 2, 1969.
Swires, Steve. "Ray Harryhausen: Farewell to Fantasy Films." *Starlog* # 127, Feb. 1988.
"This is Ray Harryhausen." *Kaleidoscope* Vol. 3 No. 1, 1967.
Turner, George E. "A Lost World of Dinosaurs." *Retrovision* # 3, Aug. 1998.
Vincelli, Ralph. "*Beast from 20,000 Fathoms*: The Essential Harryhausen." *Midnight Marquee* # 45, Summer 1993.
Warren, Bill. "*The Valley of Gwangi*." *Photon* # 18, 1969.
"When Lizards Ruled the World." *Mechanix Illustrated* Vol. 52 No. 12, Dec. 1956.
Wolf, Mark. "Ray Harryhausen's Aerial Brace Creations." FXRH (Special Visual Effects created by Ray Harryhausen) Vol. 1 No. 4, Spring 1974.

MISCELLANEOUS

The Animal World pressbook.
The Ashbury Park Press. Sunday Dec. 13, 1998.
Interview with Jerome Moross by Craig Reardon, dated Apr. 16, 1979.
Interview with Jerome Moross by John Caps, dated Aug. 31, 1979.
Letter to the author from Ray Harryhausen, dated Aug. 14, 1995.
The Los Angeles Daily News "L.A. Life" section. Tuesday Jan. 27, 1998.
The Los Angeles Times. Tuesday Jan. 27, 1998.
One Million Years B.C. pressbook.
Telephone conversation with Charles H. Schneer. 2001.
Telephone conversations with Ray Harryhausen. 1992-2002.
The Valley of Gwangi pressbook.
"Valley of the Mists" screenplay, dated Dec. 22, 1949.

Video / Television / Personal Appearances

A. Boyd Campbell appearance at the Monster Bash in Monroeville, PA, 1998.
Aliens, Dragons, Monsters & Me (VHS). Midwich Entertainment, Inc. / Cerberus Video, 1991.
"Dinosaur!" Arts & Entertainment Network. 1991.
Dinosaur Movies (VHS). Simitar Entertainment, Inc., 1993.
The Fantasy Worlds of Irwin Allen. The Sci-Fi Channel. 1995.
The Harryhausen Chronicles (DVD). Rhino Home Video, 2002.
Jason and the Argonauts (Laserdisc). The Criterion Collection, 1992.
The Lost World (1925)(DVD). Lumivision Corp. / The International Museum of Photography at George Eastman House, 1997.
"Movie Magic: Behind the Scenes — Dinomania." The Discovery Channel. 1996.
Mysterious Island (Laserdisc). "Ray Harryhausen Signature Collection." Columbia / TriStar Home Video, 1995.
One Million Years B.C. (Region 2 DVD). StudioCanal / Warner Home Video, 2002.
"Opening Shot: Dinosaurs." Bravo Network. 1993.
Ray Harryhausen appearance at the Modelfest in Boston, 1994.
Ray Harryhausen appearance in Cleveland, 1993.
The Sinbad Collection (Laserdisc). "Ray Harryhausen Signature Collection." Columbia / TriStar Home Video, 1995.

Index

*Numbers in **bold** refer to illustrations*

ABC-TV (American Broadcasting Company) 149
Ackerman, Forrest J (Forry) **25**, 26, 201, 202
aerial brace 123, 132, 161
agathaumas 24, **28**, 29, 30, 36, 209
The Age of the Dinosaurs 179
albertosaurus 84
Aldrich, Fred 211
Alexander the Great (1956) 141
Aliens, Dragons, Monsters & Me 28, 29, 30, 32, 34, 185, 201, 203, 204; laserdisc 202
Allen, David 64
Allen, Irwin 87, **90**, **93**, 96–97, **98**, 109, 212
Allied Artists 80
allosaurus 7–8, 10, 23, 24, 28, 29, **32**, 33, 34, 35, 36, **42**, 43, 50, 61, 88, 90, 92, **93**, 94, 96, 100, 113, 120, 121, 122, 123, **123**, **124**, 125, 126, 128, 132, 145, 146, 147, **149**, 152, 153, 155, 157, 158, 159, 160, 163, **164**, 165, 166, 167, 168, 169, 171, 172, 173, 174, 175, 177, 178, 179, 181, 182, 184, 188, 189, 190, 195, **199**, **201**, 209, 210
Amazing Stories 104
American Cinematographer 66
American Movie Classics (AMC) 150
American Museum of Natural History 6, 11, 88, 133
ammonite 107, 108, **109**, 210
Andress, Ursula 138, 139
Andrews, Roy Chapman 11
Angelinetta, Olga 212
The Animal World (1955) 3, 34, 86, 87, **88**, **89**, 90–**110**, 124, 126, 133, 151, 153, 172, 185, 204, 205, 210, 212; pressbook 91, 93
Animals 179, **180**
Animato! 71, 77, 104, 141
apatosaurus *see* brontosaurus
aperture 121

archelon 117, **118**, **119**, 132, 140, 146, 147, 151, 167, 196, 198, 202, 210
Archer, Steven 87, 153
Arden, Curtis 153, 162, 182, 213
Argosy Pictures 38
armature 2, 21, 23, 24, 29, 37, 40, 51, 52, 80, 82, 84, 89, 105, 108, 116, 119, 125, 132, 133, 134, 158, 159, 166, 205
Armstrong, Robert 12, 19, 38, 39
arsinoitherium **12**, 19, **20**, 23, 196, **197**, 210
Associated British Picture Corporation 141, 149
Asterix and the Big Fight (1989) 203
Atala 25
Atomic Submarine (1959) 83
Aupperle, Jim 64, 189
Australopithecus 144

Babelsberg StudioTour 202
background plate 35, 56, 64, 69, 72, 79, 83, 86, 121, 131, 135, 136, 138, 140, 147, 157, 175, 178, 186, 188, 189, 198; *see also* rear-projection plate
Bagdad (1949) 67
Baker, George 143, 212
Baker, Ivy 212
Baker, Roy 212
Baker, Tom 192
Ballentine, John 150
Barabbas (1962) 141
The Barefoot Contessa (1954) 141
Barnes, Alan 146
Barron, Craig 202
Barrye, Emily 153
Bast, William E. 153, 183, 213
The Battleship Potemkin (1925) 175
Bavaria Studios 203
BavariaFilmPark 202
BBC (British Broadcasting Corporation) 95, 96, 204
beam-splitter 67, 78; *see also* semi-transparent mirror
The Beast from 20,000 Fathoms

(1953) 3, 6, 27, 44, 45–86, 47, **49**, **86**, 95, 100, 108, 146, 157, 168, 185, 196, 204, 210, 211; Bradbury story 73
The Beast of Hollow Mountain (1956) 83, 152
Beery, Wallace 6
Behemoth, the Sea Monster 84; *see also The Giant Behemoth*
Belcher, Robert A. 212
Beneath the Planet of the Apes (1970) 181
Berg, Jon 184
Berman, Monty 145, 212
Berman's of Hollywood 211
Berry, Mark F. 71, 100
Bertera, Denis 212
Best, James 211
Beswick, Martine 112, 138, 139, 212
Beyond the Poseidon Adventure (1979) 97
The Bible 25
The Big Circus (1959) 96, 97
The Big Country (1958) 183
The Big Sleep (1978) 199
Billy Budd (1962) 139
Bingham, James R. 73
bi-packing 136
The Bishop's Wife (1947) 183
Bissette, Stephen 104, 149
The Black Scorpion (1957) 54, 71, 86, 97, 109
Blackwell, George 134, 212
Block, Irving 83
blue-backing (traveling matte) 131, 134, 135–**136**, 137, 178
Boardman, Eric 202
Bogart, Humphrey 141
Bottomley, Philip 213
Bowie, Les 135, 212
Boyle, Edward 211
brachiosaurus 7, 83
Bradbury, Ray **25**–26, 73, 85, 203, 205, 206, 207, 211
The Brave One (1956) 43; pressbook 43
Bravo Network 204
Bray Studios 142

219

Brides of Dracula (1960) 182
Bringing Up Baby (1938) 72
British Museum of Natural History 133
Brodie, Steve 211
Bronco Billy (1980) 72
Bronson, Charles 199
brontosaurus 1, 7, 8, 9, 10, 15, **20**, 21, 23, 24, 27, 28, 29, 30, **32**, 33, 34, 36, 50, 60, 79, 83, 88, 92, **93**, 96, 99, 100, **101**, 112, **114**, 116, **117**, 145, 170, 180, 209, 210
Brosnan, John 135
Brown, Robert 111, 139, 212
Brown, William Lyon 113, 139, 212
Budd, Roy 198
build-up procedure (modelmaking) 10, 24, 40, 51, 82, 89, 90
Burgos, Jose 155, 156, 182, 213
Burton, Bernard W. 72, 211
Buttolph, David 70–71, 77, 211

Cabot, Bruce 12
Callan, Michael 106
Calvin, Sam 66
camarasaurus 116
Camp, Charles L. 95
Capra, Frank 37
Caps, John 184
Captain Sindbad (1963) 71
Carlson, Richard 154, 181, 212
Carnera, Primo 39
Carreras, Enrique 142, 143
Carreras, James 142, 143
Carreras, Michael 117, 121, 141, 142, 143, 144, 145, 212
Carson, Rachel 87
"Cashing In on a Fantasy" (*Popular Mechanics*) 37
casting: bronze 205; Fiberglass 119; foam latex injection 50, 51, 82, 89–90, 91, 125, 134, 179; resin 90
Catch as Catch Can (1967) 181
cave bear 19, **20**, 21, 22, 23, 29, 209
Caveman (1981) 151
The CBS Late Movie 190
centrosaurus 24, 165
ceratosaurus 34, 88, **89**, **90**, 91, 93, 94, 95, 96, **99**, 100, **102**, 110, 114, 115, 125, 126, **127**, **128**, 129, 131, 145, 159, 168, 173, 198, 199, **201**, 205, **206**, 210
Chaffey, Don 144, 212
Chamberlain, Richard 181
Chaney, Lon, Jr. 111
Chang (1927) 18
Chang, Wah 31
Chaplin, Charlie 72

Charlie's Angels 144
chasmosaurus 146, **148**
Cheap Tricks and Class Acts 97
Chester, Hal 45, 65, 68, 70, 71, 72, 73, 211
Christian, Paul *see* Hubschmid, Paul
Cinefantastic: Babelsberg Studio-Tour 203
Cinefantastique 12, 20, 27, 33, 36, 45, 50, 64, 66, 70, 78, 86, 92, 103, 120, 179, 204
Cinefex 109, 204
Cinemagic 54, 56, 71, 73
CinemaScope 77
Cinerama 44
Citizen Kane (1940) 183
Clark, Ed 211
Clash of the Titans (1981) 84, 104, 119, 133, 161, 166, 178, 182, 185, 199, 210
Claymation 2
Clifton's Cafeteria 25
Close-Up (1948) 183
Coca, Imogene 68
Cohan, William 181
Collectable Toys & Values 19
Colonial Pictures 152, 153
color-difference 137
color timing 189
color wheel 178
Colossa 52
Columbia Pictures 105, 181, 185, 190, 192, 193
Conan Doyle, Sir Arthur 6, 9
Conquest Pictures 10
contrast (film) 64, 91, 135, 137
Cook, Randy 64
Cook, Willis 67, 211
Cooper, Merian C. 12, 18, 38, 42, 44, 210
Cooper, Wilkie 131, 144, 190, 212
Corman, Roger 73
counter-matte 64
Cox, Alfred 212
Crabbe, Byron 18
Craig, Michael 106
Crawford, Joan 99
Creation (1931) **12**, 18–19, 196
Creature from the Black Lagoon (1954) 181
Creatures the World Forgot (1971) 142, 144, 146
Creed, Bill 213
Criterion *Jason and the Argonauts* (laserdisc) 6, 11, 22, 24, 26, 78, 202
Cro-Magnon 144
Cronkite, Walter 204
Cunningham, Harry 66
The Curse of Frankenstein (1957) 142

Curtis, Donald 79
Curtis, Patrick 138

D-Day, the Sixth of June (1956) 68
Dalton, Tony 204
Danforth, Jim 64, 92, 100, 109, 146, 205
Dante's Inferno 25, 130
Darabont, Frank 146
Dark Horse Comics 43, 203, 205
David and Goliath 27
Davis, Desmond 84
Dawley, Herbert M. 10
DC Comics 190
Dead End Kids 71
Death Wish (1974) 199
de Barros, Mario 155, 182, 213
The Defiant Ones (1958) 68
De Laurentiis, Dino 150
Delfs, Holger **201**, **202**, 204
Delgado, Marcel 10, 18, 19, 40, 51, 89, 109, 153
Del Vecchio, Deborah 133
DeMille, Cecil B. 97
DeMond, Henry L. 212
de Packh, Maurice 71, 211
de Rauch, Micky 139, 212
DeWitt, Louis 83
Diamond, David 81
The Diary of a Chambermaid (1946) 72
diatryma 10, 163, **164**
Dicken, Roger 100
Dietz, Jack 45, 65, 70, 71, 73, 77, 78, 91, 210, 211
dimetrodon 24, 60, 124
"Dinomania" (*Movie Magic*) 204
Dinosaur (*Starlog*) 43, 50, 67, 153, 183
Dinosaur! 204
The Dinosaur and the Missing Link (1915) 3, 10
The Dinosaur Filmography 71, 100, 160
Dinosaur Movies 204
The Dinosaur Scrapbook 95, 131
Dinosaur Valley Girls (1997) 151
"Dinosaurs on the Hall Cupboard" (*Supernatural*) 201
Dinosaurus! (1960) 152
Diplodicus 116
dire wolf 5
The Dirty Dozen (1967) 142
Discovery Channel 204
Disney 9, 36, 105
Dr. Jekyll and Sister Hyde (1971) 139
Dr. Kildare 181
Dollywood studio 30
Domergue, Faith 79
Don Quixote 25
Donovan, King 46, 68, 211

Doré, Gustave 25, 27, 33, 43, 78, 130, 163, 193
Double Dynamite (1951) 96
double-framing 92; *see also* shooting on twos
double-printing 53, 58, 59, 177
Douglas, Kirk 105
Down Place *see* Bray Studios
Dracula (1958) 142
Duchess of Idaho (1950) 68
Duel in the Sun (1946) 41
Dunn, Linwood 109, 205
The Dunwich Horror (1970) 69
Dynamation 66, 67, 91, 105, 108, 117, 120, 121, 126, 144, 169, 170, 176, 178, 186; *see also* static matte rear-projection composite
Dynarama 66; *see also* Dynamation

Earth Vs. the Flying Saucers (1956) 54, 57, 59, 67, 80, 102, 185
East Side Kids 71
Easton, Robert 211
Easy Rider (1969) 190
Edeson, Arthur 9
The Edge of the Sea 87
Ege, Julie 146
The Elementals 77, 102, 130, 210
Elliott, Ross 46, 68, 211
Elliott, Walter 212
Elstree Studios 141
Emilio and Guloso 43
Emmerich, Roland 203
Endfield, Cy 106
Enemy Mine (1985) 140
Engel, Roy 211
eohippus 154, 155, 160, **161**, 164, 167, 181, 187, 189, 202, 210
Eppleton, Lou 185
eryops 24
Evans, Gene 80, 81
Evolution (aka *Evolution of the World*) 31–**32**, **33**–36, 37, 38, 45, 87, 90, 91, 94, 120, 124, 209
Exclusive Films 142, 143
Execution (1968) 139

Fairbanks, Douglas 9
Fairfax, Marion 9
Fairy Tales (Harryhausen) 24, 37, 44, 45, 91, 102
Famous Monsters of Filmland 25
Fantasia (1940) 2, 36–37, 180
Fantastic Voyage (1966) 138
The Fantasy Worlds of Irwin Allen 97
Farnum, Franklyn 211
Feilberger, Dan 20
Ferguson, Frank 211

Film Fantasy Scrapbook 19, 24, 27, 40, 41, 67, 102, 116, 117, 133, 161, 181, 186, 204
film gate 121, 136, 137
Filmfax 68
Filmmuseum Berlin (Sony Center) 202, 203, 204, 205
Films Illustrated 104
Firebird Suite 94
First Men in the Moon (1964) 53, 90, 103, 135, 143, 144, 148, 185, 196, 198
First National 6, 11
The 500 Pound Jerk (1972) 181
Five Weeks in a Balloon (1962) 97
Flowers, Bess 211
The Fly (1958) 97
foam latex (rubber) 2, 26, 37, 51, 89, 90, 125, 128, 134
"The Fog Horn" (Bradbury story) 73; *see also The Beast from 20,000 Fathoms*
For a Few Dollars More (1967) 68
Forbes, Don 87
Ford, John 38, 68
Forest Park Productions 153
Fort Apache (1948) 38
The Four Feathers (1929) 18
The Four Musketeers (1974) 138
Fox (studio) 70
Fox, Michael 49, 69, 211
Franciscus, James 153, 174, 176, 177, 181, **182**, 187, 212
Freiberger, Fred 45, 74, 211
Freie Universität Berlin (Free University Berlin) 203
Frickert, Joseph 143, 212
From Russia with Love (1963) 139
From the Land Beyond Beyond 21, 24, 26, 31, 66, 94, 100, 104, 107, 119, 122, 140, 187, 202, 204
front-projection 41, 67, 78
Fulton, Fitch 41
Funeral in Berlin (1966) 68
Furness, John 213
Füsilier Wipf (1938) 67
FXRH 28, 66, 132, 161, 176, 184, 204

Gable, Clark 67, 68
Gahagan, Helen 53
gallimimus 163
Gardner, Ava 141
George Eastman House 9
Gertie the Dinosaur (1914) 2
The Ghost of Slumber Mountain (1919) 3, 10
The Giant Behemoth (1959) 72, 80–**82**, 83–84, 109, 168
giant ground sloth 5

The Giant Ymir 77, 102, 210
Giesen, Rolf 4, 132, 157, 198, 199, 203–204, 205
Gil, Carlos 213
Gil, Miguel 213
A Girl in Every Port (1952) 96
Globe Theater 193
Glut, Don 95, 131, 204
Godzilla 85
Godzilla, King of the Monsters! (1956) 85
Gojira (1954) 85
Golan, Gila 154, 181, **182**, 187, 212
Golden Apples of the Sun 73
The Golden Voyage of Sinbad (1974) 27, 78, 130, 132, 133, 161, 182, 184, 192–193, 198
Goldenburg, Miriam *see* Golan, Gila
Goldner, Orville 205
Goldsmith, Gladys 212, 213
The Golem 6
Gone with the Wind (1939) 26
The Good, the Bad and the Ugly (1967) 68
Gorcey, Leo 71
Gordon, Robert 80
Gordon E. Sawyer Award (Oscar) 206
Gorgo (1961) 72, 84
gorgosaurus 84
grain (film) 64, 189
The Grand Illusion (1937) 71
Grass (1925) 18
Grauman, Sid 11
Grauman's (Mann's) Chinese Theatre 11, 19, 25, 205
Gray, Joe 211
The Great Adventure 44, 210
The Great Rupert (1950) 45
The Greatest Show on Earth (1952) 97
The Greek Tycoon (1978) 181
Green, Nigel 108
Greenman, Alvin 69, 211
Greenwood, Joan 106
Gremlins 2: The New Batch (1990) 68
Grenadier Guards 143
Griffin, Merv 69, 211
Griffith, D.W. 111
Groves, George 211
Guadalcanal 37
The Gun That Won the West (1955) 68
Gunsmoke 183
Gwangi (1941–1942) 37, 42, 91, 97, 152–153, **156**, 161, **171**, 184–185, **186**, 210
Gwangi 28, 61, 91, 100, 124, 129, 152, 155, **156**, 157, **158**, **159**, 160, 163, 164, 165, **166**, 167,

168, 169, 170, **171**, **172**, **173**, **174**, 175, **176**, 177, 178, **180**, 181, 182, 184, 185, **186**, **187**, 188, 189, 190, **201**, 202, 210; *see also* allosaurus

Haggard, H. Rider 199, 200, 210
Hail, Hero! (1969) 183
The Hairy Ape (1944) 71
half-silvered mirror 67; *see also* semi-transparent mirror
Hall, Huntz 71
Hammer Films 110, 111, 135, 138, 139, 140, 142–143, 144, 145, 149, 150, 151, 178, 190, 210, 212
Hammer Films: An Exhaustive Filmography 133
Hammer, House of Horror: Behind the Screams 141
The Hammer Story 146
Hammeras, Ralph 10–11
Hand of Death (1962) 68
Hankin, Mike 52
Hanks, Tom 206
Hansel and Gretel (1950) 45
Harcourt, David 212
Hardy, Oliver 203
Hardy, Sam 12
Harris, Richard 212
Harrod's 108, 202
Harryhausen, Diana 202, 205, 206
Harryhausen, Fred 5, 24, 51
Harryhausen, Martha 5, 11
Harryhausen, Vanessa 202, 206
The Harryhausen Chronicles (aka *The Ray Harryhausen Chronicles*) 78, 107, 202, 204; DVD 32, 35–36, 204
Have Gun Will Travel 183
Hawdon, Robin 146
Hayden, Frank 139, 212
Hayward, Arthur 133, 178–179, 204, 212, 213
Hearn, Marcus 146
Heindorf, Ray 71, 211
Heinlein, Robert 25
Hell Boats (1970) 181
Herbert, Percy 111, 139, 212
Herrmann, Bernard 107, 141, 183–184
Hessler, Gordon 192
High Noon (1952) 68
The Hill (1965) 142
Hill, Mary 211
Hillier, Erwin 190, 213
Hinds, Anthony 142
Hinds, Will 142
Hitchcock, Alfred 183
holdout matte *see* matte/counter-matte
Hollywood Merry-Go-Round 96

Hopper, William 103
Horner, Yvonne 139, 212
Horrors: From Screen to Scream 85, 141, 186
The Horse Soldiers (1959) 70
Hotel Esplanade 203
Hough, Horace 211
A House Is Not a Home (1964) 138
House of Hammer 135
House of Wax (1953) 77
The House That Hammer Built 50, 138, 157
How to Bridge a Gorge 37
The Howling (1980) 68
Hoyt, Arthur 6
Hoyt, Harry O. 9
Hubschmid, Paul 46, 67, **69**, 204, 211
Hudson, Earl 9
Hughes, Lloyd 6
The Human Beast (1938) 71
Hume, Cyril 44
Hunt, Peter 139
Hush…Hush, Sweet Charlotte (1964) 68
Hutchinson, Max 211
Hyke, Ray 211
Hyman, Elloit 142, 190
Hyman, Kenneth 142, 190, 212
hyracotherium *see* eohippus

Image Entertainment 150
Imagi-Movies 120, 145, 204
Imagination 26
L'Incroyable Cinema 158
internegative (IN) 137
interpositive (IP) 137
Invasion of the Body Snatchers (1956) 68
The Invisible Boy (1957) 83
It Came from Beneath the Sea (1955) 68, 78–**80**, 107, 157, 185
It Came from Outer Space (1953) 181
It's a Mad, Mad, Mad, Mad World (1963) 109

Jackson, Freda 154, 182, 213
James, Richard 115, 139, 212
Janus Company 205
Jason and the Argonauts (1963) 24, 78, 90, 108, 130, 132, 135, 137, 141, 144, 169, 170, 177, 182, 183, 185, 191, 193, 198
Jasper (Puppetoons) 31
The Jayhawkers! (1959) 183
Jein, Gregory 202
Jensen, Paul M. 41, 42, 74, 104, 191
Jim Dandy (Puppetoons) 31
"Joe Palooka" 71, 72

Joey (aka *Making Contact*) (1985) 203
Johnson, Ben 38, 39
Johnson, John 97
Johnson, Tom 133
Jones, Jennifer 41
Jones, Robert 212
Journey to the Lost City (1959) 68
Juilliard School of Music 70, 183
Jungle Manhunt (1951) 111
Juran, Nathan 103
Jurassic Park (1993) 3, 60, 163, 191, 207
Jurassic Park films 95

Katzman, Sam 185
Kellaway, Cecil 46, 68, **69**, 211
Kellison, Phil 82
Kelly's Heroes (1970) 68
Kemp, Kenner G. 211
Kilbane, Dennis 155, 182, 213
King Brothers 84
King Kong (1933) 3, 11, 12–19, 21, 22, 25, 26, 28, 33, 35, 37, 38, 40, 41, 42, 44, 51, 65, 66, 70, 85, 89, 103, 105, 108, 109, 127, 150, 153, 157, 168, 170, 176, 177, 184, 196, 200, 203, 205, 207
King Kong (1976) 150
King Kong (Harryhausen) 150, 210
King Kong Vs. Frankenstein 85
King Kong Vs. Godzilla (1963) 85
King Solomon's Mines 199
Kinney National Service 190
KLAC 96
Knight, Charles R. 1, 5, 24, 61, 95
Knight, Charlotte 24, 102
Knoth, Fred 111, 120
Kodak Cine II (camera) 31
Kossoff, David 212
Krakatoa, East of Java (1969) 72
Kronos (1957) 83
Kunert, Arnold 206

L.A. Life 180
La Jolla High 138
Lamb, Harold 153
Land of the Giants 97
Land Raiders (1969) 182
Landau, Richard 43
Landis, Carole 111, 145, 146
Landis, John 205
Larrinaga, Juan 153
Larrinaga, Mario 18
Lasky, Jesse, Jr. 43
Lasky, Jesse, Sr. 43
Lasky, William 43
Laurel, Stan 203
Lavelly, Marjory 212

Law, John Phillip 192
Lazenby, George 139
Lemuria 27, 192, 209
Lexikon der Special Effects 203
Lexikon des Phantastischen Films: Horror, Science Fiction, Fantasy 203
Limelight (1952) 72
Litchenfield, Lou 41
Little Red Riding Hood (1949) 45, 102
Lofgren, George 41, 67, 105, 133
Lom, Herbert 106
Longstreet 181
Look 19
Los Angeles City College (LACC) 23, 31, 102
Los Angeles County Museum of Natural History 5, 6
Los Angeles Daily News 180
Los Angeles Museum of Art 23
Los Angeles Science Fiction Society 25, 27
The Lost Continent (1951) 45
The Lost Continent (1968) 140, 142, 143, 178
Lost in Space 97
The Lost Volcano (1950) 68
The Lost World (1925) 3, 6–7, 8–9, 10, 11, 18, 22, 24, 27, 40, 43, 50, 51, 79, 96, 153, 179
The Lost World (1960) 97, 109
The Lost World (Shepard DVD) 9
Lourié, Eugene 45, 50, 66, 68, 69, 71–72, 73, 74, 77, 78, 80, 81, 83, 84, 85, 211
Love, Bessie 6
Lucas, Tim 119
Luigi, Pierre 145, 212
Lumivision *The Lost World*: DVD 9; laserdisc 9
Lumkin, A.W. 212

MacGyver 144
Mack, Helen 19, 53
MacQueen, Scott 9
The Magnetic Monster (1953) 68, 69, 181
Maidment, Terence 139, 212
Majan, Juan 213
"Making Fossils Live" (*Animals*) 179
Maltin, Leonard 84, 151, 186, 197
mammoth (woolly mammoth) 5, 24, 35, 37, 111, 209
The Man Who Shot Liberty Valance (1962) 38, 68
Mandell, Paul 43, 50, 54, 56, 66, 67, 71, 73, 153, 183, 210
Mankiewicz, Joseph L. 141
Manual Arts high school 22
Manuelli, Pasqual 89, 91, 212

Marooned (1969) 181
Martell, Philip 212
Marx, Chico 97
Marx, Groucho 97
Marx, Harpo 97
Mason, James 105
Massaro, David 27–28, 29, 30, 36
mastodon 47
matte/counter-matte (matte/reverse-matte) 135, 136, 137, 178
Mature, Victor 111, 145, 146
Maxford, Howard 141
McFarland & Company, Inc., Publishers 203
McKenzie, Nicolette 138
McVey, Tony 133
The Men Who Made the Monsters 41, 74, 104, 191
Mercury Theater 68
Merrill, Gary 106
Metropolis (1927) 6
Metropolitan Museum of Art (New York) 201
MGM (Metro-Goldwyn-Mayer) 22, 23, 199
Michelet, Michel 70–71
Midnight Cowboy (1969) 190
Midnight Marquee 66
Midwich Entertainment 28, 185, 201
Mighty Joe Young (1949) 38–43, 44, 45, 61, 62, 66, 67, 68, 85, 89, 91, 109, 133, 152, 153, 191, 205, 209
Mills, Alec 213
Mills, Jack 212
Miracle on 34th Street (1947) 69
Mirissis, Richard 149
Mr. Joseph Young of Africa 38; see also *Mighty Joe Young*
Mitchell (camera) 66
monoclonius (agathaumas) 29
The Monster from Beneath the Sea 73; see also *The Beast from 20,000 Fathoms*
Monstrous Movie Music 71
Moon Zero Two (1969) 143
Moore, Terry 38, 39, 205
More, Julian 153, 213
Morell, André 80, 81
Morheim, Lou 45, 74, 78, 211
Morningside Productions 102, 185, 213
Moross, Jerome 183–184, 213
Morpheus Mike (1917) 10
mosasaurus 146, 201
moschops 200, 210
Mother Goose Stories (1946) 37–38
Motion Picture Center 70, 72, 73
Movie Magic 204

The Mummy (1959) 142
Munro, Caroline 192
Museum of the Moving Image (MOMI) 201–202, 203
Mutiny on the Bounty (1935) 68
Mutiny on the Bounty (1962) 139
Mutual Pictures of California 71, 72, 211
My Fair Lady 68
My Work in Films 72, 81
Mysterious Island (1961) 3, 105–**107**, 108, 137, 139, 163, 177, 182, 185, 191, 210; laserdisc 107

Naha, Ed 85, 141, 186
Naismith, Laurence 154, 182, 212, 213
Nappi, Malya 112, 139, 212
Nascimbene, Mario 141–142, 148, 212
Nassour brothers 43, 152
Natale, Mike 176
Nazi Propaganda Films 203
Neanderthal 36, 144, 195
Needs, James 212
Nevada Test Site (NTS) 76
The NeverEnding Story (TV series) 203
The NeverEnding Story II (1990) 203
New York University School of Music 183
Newman, Alfred 70
Newsom, Ted 27, 33, 36, 50, 64, 66, 70, 92, 103–104, 179, 204
Night of the Demon (1957) 71
A Night to Remember (1958) 182
No Time for Flowers (1952) 68
North by Northwest (1959) 183
nothosaur 200, 210
Novak, Mickell 143, 212

Oakley Court 142
O'Brien, Darlyne 30, 43, 86, 205
O'Brien, Willis H. (Obie) 3, 10, 11, 18, 21, 22, 23, 25, 26, 27, 30, 31, 37, 38, 40, 41, 42, 43, 45, 62, 64, 71, 82, 83, **84**, 85, 86, 87, 89, 91, 92, 93, 95, **98**, 108, 109, 151, 152, 153, 161, 184, 185, 190, 196, 199, 205, 207, 209, 210, 212, 213
O'Connolly, James 186, 213
Of Mice and Men (1939) 111
O'Hara, Maureen 67
On a Clear Day You Can See Forever (1970) 139
On Her Majesty's Secret Service (1969) 139
100 Years of Horror: Giants and Dinosaurs 204

One Million B.C. (1940) 2, 110, 111, 116, 117, 120, 124, 126, 128, 135, 141, 142, 143, 144, 146, 151, 210
One Million Years B.C. (1966) 3, 29, 35, 66, 78, 93, 110, 111–112, **113**, **114**, 115–**118**, 119–**123**, 124–**125**, 126–**128**, 129–**130**, 131–**139**, 141–**143**, 144–151, 157, 158, 159, 160, 161, 163, **164**, 165, 167, 168, 173, 177, 179, 180, 181, 184, 185, 190, 191, 192, 193, 195, 196, 198, 200, 202, 205, 210, 212; pressbook 144
Opening Shot 204
Operation Crossbow (1965) 139
optical printer 59, 64, 107, 116, 136, 137, 171, 177
ornithomimus 155, 157, 163, 164, **165**, 168, **169**, 184, **207**, 210
Our Man Flint (1965) 181
Our Town (1940) 183
The Outer Limits 45

Pal, George 22, 30
paleosaurus 80, **82**, 83, 84
Palmer, Gene 212
Panavision 144
Paradise Lost 25
Paramount Pictures 30, 43, 70
Parrondo, Gil 213
Pathe Limited 149, 212
Paul, Gregory S. 126
pelycosaur 60
Pennick, Jack 46, 68, 211
People of the Mist 199–200, 210
Peter Pan (1953) 77
Peterson, Pete 40, 41, 82, 83
Pete's Dragon (1977) 144
Petterson, Selwyn 213
Pettigrew, Neil 51, 52, 53, 56, 59, 60, 96, 101, 102, 116, 128, 163, 174
Phelps, Lee 211
Phillippi, Louis 211
phororhacos 106, **107**, 163, 210
Photon 167, 184, 189, 191
Physoic, Lou 24
A Pictorial History of Science Fiction Films 167
Pirates of Tortuga (1961) 139
Planet of Dinosaurs (1978; aka *Planet of the Dinosaurs*) 75, 189
plesiosaurus 16, 146, **147**, 199, 200, 201, 210
Popular Mechanics 37, 204
The Poseidon Adventure (1972) 97
The Postman Always Rings Twice (1946) 68
Power, Taryn 193

Power, Tyrone 193
Prebble, John 105
Predatory Dinosaurs of the World 126
"Prehistoric Challenge" (Janus Company) 205, **206**
Prehistoric Peeps (1905) 1
Prehistoric Poultry (1917) 3, 10
The Prehistoric Times 50
Prehistoric Women (1967) 139, 143
Presley, Elvis 138
The Prince and the Pauper (1962) 144
The Prisoner 144
Prosser, Hugh 211
The Proud Rebel (1958) 183
Psycho (1960) 183
pteranodon 7, 16, 24, 29, 30, 115, 129, **130**, 131, 132, **133**, 137, 140, 146, 147, 152, 155, 161, **162**, **163**, 168, 169, 189, 200, 209, 210
pterodactyl *see* pteranodon, pterosaur
pterosaur 1, 78, 115, 129, 132, 147, 162, 180, 193, 210
The Public Lives of Henry the Ninth (1935) 142
Pueo, Antonio 213
Puglia, Frank 103
Puppetoons 30–31, 37
Puppets & People 51, 59, 79, 157

Quatermass and the Pit (1967) 142
The Quatermass Xperiment (1955) 142

Rabin, Jack 83
Rachel, Rachel (1968) 183
Rancho La Brea Tar Pits (Hancock Park) 5
The Ray Harryhausen Chronicles *see* *The Harryhausen Chronicles*
Ray Harryhausen: Master of the Majicks 52
Raymond, Paula 47, 68, **69**, 211
rear-projection plate 63; *see also* background plate
registration 64
Reicher, Frank 12, 19
Renoir, Jean 71, 77
replacement animation 30, 38
R.F.D. 10,000 B.C. (1917) 3, 10
rhamphorhynchus **130**, 131, 132, **134**, 146, 147, 193, **202**, 210
rhedosaurus 27, 47, 48, **49**, 50, 51, **52**, 53, 55, 56, 57, 58, 59, 60, 61, 62, 65, 66, **75**, 78, 79, 82, 83, **85**, **86**, 89, 95, 100, 157, 168, 196, 210

Rhoades, Arthur S. 89, 212
Richardson, Henry 213
Richardson, John 112, 122, 123, 126, 138–**139**, 145, 150, 212
Right to Die (1987) 138
The Rite of Spring (*Fantasia*) 36
The River (1951) 72
RKO (Radio-Keith-Orpheum) 12, 18, 20, 22, 38, 66, 72, 96, 150, 152, 153
Roach, Hal, Jr. 111
Roach, Hal, Sr. 111, 120, 142, 149, 212
The Robe (1953) 77, 111
Roberts, Jack 21
Roberts, Luis 213
Rojo, Gustavo 154, 162, 182, 213
Romancing the Stone (1983) 51
Roosevelt Hotel 205
Rose, Ruth 38, 44
Ross, Steven 190
Rothacker, Watterson R. 10
Roustabout (1964) 138
Rovin, Jeff 31, 94, 104, 107, 119, 122, 167, 187, 204
Rowe, Bill 212
Rózsa, Miklós 192
Russell, Jack 211

saber-tooth tiger 5, 195, **196**, 198, 210
Sagenhafte Welten: der Trickspezialist Ray Harryhausen 203
Samson and Delilah (1949) 111
The Saturday Evening Post 73, 211
Saura, Antonio 213
Sawtell, Paul 97, 153, 212
Schaefer, George 152
Schneer, Charles H. 66, 78, 102, 104, 105, 108, 133, 143, 144, 146, 151, 152, 153, 182, 183, 184, 185–186, 190, 192, 193, 197, 199, 210, 213
Schneiderman, Wally 212
Schoedsack, Ernest B. 12, 18, 38
Schoenfeld, Bert 212
Scott, Randolph 53
Scrooge (1970) 182
The Sea Around Us (1951) 87, 97, 98
The Searchers (1956) 68
Seizure (1974) 139
semi-transparent mirror 67, 78; *see also* beam-splitter
Serpico (1973) 199
Seven Arts 142, 149, 152, 190, 212, 213
7 Faces of Dr. Lao (1964) 30
The 7th Voyage of Sinbad (1958) 51, 52, 66, 90, 91, 103, 105, 116, 133, 144, 157, 166, 182,

185, 190, 191, 192, 193, 195, 203
Seymour, Jane 193
SFX 205
Shaw, Jack 41, 91, 153
The Shawshank Redemption (1994) 146
She (1935) 53, 196
She (1965) 138, 142
She (Haggard novel) 199
She Wore a Yellow Ribbon (1949) 68
Shepard, David 9
Shilton, Len 212
Ship of Fools (1965) 181
shooting on twos 92
Signal Corps 37, 185
Simpson, Tom 212
Sinbad and the Eye of the Tiger (1977) 3, 27, 53, 133, 135, 166, 185, 193–**197**, 198, 210
Sinbad and the Seven Wonders of the World 198
Sinbad at the World's End see *Sinbad and the Eye of the Tiger*
Sinbad Goes to India see *The Golden Voyage of Sinbad*
Sinbad Goes to Mars 198
Sinbad trilogy 185
Sink the Bismarck! (1960) 182
Smilodon *see* saber-tooth tiger
Smith, Robert 211
Society for the Prevention of Cruelty to Animals (SPCA) 124
sodium-backing (traveling matte) 133, 137–138
Solomon and Sheba (1959) 141
The Son of Kong (1933) 19, 41
Speaks, John 152
The Spy Who Loved Me (1977) 139
Stagecoach (1939) 38
Star Trek 45
Starlog 43, 50, 67, 153, 183, 199, 200
static matte **21**, 22, 27, 28, 29, 35, 56, 79
static matte rear-projection composite 53, 55, 56, 58, **62–63**, 64, **65**, 66, 85, 86, 91, 92, 108, 117, 118, 132, 135, 169, 174, 175, 189; *see also* Dynamation
stegosaurus 1, 7, 14, **17**, 19, **22**, 23, 29, 88, 89, 92, 95, 100, 104, **110**, 199, 210
Steiner, Max 70–71
Stevens, Janet 133
Steward, Malcolm 213
Stone, Lewis 6
The Stop-Motion Filmography 51, 52, 53, 56, 59, 96, 101, 116, 128, 163, 174

Storm, John 97, 212
The Story of Mankind (1957) 96–97, 98
The Story of Rapunzel (1951) 45
Stravinsky, Igor 36
struthiomimus 163
styracosaurus **15**, 19, 24, 95, 100, 129, 146, 155, 159, 165, **166**, **167**, 168, 169, 171, 172, 173, **174**, 178, 184, 188, **189**, 198, 199, **201**, **207**, 210
Superdynamation 66, 108; *see also* Dynamation
Supernatural 91, 201
The Swarm (1978) 97
A Swingin' Summer (1965) 138
Swink, George E. 212

Tait, Kenneth McCallum 212
Tarantula (1955) 68
Taylor, Joan 103
Teenage Caveman (1958) 111
Tejada, Jo Raquel *see* Welch, Raquel
The Terror of the Tongs (1961) 142
Them! (1954) 76
The Thief of Baghdad (1924) 9
The Thief of Venice (1950) 68
The Thing from Another World (1951) 68
13 Ghosts (1960) 68
13 Rue Madeleine (1946) 70
This Gun for Hire (1942) 70
Thomas, Lisa 112, 139, 212
3 Godfathers (1948) 68
The 3 Worlds of Gulliver (1960) 105, 133, 137, 178, 182
Thunderball (1966) 139
Time 138
The Time Machine (1960) 30
The Time Tunnel 97
Tippett, Phil 64, 202
Tobey, Kenneth 46, 68, 79, 211
Toms, Carl 145, 212
El Toro Estrella (*The Star Bull*) 43
Tourneur, Jacques 71
The Towering Inferno (1974) 97
traveling matte 6, 118, 126, 128, 131, 134, 135, 144, 147, 148, 177, 188, 198; *see also* bluebacking, sodium-backing
triceratops 1, 7, 10, 18, 19, **22**, 24, 28, 29, **33**, 34, 35, 36, **42**, 43, **55**, 88, 89, **90**, **93**, **94**, 95, 101, **101**, 111, 114, 115, 124, **125**, 126, 127, **128**, **129**, 145, 146, 152, 165, 166, 168, 172, 173, 184, **201**, **207**, 209, 210
Trog (1970) 99–100, 101
Troughton, Patrick 193, 198
"Turkey in the Straw" 107

Tuttle, Bert 212
20 Million Miles to Earth (1957) 3, 24, 102, **103–104**, 105, 157, 166, 167, 175, 185, 210
20th Century-Fox 97, 138, 149, 212
20th Century Pictures 70
20,000 Leagues Under the Sea (1954) 105
A Twist of Sand (1968) 144
Two Lost Worlds (1950) 111
2001: A Space Odyssey (1968) 99
two-way mirror 67; *see also* semi-transparent mirror
tyrannosaurus (Tyrannosaurus rex) 1, 2, 7, **15**, 19, 28, **33**, 34, 35, 36, 50, **75**, 84, 88, 89, 90, 95, **101**, 102, 111, 120, 126, 127, 152, 157, 165, 184, 205, 206, 209, 210

UFA studios 202
Ullman, Daniel 105
Under the Sea-Wind 87
U.S. Fish and Wildlife Service 87
Universal Pictures 142, 185
University of California 95
University of Southern California (USC) 24, 31
unmade Sinbad project (1970s) 198, 210

The Valley of Gwangi (1969) 3, 29, 37, 61, 78, 95, 100, 105, 120, 121, 129, 132, 133, 146, 151, 152–153, **154**, 155–**163**, 164–166, 167–172, **173**, **174**, 175, **176**–192, 197, 202, 210, 212–213; pressbook 157, 183
Valley of the Mist 42, 43, 153, 209
The Valley Where Time Stood Still see *The Valley of Gwangi*
Van Cleef, Lee 49, 68, 211
velociraptor 60
The Vengeance of She (1968) 139
Verne, Jules 105
Vertigo (1958) 183
Vetri, Victoria 146
Vidal, Pedro 213
Video Watchdog 149
View-Master 100–101, 102
The Viking Queen (1967) 139, 144
The Vikings (1958) 141
Vincelli, Ralph 66
VISFX 26, 51
Visual Effects Society 203
Vlahos, Petros 137
von Eltz, Theodore 87, 97, 212
Voyage to the Bottom of the Sea (1961) 97

Voyage to the Bottom of the Sea (TV series) 97

Walking with Dinosaurs 3, 95, 96
Waller, Hal 211
Wanamaker, Sam 193
War Eagles (1939) 23, 153, 199, 210
War Eagles (Harryhausen) 210
War of the Satellites (1958) 69
The War of the Worlds (1953) 30
The War of the Worlds (Harryhausen) 104
Warner, Jack 77, 190
Warner Bros. 69, 70, 71, 73, 76, 77, 87, 89, 93, 152, 190, 192, 211, 212, 213
Warner Home Video 86, 191
Warren, Bill 167, 184, 189, 191
Wayne, John 38, 68, 193
Wayne, Patrick 193, 197
Welch, James 138
Welch, Raquel 112, 126, 130–131, 137, 138, **139**, **140**, **145**, 150, 151, 161, 212

Welles, Orson 68
Wellman, Harold 92, 212
Wertheim 202
What Ever Happened to Baby Jane? (1962) 142
When Dinosaurs Ruled the Earth (1970) 92, 100, 140, 142, 144, 146, **147**, 206
When Time Ran Out (1980) 97, 181
When Worlds Collide (1951) 95
Where Danger Lives (1950) 96
Whiting, Margaret 193, 198
Whitlock, Albert 203
Why We Fight 37
Wilber, Crane 105
Wilcox, John 212
Willis O'Brien: Special Effects Genius 87, 153
Wilson, Harold 89, 91, 212
Wilson, S.S. 51, 59, 79, 157
window matte *see* matte/counter-matte
Windsor Productions 87, 212
The Wings of Eagles (1957) 68
Winner, Michael 199–200, 210

Wladon, Jean 112, 139, 212
Wobber, Herman 10
Wolf, Mark 132, 161
The Wolf Man (1941) 111
Wonder 20, 26, 199
Woods, Donald 48, 68, 211
Woodson, William 211
Working with Dinosaurs 204
Wray, Fay 12, 205
Wright, Paula Remona *see* Raymond, Paula
Wright, Tony 77
Wuthering Heights (1939) 68

Yale University 181
Yank 37
yellow-backing *see* sodium-backing
You Must Be Joking! (1965) 143, 199
Young, Aida 142, 212

Zanuck, Richard 138
Zastupnevich, Paul 97
Zulu (1964) 106

www.ingramcontent.com/pod-product-compliance
Ingram Content Group UK Ltd.
Pitfield, Milton Keynes, MK11 3LW, UK
UKHW050532150426
5217IPUK00026B/1903